the psychologists

the psychologists

VOLUME ONE

edited by **T. S. KRAWIEC**

SKIDMORE COLLEGE

New York   **OXFORD UNIVERSITY PRESS**

London   1972   Toronto

Preface

One way to learn about and understand psychology is to study psychologists as they reveal themselves in writing about their lives. This book came about because the editor felt that contemporary introductory psychology texts give the student little opportunity to explore in depth the thinking—the frustrations as well as the insights—of the individuals working in the field.

Those represented in this volume are all distinguished by virtue of their achievements and their total involvement and participation in the various areas of psychology in which they have chosen to work. Each is significant in at least one facet of the discipline, be it research, teaching, editing, or writing, and brings to his essay a lifetime of study in his field of special interest.

The chapters are varied, the authors having been free to choose not only their manner of presentation but also the aspects of their lives they wished to emphasize. In their accounts they have referred to people who have influenced their lives and their work. Brief sketches of some of these people are included in the Biographical Index.

I am profoundly indebted to the authors of the chapters for their excellent contributions.

T. S. K.

Saratoga Springs, New York
January 1972

Contents

the psychologists

1

Reminiscences
of a Differential Psychologist

ANNE ANASTASI

I would rather write about psychology than about myself. But in keeping with my own conviction regarding the importance of experiential background in shaping an individual's development, I must recognize the relevance of a psychologist's own experiences to an understanding of his contributions. Hence the first section of this chapter brings together some salient facts from my own experiential background. In the remaining sections, I have tried to identify major themes underlying my research, writing, teaching, administrative activities, consulting work, and participation in psychological associations. If I were to carry out a second-order factor analysis among these major themes, I would undoubtedly find a single factor running through them all, a basic theme that can best be described as the recognition and maximum utilization of individual differences.

EXPERIENTIAL BACKGROUND

Early Education. Although the work of psychologists is much more familiar to the general public today than it was when I entered college, it is probably still true that most decisions to pursue a career in psychology are not reached until the college level or later. Such was certainly true in my case. Prior to my admission to Barnard College in 1924, I must confess, I would have been unable to give a satisfactory definition of psychology. Not only was psychology not taught in high schools at that time, but I was also not a high school graduate. In fact, I was a high school dropout.

After graduating from P.S. 33 in New York City with the "gold medal for general excellence"—awarded to one member of each graduating class—I entered a public high school along with many of my classmates. My elementary school days were happy days—I loved school. The move to high school changed all that. The particular high school we entered was overcrowded. In fact, it had so clearly outgrown its existing building that the year I was admitted the entire freshman class was assigned to an annex housed in an unsuitable elementary school building. To reach this school required a fifteen-minute trolley-car ride (an early version of bussing?). In addition, classes were held on a double shift, one-half of the students attending in the morning and one-half in the afternoon. Despite these ingenious devices, classes were still grossly overcrowded, teachers were overworked and consequently remote and impersonal, and the physical surroundings were unattractive and downright uncomfortable. I stood all this for just two months.

During my dropout phase, there were many discussions and family conferences about what I should do next. One evening, a friend of the family offered the bold suggestion that what I should really do was go to college, not high school. There were alternative routes, she pointed out, such as the series of examinations administered by the College Entrance Examination Board. At that time these examinations were designed for very specific courses, such as elementary algebra, solid geometry, or third-year French. There were, in addition, certain schools that taught courses in just those subjects required for college admission, with no such "frills" as extracurricular activities, physical education, or high school diplomas. Through a careful selection of the required subjects in such a school I was able to qualify for admission to Barnard in only two years. As a result, I entered college at the age of fifteen, graduated at nineteen, and received my Ph.D. from Columbia University at twenty-one.

A further bonus of this unorthodox education was that I entered Barnard with additional college credits in mathematics and was placed in advanced classes not only in mathematics but also in French literature and Latin poetry. My Barnard years picked up where elementary school had left off: classes were fun again and on graduation I won the Caroline Duror Memorial Fellowship, "awarded to that member of the graduating class showing greatest promise of distinction in her chosen line of work." To this day, I am not convinced that high school is necessary!

Choice of Psychology. Throughout all this account I have not yet answered the question: Why psychology, or when, or how? In elementary school my first love was mathematics. Not only did I enjoy mathematics more than any other subject in the regular curriculum, but I also entertained myself during vacations by devising numerical games or by working our shortcut procedures for the operations we had been taught in class. One summer when preparing for college, I purchased a textbook of plane and spherical trigonometry and solved all the problems in it. Then I decided I might as well take the CEEB examination in this subject, along with the others. My grade on this examination was one of the bases for my advanced credit in college mathematics. In my freshman year at Barnard, I filled out a form indicating that I planned to work for a B.S. degree with a major in mathematics and a double minor in physics and chemistry. My faculty adviser assured me that I did not need to fill out this form until the end of my sophomore year. But I was so confident in my choice that I did not wish to postpone my commitment.

During the freshman year, I took a required introductory philosophy course in the fall semester, followed by a required introductory psychology course in the spring—both taught by the same instructor, a bright and attractive young woman with a degree in philosophy. Nevertheless, the psychology course offered solid scientific fare (the text was by Pillsbury). I enjoyed the course thoroughly and felt more at home in it than I had in the philosophy course. But I certainly did not at that time entertain the idea that I might find my life work in psychology.

Two significant events occurred in my sophomore year: I took a course in developmental psychology with Harry L. Hollingworth, then chairman of Barnard's Psychology Department; and I happened to read an article by Charles Spearman. Hollingworth was a fascinating lecturer, with a lively curiosity about all natural phenomena. He was an individualist who pursued his own theoretical bent with vigor and independence. He was also one of the last of the generalists in psychology. Years later, a classmate reminded me that after one of "Holly's" classes I remarked, "Once I get my Ph.D. in math, I'm going back to take some more psych. courses." Then the Spearman article really clinched matters. In it I learned not only about correlation but also about some fascinating relationships among correlation coefficients that later led Spearman to develop his rationale for the tetrad equation, itself an early step toward modern techniques of factor analysis. Here, then, I saw a way of enjoying the best of two possible worlds: I could remain faithful to my first love and espouse the newcomer too. I filled out new forms for a major in psychology and embarked upon the work of a lifetime.

Special Influences. I have thus far singled out two psychologists, Hollingworth and Spearman, because their influence happened to come at a critical stage in my career choice. Obviously, my subsequent development in psychology, my eventual concentration on certain areas of specialization, and my theoretical orientation have been shaped by many other contacts in graduate school and throughout my career. At the time when I was a graduate student at Columbia (and during the following years when I was an instructor "across the street" at Barnard), the Columbia Psychology Department was one of the most active in the country. I owe much to my contacts with faculty and fellow students; several of the latter went on to become distinguished colleagues in many parts of the country.

Those were exciting times in the burgeoning science of psychology. The journals bristled with vigorous controversies on topics ranging from Gestalt psychology to factor analysis. The New York State Psychiatric Institute had just been established in its new quarters in the Columbia Medical Center and it offered great promise of interdisciplinary research. The Institute of Human Relations had recently been opened at nearby Yale University, with such leaders as Gesell, Hull, and Yerkes. There was much commuting between New York and New Haven by faculty, students, and postdoctorals. In 1929, as a second-year graduate student, I enjoyed the heady privilege of attending the International Congress of Psychology at Yale (the last to be held in the United State for over three decades), where we saw and heard the real persons attached to such familiar names as Pavlov, Spearman, Pieron, and McDougall.

The summer of 1929 was truly memorable for me. It began with a research assistantship at the Carnegie Institution of Washington in Cold Spring Harbor, Long Island, under Charles B. Davenport (who had taught biology in college to R. S. Woodworth, one of my professors at Columbia). It ended with the International Congress at Yale. And sandwiched in between were six weeks of summer school in which I took two courses with Clark Hull. At that time, Hull was just moving from Wisconsin to Yale, and on the way he taught Summer School at Columbia. My contacts with Hull continued long after the completion of those summer courses, through correspondence, exchange of reprints, meetings, and personal counsel. I recall vividly his wise advice against my taking a job in a certain type of organization where "trying to get anything done is like swimming in glue."

In trying to identify the specific manifestations of Hull's influence on my psychological development, I can point to at least two. Both represent general attitudes toward psychology. One is a deep respect for rigorously controlled experimental approaches to hypothesis testing. The other is a firm conviction that learning theory is the heart of psychology and that study of learning is what primarily differentiates psychology from other disciplines concerned with living organisms. Although I have not worked directly in the area of learning, this orientation has provided a setting into which my own work could be fitted and more broadly interpreted.

Another influence that I consider to be of primary importance was more indirect. It is the influence of J. R. Kantor of Indiana University. In some ways, Kantor resembles Hollingworth. He, too, is one of the last of the generalists in psychology, with a remarkable breadth of knowledge extending over psychology and related fields. He, too, formulated a comprehensive theoretical system for psychology. And he, too, pursued his interests with vigor and independence. It is, however, his emphasis on the role of environment and his explication of the specific operation of environmental factors in individual development that I recognize as the predominant influence on my own work.

My special interest in studying Kantor's published works and my opportunities for personal contacts with him stem from an event in my personal life. In the summer of 1933 I married one of Kantor's former students, John Porter Foley, Jr., of Bloomington, Indiana. After receiving the Bachelor's degree in psychology from I.U., John obtained the Ph.D. degree at Columbia, where we met. In many ways, John's experiential background complemented and thereby enriched mine. His Indiana upbringing and I.U. degree certainly provided the much needed broadening of my ultralimited New York City environment. I had, indeed, done what I advise my students against: taken my undergraduate and graduate degrees at the same institution and lived throughout in my native city. Within psychology itself, John not only stimulated my exploration of Kantor's ideas, but also encouraged my interest in areas in which I had had limited preparation. For example, as a graduate student at Columbia and for several years in his own subsequent research and teaching, he worked largely in animal psychology, a specialty I had touched upon only lightly in my own training. Similarly, his studies in anthropology and his research with Franz Boas strengthened my own interest in a field that is most relevant to differential psychology. Professionally, my marriage has thus meant that I had the benefit of not one but two Ph.D.'s in psychology.

RESEARCH INTERESTS

The Role of Environment. A major theme underlying my research is the operation of experiential factors in the individual's
psychological development. An early example is provided by an
exploratory study in which the factor pattern represented by the
intercorrelations among a set of test scores was experimentally altered through the interpolation of a brief relevant experience
(1936b). The subjects were 200 sixth-grade school children.
Factor analyses of parallel forms of the tests administered in
pre-test and post-test sessions revealed several changes in the antici-
pated direction. The interpolated experience was a capsule version of the sort of instruction in problem-solving techniques that is
provided over much longer periods in ordinary school work.

The same approach was illustrated in my paper, "The Nature
of Psychological 'Traits,'" which surveyed published research
demonstrating the effect of group differences in prior experience
upon the emergence and organization of intellectual traits, as well
as the results of a few more direct investigations of experimentally
interpolated experiences (1948c). The relevant literature was again
surveyed in a later paper entitled "On the Formation of Psychological Traits" (1970b). By this time a considerable body of research had accumulated, both from comparative analyses of
groups with differing educational, socioeconomic, occupational, or
cultural backgrounds and from experimental investigations utilizing a variety of procedures. The results generally supported the
hypothesis that not only does the nature of one's antecedent experiences affect the degree of differentiation of "intelligence" into
distinct abilities, but it also affects the particular abilities that
emerge, such as verbal, numerical, and spatial abilities. Thus, experiential factors affect not only the level of the individual's intellectual development, but also the very categories in terms of
which his abilities may be identified.

The influence of environmental factors upon intellectual development was investigated from a different angle in a set of studies

of Puerto Rican and Negro children in New York City conducted jointly with some of my graduate students. In an investigation of Negro and white preschool children in language development and Draw-A-Man Test performance (1952b), the experimental design permitted a simultaneous comparison with regard to race, sex, and type of neighborhood (uniracial vs. interracial). The results revealed some interesting interactions among these three variables, which were consistent with environmental hypotheses. For instance, several indices of language development revealed significant differences between Negroes and whites living in uniracial neighborhoods, but not between the samples living in interracial neighborhoods.

Two studies of Puerto Rican children in New York City—one on preschool children and one on elementary school children—threw some interesting light on the manifestations of bilingualism (1953f, 1953g). For example, when children are exposed to one language at home and another in school, as was true of these children, they manifest a characteristic "linguistic bifurcation," that is, they tend not to learn either language fully and are thereby handicapped in both languages. Thus, whether tests were administered in English or Spanish made no difference in the performance of the Puerto Rican children. On the other hand, when the spontaneous speech of Puerto Rican preschool children was studied by a bilingual examiner and the children were completely free to use a combination of English and Spanish, they demonstrated superior linguistic maturity in terms of such indices as sentence length and sentence structure.

Still another approach to the same underlying question is illustrated by a long-term project on the role of experiential factors in the development of creative thinking in children and adolescents carried out in collaboration with several students and former students (1968f, 1969c, 1970a, 1970c, 1971f, 1971g). This series of studies utilized three basic procedures. First, the personal characteristics and experiential backgrounds of highly creative high school boys and girls were investigated through biographical inventories and tests. Second, an exploratory study was conducted of the home environments and child-rearing practices associated with creativity among elementary school children. Third, an intensive program of creativity training for the elementary school ages was developed and evaluated through follow-up studies.

In the first study, students selected on the basis of outstanding creative achievement were found to differ significantly from comparable control groups in a number of variables. With these differences before us, we could sketch a tentative picture of conditions conducive to creative productivity in adolescent boys and girls. Additional related information was provided by the second procedure, in which data were gathered by home visits and interviews with mothers of creative and equated control children. This study helped to fill in the picture from a different source and at a younger developmental level. The third procedure demonstrated that creative attitudes can be encouraged and creative achievement improved significantly by an appropriately devised set of experiences presented within the school situation.

The Psychology of Art. Certain exploratory inquiries into the psychology of art considerably antedated the broader creativity project. In fact, my first publication (1928), based on an honors project conducted in my junior year at Barnard, reported a minor experimental study of the effect of familiarization upon aesthetic judgment. Several later publications with my husband reflected our joint interest in children's art, in the artistic productions of self-taught "Sunday painters," and in cultural differences in artistic expression (1936d, 1938e, 1938f, 1940e). Soon this interest led us both to a long-term project on the relation of art and abnormality (1940f, 1941f, 1941g, 1941h, 1941i, 1942e, 1943b, 1944b). Our decision to carry out this project was bolstered by our dissatisfaction with the many unsupported claims regarding the identification and interpretation of pathological "signs" in art products. The extensive literature on this topic ranges from fanciful psychologizing about paintings by eminent artists who have suffered psychotic episodes to the use of drawing tests as projective techniques for personality assessment. Our own efforts to test some of the alleged indices of abnormality, under more nearly controlled conditions, demonstrated that a number of such indices were related not to pathology but to educational, occupational, or cultural differences.

Statistics, Tests, and Traits. Much of my research has been concerned with the application of statistical techniques to the development and evaluation of psychological tests and to analyses of intercorrelations of test scores in the effort to identify intellectual traits. Remember that it was through statistics that I entered psychology as a life work. Understandably, my Ph.D. dissertation at Columbia (my second publication) utilized an adaptation of Spearman's tetrad equations in the identification of a group factor or "trait" of immediate associative memory (1930). This research had left a number of unanswered questions which I pursued during the next two years (1932a). The results indicated the presence of several, relatively independent memory factors, a finding that has been confirmed and elaborated by later investigators.

Several projects were concerned with the development and evaluation of tests for specific practical purposes (1952c, 1954f, 1960g). Some studies were more broadly oriented, dealing with the empirical procedures and statistical techniques of item analysis (1953a) or test reliability (1934a, 1954e), for example. Any account of my involvement with psychological tests would be incomplete without mention of the test evaluations I prepared for each volume of the *Mental Measurements Yearbooks* (*MMY*) since the inception of the series (1938a, 1938b, 1940a, 1940d, 1949a, 1949b, 1949d, 1953b, 1953d, 1959c, 1959d, 1965b, 1965c). When Oscar K. Buros began the publication of these yearbooks in 1938, he launched an enterprise that has done much to raise the standards of test publishing. I consider it a privilege to have been among the many psychologists participating in this monumental project.

The task undertaken single-handed by Buros is impressive in both its magnitude and its daring. The numerous problems encountered in carrying it out can be gleaned from the Introduction to the 1940 *MMY*, which provides fascinating reading. One example will suffice to give the flavor of the operation. In his characteristic quest for accuracy and objectivity, Buros submitted to test publishers copies of the reviews of their tests, without the reviewers' names, prior to publication. Excerpts from a sample of replies, including some quite hostile responses from publishers whose tests had been adversely evaluated, are reproduced in the Introduction to the 1940 *MMY*. It happened that one of my own early reviews was the object of such an irate reply. The lengthy letter, objecting vigorously to the criticisms of both of the reviewers evaluating this test, concluded with the following impassioned phrases: "I appeal to you in the name of common decency to withhold from publication . . . the 'reviews' submitted by Reviewers A and B. On the other hand, in the event that you . . . publish the 'reviews' . . . I must comfort myself with the thought that we are not the first people who have been maligned and grossly misrepresented in a most unfair and scurrilous manner. . . . At any rate, I am happy in the knowledge that I am spared the personal acquaintance of these two brave lads, A and B." I have often wondered what the writer of this letter thought when he saw the printed review and discovered that one of the two brave lads was female.

Miscellany. Besides the relatively coordinated and continuing research interests described thus far, there are scattered studies falling outside any broadly conceived plan. These were undertaken to satisfy curiosity about specific questions and may be regarded as the research counterparts of the "electives" in a college student's curriculum. Then, too, they may reflect a reaction against undue specialization, arising from my generalist predilections. Examples of this type of research range from a study of the effect of shape upon the perceived area of two-dimensional figures (1936a) to an investigation of fear and anger in college girls by the diary method (1948b, 1948e), a factor analysis of learning behavior in several breeds of dogs (1955c), and a case study of a musically talented "idiot savant" (1959e).

WRITING AND TEACHING

Whereas the primary object of research is to advance the discovery of truth, the chief purpose of both teaching and writing is communication. It thus seemed natural in this account to group teaching activities with those publications concerned, not with the reporting of my own research, but with surveys of available information on a topic (as in textbooks) or theoretical analyses of certain areas of psychology. The connection appears all the clearer when we consider that textbooks are designed for teaching and are thus an extension of one's own classroom teaching. Similarly, several of my theoretical papers are the published versions of lectures given before various organizations.

Textbooks. My books, even more than my research reports and journal articles, reflect my underlying interest in the nature and origins of individual differences and in techniques for measuring them. Such interest is illustrated in the successive editions of *Differential Psychology* (1937a, 1949d, 1958a) and *Psychological Testing* (1954c, 1961c, 1968e). Two volumes I have edited likewise fall into the same general area. *Individual Differences* (1965a) is a collection of excerpts illustrating the historical development of major topics in differential psychology over approximately a century. *Testing Problems in Perspective* (1966e) is a collection of the most significant papers presented over a twenty-five-year period at the Annual Invitational Conference on Testing Problems sponsored by Educational Testing Service.

Because my interest in differential psychology pervades so much of my work, it may be well at this point to examine this area more closely. First, a word about the term "differential psychology." Prior to the publication of the first edition of my book by that title in 1937, the area was commonly referred to as "individual differences." I felt that the broader term "differential psychology" was more appropriate. This title was a direct translation of a term proposed by William Stern in 1900 in a German book on the subject (Stern, W. *Über Psychologie der individuellen Differenzen: Ideen zur einer "Differentielle Psychologie."* Leipzig: Barth, 1900). To my knowledge, however, this term had not been previously used in any publication in the English language.

A basic question underlying much of differential psychology

pertains to the contribution of hereditary and environmental factors to individual differences in psychological traits. Research on this question has utilized a wide diversity of approaches, ranging from statistical studies of family resemblances and differences to selective breeding experiments with white rats and fruit flies. A related question concerns the relation of behavioral to organic differences, including anatomical, physiological, and biochemical characteristics of the individual. Investigations of behavioral changes associated with growth and with learning provide relevant data from other angles. Differential psychology is also concerned with the identification and organization of psychological traits (as in factor-analytic research) and with their distribution in the general population. Special attention has been focused on the extremes of the distribution of intellectual traits, as illustrated by the mentally retarded at one end and the intellectually gifted and creative at the other.

A major part of differential psychology deals with group differences in behavior, covering studies of sex, racial, national, socioeconomic, regional, and other types of groups. An important finding of all such group comparisons is the extensive overlapping of the trait distributions of whatever groups are compared. In other words, even when large and significant differences in mean scores are demonstrated between two groups, many individuals in the lower-scoring group equal or excel individuals in the higher-scoring group. Another important point to bear in mind is that the presence of a group difference in any psychological trait does not in itself imply a causal explanation for such a difference. Insofar as the groups under investigation differ in environmental background and have been reared under different cultural conditions, the observed behavioral differences may have resulted from such environmental dissimilarities. Although it is difficult to disentangle hereditary from environmental influences in human research, those experimental designs permitting some isolation of these variables have generally shown environmental factors to play a major role in the existing group differences in psychological traits.

It can be seen that the field of differential psychology ranges widely. A vast amount of descriptive information has been accumulated about individual and group differences in a broad spectrum of psychological traits. The fundamental aim of differential psychology, however, is not description. Its aim is similar to that of all psychology, namely the understanding of behavior. Differential psychology approaches this task through a comparative analysis of behavior under varying environmental and biological conditions. By relating the observed differences in behavior to other known concomitant circumstances, it should be possible to tease out the relative contribution of different factors to behavioral development. If we can discover why one person (or group of persons) behaves differently from another, we shall advance our knowledge of what makes each behave as he does.

Both *Differential Psychology* and *Psychological Testing* are textbooks, designed for class use. As such they grew out of courses I had taught for many years. Writing a text based on one's courses is a practice common to many textbook writers, I understand. A course I had taught repeatedly at both undergraduate and graduate levels was likewise the principal incentive for my writing *Fields of Applied Psychology* (1964c). The preparation of such a book also appealed to my generalist tendencies because it enabled me to bring together several disparate and apparently unrelated areas of psychology. The aim of the book was to introduce the student to the work psychologists do outside the classroom or university laboratory.

A byproduct of taking such a comprehensive look at applied psychology is the emergence of relations among the findings of different approaches. Fresh insight may be gained from the juxtaposition of similar problems studied in diverse contexts. For instance, research on teacher effectiveness in the classroom and supervisory effectiveness in industry revealed some interesting parallels in the dimensions of effective behavior that were identified. Furthermore, the operation of individual differences in both types of contexts was evidenced in interactions between teacher or supervisor behavior, on the one hand, and the nature of the task or the characteristics of the individual pupil or employee, on the other. In other words, the *relative* effectiveness of different teaching or supervisory procedures varied with task and individual characteristics. This concept of interaction of variables is widely applicable to many situations.

My texts have enjoyed extensive use in foreign countries, probably because their characteristically broad orientation provides convenient surveys of contemporary developments in American psychology. In addition to translations into several languages (see 1958a, 1961c, 1964c), the American editions themselves are in use in a number of countries in which English is either the principal language or sufficiently familiar in university circles. As a result, I have been put in touch with colleagues in several countries, from whom I regularly receive publications. Within my own areas of specialization, the opportunity thus to learn about current research in England, France, Germany, Israel, and Sweden has proved particularly helpful. With the overpowering communication explosion in science today, I have found such personal correspondence and exchange of reprints a great boon in my efforts to keep abreast of developments in the field.

Articles. Several of my theoretical articles, as well as some of the topics covered in my books, were suggested by the confusions and controversies I observed in discussions among psychologists with differing orientations or in questions directed to psychologists by persons in other fields. My goal in such cases was clarification of concepts and a systematic attempt to work out the implications of a given theoretical position. A case in point is the confusion between "hereditary" and "organic" causes of behavior (1948f, 1954a, 1958b). This confusion is compounded by the ambiguity of such common terms as "constitutional," "innate," and "inborn." "Constitutional" is used by some to refer to behavior characteristics having an organic basis and by others as a synonym for "hereditary." Similarly, "innate" and "inborn" often refer to that which is present at birth; but sometimes these terms, too, are employed interchangeably with "hereditary." What needs to be considered, of course, is that environmental factors may produce an organic condition leading to behavioral deviations. Moreover, such environmental factors may operate prenatally. Obviously the existence of a condition at birth does not necessarily imply a hereditary origin.

My efforts to clarify these distinctions led eventually to a reformulation of certain questions about the role of heredity and environment in behavior development. Thus it became apparent that for such traditional questions as *"What* is inherited and *what* is acquired?" or *"How much* do heredity and environment contribute to behavior?"* we could more profitably substitute the question, *"How?"* The first two questions are meaningless and unanswerable. From both theoretical and practical standpoints, the more fruitful questions pertain to the *modus operandi* or the specific mechanisms whereby hereditary and environmental factors interact in the development of behavioral differences (1958b).

Similarly, I have been deeply concerned about the frequent misuse of psychological tests or misinterpretations of test scores and more particularly about the prevalent misconceptions about "culture-free" or "culture-fair" tests. A psychological test is no more than an objective and standardized measure of a sample of the individual's behavior. Hence it follows that any factors that influence behavior will and should be reflected in test scores. Whether or not cultural differentials should be eliminated from a test depends upon the *breadth* of the cultural differences in performance: is the difference narrowly restricted to the test or does it extend to the broader behavioral domain the test is designed to assess? Any attempt to rule out cultural differences in the latter case will serve only to lower the validity or usefulness of the test and to discard information needed to help the individual overcome environmental handicaps (1950f, 1960a, 1961d, 1964a).

Broader issues regarding the interpretation of test results include the need for validation research (covering construct as well as criterion-related validity) as a basis for specifying the meaning of a test score (1950a, 1964d). Similarly, the loose use of such global terms as "intelligence" or (even worse) "IQ" must be scrutinized in the light of factor-analytic research on the identification and organization of such intellectual traits as verbal, numerical, and spatial abilities (1954b). In a later paper (1967b), I developed the theme that misuses and misinterpretations of tests often stem from a gradual dissociation of test development from the mainstream of psychological research. Testing specialists have made great advances in the refinement of test construction techniques and statistical analysis, without sufficient consideration of the substantive findings about the human behavior measured by the tests. This situation has probably contributed to the public expressions of antitest attitudes so prevalent in the 1960s. The partial isolation of testing from other relevant developments in psychology undoubtedly reflects the increasing specialization of psychologists. Its adverse effects provide an eloquent plea for the cultivation of a few generalists in our midst.

Teaching. Like many of my colleagues, I engage in a diversity of psychological activities. Research and writing have already been described. Administration, committee appointments, consulting work for various private or governmental organizations, and participation in the functions of psychological associations will be touched upon in the next section. Nevertheless, university teaching is my occupation, and teaching has been the central activity of my professional life since 1930. Beginning as an instructor at Barnard during the economic Depression, I moved to Queens College of the City University of New York as the first and only member of its newly established psychology department in February 1939. There I remained as chairman of a steadily growing department, through World War II and a few of the post-war years. In 1947, I joined the faculty of the Graduate School of Fordham University, which continues to be my academic home.

Although in a number of respects, university students are a more homogeneous group than the general population, the goals of teaching a given subject differ for different academic subgroups. A distinctive need of the *graduate student,* for example, is that he learn to conduct research. On the basis of more than two decades of contact with graduate students, what advice would

I give the research neophyte? Here are a few random suggestions. First, in trying to identify a problem, look at inconsistencies among the findings of different investigators and at current controversies in the literature; look at the loose ends left dangling in published studies. Second, formulate answerable questions. A vague malaise about a topic or a strong conviction that "something should be done" to solve an important social problem is not enough. Nor does access to a population "that should be interesting to study" constitute a problem for research, although observation of such a population may suggest problems. Third, whittle down the problem to manageable size. Beginners are apt to underestimate the magnitude of the problems they choose.

Fourth, make sure that you are asking scientifically meaningful questions. Your hypotheses should be so formulated and your research design so planned that the hypotheses can be disproved if they are incorrect. It is well to ask yourself what sort of results would lead to an acceptance of the hypothesis and what sort of results to a rejection. Otherwise, you may be operating on the principle that "heads I win, tails you lose." Fifth, be prepared for false starts and be alert for unanticipated leads. The path of true research is neither straight nor smooth. Finally, remember individual differences. Do not try to imitate someone else's approach if you find his research "style" uncongenial. There is enough latitude in research for each individual to make his unique contribution.

In the teaching of *undergraduate majors,* an advantage of psychology, in comparison with older sciences, is the greater closeness of contemporary psychology to the foundations of its own scientific edifice. This circumstance can be utilized in stimulating enthusiasm and encouraging the student to identify with the scientist. Thus the serious student of psychology can readily become acquainted with the procedures whereby particular psychological facts were gathered, hypotheses developed and tested, and generalizations formulated. In presenting the facts and principles of psychology, it is customary to report at least some of the original experiments through which they were derived. Often such reporting is accompanied by critical evaluations of the experiments and a discussion of how the procedure could have been improved. The student thus has a direct opportunity to learn what sort of questions to ask in evaluating results; what pitfalls should be avoided in gathering data; and what conditions may limit generalizations from observed facts. Hence the relative youth of modern psychology and the rapid development it is undergoing should provide powerful safeguards against accepting a statement as true because it appears in print, or because "authorities agree."

What of the non-major and the *educated layman*? What is the role of psychlogy in a liberal education? What does the general student, who is not preparing for a career in professional psychology, expect from exposure to this field? A common answer is that he expects to increase his understanding of himself and his associates and thereby improve the management of his own feelings and actions. I would certainly not deny that courses in psychology may be relevant to these objectives. But the contribution that a knowledge of psychology can make along these lines is at best indirect. It is in a class with what a knowledge of optics can contribute to the production of a painting, or what a knowledge of physiology can contribute to a medical diagnosis. The sort of personal development popularly sought from psychology can be more directly fostered by literature, art, philosophy, or the experiences in leadership and other interpersonal behavior available outside the classroom.

A second reason for studying psychology is to be found in the need for information about the increasing functions served by professional psychologists in modern society. Psychology now constitutes a significant part of the contemporary scene with which the educated man should be familiar. He should, for example, know what services psychologists can properly provide; he should be aware of what can and what cannot be accomplished with such instruments as psychological tests; and he should be able to detect unfounded claims and charlatanism. A course in psychology for the general student should certainly include a consideration of the earmarks of charlatanism and a discussion of how the reputable psychologist can be differentiated from the untrained or unscrupulous practitioner.

Finally there is a third type of contribution that psychology can make to a liberal education—one that I myself consider to be the most significant. This contribution stems from psychology's nature as a basic science, rather than as an applied science or as an area of professional practice. Psychology is in a peculiarly favorable position to introduce the student to the nature of scientific method and to demonstrate the applicability of this method to his own thinking and problem-solving. For example, research on perception and memory has demonstrated the selectivity of both of these processes. Of all the stimuli impinging upon our senses at any moment, we are most likely to notice and recall those that fit in with our expectations, hypotheses, or biases. This selectivity contributes to the survival of superstitions as well as social stereotypes. The isolated supporting instances are perceived and retained, while the more frequent contradictory instances are overlooked and forgotten.

Similarly, the application of the scientific method to behavioral data highlights the multiplicity of variables that need to be controlled—or at least recognized—when drawing conclusions about causal relations. Some of these variables may pertain to subtle attitudinal or interpersonal differences that may easily escape notice. An example is provided by the "Hawthorne effect," which refers to the side effects of participation in an experiment (see 1964c, pp. 133-135). Merely being a subject in a particular investigation may in itself involve special interpersonal relations with the research staff, as well as associated changes in status or self-concept, over and above the experimentally controlled variables. Any resulting differences between the reactions of experimental and control subjects may thus arise from these incidental variations rather than from the deliberately introduced experimental changes.

Another example is the "self-fulfilling prophecy," or the fact that what is expected of an individual affects his immediate behavior as well as his subsequent emotional and intellectual development (see 1958a, p. 553). This mechanism is likely to influence the achievement of individuals or groups about whom social stereotypes exist within a given culture. Similarly, it tends to augment parent-child resemblances in any psychological trait, from mathematical talent to neuroticism.

ADMINISTRATIVE, CONSULTING, AND ASSOCIATIONAL ACTIVITIES

The functions grouped together in the present section are obviously miscellaneous and indubitably ancillary to my primary professional objectives. Nevertheless, they must be included in this account to provide a realistic picture of typical professional roles and day-by-day activities of academic psychologists.

Administration. At the time of my move from Queens College to Fordham University, I was convinced that administration rated very low in my scale of personal preferences. In fact, I begrudged the time my duties as Chairman of the Queens College Psychology Department had taken away from the far more gratifying activities of teaching, research, and writing. Because this view of administration is shared by many of my fellow psychologists, my own opinion was repeatedly reinforced over the intervening years. Eventually, however, I came to recognize that administration, like so many other occupational functions, covers a wide spectrum of activities and varies greatly in different contexts. Local circumstances may be such as to overload an administrative post with the less attractive aspects of the job. Because of insufficient supporting personnel or an overelaboration of formal procedures, too much time may be required for mechanical, dull, and uninspiring details. Or long hours may be spent in futile committee meetings that lead to little or no action. These seem to be the most common complaints of disillusioned administrators.

When in 1968 Fordham University, in accordance with its policy of rotating department chairmanships, invited me to assume this office I was psychologically ready to reconsider the possibility. Hence I accepted the offer and have had no regrets. Among the most challenging and rewarding aspects of a department chairmanship, I would list curriculum development and faculty selection and allocation. It is an exciting experience to work with faculty colleagues and students in formulating long-range departmental plans; to identify gaps to be filled in the existing courses and personnel; and to have the opportunity to begin actual implementation.

Even more stimulating to me is a study of the varied patterns of interests and talents provided by the members of any one department. Ten or twenty persons, all of whom have a Ph.D. in psychology and have chosen a career in college teaching, can be so very different from one another! Each is equipped to make diverse contributions to the total departmental picture. The challenge is to so structure the working environment as to encourage the maximum utilization of these individual differences. There is room for a wide variety of teaching styles, whose relative effectiveness is a function of the subject matter, nature of the course, student level and orientation, and instructor predilection and skills. Here again we see the applicability of the concept of *interaction* among student, instructor, and subject matter variables. How much richer is the result when every instructor has an opportunity to "do his own thing" than when some uniform set of "good teaching principles" is held up as a universal pattern to emulate!

The late 1960s and early 1970s have been lively years on university campuses. There was little time for quiet concentration. Traditional references to the ivory tower and the ivy-covered walls seemed most remote and alien to the prevailing climate. Student protest, Black Studies and Afro-American Institutes, and Women's Lib had taken their place.

At times, the galloping pace of change threatened to destroy what was worth preserving, along with what was outworn and in need of revision. But by 1971 there was some cause for optimism. The situation seemed to have achieved some balance; and sanity prevailed in academia. The major effect in most universities was a healthy and constructive increase in faculty and student participation in policy-making and administrative decisions. I was privileged in being involved in many of these innovations in my own university. In addition to serving on special committees, I was elected to the first faculty senate, on which I served for several subsequent terms. I was also in the first set of faculty representatives chosen to serve, along with student representatives, on the committees of the Board of Trustees.

Consulting Activities. Over the years I have served as an individual consultant or member of an advisory committee for a number of government agencies at the city, state, and federal levels; for private foundations; and for educational, industrial, and other types of private organizations. Of special interest to me was my work for the College Entrance Examination Board, both as research consultant and as a member and subsequently chairman of its Research and Development Committee. I also recall with particular pleasure my service on the Advisory Committee on Science Education of the National Science Foundation, which brought me into contact with representatives of other sciences, and the busy summer I spent as overseas consultant for the Ford Foundation at the Fundação Getúlio Vargas in Rio de Janeiro.

Much of my consulting work has been concerned with such problems as test development and evaluation; design of research utilizing tests and other assessment instruments; and the interpretation of individual or group differences in test performance. In these connections, I am reminded particularly of two popular misconceptions that I repeatedly encountered and endeavored to mitigate. One is what I regard as an internally inconsistent view of the operation of environment. On the one hand, environmental conditions are looked upon as a major source of existing group differences, as illustrated by the effects of disadvantaged environments on the development of minority group children. On the other hand, the cumulative effects of these adverse environmental conditions upon the individual are minimized or ignored in plans for social action. Thus an individual whose antecedent experiences have failed to provide the prerequisite information, skills, and attitudes is expected to achieve successfully in college courses, on jobs, or in other situations for which he lacks the necessary qualifications. Such procedures can serve only to heighten the frustration and further undermine the self-confidence of the individual and to perpetuate discriminatory social stereotypes among his associates. A more constructive and logically defensible approach would stress: (a) remedial programs to reduce the effects of cultural deficits; (b) concentration of effort on the improvement of environmental conditions at early life stages, when the cumulative effects of adverse environment are minimal.

A second and related fallacy is illustrated by the all-too-frequent recommendation that any test or other assessment device revealing a significant group difference is *ipso facto* discriminatory against the lower-scoring group and should be discontinued. I have touched upon this fallacy from another angle in connection with research on "culture-fair tests." At this point, let me add only that this reaction to tests is analogous to requesting a physician that he discard his thermometer because it often registers an undesirable deviation from the norm when applied to children who are ill, and therefore discriminates against sick children.

Associational Activities. The first office I held in a scientific association was the secretaryship of the Psychology Section of the New York Academy of Sciences in the mid-1930s. This was followed a couple of years later by the chairmanship of the section. In the latter office, my principal duty was the enjoyable one of inviting eminent speakers for the monthly meeting of the section.

For varying periods of time I have been a member and served in various capacities in the following additional organizations: American Psychological Association, Eastern Psychological Association, New York State Psychological Association, Psychometric Society, Psychonomic Society, Psychology Section of National Research Council, Board of Trustees of the American Psychological Foundation, and local university chapters of Phi Beta Kappa and Sigma Xi. Besides membership on innumerable committees and the chairmanship of some, I have over the years held various offices in one or more of these organizations. Those I recall most clearly are the presidencies, probably because (with the exception of the presidency of the American Psychological Foundation), each involved the preparation, delivery, and publication of a presidential address. These presidencies (and the references to the corresponding published addresses) include: Eastern Psychological Association (1948c), Division of General Psychology, APA (1958b), and Division of Evaluation and Measurement, APA (1967b). In 1970 I was elected to the presidency of the American Psychological Association, which includes one year as President-elect (1970-71), one year as President (1971-72), and one year as Past President (1972-73). I am expected to deliver a presidential address in September 1972.

In commenting upon my experiences in these associations, I shall single out the APA, with which I have been associated for the longest time and in the widest variety of capacities. My contacts with the APA began when I became an associate member in 1931 and a fellow in 1934. I was elected to the Council of Representatives in 1947, shortly after its formation, and I have served on it repeatedly since then as representative of two divisions, a member of the Board of Directors, Recording Secretary, and President. This experience, in combination with service on a number of divisional and association-wide committees and boards, has given me a view of the Association from many levels and over a period when great changes were taking place in both the APA and psychology itself. When I joined, the APA had 1,267 members, most of whom were university professors. In 1971, the total membership was 31,917, and more than half were employed in such nonacademic settings as government agencies, industrial organizations, school systems, hospitals, clinics, prisons, counseling centers, consulting firms, and private practice.

If I ask myself what have been the most persistent concerns of the Association's governing structure over this period, three problems stand out most vividly in my impressions. The first pertains to ways of ensuring wide representation and participation by the membership in association affairs. This concern is repeatedly manifested, for example, in the preparation of slates for various boards and committees. Invariably the question is raised about bringing in "new blood" and valiant efforts are made to achieve this objective. One year the Board of Directors established a "Committee on Participation in Association Affairs," whose function was to seek out persons with the particular qualifications or expertise required for each board or committee, who were willing to serve but not sufficiently "visible" to have been nominated in the normal course of events. This procedure yielded some promising slates, but unfortunately the less visible nominees were infrequently elected when appearing on a slate with more familiar names.

The following year another device was tried: the less visible names were marked with an asterisk, indicating that these candidates had been specially chosen because of their relevant qualifications and as a means of encouraging participation by persons who had not heretofore been active in APA affairs. Many of these persons, of course, had low visibility because they were young, had not published extensively, or had had limited contacts with other psychologists. Although efforts such as those cited have undoubtedly helped to broaden the base of APA participation, the problem remains and the APA governance continues to attack it with vigor and ingenuity.

A second major concern is the achievement of balance among the conflicting pressures exerted by a highly diversified membership. This is illustrated by the varied interests and objectives represented by the different divisions as well as the affiliated State Associations. The Division of Experimental Psychology or the Division of Physiological and Comparative Psychology, for example, expects different services from its national association than does the Division of Clinical Psychology or the Division of School Psychology. A broader and more pervasive differentiation is that among members with a predominantly scientific, professional, or social-action orientation. Spokesmen for each of these three orientations have repeatedly argued that APA should devote proportionately more of its resources to services and activities consistent with their own orientation.

A third problem is that of coping with the sheer magnitude of the APA and modifying its structure and operation to keep pace with its rapid growth. The increasing size and heterogeneity of the membership have led to periodic reexaminations of the organization of the APA. Thus in 1945, when the APA merged with the American Association for Applied Psychology, the present differentiation into divisions was introduced in recognition of the diversity of interests and professional activities of psychologists. At the same time, the Council of Representatives and the Central Office were established to facilitate the administration of the complex and rapidly expanding Association. More recently, a plan for the reorganization of the Council of Representatives was carefully developed and widely evaluated prior to its full implementation in 1972. The chief objectives of this plan were to increase the functioning effectiveness of the Council and to ensure fuller representation of all the membership, while keeping the size of the Council within workable limits.

Further reorganizations of the entire Association are now under serious consideration at several levels. The administrative complexities of the Association, its present and projected size, and the sharpened diversification of member interests and goals have once more combined to exert conspicuous strain on the current organizational structure. We can anticipate another period of active discussion of alternative solutions. At this critical stage in the development of both the Association and psychology as a whole, it is to be hoped that whatever solution is adopted will provide sufficient flexibility or autonomy to allow full scope to the wide individual differences among psychologists, while at the same time retaining a firm grasp on the distinctive contribution that psychology—in contrast to other disciplines—can make to human problems.

PUBLICATIONS

1928   With F. H. Lund. An interpretation of esthetic experience. *American Journal of Psychology, 40,* 434-448.

1930   A group factor in immediate memory. *Archives of Psychology,* No. 120. Pp. 61.

1932   (a) Further studies on the memory factor. *Archives of Psychology,* No. 142. Pp. 60.

(b) Review of H. B. Reed, The influence of training on changes in variability in achievement. *American Journal of Psychology, 44*, 842-843.

(c) With H. E. Garrett. The tetrad difference criterion and the measurement of mental traits. *Annals of the New York Academy of Science, 33*, 233-282.

1934 (a) The influence of practice upon test reliability. *Journal of Educational Psychology, 25*, 321-335.

(b) Practice and variability. *Psychological Monographs, 45*(204). Pp. 55.

1935 Some ambiguous concepts in the field of mental organization. *American Journal of Psychology, 47*, 508-511.

1936 (a) The estimation of area. *Journal of General Psychology, 14*, 201-225.

(b) The influence of specific experience upon mental organization. *Genetic Psychology Monographs, 18*(4), 245,355.

(c) Review of D. H. Cooke, Minimum essentials of statistics as applied to education and psychology. *American Journal of Psychology, 48*, 557-558.

(d) With J. P. Foley, Jr. An analysis of spontaneous drawings by children in different cultures. *Journal of Applied Psychology, 20*, 689-726.

1937 (a) *Differential psychology*. New York: Macmillan. Pp. 615.

(b) Review of G. D. Higginson, Psychology. *American Journal of Psychology, 49*, 324-325.

1938 (a) American Council on Education Psychological Examination for College Freshmen. *Mental Measurements Yearbook*, 95-96.

(b) Detroit Tests of Learning Aptitude. *Mental Measurements Yearbook*, 108-109.

(c) Faculties versus factors: A reply to Professor Thurstone. *Psychological Bulletin, 35*, 391-395.

(d) Review of S. D. Porteus, Primitive intelligence and environment. *American Journal of Psychology, 51*, 192-194.

(e) With J. P. Foley, Jr. A study of animal drawings by Indian children of the North Pacific Coast. *Journal of Social Psychology, 9*, 363-374.

(f) With J. P. Foley, Jr. The work of the children's federal art gallery. *School and Society, 48*(1253), 859-861.

1939 Individual differences. *Fifth Yearbook, National Commercial Teachers Federation*, 26-35.

1940 (a) Henmon-Nelson Test of Mental Ability. *Mental Measurements Yearbook*, 220-221.

(b) The nature of individual differences (Ch. 12); Major group differences (Ch. 13). In J. P. Guilford (Ed.), *Fields of psychology*. New York: Van Nostrand. Pp. 251-284; 285-314.

(c) Review of E. L. Smith, Tides in the affairs of men. *American Journal of Psychology, 53,* 629.

(d) Terman Group Test of Mental Ability. *Mental Measurements Yearbook, 250.*

(e) With J. P. Foley, Jr. The study of "populistic" painters as an approach to the psychology of art. *Journal of Social Psychology, 11,* 353-368.

(f) With J. P. Foley, Jr. A survey of the literature on artistic behavior in the abnormal: III. Spontaneous productions. *Psychological Monographs, 52*(6). Pp. 71.

1941 (a) Abstract of C. Burt, The factors of the mind. *Psychological Abstracts, 15,* 349.

(b) Review of C. Burt, The factors of the mind. *American Journal of Psychology, 54,* 613-614.

(c) Review of E. R. Carlson, Born that way. *American Journal of Psychology, 54,* 629-630.

(d) Review of L. P. Thorpe, Personality and life. *Psychological Bulletin, 38,* 769-770.

(e) Review of P. E. Vernon, The measurement of abilities. *American Journal of Psychology, 54,* 154-155.

(f) With J. P. Foley, Jr. A study of spontaneous artistic productions by the insane. *Psychological Bulletin, 38,* 538-539.

(g) With J. P. Foley, Jr. A survey of the literature on artistic behavior in the abnormal: I. Historical and theoretical background. *Journal of General Psychology, 25,* 111-142.

(h) With J. P. Foley, Jr. A survey of the literature on artistic behavior in the abnormal: II. Approaches and interrelationships. *Annals of the New York Academy of Science, 42*(1). Pp. 112.

(i) With J. P. Foley, Jr. A survey of the literature on artistic behavior in the abnormal: IV. Experimental investigations. *Journal of General Psychology, 25,* 187-237.

1942 (a) Abstract of E. Newbury, The genetics of intelligence. *Psychological Abstracts, 16,* 341.

(b) Abstract of H. E. Rees, A psychology of artistic creation as evidenced in autobiographical statements of artists. *Psychological Abstracts, 16,* 551-552.

(c) Review of V. Case, Your personality—introvert or extrovert? *American Journal of Psychology, 55,* 305-306.

(d) Review of D. Wechsler, The measurement of adult intelligence. *American Journal of Psychology, 55,* 608-609.

(e) With J. P. Foley, Jr. An experimental study of the drawing behavior of adult psychotics in comparison with that of a normal control group. *Psychological Bulletin, 39,* 462-463.

1943 (a) Review of W. H. Sheldon, The varieties of temperament. *Psychological Bulletin, 40,* 146-149.

(b) With J. P. Foley, Jr. An analysis of spontaneous artistic productions by the abnormal. *Journal of General Psychology, 28,* 297-313.

1944 (a) Abstract of B. Morris, The aesthetic process. *Psychological Abstracts, 18,* 87.

(b) With J. P. Foley, Jr. An experimental study of the drawing behavior of adult psychotics in comparison with that of a normal control group. *Journal of Experimental Psychology, 34,* 169-194.

1945 With J. P. Foley, Jr. Review of J. H. Sanders, Chains of shadows. *Journal of Social Psychology, 21,* 295-296.

1947 The place of experimental psychology in the undergraduate curriculum. *American Psychologist, 2,* 57-62.

1948 (a) Individual differences (Ch. 18); Heredity and environment (Ch. 19). In E. G. Boring, H. S. Langfeld, & H. P. Weld (Eds.), *Foundations of Psychology.* New York: Wiley. Pp. 393-435; 436-458.

(b) A methodological note on the controlled diary technique. *Journal of Genetic Psychology, 73,* 237-241.

(c) The nature of psychological "traits." *Psychological Review, 55,* 127-138.

(d) Review of L. M. Terman & M. H. Oden, The gifted child grows up. *Psychological Bulletin, 45,* 363-366.

(e) With N. Cohen & D. Spatz. A study of fear and anger in college students through the controlled diary method. *Journal of Genetic Psychology, 73,* 243-249.

(f) With J. P. Foley, Jr. A proposed reorientation in the heredity-environment controversy. *Psychological Review, 55,* 239-249.

1949 (a) Adaptability Test. *Third Mental Measurements Yearbook,* 302-303.

(b) California Capacity Questionnaire. *Third Mental Measurements Yearbook,* 294-295.

(c) Thurstone Test of Mental Alertness. *Third Mental Measurements Yearbook,* 344-345.

(d) With J. P. Foley, Jr. *Differential psychology.* (2nd ed.) New York: Macmillan. Pp. 894.

(e) With S. Miller. Adolescent "prestige factors" in relation to scholastic and socioeconomic variables. *Journal of Social Psychology, 29,* 43-50.

1950 (a) The concept of validity in the interpretation of test scores. *Educational and Psychological Measurement, 10,* 67-78.

(b) The nature of individual differences (Ch. 12); Major group differences (Ch. 13). In J. P. Guilford (Ed.), *Fields of psychology.* (2nd ed.) New York: Van Nostrand. Pp. 331-373; 374-412.

(c) Review of R. Mukerjee, The social function of art. *Journal of Abnormal and Social Psychology, 45,* 569-572.

(d) Review of N. Pastore, Heredity and environment. *Science, 111,* 45-46.

(e) Review of G. Smith, Psychological studies in twin differences. *Psychological Bulletin, 47,* 80-81.

(f) Some implications of cultural factors for test construction. *Proceedings, 1949 Invitational Conference on Testing Problems, Educational Testing Service,* 13-17.

1951 (a) Cultural factors in the concept of genius. *Yearbook, New York Society for the Experimental Study of Education,* 58-64.

(b) With J. P. Foley, Jr. *Human relations and the foreman.* New London, Conn.: National Foreman's Institute. Pp. 251.

1952 (a) Review of P. E. Vernon, The structure of human abilities. *American Journal of Psychology, 65,* 143-145.

(b) With R. Y. D'Angelo. A comparison of Negro and white preschool children in language development and Goodenough Draw-A-Man IQ. *Journal of Genetic Psychology, 81,* 147-165.

(c) With J. P. Foley, Jr. The Human-Figure Drawing Test as an objective psychiatric screening aid for student pilots. *USAF School of Aviation Medicine, Project No. 21-37-002, Report No. 5.* Pp. 30.

1953 (a) An empirical study of the applicability of sequential analysis to item selection. *Educational and Psychological Measurement, 13,* 3-13.

(b) The Guilford-Zimmerman Aptitude Survey. *Fourth Mental Measurements Yearbook,* 693-695.

(c) Individual differences. In *Annual Review of Psychology,* Vol. 4. Stanford, Calif.: Stanford University Press. Pp. 137-156.

(d) Primary Mental Abilities. *Fourth Mental Measurements Yearbook,* 700-703.

(e) Psychological traits and group relations (Ch. 3). In M. Sherif & M. O. Wilson (Eds.), *Group relations at the crossroads.* New York: Harper. Pp. 74-98.

(f) With F. A. Cordova. Some effects of bilingualism upon the intelligence test performance of Puerto Rican children in New York City. *Journal of Educational Psychology, 44,* 1-19.

(g) With C. de Jesús. Language development and nonverbal IQ

of Puerto Rican preschool children in New York City. *Journal of Abnormal and Social Psychology, 48,* 357-366.

1954   (a) The inherited and acquired components of behavior. *Proceedings of the Association for Research in Nervous and Mental Diseases,* 67-75. (Ch. V.)

(b) The measurement of abilities. *Journal of Counseling Psychology, 1,* 164-168.

(c) *Psychological testing.* New York: Macmillan. Pp. 682.

(d) Tested intelligence and family size: Methodological and interpretive problems. *Eugenics Quarterly, 1,* 155-160.

(e) With J. D. Drake. An empirical comparison of certain techniques for estimating the reliability of speeded tests. *Educational and Psychological Measurement, 14,* 529-540.

(f) With J. P. Foley, Jr., & H. Sackman. Psychiatric selection of flying personnel: An empirical evaluation of the SAM Personality-Sketch Test. *USAF School of Aviation Medicine. Project No. 21-0202-0007, Rep. No. 6.* Pp. 51.

1955   (a) Review of C. J. Adcock, Factorial analysis for non-mathematicians. *Educational and Psychological Measurement, 15,* 520-521.

(b) Review of R. J. Williams, Free and unequal: The biological basis of individual liberty. *Human Biology, 27,* 243-246.

(c) With J. L. Fuller, J. P. Scott, & J. R. Schmitt. A factor analysis of the performance of dogs on certain learning tests. *Zoologica, 40*(3), 33-46.

1956   (a) Age changes in adult test performance. *Psychological Reports, 2,* 509.

(b) Intelligence and family size. *Psychological Bulletin, 53,* 187-209.

(c) A suggested modification of T-scores: Comments on the article by D. Mahanta. *Education and Psychology* (Delhi, India), *3,* 31-32.

1957   Tested intelligence and family size: Methodological and interpretive problems. *Proceedings of the World Population Conference* (E/Conf./13/418). New York: United Nations. Vol. VI. Pp. 689-702.

1958   (a) *Differential psychology.* (3rd ed.) New York: Macmillan. Pp. 664. (Translations: Hindi, Italian, Portuguese, Spanish.)

(b) Heredity, environment, and the question "How?" *Psychological Review, 65,* 197-208.

(c) Review of A. M. Shuey, The testing of Negro intelligence. *Science, 128,* 297.

1959 (a) Differentiating effect of intelligence and social status. *Eugenics Quarterly, 6,* 84-91.

(b) Discussion of H. Knobloch & B. Pasamanick, Distribution of intellectual potential in an infant population. *Epidemiology of Mental Disorder. Publication No. 60, American Association for the Advancement of Science,* 264-267.

(c) Holzinger-Crowder Uni-Factor Tests. *Fifth Mental Measurements Yearbook,* 700-702.

(d) Yale Educational Aptitude Test Battery. *Fifth Mental Measurements Yearbook,* 717-719.

(e) With R. F. Levee. Intellectual defect and musical talent. *American Journal of Mental Deficiency, 64,* 695-703.

1960 (a) Cultural differences. *Encyclopedia of Educational Research.* (3rd ed.), 350-358.

(b) Differential psychology. *Encyclopedia Britannica,* 367-369.

(c) Estableciendo normas de conducta. *Revista de Psicologia General y Aplicada, 15,* 863-865.

(d) Psychological research and educational desegregation. *Thought, 35,* 421-449.

(e) Review of L. M. Terman & M. H. Oden, The gifted group at midlife: Thirty-five years' follow-up of the superior child. *Contemporary Psychology, 5,* 46-47.

(f) Standardized ability testing. In P. H. Mussen (Ed.), *Handbook of research methods in child development.* New York: Wiley. Pp. 456-486.

(g) With M. J. Meade & A. A. Schneiders. The validation of a biographical inventory as a predictor of college success. *College Entrance Examination Board, Research Monographs,* No. 1. Pp. 81.

1961 (a) L'établissement de normes de comportement. *Revue de Psychologie Appliquée,* 11, 87-90.

(b) Psychological research and educational desegregation. In J. E. O'Neill (Ed.), *A Catholic case against segregation.* New York: Macmillan. Pp. 116-145.

(c) *Psychological testing.* (2nd ed.) New York: Macmillan. Pp. 657. (Translations: Italian, Portuguese, Spanish.)

(d) Psychological tests: Uses and abuses. *Teachers College Record, 62,* 389-393.

1962 (a) Intelligence. *Collier's Encyclopedia, 13,* 92-95.

(b) The longitudinal study of populations. *Indian Psychological Bulletin,* 7 (Part II), 25-28.

(c) Mental deficiency. *Collier's Encyclopedia, 15,* 696-699.

(d) Mongolism. *Collier's Encyclopedia, 16,* 455. (rev. 1963)

(e) Psychological testing. *Collier's Encyclopedia Yearbook,* 515-520.

1964 (a) Culture-fair testing. *Educational Horizons, 43* (1), 26-30.

(b) Differential psychology. *Encyclopedia Britannica,* 419-421.

(c) *Fields of applied psychology.* New York: McGraw-Hill. Pp. 621. (Translations: Chinese, Dutch, German, Italian, Japanese, Portuguese, Spanish.)

(d) Some current developments in the measurement and interpretation of test validity. *Proceedings, 1963 Invitational Conference on Testing Problems, Educational Testing Service,* 33-45.

1965 (a) *Individual differences.* (Ed.) New York: Wiley. Pp. 301.

(b) IPAT Children's Personality Questionnaire. *Sixth Mental Measurements Yearbook,* 256-257.

(c) The Jastak Test of Potential Ability and Behavior Stability. *Sixth Mental Measurements Yearbook,* 1030-1031.

(d) Male vs. female attitudes. In W. C. Bier (Ed.), *Marriage: A psychological and moral approach.* New York: Fordham University Press. Pp. 57-66.

1966 (a) Differential psychology: Individual differences (Ch. 8); Differential psychology: Group differences (Ch. 9). In J. P. Guilford (Ed.), *Fields of psychology.* (3rd ed.) Princeton, N. J.: Van Nostrand. Pp. 133-154; 155-173.

(b) Psychology and guidance. In T. C. Hennessy, S. J. (Ed.), *The interdisciplinary roots of guidance.* New York: Fordham University Press. Pp. 24-25.

(c) *Testing problems in perspective.* (Ed.) Washington, D. C.: American Council on Education. Pp. 671.

1967 (a) Psychological testing of children. In A. M. Freedman & H. I. Kaplan (Eds.), *Comprehensive textbook of psychiatry.* Baltimore: Williams & Wilkins. Pp. 1342-1356.

(b) Psychology, psychologists, and psychological testing. *American Psychologist, 22,* 297-306.

1968 (a) Applied psychology. *International Encyclopedia of the Social Sciences, 13,* 84-95.

(b) Individual differences. *International Encyclopedia of the Social Sciences, 7,* 200-207.

(c) A inteligência: Sua natureza e origens. *Arquivos Brasileiros de Psicotécnica, 20* (4), 11-24. (transl. by A. M. Arruda & M. I. Garcia de Freitas)

(d) Psychological differences between men and women. In W. C. Bier, S. J. (Ed.), *Woman in modern life.* New York: Fordham University Press. Pp. 42-54.

(e) *Psychological testing.* (3rd ed.) New York: Macmillan. Pp. 665.

(f) With C. E. Schaefer. A biographical inventory for identifying creativity in adolescent boys. *Journal of Applied Psychology, 52,* 42-48.

1969 (a) Comparative analysis of Council representatives from divisions and state associations. *American Psychologist, 24,* 1115-1118.

(b) La psychologie, les psychologues, et les test psychologiques. (transl. by D. Bonoro) *Bulletin de l'Institut National du Travail et d'Orientation Professionnelle,* 2° ser., 25(1), 3-20.

(c) With C. E. Schaefer. Biographical correlates of artistic and literary creativity in adolescent girls. *Journal of Applied Psychology, 53,* 267-273.

1970 (a) Correlates of creativity in children from two socioeconomic levels. *Final Report, Center for Urban Education Subcontract No. 2* (Contract No. OEC-1-7-062868-3060). Pp. 76.

(b) On the formation of psychological traits. *American Psychologist, 25,* 899-910.

(c) With S. Urbina, J. Harrison, & C. E. Schaefer. Relationship between masculinity-femininity and creativity as measured by the Franck Drawing Completion Test. *Psychological Reports, 26,* 799-804.

1971 (a) Differentielle Psychologie. *Lexicon der Psychologie, 1,* 378-388.

(b) More on heritability: Addendum to the Hebb and Jensen interchange. *American Psychologist, 26,* 1036-1037.

(c) Reply to Brandt. *American Psychologist, 26,* 513-514.

(d) Review of R. L. Thorndike (Ed.), Educational measurement. (2nd ed.) *Contemporary Psychology, 16,* 694-695.

(e) Standardized tests. *Encyclopedia of Education, 8,* 391-395. (Also Editorial Advisor, articles on Measurement and Testing.)

(f) With C. E. Schaefer. The Franck Drawing Completion Test as a measure of creativity. *Journal of Genetic Psychology, 119,* 3-12.

(g) With C. E. Schaefer. Note on the concepts of creativity and intelligence. *Journal of Creative Behavior, 5,* 113-116.

2

A Venture in Autobiography

IRWIN A. BERG

In February 1929 I was expelled from high school for squirting water on the vocational shop teacher and that event triggered a series of others which led to my becoming a psychologist. The second semester of my sophomore year had just started when a friend and I were amusing ourselves at two water fountains which were diagonally across the hall in the high school basement. By turning on the faucet full force and with careful manipulation of a thumb pressed over the outlet, we were able to douse each other with arching streams of water. Neither would call quits and both of us as well as the floor were quite drenched when the vocational shop teacher burst out of a nearby room, perhaps in response to our happy squealing, right into our cross-streams. He came out with such speed that he lost his footing on the wet floor and exhibited a brief ballet complete with *glissades, arabesques,* and *tour jetés.* He regained his balance, literally collared us, and, shaking water from his enpurpled face, he propelled us upstairs into the dean of boys' office. There he told the dean all about our misbehavior and, through clenched teeth, demanded that we be "disciplined—drastically."

During my ensuing interview with the dean, I was genuinely repentant and expressed a desire to apologize to the vocational shop teacher. There was a period of dead silence while the dean, whose name was Anderson, sat rigidly erect and glared balefully down at me. Hoping to lighten the looming punishment, I sought to curry favor with the naïveté of a fifteen year old by remarking that three of my four grandparents were named Anderson and wondered whether his people came from the same part of Sweden as mine. It was the wrong thing to say. He snapped that there were no lounge-lizard hooligans (popular phrase of that day) in his family. He instructed me to return the next day with my mother, which I did. With woeful face he said that he knew how hard it was for a widow to raise a son in those times and that it would be best if I stayed out of school for one month. He told me to come to see him, emphasizing *only* "him" (the dean), when the month was up and he would reinstate me unless he heard that I had been in further mischief.

The penalty was a disaster at the time. I could not possibly stay out of school for a month and still pass my courses and the dean knew it. In later years I was given some indication that he may have been under heavy faculty pressure to do something about "those kids who were always horsing around." Surely there could be no doubt about what the sodden shop teacher demanded. Also, I believe he simply "resigned" me by getting us to sign something and followed no formally established expulsion procedure. That is, the dean recorded me as a dropout but told me I was expelled which, in my ignorance of the regulations, I accepted without question. (Recently, by writing to the school I learned that my transcript did carry the record of dropout.) I do recall being quite angry at the time because there previously had been closely similar offenses by others and the penalty in those cases had been, "Boys, you've had your fun. Here's a mop and a bucket. You're going to put in three hours after school getting those floors clean enough to eat from." In retrospect it seems to me that water fights in the gym, the halls, and the lavatories, all strictly forbidden, were our way of thumbing our noses at the establishment of those days—and fun, too. I would note that the incident I describe, which was for me critical, was not my first offense, just the first time I was caught. Usually we had a lookout who, in the jargon of the day, "gave Jiggs" as a signal to scatter at the approach of anyone in authority. Be that as it may, the rather severe penalty turned out to be a favor to me although for the wrong reasons.

I LEARN WHAT PSYCHOLOGY IS

The national economy was booming at the time of my enforced departure from high school and, within several days, I obtained a job as a messenger at the Western Electric Company in Chicago. After a short time I was promoted to office boy and my duties included errands to every part of that enormous plant, which then had over 40,000 employees. On one errand I was sent to deliver some training material to the psychologists in another department. I had never known just what a psychologist was; so when I delivered my package, I said to the man who signed my receipt that I would like to ask a question if he wouldn't think I was a *dumboom*. The man threw back his head and roared with laughter and said he certainly wouldn't think any Swede was a *dumboom* for asking a question. The word means a stupid or silly person in Swedish and I had used it naturally, for we often spoke Swedish at home. Even today, I catch myself using Swedish phrases when exasperated or delighted, a cultural heritage from my Swedish-born parents. At any rate, the man I questioned turned out to be of Swedish ancestry and, more importantly, a psychologist. I never learned what his level of training was except that he was a *college graduate,* a designation which was used as a title of respect and almost as an occupational label by us office boys. He listened carefully when I told him I had heard the word "psychology" but didn't really know what the field of study was. He took my question seriously and showed me a book which I think may have been Pillsbury's *Fundamentals of Psychology*. His comments made it clear to me that psychology was centrally concerned with all forms of behavior but the book seemed to me to devote a great deal of space to the nervous system and sensation. The Pillsbury book, my new-found friend remarked, was probably a bit technical for me but he had a popular book on psychology which he would lend me. It was *Exploring Your Mind* by Albert Edward Wiggam and it opened a new world for me.

Each of the chapters of Wiggam's book, published in 1928, was based upon an interview with persons such as E. L. Thorndike, Donald A. Laird, Lewis L. Terman, Carl E. Seashore, James McKeen Cattell, Henry Foster Adams, Hugh Hartshorne, and Mark A. May, among others. The presentation of each topic was Wiggam's and he wrote clearly, but the ideas and opinions were those of leading psychologists of the day, most of whom later earned a permanent niche in psychology's hall of fame. Wiggam may have glossed over some of the intricacies of the topics presented by the psychologists he interviewed but he offered a readable treatment of psychology in 1928. It was just what I needed at the time and I read and re-read the book, even buying my own copy (which I still have) a year or so later.

Wiggam was an American Psychological Association member, so he probably had training in psychology, but his specialty seemed to be biology. He published for years a widely syndicated newspaper column under the "Exploring Your Mind" title. Each column presented a couple of questions on psychological topics and then answered the questions by quoting the findings of a relevant study published in one of the professional journals of psychology. His columns had an enormous readership and presented psychology in flattering terms. In the 1950s, four or five of his columns quoted some of my published researches and I received letters afterward from acquaintances in many parts of the world. Wiggam had a sound enough approach but it exasperated some academic psychologists whose students quoted Wiggam in rebuttal to points made in their lectures. To my way of thinking, Wiggam did as much as anyone to make psychology a household word and to nurture the "can do" attitude of a later generation of psychologists with respect to human problems of all kinds. Be that as it may, I know that at age sixteen I read Wiggam's popular book and from that time on I knew what I was going to be—a psychologist. I didn't know how nor exactly what I had to do but I did know what my goal was.

THE RETURN TO SCHOOL

The Great Depression had numbed our nation and what was a catastrophe for most was for me a disguised blessing because it forced the issue of my return to school. The Western Electric Company had shortened its work week and laid off thousands of employees. My mother had been urging me to return to school and her wishes began to coincide with mine. I knew that I would soon be laid off and I also knew that I had to resume my education if I really wanted to be a psychologist. Various acquaintances had given me a pretty fair idea of what I had to do. First I had to finish high school and then I had to finish college. With a college degree in psychology, I was told, I could probably get a job as a personnel man because the Depression would be soon over. I also learned what the master's degree level of education entailed and something about the Ph.D. The Ph.D. in my circle of aquaintance was always referred to in rather awesome tones and pronounced "Ph.DEE" with a slurring of the "Ph." and an emphasis on the "D." No one recommended shooting for this remote academic star because that degree, it was explained to me, required that one "write a book on something he himself had discovered that nobody had ever known before."

I returned to high school in 1931 and in a year and a half I completed the four-year program, making a total of three years and part of a summer for the diploma. Previously I had been an indifferent student at best but now everything was exciting because it led to college. This marked change in my attitude and motivation as well as my grades remains something of a puzzle to me. In part it was a new relationship with my teachers. They were about the same ones I had had two years before but they responded positively, as teachers do, to an eager student. Several of them even became my friends in later years. In the main I think the most significant factor in my improved motivation in school was a circle of new friends among my fellow students. We were a motley group in terms of background: Czechs, Poles, Germans, Irish, English, Swedes, etc. All of us were American-born but most of our parents were "from the old country." The things we had in common were an unshakable conviction that education was the way to success and a fondness for reading and discussing what we had read. Discussion is an utterly inadequate description of our exchanges. We often shouted at one another and it is hard for me now to understand why conversations about John Ruskin, Freud, or technocracy (a proposed social order based on engineering principles) would evoke outbursts like, "You're full of crap—crap up to your ears!" "Your goddamn roof leaks!" or more restrained cries of "Baloney!" and "Horsefeathers!" Periodically we agreed to remain silent but that did not stop us from silently gripping our noses with forefinger and thumb while waving the free hand at the earnest speaker. We weren't angry but rather it was our teenage way of taking exception and expressing our involvement with the issues being considered. Perhaps it was the Chicago atmosphere which permeated its middle-class, western suburb of Berwyn where we grew up. Chicago is a town, as Phillip Wylie remarked, where a burp brings down the house. It was also a town where superb art galleries, aquariums, planetariums, theaters, and libraries were all available to us by taking a ride on the "L" into the Loop. Anyway, all the members of our group eventually finished college and most of them earned an M.D. or Ph.D.

PLANS FOR COLLEGE

My mother expressed deep satisfaction at my interest in college. She told me that it would be very difficult financially but she was determined to see me through. She asked only one thing—that I work hard and earn good grades. She got out my father's diploma and report cards from his school in Sweden and gave them to me with a touching display of reverence. The school was a kind of veterinarian-farrier school where both horseshoeing and elementary veterinary medicine were taught. The curriculum seemed largely concerned with blacksmithing with some courses dealing with the treatment of animal ailments—probably typical for such turn-of-the-century training. A requirement for graduation from this school was that the students make by hand their own com-

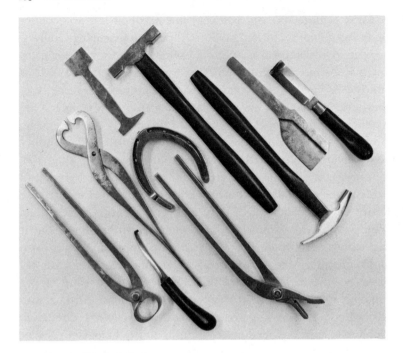

FIGURE 2-1. Farrier's tools

plete set of farriers tools, using only anvil, hammers, and files. Figure 2-1 shows the set of tools my father made at age eighteen for his final examination. The tools were never used because he emigrated to America shortly afterward. What a remarkable commentary these tools represent with regard to vocational training at the turn of the century. My father never worked as a veterinarian but stayed with blacksmithing, probably because his people in Sweden had operated a small blacksmith shop for generations. At the time of his death he was general superintendent of a medium-size steel-forging plant in Chicago. In this manner the way to college was paved for me. I had the promise of all the support my widowed mother could offer, an admonition to "make something of myself," and the example together with mementoes of a dead father who had "done all right" because he had a bit more education than was common at the time.

Knox College was and is a very fine small liberal arts college and it was there that I had my introduction to psychology courses. I went to Knox because it was recommended by my chemistry teacher, a Knox alumnus, and two of my close friends liked it as much as I. There was only one psychology professor at Knox, Ray Starbuck Miller, who had earned his Ph.D. at Iowa under Carl Seashore. Miller offered a full array of psychology courses and he taught about fifteen or twenty hours a week plus another twenty hours talking individually to students and supervising their special projects, reserving his evenings for grading papers. He didn't pretend to know all areas of psychology but he had an attitude which I found contagious. When a difficult question came up, he would say, "I don't know. Let's see what we can find out about it right now." He would drop what he was doing and pull down books, handing me books with a grin and request, "You try these," while he looked in others. If we found no answer, we would walk over to the library together and search further, usually with success. A larger department of psychology would undoubtedly have provided better training in psychology but Miller as a one-man department provided a better *education* and I gained immensely from his highly personal approach. I graduated from Knox in 1936 with a Phi Beta Kappa key and with more semester hours in English than in psychology, with virtually no laboratory experience in experimental psychology, and with an unusually broad background of reading in the original source reports in the journals of psychology. Just recently, I learned from Knox College psychology professor Robert S. Harper that between 1837 and 1936 I was the second Knox graduate to go on for the Ph.D. in psychology. Dr. Edna Heidbreder, Knox 1911, was the first.

A JOB AT THE WESTERN ELECTRIC COMPANY

Despite my new bachelor's degree, I knew that I really wasn't a psychologist. I hadn't done the things that Ebbinghaus, Müller, and Pilzecker described in their wretched German prose, which

made me inch through their articles, nor had I done anything re-
motely akin to the studies of Pavlov, Watson, Thorndike, Lashley, and others. I wanted to go to graduate school but could not,
for I had no money and owed $150. So I had to find a job at a
time when our nation was just barely beginning to come out of
the pall of the Great Depression. By a stroke of luck I managed to
return to the Western Electric Company. I was hired as a cost accounting clerk, a field about which I knew absolutely nothing.
The employment office interviewer was slightly acquainted with
me and knew how desperately I wanted a job. When I asked
whether there were any openings in personnel, he said that in six
months to a year there might very well be personnal interviewer
openings but at that time he had exactly one office job vacancy in
the entire plant—for a cost accounting clerk. I must have looked
profoundly woebegone because he looked at me sympathetically
and said, "Of course, I understand you haven't had the advanced
courses in cost accounting but I believe you could handle the job
with a little review before you begin work." Accounting practice
in any form, elementary or advanced, was a mystery to me but I
was grateful for the unspoken conspiracy which enabled me to get
a job for which my employment referral card identified me, "Has
had no advanced accounting courses." For two weeks I boned up
on accounting and cost accounting, learned to distinguish a credit
from a debit (not always easy, I found out), and learned some accountant's jargon that I hoped would conceal part of my ignorance. I needn't have worried. Western Electric had switched to
an IBM punch card system (Hollerith cards we called them at the
time) and all I had to do was master the charge codes for the accounting system that some remote super-accountant had programed. I did learn about the IBM system which was to be of
considerable help to me in handling masses of behavioral data
in later years. But that's about all I got from my accounting work,
except for a feeling which came decades later when I wondered
why I was so stupid as not to buy at least a few shares of IBM.

I was transferred to a personnel research department where I
had my eyes fully opened to what applied behavioral research

meant on a large scale. The department was carrying forward the Hawthorne Study which was later to become world famous in the field of industrial relations when the book *Management and the Worker* by Roethlisberger and Dickson was published in 1939. W. J. Dickson was the head of my department and Fritz Roethlisberger was a Harvard professor who periodically visited the department as a consultant. My immediate supervisor was Burleigh B. Gardner, who had a Harvard Ph.D. in anthropology and whose book, *Deep South*, co-authored with Allison Davis, was to become a standard reference in cultural anthropology.

A SUPPORTIVE ENVIRONMENT

It was a splendid place to keep alive my aspiration for a doctorate. In an adjacent department was Harold C. Taylor, a Yale Ph.D., who taught me to operate a Monroe calculator and also told me something of what graduate study entailed. Taylor later achieved national prominence when he left Western Electric to become director of the W. E. Upjohn Institute of Community Research. There were also two graduate psychology students at the University of Chicago. Frederic Wickert, now a Michigan State University professor, and Ruth Bishop, now in private practice as Mrs. Karl Heiser. While I did not know them particularly well at the time, they added to the advanced education aura that pervaded personnel activities at Western Electric.

This all sounds as if I were unswervingly devoted to following my star with eyes raised heavenward, seeking the Ph.D. like the Holy Grail. It wasn't like that at all. I talked very little of my aspirations for graduate study and I thoroughly enjoyed my coworkers while learning some useful new skills. It seems to me now that much of our spare time on the job was spent in exchanging bawdy stories and that we were as ribald a bunch—young and old, male and female—as I have ever encountered before or since. In the five years during my two stints at the Western Electric Company I heard more salacious stories than I had heard before or since. As a matter of fact, most of the jokes I have heard since then are the same ones I heard at Western Electric except that Raquel Welch is now substituted for Mae West, Spiro Agnew replaces Franklin D. Roosevelt, etc.

One of the skills I acquired at Western Electric was the result of the training in what Roethlisberger and Dickson called nonauthoritarian interviewing. It was Rogerian nondirective or client-centered counseling but about five years ahead of Rogers in the sense of a formal statement. Rogers worked out his conceptual framework much more completely than Roethlisberger and Dickson had and he provided the historical background of the procedure. But the method and the rationale were about the same and in 1937 the Western Electric personnel counselors used a privately printed version of what became Chapter XIII, "The Interviewing Method," in the 1939 book *Management and the Worker.*

Over the years I have found the nondirective or nonauthoritarian technique exceedingly useful in any emotion-laden situation, at least for the initial personal contacts. Accordingly, in teaching my courses which dealt with the interview, I have insisted that the first few interviews with a client or patient be nondirective. The counselor or clinician is able to perceive the problem as the client or patient sees it and, more importantly, he will not harm the patient by opening old wounds or rending asunder defenses which have been supporting him, however precariously. But after the first interview or two I believe it best to become more interpretive and eclectic in procedure. The chief factor is time, as I see it, for straight nondirective treatment can stretch out to an interminable series of interviews. Nevertheless every clinician should understand and achieve competence in the procedure and use it during the early interviews. Also, every clinician needs an anchorage point for his approach to helping patients and the nondirective technique, in my estimation, is ideal for this purpose. The clinician is provided with a rough gauge for assessing the kind of pressure his patient is experiencing during any other therapeutic process when he has observed the patient under nondirective interviewing conditions. But I decline to stick exclusively to nondirective procedure and that may well be a commentary on my own personality.

MARRIAGE AND PLANS FOR GRADUATE TRAINING

While at Western Electric I had been corresponding with my oldest and closest friend, Vincent Tomas, who was a graduate student in philosophy at Brown University—where he still is, having served some years as chairman of that department. He urged me to get off my dead center, as he approximately put it, and apply to a graduate school. There was, however, a complication. I had met, fallen in love, and became engaged to Sylvia, a lovely girl. I didn't know how she might feel about the idea of graduate school and the straitened circumstances such study would entail. But I broached the subject to her and before I finished my preamble she was urging me to enroll in a graduate school. Since she was working in Michigan, I applied to Ann Arbor, where I was accepted and awarded a modest assistantship. With this encouragement we married in March 1939. That was over thirty years ago and it sounds old-fashioned but is nevertheless quite true to observe that we continue to enjoy each other's company as much as ever. This happy state, my family and friends frequently remark, is due entirely to her, not to me.

As I reflect upon the matter, it strikes me as odd that nothing stands out as especially eventful or unusual during my graduate-student days at the University of Michigan. It all seemed very business-like to me at the time. When I registered, my deficiencies in preparation for graduate work in psychology were assessed (quite correctly as I now realize) and I was enrolled in experimental psychology among other courses and also as an auditor in statistics to correct my shortcomings. The teaching was very good and the professors were friendly; yet I had then and have now the feeling that the graduate students taught one another about as much as the professors did. This feeling may actually be an unwitting tribute to teaching of an unusually high order. The educational pattern involved our going to class while the professor presented a tightly organized lecture, usually on a single topic and with copious references to original articles. Then some of us would usually discuss the lecture after class, compare and expand our notes, and read some of the journal articles mentioned. We made skillful use of each other's special abilities. Seymour Wapner, now a Clark University professor, took the most complete notes, while Robert W. Kleemeier, late Washington University professor, was very good at translating German. Stan E. Wimberly, late vice president of Florida Atlantic University, had a positive genius for spotting what each professor thought was important enough for a final-examination question or, equally important, what the professor would *not* ask.

STUDENTS AND PROFESSORS AT MICHIGAN

Highly informal, Michigan bore no semblance to a structured traditional school yet it was highly educational for us. Thus Wimberly might tell me, "Bill Gilbert says Norman Maier always asks about his theory of stimulus intensity and elicited response—know it cold." I would then tell Wapner and others, who presumably would tell still others. Through such casual contacts we learned that Professor J. F. Shepard detested psychoanalysis and took a dim view of statistics as a substitute for experimentation; hence one was unlikely to be quizzed on such topics but, if one was, a sharply critical approach was in order. Department Chairman W. B. Pillsbury, who had served as president of the American Psychological Association in 1910, was a scholarly gentleman who appreciated a graceful turn of phrase and enjoyed foreign phrases, especially Latin and Greek, if appropriately employed. Henry F. Adams was sold on the "new" factor analysis of data and N. R. F. Maier wanted every statement buttressed by reference to experimental studies, while Wilma T. Donahue was oriented toward clinical applications. We depended on the graduate students a year or two ahead of us for much of our tutoring. My roommate during my first year was Tooi Xoomsai, a Thai who is now the retired dean of Chiang Mai University, and he helped me immensely with factor analysis and with French translations of articles. I am not sure that our self-tutoring really helped us very much in passing our examinations, for it probably was like adding only twenty points to everyone's examination score. But I am sure we all acquired an enormous amount of knowledge in our field which was untested by any course examinations.

There was another aspect of student relations which contributed to our education. This was a fondness among us for performing some sort of minor experiment or helping another student with his experiment. The experiments were often not related to a thesis or dissertation nor were they for any course credit. The first psychological study I ever published was a rat experiment on Clark Hull's goal-gradient hypothesis which I did with a fellow graduate student, Raoul Weisman, who is now a practicing physician. Weisman and I got to arguing about a point in Hull's hypothesis and ended up by borrowing J. F. Shepard's rat maze for a month or two of evenings.

DOCTORAL DISSERTATION DISCOURSE

The same sort of *laissez faire* but ask-for-help-if-you-need-it prevailed when I was ready to begin my doctoral dissertation. I outlined my study in a conference with J. F. Shepard and W. B. Pillsbury, they accepted it, and assigned laboratory quarters and equipment to me. That was it. I was asked for no progress reports but when I volunteered them I got full attention and whatever help I asked for. My study was in the area of physiological psychology, one of the favored areas of investigation at pre-World War II Michigan. One had a severely limited choice of areas for a dissertation topic. Comparative and physiological psychology were highly acceptable and so was learning—animal and human. There were a few doctoral dissertations completed in other areas but those pioneering spirits who wanted to work on personality, clinical, social, or statistical problems seemed to have a hard time assembling a committee. There was no opposition, just disinterest. With a little cleverness one could merge areas and engage the professor's interest. William M. Gilbert, now a University of Illinois professor, used hypnosis, which fascinated him, to study the retroactive effect of interpolated learning under hypnotic and normal waking conditions. But most of us chose traditional topics, lacking either the incentive or ingenuity to do otherwise. Things at Michigan are, of course, quite different now.

My own dissertation study was centered on hormonal control of the leg elevation pattern during urination in the male dog. In addition to various controls which included hormone injections, orchidectomies, etc. I used motion pictures as part of my data collection which was not then common in such studies. It was a most satisfying piece of research. Male puppies whose littermates still squatted when urinating could be made to elevate the leg by appropriate injection of testosterone propionate. Castrated males still squatted in the puppy posture while their normal male littermates raised the leg when urinating. There was even a canine leg elevation preference, akin to handedness in humans. Under certain hormonal conditions females elevated the leg when urinating, a most inefficient procedure for them. What was so satisfying was that the data were definite. If the behavior I was studying appeared, it was clearly and demonstrably present—no teasing out of .01 or .05 probability levels. Also satisfying later was the replication by other researchers of my research in two different studies and with the same findings as I had reported in a *Journal of Experimental Psychology* article.

At times, I wonder why I did not continue as a physiological psychologist. I did later publish several physiological and animal studies but I drifted into the more applied fields of testing and counseling, due largely to my job situations and my Western Electric experience. But there were later opportunities to return to the physiological psychology fold but I never did.

By the time I was nearing the completion of my doctorate, America had entered World War II. Like most communities, Ann Arbor had a large, noisy group of anti-war demonstrators who raised hell in somewhat less violent but otherwise quite similar fashion as the anti-Viet Nam War factions today. With Pearl

Harbor all protest ended as dramatically as a complete power failure on Broadway at midnight. I was completely deaf in one ear,
the result of a childhood illness, and I also had a child, my daughter Karen, who was born during the summer before Pearl Harbor.
Thus it seemed to me that I was unlikely to be acceptable for
military service although I did try to enlist for officer's training.

My first job was at the State Prison of Southern Michigan in
Jackson, Michigan. I had met the director of corrections in Michigan, Dr. Garrett Heyns, through his son who was two years behind
me in graduate school and about to join the army. The son was
Roger Heyns, who later served as chancellor of the University of
California at Berkeley. I stayed in prison work only a short time
but did manage to gather data for three or four studies on forgers,
car thieves, and murderers, which were published in due course.
The chief factor in my decision to leave correctional work was a
position at the University of Illinois which had great appeal to me
because it combined some teaching with counseling students and
at the same time provided opportunities for research.

ANY PSYCHOLOGIST CAN DO RESEARCH—IF HE WANTS TO

Every now and then I meet psychologists who bemoan the fact
that they have no time for research or no facilities for research.
Frankly, I have no patience with them. Psychology is one field in
which a useful research contribution can be made wherever one
is. As Benton J. Underwood once remarked to me, "John Mc-
Geogh said you can do research with some chalk and a piece of
string and he's right." My sentiments exactly. There are always
studies to be done by persons with the interest to do them and the
willingness to work with what is at hand. At Michigan it was easy
to work with animals and so I did. At the prison in Jackson there
were inmates that could be studied, and at Illinois I had a wealth
of psychological and other test data available to me for investigation. So I took what was at hand and thoroughly enjoyed myself
with such different areas of research. This is not to say that every
psychologist should engage in research but it is saying that he

needn't rationalize by bellyaching about lack of time or facilities.

I learned one thing about research during my tenure at the University of Illinois which may be worth mentioning. That is that one should never discuss with colleagues his findings or emerging interpretations in any detail while a study is in progress. Wait until it is *finished and written*. As I see it, one builds up a head of steam that sustains one while working on a project. But lengthy discussions of the project seem to provide a release and the same satisfaction that completing the research and writing up the results do—a kind of *affective drainage* in terms of McDougall's old theory. Talking about the project seems to provide a feeling that the unfinished task is really completed when it isn't. Conversely, keeping quiet about it seems to function as a drive like Zeigarnik's uncompleted tasks. Be that as it may, I do know that I have a number of file folders with partially completed studies that I lost interest in after telling about them to everyone who would listen. In this connection I have often wondered whether this is not a factor in understanding why so many doctoral dissertations are never published. The student over a long period had lived so intimately with and had to discuss so frequently his doctoral study that his drive to take the final step of publication had evaporated.

The consequence, as I see it, was that the majority of the studies I published during my five years at the University of Illinois were rather pedestrian. There was nothing wrong with them but nothing particularly exciting either and so not likely to be discussed at length. But several promising studies were never completed because I found satisfaction and release in talking about them with colleagues. Some of these colleagues such as Raymond B. Cattell, Donald M. Johnson, L. L. McQuitty, P. T. Young, and L. A. Pennington were themselves very active researchers and interested in everything. So it was easy to talk to them. But it seems to me now that they never went into any detail concerning their own studies until they had written a first draft. Consciously or unconsciously I think they knew the disengagement that followed too much discussion of their emerging research findings.

THE BEGINNINGS OF THE ORGANIZING
OF THE FIELD OF CLINICAL PSYCHOLOGY

While at the University of Illinois, L. A. Pennington and I began planning a book on clinical psychology. We prepared the chapter and topical outline of what we intended to put in the book and, as an afterthought, decided to write to a couple of dozen clinical psychologist friends about their work. We asked each to describe how their time was spent in a typical day as a working clinician. The replies came in and wrecked our neatly outlined book. Pennington and I had had considerable experience with a wide variety of psychological tests and we both had done a good deal of clinical counseling and psychotherapy with young adults. The working clinicians we wrote to in 1946 did all of that, of course, but as a group they routinely encountered such problems as mental retardation, slow learning in children, physical handicaps, sensory handicaps, speech difficulties, senility, and so on and on. Pennington and I knew what *we* knew about clinical psychology and we also knew what we didn't know—much of which was included in the replies. We were discussing the replies from our clinician friends and considering abandoning the project when Pennington said in effect, "Look, no single clinician is competent in all of these areas. What we have is a composite of clinical activities. These replies are really an operational definition of clinical psychology. They are an *organization*. So let's assign experts to each broad area and ask them to write a chapter and build the definition of the field that way. If the book is ever revised we can operationally redefine the field in the same way." So we went about doing just that and the book was a success. In later years a second and then a third edition were published and each time we redefined the field operationally in terms of what clinicians were currently doing. As an aside, I would note that some of the changes in clinical activity are vast. It is now a rare clinician who works regularly with aptitude, achievement, or interest-testing to any great extent—quite a change from the clinical activities of 1946. But no clinician in 1946 knew anything about psychopharmacology, behavior therapy, computer processing of personality data, etc., things which are so commonplace today.

In 1947, I left the University of Illinois to join the faculty at Pomona College in Claremont, California. My reasons for leaving Illinois are obscure to me; however I had a yen to teach in a small college like Knox and Pomona seemed to fill this need. The Pomona students, taken as a group, were remarkably bright and interesting to teach but Claremont at the time seemed somehow isolated to me and a bit stuffy. I did have time to finish with Pennington the tag ends of *An Introduction to Clinical Psychology* and it was published in 1948—with a remarkably large sale for an advanced psychology book. I also began some exploratory studies on response bias which I had been thinking about the year before. These casual studies eventually led to a lengthy series of publications on the deviation hypotheses. More of that later. But there were relatively few psychologists at Claremont and I missed the stimulation of a large department. So, when my family and I were driving through Palo Alto, we dropped in on E. K. Strong of the famous vocational interest blank. to discuss my feelings of professional loneliness. I had met Dr. Strong when he visited his daughter Margaret and her husband Thomas Harrell, now at Stanford University, who had been colleagues of mine at the University of Illinois. I don't know what magical words I expected, probably something that would rival the Sermon on the Mount. But all Dr. Strong did was listen silently while I talked and then said gruffly, "Irwin, you *know* what you want to do. Do it. Now let's talk of other things." And we did and he was absolutely right. I did know that I wanted a lot of psychologists around me on a daily basis.

NORTHWESTERN UNIVERSITY
AND WONDERFUL COLLEAGUES

When I was invited to Northwestern University in 1948, I jumped at the chance to return to my home stamping grounds. My wife was a Northwestern graduate and I was acquainted with most of the Psychology Department faculty; so the opportunity seemed most enticing. We were not disappointed. My wife was back among family and friends and I quickly became integrated into the most delightful department of psychology I had ever encountered anywhere. Nearly everybody was busy on some project that required work at night and on weekends but all of us saved time during the day to interact with each other. The interaction was sometimes serious discussions of psychological topics but equally often it was a series of Rabelaisian exchanges usually expressed in lurid language. After William A. Hunt, Carl P. Duncan, and I were probably the worst offenders in this latter respect and in that order. Our language habits at the time were sometimes handicapping however. I recall one time when I was describing the machinations of some prominent but crooked politician when Duncan exploded, "Why that-that-that *scoundrel!*" Janet A. Taylor (Mrs. Kenneth W. Spence), now chairman of the Psychology Department at the University of Texas, looked thoughtful for a moment and then said to the group, "You know, I always wondered what Dunc considered to be a dirty word."

In addition to William Hunt, Carl Duncan, and Janet Taylor Spence, there were Donald B. Lindsley, Benton J. Underwood, Donald T. Campbell, T. W. Richards, Robert I. Watson, Claude Buxton, E. L. Clark, A. R. Gilliland, Bettye M. Caldwell, and Donald J. Lewis with whom I associated fairly closely while they were at Northwestern. A. R. Gilliland, a founder of the Midwestern Psychological Association has died, and E. L. Clark has retired while the others have gone on to win considerable professional recognition at Northwestern or elsewhere.

At any rate, it was a highly productive department and part of this, I think, was due to a sense of historical continuity of psychology at the university. Walter Dill Scott, pioneer in personnel and management psychology, had been president of the university. Although retired, he still lunched with some of us several times each week at the University Club. Robert H. Seashore, the son of Carl E. Seashore of Iowa, was chairman of the Northwestern Department of Psychology until his death and he had grown up with the field of psychology. For a time the Seashores, father and son, W. D. Scott, E. L. Clark, and I lunched quite regularly, and Clark and I reveled in the reminiscences of these distinguished figures in psychology.

While the sense of historical continuity helped shape the Northwestern Department of Psychology, I believe the chief influence in making the department so interesting was William A. Hunt, who succeeded Robert Seashore as chairman. Hunt is an affiliative person with a wide circle of friends, nearly all of them close. This gift of friendship has puzzled some of us who know him well for he could not be described as charming. Indeed, he can upon different occasions be petulant, suspicious, angrily disputative, and so forth. At other times he can be overwhelmingly generous, cause you to roar with laughter, or exhibit some remarkably acute insight into a problem. He is a brilliant person and enormously complicated in personality. Hunt is undoubtedly a major contributor to psychology and, remarkably, in both the experimental and clinical areas.

CHAIRMAN OF PSYCHOLOGY
AT LOUISIANA STATE UNIVERSITY

In 1951 Nicholas Hobbs, who later served as President of the American Psychological Association, wrote me that he was leaving the chairmanship of psychology at Louisiana State University and asked if I would be interested in LSU. I wasn't because my daughter Karen was nicely settled in grammar school and we were unwilling to consider a change at that time. In 1955 the offer from LSU was renewed through the offices of LSU Professor T. W. Richards, a former Northwestern colleague who reminded me that Karen was completing grammar school and the time to move was propitious since she had to change schools anyway.

Louisiana State University had had a graduate program in psychology since 1916 but had turned out only five Ph.D.'s by 1955 and about a hundred M.A.'s. The undergraduate psychology program was sound and increasing steadily in student acceptance, owing largely to the efforts of Nicholas Hobbs and Paul C. Young. My task, as I understood it, was to develop the graduate program. There were solid psychologists to join with me in the effort—in the early years, men like Bernard M. Bass, Donald J. Lewis, Brendan A. Maher, Robert Thompson, and others. Only Thompson and I remain from that early period; for the others went on to larger responsibilities and are serving at other universities as a director, a department head, and a graduate dean respectively. They and those who followed worked effectively, for the total number of Ph.D.'s awarded increased from five in 1955 to well over a hundred by the present time. The number of undergraduate psychology majors was thirty-four in 1955 and currently is over three hundred. Most of those who earned the Ph.D. at LSU went into academic work and they have done quite well in a variety of institutional settings.

THE DEVIATION HYPOTHESIS

In the meantime I had been working on what I called the deviation hypothesis. Broadly stated, the idea was that any behaviorally valid deviant state is part of a much larger pattern of deviant responses. Clinicians typically attend to only a few critical or key symptoms in appraising deviant behavior and ignore a vast array of other symptoms which are noncritical but nevertheless a part of the atypical condition. Thus the deviation hypothesis would view a deviant state like mental retardation as much more than a low IQ, schizophrenia as much more than flattened affect with possible delusions or hallucinations, etc. These are the critical symptoms, of course, but there are many other noncritical responses associated with such conditions and they are often remote from the key symptoms. For example, there is a very high percentage of left-handedness among mental retardates and there is a much wider range of oral-anal temperature differential in schizophrenics as compared to normals. Accordingly, the obvious symptoms of deviant conditions are only part of a more general pattern of deviant responses. By identifying the broad or general pattern of deviant responses, it is believed possible to develop a better method of diagnosis and therapy, a system of differential diagnosis, and eventually a theoretical model for understanding deviant behavioral states. Finally, it should be possible to express the dimensions of personality in mathematical terms by focusing on response strength or variability in various patterns. I believe this has been partially demonstrated in published reports.

There have been more than a hundred articles published which deal with the deviation hypothesis, about half of them written by my students and/or myself. About a fourth of the articles take issue with aspects of the hypothesis and a few of them are sharply critical. I think now that on some points I was not clear and drew in some distracting side issues. Be that as it may, for those who are interested I would refer them to some of the broad statements of the deviation hypothesis in the list of publications cited at the end of this chapter. The fullest single account is my chapter in *Response Set in Personality Assessment* published by Aldine in 1967. My favorite account (but admittedly quite incomplete) is the light-hearted essay I wrote in 1957 for the *Journal of Counseling Psychology* when Harold B. Pepinsky was editing the research news for that journal (see references at the end of this chapter).

SEARCH FOR NEW DIRECTIONS

In the early spring of 1964 I went through a kind of nostalgic self-analysis. A combination of things brought it on but the triggering events, I think, were the marking of my fiftieth birthday the previous October and the celebration of my wife's and my twenty-fifth wedding anniversary in March. It began with a review of my present state which was accompanied by a pervasive feeling of gratitude. I realized that my wife and I had had an exceedingly happy marriage and that the few quarrels we had ever had were over the handling of money, something that was no longer a pressing problem. Also, I felt a bit abashed to realize that our happy relationship was due chiefly to her cheerful forebearance and so was the development of our well-adjusted daughter, who has now married and had children of her own. I had had more professional recognition than I felt I deserved; yet there was furtive pleasure in recalling some of my past honors. Included among the offices I had held were president of the Illinois Psychological Association, president of the APA Division of Counseling Psychology, president of the Southeastern Psychological Association, president of the Southwestern Psychological Association, three different terms of three years each as a member of the APA Council of Representatives, chairman of the APA Convention Committee, chairman of the APA Sub-Committee on Evaluation, book review co-editor of the *Journal of Counseling Psychology,* editor of *Counseling News and Views,* program chairman of the National Vocational Guidance Association, and membership on a wide range of APA and other professional committees. I had written over a hundred professional articles and written or edited five books, some of which went into several editions, and I was listed in a variety of national and international biographical directories. But I was restive.

In my review of things past it seemed to me that the psychology department where I had served as chairman since 1955 was in good shape and, quite frankly, I was now bored with the job. After talking over my feelings with my wife, I resolved to relinquish the chairmanship and accomplish the following things before I retired: (a) prepare a third edition of *Clinical Psychology* with Pennington (this was completed in 1966); (b) organize a symposium of experts on response set in personality assessment and publish it as a book with my own chapter included (this was completed in 1967); (c) write an elementary psychology textbook for unworthy pecuniary motives (only one chapter was written); (d) write a novel with a setting in ancient Viking days (nothing was done); (e) write several articles and a book in the deviation hypothesis which would present a theory of personality (nothing was done); (f) travel (six trips to Europe thus far, 1971). It is now apparent to me that I probably will not finish all the writing I had planned to do. The chief reason is that in 1965 I was appointed dean of the College of Arts and Sciences.

COLLEGE ADMINISTRATION AND
LESS TIME FOR PSYCHOLOGY

The deanship came about when Cecil G. Taylor, then Dean of Arts and Sciences, was appointed chancellor for the Louisiana State University Baton Rouge campus in April 1965. He and I had always worked very comfortably together all the years I was chairman of the Psychology Department and I welcomed the idea of continuing the old pattern of seeing him casually and often. So, when offered the deanship, I accepted with alacrity, only to discover that both Taylor and I became so busy that we saw one another less often than before. The chief reason was that 1965 marked the explosion of student activism and that, among other things, took up an immense amount of time for both of us.

All things considered, I have enjoyed college administration. Of course, there are aspects which have bothered me but these are largely due to shortcomings in my own personal make-up. I tend to be blunt and also to talk too much. Also, if something seems important, I like to see things move and become obviously impatient when they do not. Psychologist John Gustad, a friend and former dean who is now president of Kansas State College, once quoted somebody who said approximately, "to be a good dean requires much patience and a certain degree of low cunning," I have neither and it periodically causes me trouble that could have been avoided. But most people I regularly deal with have come to accept and, in many cases, seem to appreciate my verbose candor.

PLUS ÇA CHANGE, PLUS C'EST LA MÊME CHOSE

College administrative work meant that I was inescapably drawn away from active participation in psychology; yet this was not without its compensations. I was able to view the field in broad perspective and, I think, obtain a sense of proportion that is difficult to achieve when one is immersed in a discipline on a daily basis. Recently, Raymond Fowler, president of the Southeastern Psychological Association and Psychology Department chairman

at Alabama, wrote me to inquire what things stood out in psychology when I had been SEPA president ten years before. The tenor
of my reply illustrated the kind of perspective one obtains, for
better or worse, when viewing issues and events from a distance in
time and role. The hot issue when I was SEPA president was what
the young turks in psychology were heralding as the ER which
meant the educational revolution. According to them, learning-
teaching technology was going to enable students to learn much
faster, remember longer, and do it all with fewer teachers plus
some machines. My enthusiasm was not kindled for I had years
before seen Sidney L. Pressey's hand-operated teaching devices at
Ohio State University and E. L. Clark's somewhat similar devices
at Northwestern University. I also recalled other so-called discoveries which were offered in their time as "final answers" or "the
solution" to some psychological problem. About the time I entered puberty in the 1920's, for example, I went around intoning,
"Day by day in every way I'm getting better and better" because
a Frenchman named Coué was all the rage with his new *Auto-
suggestion* which virtually guaranteed to make everyone nigh perfect. In the early thirties psychoanalysis was the complete solution
to problems of human adjustment for us college students and
we immersed ourselves in Freud's writings. We talked much of
Women's Lib but we meant *libido,* not liberation, by *lib.* The
economic depression was full upon us about that same time and
a group of engineers offered seriously to cure all social and economic ills and the associated problems of human adjustment by
engineering principles—a conceptual system called technocracy.
For a while many of us youngsters saw this notion as the final
answer. Since then I have had my attention engaged, to a varying
degree, by other complete answers to various human problems—i.e.
the Hawthorne-Western Electric research, client-centered counseling, dianetics, group therapy, behavior-therapy, sensitivity training, personal encounter therapy, etc. All of them were presented
as *the* answer to certain problems. They all probably contributed
something to our knowledge but none was ever *the* answer. It all
reminds me of the Broadway musical *Gypsy* I saw some years ago.

An experienced stripper was explaining her art to the novice stripper Gypsy Rose Lee. The experienced stripper pressed a concealed switch on her scanty costume and suddenly lights began to flash on her chest and pelvic area. "See," said the old stripper, "Ya gotta have a gimmick," and she then sang a song with that refrain while her chest and pelvis sparkled with winking lights. So it is with the new "complete answers" to certain problems in human behavior. You have to have a gimmick. Then lights flash as a sign of enthusiasm and many people applaud while some do not. Any innovation is motivating and looks promising—for a while. But we do gain some new knowledge and experience some relief—but never the *final* answer.

GOD BLESS AMERICA

If I have any single reaction which characterizes my feelings about my life as a psychologist in America, I would say it is one of gratitude—gratitude to America which gave me a chance to do what I wanted to do. There are many things in America today that need improvement but I am confident that the needed changes will come about, just as in the past. There will be continuing upheaval and uproar along social class lines and I should guess it will last for a decade or more. But each convulsion provides options, offers further freedom of choice for those who seek it. This happened to me and I am grateful. I know full well what I should have been had my parents stayed in Sweden. I should have been a blacksmith. Had their parents or grandparents stayed in Europe a similar predestination of role would have been the fate of those close to me. My wife would have been a farmer's daughter on a steading that had been in her father's family for several generations in central Finland. The friends of my childhood, instead of being the doctors, lawyers, professors, and the executives they are, would have been tailors, carpenters, peasants, shepherds, etc., just as their relatives in Europe are today. Of course, the same is true of all Americans, whether they came to America last year or three hundred years ago. As President Franklin D. Roosevelt said, "We are all immigrants here." He could have added that sooner or later we all get a chance to shape our destinies.

REFERENCES

Bass, B. M., and Berg, I. A. (Eds.). *Objective personality assessment.* New York: Van Nostrand, 1959.

Berg, I. A. Development in behavior. *Journal of Experimental Psychology,* 1944, *34,* 343-69.

Berg, I. A. Chronic vitamin B deprivation in dogs. *Science,* 1947, *105,* 252.

Berg, I. A. The use of human subjects in psychological research. *American Psychologist,* 1954, *9,* 108-11.

Berg, I. A. Response bias and personality: The deviation hypothesis. *Journal of Psychology,* 1955, *40,* 61-72.

Berg, I. A. Deviant responses and deviant people. *Journal of Counseling Psychology,* 1957, *4,* 154-61.

Berg, I. A. Cultural trends and the task of psychology. *American Psychologist,* 1965, *20,* 203-7.

Berg, I. A. (Ed.). *Response set in personality assessment.* Chicago: Aldine, 1967.

Berg, I. A., and Adams, H. E. The experimental bases of personality assessment. In A. J. Bachrach (Ed.), *Experimental clinical psychology.* New York: Basic Books, 1962. Pp. 52-93.

Berg, I. A., and Bass, B. M. (Eds.). *Conformity and deviation,* New York: Harper, 1961.

Berg, I. A., and Hesterly, S. O. Deviant responses as indicators of immaturity and schizophrenia. *Journal Consulting Psychology,* 1958, *22,* 389-93.

Berg, I. A., and Weisman, R. The goal gradient in a maze of variable path length. *Journal of Psychology,* 1942, *14,* 307-15.

Berg, I. A., and Pennington, L. A. (Eds.). *An introduction to clinical psychology.* (3rd ed.) New York: Ronald Press, 1966.

Pennington, L. A., and Berg, I. A. (Eds.). *An introduction to clinical psychology.* New York: Ronald Press, 1948.

3

Epistemology, Rationality, and Utility in Psychology

WENDELL RICHARD GARNER

CAREER OVERVIEW

It might be useful to provide a quick overview of my career, so that as several themes or aspects of my professional life are discussed later, these can be fitted into the broad perspective. My undergraduate training—and this was the beginning of my professional life—was obtained in Lancaster, Pennsylvania, at Franklin and Marshall College, at that time an all-male, liberal arts college, with an enrollment of about a thousand students. I obtained a B.A. degree in 1942, with a major in psychology, and immediately went on to graduate school at Harvard University, obtaining the M.A. degree one year later. Then came full-time work as a research psychologist in several laboratories at Harvard, all involved in war research. These were the Radio Research Laboratory, where I did research designed to help "jam" (i.e. make difficult to perceive targets on) enemy radar. Then there was research on aircraft communications and the auditory perception of radar at the Psycho-Acoustic Laboratory. Finally I worked on problems of shipboard communication at the Systems Research Laboratory, operated by Harvard University, but physically located in Rhode Island. During this time I had managed to complete a few remaining requirements for the Ph.D. degree, which Harvard was gracious enough to award me without further ado in 1946, shortly after the end of World War II.

The next twenty-one years were spent at The Johns Hopkins University, except for a sabbatical year at Stanford University and another at the Applied Psychology Research Unit in Cambridge, England. During this time at Hopkins I went through the usual progression of academic rank, becoming professor in 1955. Additional functions were the directorship of the Psychological Laboratory at the Institute for Cooperative Research from 1949 to 1955, and the chairmanship of the Department of Psychology from 1954 to 1964. In 1967 I accepted appointment as James Rowland Angell professor of psychology at Yale University.

There is very little explaining that needs to be done about this bare outline of my career. The choice of Franklin and Marshall College was made because I lived in Lancaster and had a job there, so it was economically feasible for me to go to my local college. Pennsylvania has many such local colleges, and this was a common educational pattern at that time. Harvard, then as always, had an excellent department of psychology, and when they offered me a graduate fellowship to go there, it was easy to decide to accept. Careers during World War II were fashioned more by the military needs than by individual choice. My move to Baltimore was made for the simple reason that only Johns Hopkins actually offered me a position. At that time there was no department of psychology at Hopkins; it had died shortly before World War II, and the university was in the process of rebuilding it. Clifford T. Morgan, under whom I had done some work at Harvard, had been invited there, and he in turn invited me. Since there was no department at that time, however, we were appointed (instructor in my own case) in the Department of Biology. Psychology became a proper department again about a year later.

Then twenty-one years later came the move to Yale. It is difficult to state all of the reasons for the move, and a major one was that it was convenient for me to move to New England for personal family considerations. Of the more professional reasons, the honor of the appointment certainly had some influence, but probably the most important was simply the challenge. Yale was a distinguished department, but it had very little strength in human experimental psychology, or more particularly in perception and cognition. Thus adding and building strength in what had been a vacuum offered me a challenge, and meeting it has been satisfying. It is interesting to me that the same sort of challenge, although broader, existed when I first started at Johns Hopkins, since there we were faced with the problem of building an entire department where none existed at all.

Throughout my career I have maintained an active research program, with topics ranging from auditory psychophysics through problems of judgment, to information theory, human information processing, and the perception of auditory and visual patterns. There have been a few forays into the field of human learning, but only when the problem has seemed close to perception. In the broader sense my research has been on cognitive processes.

EDUCATIONAL INFLUENCES AND CHOICES

It is usual to speak of the influences which education has on us. Certainly individual people have had great influence on my life, and yet from my present perspective I am inclined to think that college and graduate school influenced me more in an indirect rather than direct fashion. By making certain choices available to me, both Franklin and Marshall College and Harvard University clearly helped shape the nature of my career. But the choices I made, it now seems to me, showed a consistency which indicated that the basic themes of my life were already well established by the time these choices were made. Thus the courses and subject matter I chose were indications of what I was rather than determiners of what I was going to be. But perhaps it is better simply to illustrate the point.

When I entered college, my intended major was mathematics. That had been my favorite subject in high school, where I had taken every math course available. I continued to like math in college, and yet changed my major after one year, and never took another formal course in mathematics—a decision I later regretted. The reason for the change was that at that time it seemed to me that higher mathematics had very little area of application, but was simply a self-contained subject. But I wanted to *use* the mathematics, not just to know it. Today, of course, there are many areas of application of higher mathematics, and it is clear that I could have enjoyed several of them. But the point is simply that my reason for dropping mathematics was its lack of clear application.

My next major was economics. Certainly here was a discipline which was useful, which could be applied, and which would make a difference in the world. So it seemed to satisfy my need for usefulness. In fact my plan was to become a labor union economist, a career which left me with no doubts about usefulness. It provided usefulness in two ways: one, the knowledge could be applied to practical problems, and two, the application would help people.

Even though economics provided practical application, at that time it had relatively little rationality in it of the kind provided by mathematics, so I was not really satisfied. Once again, I changed majors, even though economics has since developed into a highly mathematicized discipline. But what matters is that I dropped it for lack of that rationality then.

In my third year I had taken my first course in psychology, taught by Paul L. Whitely. He taught a relatively "hard" course, and even wrote equations on the blackboard. In particular I can remember his writing the equation which expresses Fechner's law: $S = k \log R$, which states that sensation magnitude is proportionate to the logarithm of stimulus intensity. I have since learned that Professor Whitely had little fondness for mathematics himself, so his influence on my career, which I consider greater than any other single person's, was still not the kind of direct influence of getting me to like what he liked, but rather was the indirect influence of showing me choices which I might make. So psychology became my choice of major subject because it satisfied my desire for both rationality and applicability.

This last point can be clarified a bit more. I have remarked that I wanted applicability, but also applicability of the sort which rather directly helps people. (This social conscience comes to me naturally, since I come from a family of ministers.) My application to graduate school stated that I intended to become a clinical psychologist. This was how one helped people directly. After just a few months in graduate school, however, it became clear to me that I was not temperamentally suited to clinical work. I liked the *idea* of directly helping people, but I did not enjoy the actual process at all. I needed a career that provided work I truly enjoyed on a day-by-day basis, so I ended up studying experimental psychology. I think many potential patients of mine as a clinical psychologist should be grateful that I made this choice.

But to return to college subject matter: other than changing majors to find one which satisfied the rationality plus applicability needs, my other choices are of interest as well. All students were required to take at least one course in "science," and my requirement was satisfied with chemistry. But not another single science course can be found on my transcript. Science to me seemed to be preoccupied with technique rather than with knowledge, and knowledge was what I sought. Clearly this attitude on my part was a reflection of the heavy emphasis on laboratory training in the natural sciences. Several courses in philosophy seemed to satisfy my needs, and although I never even considered a major in philosophy, it is clear that I was concerned with the nature of knowledge—with epistemology.

So my choice of psychology as a field of specialization was not at all a choice to study a science. Rather it was the choice of a field of knowledge, a field of knowledge which itself was concerned with the nature of knowledge acquisition (i.e. how do people perceive and learn?), but which included rationality and had applicability. These themes of epistemology, rationality, and applicability seem to me to have been continuously in evidence throughout my professional career.

PSYCHOLOGY AS SCIENCE

Thus I am a scientist who never really chose to be one. From the beginning my choice of psychology has been a choice of subject matter, a field of knowledge, and not a choice to engage in a particular form of activity called science. Yet also from the beginning my choice of particular subject matter within psychology has been of the topics usually considered most scientific within the broader field of psychology. Various labels have been used by others at times to designate the scientific nature of my subject matter, but the only professional designation I have ever used for myself is simply psychologist.

A professional identity is universally needed, and in every profession the identifying acts and labels occur continuously throughout the professional career. It has always been somewhat amusing to me that these identifying things have so consistently been as scientist for me, even though I never made a definite decision to be a scientist, either overtly or to myself. The identity was first established for me during World War II, when by official action of the appropriate agencies in Washington psychologists were not designated as scientists, thus could not be officially deferred for scientific research, since scientific research clearly could be done only by scientists. So during the war years, while working in the various laboratories, I was a "psychophysicist," not a psychologist, because psychophysicists were scientists and thus could engage in such activities as figuring out how to jam enemy radar, preventing our submarine radar from being detected by the enemy, and determining how to arrange communications systems aboard warships. So very early in my career it was made clear that the distinction between scientist and nonscientist was an important one, and that I was a scientist. I do not really mind being called a scientist, although the distinction between scientist and nonscientist has never seemed important to me.

But the labeling as scientist continued. While still a graduate student I joined the American Association for the Advancement of Science and became a regular weekly recipient of the journal called *Science*. Early in my years at Johns Hopkins I became listed in the biographical reference *American Men of Science,* and I have since been listed in other national and international listings of scientists. In 1964 I received the Distinguished Scientific Contribution Award from the American Psychological Association, and in the following year received the ultimate in scientific labeling, membership in the National Academy of Sciences. So scientist I am, not by my choice of psychology itself, but by my choice of subject matter within the broader field of psychology.

Nevertheless, my field of specialization reflects as much my interest in epistemology as it does an interest in science. Today the broad designation of cognition is used to describe much of human experimental psychology, and the literal meaning of cognition is knowing. My special field of interest has always been one of understanding how we perceive, i.e. come to know, the real world. In order to emphasize perception as knowing, the title of the talk I gave in acknowledgment of the Distinguished Scientist Award was "To Perceive Is To Know." By that title I was trying to emphasize perception as knowing rather than as doing. Perceiving is not just responding or discriminating—it is knowing. It is true that the experimental psychologist's approach to the study of knowing is somewhat different from the philosopher's, but the psychologist's perception and cognition are close cousins of the philosopher's epistemology.

We constantly hear about *the* scientific method, as though there is some special set of actions which constitute a method of knowing for the scientist which are qualitatively different from methods of knowing used by nonscientists. In undergraduate school, the essence of this special method seemed to be manipulation of things in laboratories. Later, in graduate school, it seemed to be some precise combination of empiricism coupled with deductions from theories which defined the scientific method. But there really is no such thing as *the* scientific method, and all it takes is a scan across different sciences to see how unlike these methods are.

Until very recently, astronomers were quite unable to manipulate their subject matter: they could only observe. And yet with systematic observations over many centuries they came to know the nature of the universe very accurately. Field biologists and modern-day ethologists likewise depend heavily on systematic observation, and they have acquired great knowledge with these techniques. But the chemist manipulates in the laboratory, as do some psychologists; and for many the essence of being a scientist is this manipulation of the events the scientist wants to understand, this carrying out of an experiment. With such manipulation we can differentiate between dependent and independent variables, and possibly also can state cause and effect relations. But this method is limited to a rather small class of phenomena we might want to study, and surely it cannot be considered *the* scientific method.

To me, the scientist comes to know things in ways which are not qualitatively different from the way any person comes to know things. He has more skill at coming to know the world than does the layman, but this skill lies primarily in his being able to use techniques with greater precision, to use tools that aid his senses (such as microscopes, telescopes, and oscilloscopes), and to use more powerful analytic techniques (e.g. computers) than are available to the ordinary layman. The scientist has not, however, discovered a new way of knowing, a new epistemological technique.

SCIENCE AND PERCEPTION AS CRITICAL REALISM

The epistemological position which seems to me valid both for the scientists and the ordinary person perceiving is that of critical realism. Realism, as contrasted with idealism, is the epistemological position that knowing is of a real world. There is a reality which is independent of the perceiver, be he scientist or layman. So to know is to know reality. But one can come to know reality in different ways. The simple, or naïve, realist believes that we come to know reality directly. We directly perceive a real world, and our perceptions show the world as it is. The critical realist believes that we come to know reality by relating various types of knowledge so as to form a correct construction of the real world, but that knowledge of reality is denied us as directly given. To give a simple example, we see with one eye a static picture which is entirely two-dimensional. But if this one eye is moved across space, or through time, the total information can be critically related to produce an accurate construct of three-dimensional space. And, of course, two eyes give two such disparate but relatable inputs at once to provide the information necessary for a correct three-dimensional construction of the real world.

But this is exactly how the scientist works. He obtains various kinds of information, from as many sources as possible, and then constructs a picture of reality by inter-relating these various kinds of information. Rarely does the scientist assume that knowledge is given to him directly, or that it constitutes very important knowledge if it is.

In accepting the critical realist position, the importance of rationality can clearly be seen. Science is often considered to have empiricism as its primary defining basis, but the critical realist position is that the rules, techniques, and operations required for putting information together to construct a picture of reality are as important in the scientific process as the obtaining of empirical data itself. Translated quite specifically into the realm of behavior and the study of perception, the observable behavior (that which behaviorists emphasize as the basis of psychology as a science) is only a first step in the scientific process. Perceiving is knowing. To understand perceiving, we as scientists must use as our basic data the behavior of the perceiver. But that behavior must not be confused with perceiving. It is our starting point and from it we must construct a picture of reality about perceiving.

A scientific disagreement I had some years ago with S. S. Stevens can illustrate this issue very nicely. Professor Stevens' role in this argument has always intrigued me because he himself played an important part in my development as a critical realist, and yet he ended up arguing for the simple realist position.

Professor Stevens was director of the Psycho-Acoustic Laboratory and thus my supervisor while I worked there during World War II. One day I showed him some data I had collected, a graph that indicated an apparent anomaly under one condition. He asked me what I thought about the graph, and I replied to the effect that that's what the data showed. He then said, "Yes, but what's the truth?" This clear distinction between data and truth, or as I would put it today, the reality we as scientists are trying to construct, is the distinction between simple realism and critical realism.

The disagreement mentioned above concerned the nature of a sensory scale of loudness. I (1954a) had argued for a scale which was based both on direct estimates of the ratio of loudnesses and on interval scaling of loudnesses, feeling that a scale must satisfy both of these scaling data to be valid. Stevens, on the other hand, argued in a series of papers (e.g. 1957) that the loudness scales based on direct estimates of loudness were the valid ones. That is to say, Stevens wanted to accept the naïve realist position that verbal statements by an observer directly gave evidence concerning the magnitude of a sensation. My own position can be seen with a quotation from one paper (1954b):

> Direct validation of the numerical responses is impossible, because we have no independent measure of the sensory process itself. . . . Validation can be obtained by using converging operations to arrive at a single construct or concept. If two or more independent sets of data, involving basically different indicators of the nature of the sensory process, lead to the same sensory scale, then we have a form of validation.

This is a clear statement of the role of the scientist as critical realist, where the operations for relating empirical data are as important as those for obtaining data.

A statement of this position was later formalized and elaborated in a paper I wrote with Harold Hake and Charles Eriksen (1956), at that time colleagues of mine at Johns Hopkins University. In that period, empiricism and a simple form of operationism were quite accepted. It was widely felt that a concept was no more than the operations on which it was based. I had heard psychologists say such things as "We cannot differentiate between a perceptual process and a response process because the response is our observable, and thus the concept of perception is synonymous with the responses which constitute our data." This attitude on the part of editors had caused all three of us certain difficulties. We all agreed that it is not only permissible to consider perception as a concept independent of the operations which indicate its nature, but that as psychologists it was imperative that we do so. Editors felt differently, so we had some difficulty getting papers published when we tried to differentiate response and perceptual processes. So we wrote a complete statement of the position we shared, elaborated on the idea of converging operations as the basic conceptual method, and illustrated its use in several research areas. This paper has been given credit by many writers for making possible the current research on information processing, in which we try to differentiate not only perceptual from response processes, but in addition many other organismic processes. Fundamentally, however, the paper "Operationism and the Concept of Perception" is a statement of a critical realist position for science.

The most extensive use I have made of this idea of converging operations to allow a construction of reality which is not directly observable is in a recent paper written with Gary Felfoldy (1970). The converging-operations idea requires that we attempt to understand a process by using a variety of experimental or observational procedures, with sufficient variation that we can critically construct reality, i.e. can converge on the appropriate construct. In this research we were concerned with the attentional process, the ability in perception to disregard some dimensions of the stimulus. We felt that such an ability ought to be related to the ability to integrate information by providing better discrimination if stimulus dimensions are correlated, thus redundant. So we used the necessary control condition of measuring speed of discrimination with stimuli varying on just a single dimension, plus measurements with stimuli varying on two dimensions which are correlated (the redundancy task) plus measurements with stimuli varying on two dimensions but with discrimination to be carried out with only one dimension (the attention task). Thus we used several tasks with a given pair of stimulus dimensions. In addition, however, we also repeated the experiment with several different pairs of stimulus dimensions. This combination of stimulus and task variation allowed us to demonstrate the construct of dimensional integrality; it showed that interference in the attention task occurred when there was facilitation in the redundancy task and that this combination of effects occurred for some stimulus dimensions and not for others. The use of converging operations can indeed be a powerful tool in psychological research.

A present colleague of mine, Professor Endel Tulving, calls me a rational empiricist. This is a good term, and one comfortable for me to accept. It is, furthermore, a rather good synonym for "critical realist."

RATIONALITY IN SCIENCE

Both laymen and scientists are (or should be) critical realists. "The scientific method," if we use the term at all, applies not to a basically different epistemological position but to greater sophistication on the part of the scientist. Critical realism involves both empirical and relating operations, and the greater sophistication required for the scientist must be for both aspects of the process. His observing techniques must be improved but so also must his rational techniques.

The techniques which I would call rational are many and varied. The most obvious are those that use mathematics. Certainly one of the oldest uses of mathematics in psychology was in physical specification of the stimulus in psychophysical research. Then psychologists became quite sophisticated in the processing of data, a fact which means that psychologists all have to learn some statistics. More recently mathematics has been used to provide a model for behavior, and in this use mathematics is simply providing the language for the expression of a theory. But there is still another usage, one which I like to use myself, and that is to provide a normative model for psychologists to work with. In my book *Uncertainty and Structure as Psychological Concepts* (1962), I used the mathematics of information theory primarily this way. A quotation from that book makes the point: "Mathematics may, however, be used as a tool, sometimes a powerful tool, to examine theoretical problems without itself being a theory, nor yet becoming simply a technique for data processing. Mathematics may help us ask questions without presuming answers" (p. 15).

Thus mathematics may be used as a means to think through the nature of a problem, to see potential relations in the more exact form which mathematics can provide, and as a result frequently to state or at least clarify the nature of a proper experimental question.

Information theory deals with relations between events in a very general way because it ignores the underlying metric of the things being measured, attending only to the number of alternative things which can happen and the probability of their occurrence. This concept is, of course, the fundamental contribution of information theory: information is not a matter of what happens in an act of communication but rather a question of the number of things which could happen but do not.

One particular problem area that informational mathematics helped me to see more clearly is that of goodness of pattern. Many psychologists, in particular Fred Attneave (e.g. 1954), had felt that the formal informational concept of redundancy should be related to the gestalt concept of pattern goodness. Yet many of these attempts, while providing useful insights, seemed to provide less generality than had been hoped for. By a logical and mathematical analysis of the concept of redundancy, however, I realized that the connection between redundancy and pattern goodness lay in understanding that redundancy is related to the number of alternatives of subsets of patterns from larger defined sets. Thus good patterns should be those with few perceived alternatives. In a series of researches on both visual spatial patterns and auditory temporal patterns, I have shown that indeed "Good Patterns Have Few Alternatives," which is the title of a 1970 summary paper on this topic.

This example illustrates a point, namely that rational processes in science do not necessarily occur after empirical data have been obtained; nor is the critical realist position one which need assume a temporal priority of evidence over the rational relating processes. Rational processes, in science or in everyday life, may properly determine what data are to be collected. All combinations of data are not equally useful in providing converging operations to a construct, since some sets of data essentially establish reliability only but are not sufficiently independent to provide convergence to a construct which is not simply identical to the operations involved in data collection. Thus rational processes should be used to establish what data should be collected, and not just what to do with the data after they have been obtained.

A paper I wrote with John Morton (1969) illustrates this need to reason through the nature of the problem before doing research on the problem. And I hope it is clear that I am not talking here about the use of the deductive method in science as opposed to the inductive method, because I am trying to emphasize not deductions to a conclusion which is to be empirically verified, but rather rational and logical processes which are intended to clarify the nature of the entire problem area. The concept of perceptual independence has floated through a great deal of research concerned with multiple perceptual processes, such as listening and seeing simultaneously, or judging multidimensional stimuli. It seemed to Morton and me that a lot of apparent contradiction in the literature had to do with the definition of the nature of perceptual independence itself and that scientists had been acting as though perceptual independence were a unitary concept when in fact it was not. We showed that there are at least six logically different meanings to the concept of perceptual independence and that empirical research was not going to lead to clear answers until the research was directed at a specific kind of perceptual independence. Notice once again that the rational process is not concerned with deductions and predictions about experimental outcomes; it is concerned with determining the proper nature of a question.

I have been talking primarily about the use of rational processes before data collection, processes that let us know what the question is or should be. But it is true that we sometimes collect data when we think we know what the question is, then discover that the data don't make any sense with regard to the question. So we end up with data in search of a question, an experience common to many researchers. When this happens, what do you do? If you have a sufficiently firm belief in the primacy of the empirical process, you publish the data anyway. If, however, you feel that data cannot be understood correctly without an appropriate question, usually based on rational considerations, then you do not publish the data. You wait. My most extreme case was publication of a paper on information measurement with ratings of ambiguous materials (e.g. quality of handwriting) in 1960, although I had actually collected the data seven years earlier. Each summer I took another look at the data, then put them back on the shelf. Finally, the question which the data were answering became clear, and the paper was published.

This emphasis on the role of rationality in the scientific process should not be taken to mean that the process of adding rationality to empirical processes is necessarily very formal. Often one collects data with at best a vaguely formed question, hoping that the data themselves will help clarify what the question should have been. Certainly the process actually used by most scientists is not the formally described process wherein one has a hypothesis, translates it into an exact empirical test, collects the data, then gets a clear yes-or-no answer with respect to the hypothesis. One experience in my life will illustrate the extent to which this entire process of critical realism, or rational empiricism, is a fairly loosely structured affair for most scientists.

The American Psychological Association had appointed a committee of Donald W. Taylor, Howard F. Hunt, and me to try to arrange a seminar to discuss training for science careers in psychology. The three of us got together for a preliminary meeting in New York in 1957, none of us being very sure there was anything worthwhile we could arrange. However, one problem had been nagging me, and it was this: For several years I had been teaching graduate students how to become scientists, and I had been teaching the usual formal approach which we read about in books on the logic of science. My problem was that of several dozen research papers I had published by then, only one came close to satisfying the formal requirements. (In a paper on temporal integration of energy in the ear, I had actually worked out

Fourier analyses of energy distributions of very short tones and had deduced that the rate of energy integration was a function of the bandwidth of frequencies over which the energy was spread. The experiment was carried out, it came out just as predicted, and I had actually followed the textbook method of doing rerearch. (See Garner, 1947.) My feeling was that there was little reason for me to worry about the fact that my way of doing research was so different from what the books said. It worked for me and that was all that mattered. The fact that other people seemed to do research so differently was little reason for me to be concerned.

At this preliminary meeting I ventured to ask Professors Hunt and Taylor if possibly they too didn't do research the way the books said. They said they didn't and also felt that they were simply deviant, but since fortune smiled on their efforts, why should they worry? At any rate, we arranged a month-long seminar, attended by Leon Festinger, D. O. Hebb, Douglas H. Lawrence, Charles E. Osgood, B. F. Skinner, and Michael Wertheimer, in addition to the three organizers. The results of this seminar were published in 1959, and perhaps the most important result was the discovery that none of these people, all successful as scientists, actually did research according to the book. Rather, various informal techniques, intuitions, hunches, pilot data collections, etc., characterized the way research gets done by most successful researchers. So while I want to argue that rationality is a very large part of the scientific process, I do not think that it occurs in a highly formalized way at all. Rational and empirical processes are thoroughly intermixed, at times one dominating the activity, at times the other. But informal though the process may be, the ultimate result involves both rational and empirical components.

BASIC AND APPLIED SCIENCE

To me, knowledge which has utility (or application) has always been more interesting than knowledge which presumes to exist for its own sake. Many scientists attempt to draw distinctions between pure, basic, and applied research, and they seem to feel that some kinds are proper for universities to engage in, while others are not. There is no question in my mind that the actual application of knowledge is a process different from that of obtaining knowledge, and I think rather specialized personnel are necessary for it. However, the distinctions between pure, basic, and applied research are really rather tenuous and the bases for the distinctions are usually quite inappropriate to a proper evaluation of any research or new knowledge.

Knowledge should have generality for it to be valuable—or efficient, if you prefer. To know something that is true for a unique event or situation is obviously much less valuable than to know something that is true for many situations, or that can at least be related to many situations. Thus generality is the primary evaluative property for knowledge and the search for it, and words such as "pure" and "applied" are simply irrelevant. The concept of pure research has always been especially unpleasant to me because frequently people who use the term define "pure" as having no foreseeable application, and imply that such a state of affairs is desirable. That research should somehow be considered better because it has no possible application makes no sense. The term "basic" is a bit more congenial, because it comes closer to connoting the idea of generality, which is to me the only justifiable grounds for evaluating the quality of research.

Since my research career started during World War II, when practically all research effort was directed at the war, my early research years were necessarily concerned with applied problems. World War II showed on a quite large scale that traditional problems of experimental psychology had a substantial area of application. In the use of complex sensing devices such as sonar and radar, and complex communication apparatus—and especially in training people to use them—topics of sensation, perception, and learning were quickly enough translated into the realities of the war-time needs.

In order not to lose the impetus which the war years had provided, and with the hope of extending the applications of experimental psychology into new domains, three of us who had been active in doing research on the applications of experimental psychology during and shortly after World War II decided it would be a good idea to provide a basis of training for such work. So Alphonse Chapanis, Clifford Morgan, and I (at that time all at Johns Hopkins University) wrote a textbook *Applied Experimental Psychology* (1949), showing the relations between the more traditional experimental psychology and various types of application for it. This area has now become a recognized specialty within psychology, although terms like "engineering psychology" or "human factors research" are now more commonly used to describe the area.

As I mentioned earlier, I had finished the war years working in the Systems Research Laboratory operated by Harvard University. Clifford Morgan had also been involved in that laboratory's work. After the war, the Navy wanted to continue the research program of that laboratory; with two of its scientific personnel moving to Hopkins, responsibility for the laboratory was shifted to Hopkins. In 1948, it was decided that the laboratory itself should be moved to Baltimore. The university had organized its Institute for Cooperative Research, which was designed to provide a means for scientific cooperation between university scientists and both industry and the government. The Psychological Laboratory was formed in the institute, and a search went out for a man interested in this type of cooperative research to become its director. Hopkins was unsuccessful in finding the man it wanted, so I requested permission to take a try at it myself, even though I was a bit less established than seemed desirable. My motives were, I think, fairly simple in undertaking this directorship, leaving the straight academic role. I truly believed in the concept of research and application properly going hand in hand and wanted to participate in what I hoped would be a growing type of activity in American universities. So I changed primary function to the Institute for Cooperative Research and for six years worked in a laboratory physically separated from the main psychology department.

Ultimately we closed that laboratory, and I am still regretful. The reasons for closing had to do with the fundamental difficulties of carrying on the applied (although still basic) research in the traditional university setting. In universities, research is fitted around the needs of the academic schedule. Much applied research has to be fitted into schedules of the cooperating agency, and only by the purest luck will these coincide with the academic schedule. In addition to the scheduling problems, there are personnel problems. It soon became apparent that the people who were very good at doing academic research were not always good at doing applied research (by which I mean research in settings where ultimate application might occur), and vice versa. Personnel procedures at universities make it easy to promote somebody good at laboratory research who could not do one meaningful piece of research in the settings of a real world, but a person whose real skill is in being able to handle all the complexities of the applied setting has little chance of being rewarded for such work with academic promotion.

What are the values of such cooperative, or applied research? To me there are two major ones. The first is simply that all research and scholarly work is done in and by the consent of the society in which it lives, and which supports it. It may seem at times that the heavily endowed great universities support their research with their endowment, rather than by the consent of the society. But that endowment exists only because the society gives special tax privileges to the universities and the individuals providing it. Thus we as members of a profession have no obligation to see that the society reaps some benefit from what it pays for. This type of responsibility must be as a total profession, because each of us as an individual is not capable of providing the application or the liaison between the acquirers of knowledge and the users of it. Many of the academics, as noted above, simply are not capable of doing such work. If we are to be responsible members of the society in which we live we must see to it that capable individuals are trained to do applied research and to carry out its actual application.

The second major value of cooperative research is the more important to me personally, simply because I do work in an academic institution. It is that much very good basic research comes from discovering our ignorance in the real world. If academic research divorces itself completely from the world of potential application, new research tends to be built onto existing knowledge. But research which originates with an applied problem is built on ignorance, not existing knowledge. In the long run we will progress much faster if research is done on what we know little about than if research is done on what we know a lot about. Thus the area of application provides an essential feedback to the area of research, a feedback which defines areas of ignorance.

To give a personal example, in about 1949 several psychologists were asked this reasonable question: Aircraft controllers can directly read azimuth direction and range or distance on their radar. If we want to code altitude information for controllers to use by varying such things as the brightness or size of the spot on the radar oscilloscope, how should the coding be done to give the aircraft controller the most information? Should a small number of discrete steps of brightness be used, or should altitude be indicated as a true continuum? We did not know how to answer the question, and several of us began a research program on it. It was this program that first got me interested in information theory, because clearly information was the commodity we wanted to talk about, and Harold Hake and I (1951) worked out a way to use information measurement to obtain an answer to this question. (The answer is, incidentally, that above a small number of steps it makes little difference how many discrete steps are used. Errors will increase with an increase in number of steps, but the amount of information obtained by the aircraft controller will remain constant.) This question, showing psychologists an area of ignorance, essentially opened up a large research area concerned with information transmission as a function not just of the number of discrete steps but also of the number of dimensions, and whether the stimulus dimensions are correlated or not.

So constant contact with applied problem areas is needed not just to provide help to the society which supports scientists but also to make the efforts of the scientists maximally useful. True interaction between basic research and application is enormously valuable.

In conclusion, the themes which were evident in the decisions I made as an undergraduate student have run throughout much of my professional career: an interest in the nature of knowledge, a belief that rational and empirical processes are important in both the layman's knowledge and the scientist's knowledge, and a belief that scientific knowledge should be useful to society.

REFERENCES

Attneave, F. Some informational aspects of visual perception. *Psychological Review,* 1954, *61,* 183-93.

Chapanis, A., Garner, W. R., and Morgan, C. T. *Applied experimental psychology.* New York: Wiley, 1949.

Garner, W. R. The effect of frequency spectrum on temporal integration of energy in the ear. *Journal of the Acoustical Society of America,* 1947, *19,* 808-15.

————. A technique and a scale for loudness measurement. *Journal of the Acoustical Society of America,* 1954a, *26,* 73-88.

————. Context effects and the validity of loudness scales. *Journal of Experimental Psychology,* 1954b, *48,* 218-24.

————. Rating scales, discriminability, and information transmission. *Psychological Review,* 1960, *67,* 343-52.

————. *Uncertainty and structure as psychological concepts.* New York: Wiley, 1962.

————. To perceive is to know. *American Psychologist,* 1966, *21,* 11-19.

————. Good patterns have few alternatives. *American Scientist,* 1970, *58,* 34-42.

———— and Felfoldy, G. L. Integrality of stimulus dimensions in various types of information processing. *Cognitive Psychology,* 1970, *1,* 225-41.

———— and Hake, H. W. The amount of information in absolute judgments. *Psychological Review,* 1951, *58,* 446-59.

———— Hake, H. W., and Eriksen, C. W. Operationism and the concept of perception. *Psychological Review,* 1956, *63,* 149-59.

Garner, W. R., and Morton, J. Perceptual independence: Definitions, models, and experimental paradigms. *Psychological Bulletin,* 1969, *72*, 233-59.

Stevens, S. S. On the psychophysical law. *Psychological Review,* 1957, *64,* 153-81.

Taylor, D. W., et al. Education for research in psychology. *American Psychologist,* 1959, *14,* 167-79.

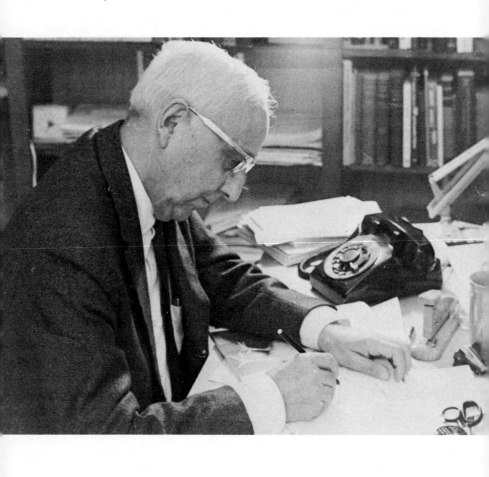

4

Some Highlights
of an Intellectual Journey

HARRY HELSON

The writing of an autobiography should do more than serve as a catharsis or ego-builder for its author. It should serve some useful purpose to the reader and this means that it should do more than entertain him or titillate his fancy. There are other forms of literature that can do such things much better than biography. Various forms of fictional writing are not subject to the constraints of biography and thus have the advantage of unfettered imagination. Biography has the advantage of being true (insofar as one can see himself and others truly) and truth, as has so often been pointed out, can be stranger and more exciting than fiction. In a good novel everything that happens to its characters is supposed to follow as a natural development of their inner nature. In the work of fiction little is left to chance or accident, but these often play important roles in actual life. I begin on this note because I often wonder what my life and career would have been had it not been for various chance factors.

EARLY YEARS

Practically all the conditions for a very different kind of life from the one I have had were present during my early years: a broken home, separation from parents, poverty (with no governmental sources of support or relief), and little external motivation to pursue an intellectual career. Until I reached the sixth grade I went to a number of different schools in Bangor, Maine, where I finished grammar school, followed by four years of high school. My years in the seventh and eighth grades were extremely unhappy ones owing to the fact my teachers were, to say the least, unsympathetic. I was regarded as a disciplinary problem by them but not by any of my teachers before or afterward. In seventh grade I had great difficulty learning grammar until one day it suddenly became clear and easy. It is hard to explain such sudden learning by insight since this is a subject governed by arbitrary rules (except to a philologist!). Perhaps the dissipation of my difficulties was a matter of disinhibition of blockages that prevent mechanical as well as insightful learning. Contemporary learning theory throws little or no light on such mechanisms. In the ninth grade I had a sympathetic teacher and the difficulties of my grammar school days were over.

In high school, to use current slang, I had a ball. Rooms, teachers, and subjects changed every hour and I was never bored. In high school there were also outside activities in which I participated: orchestra, in which I played violin, debating, public speaking, school plays, and the monthly magazine, *Oracle,* of which I became editor in my senior year. Most of my last year was taken up with editing and I spent more time in the composing room of the printing shop than in classes. Absences from class were automatically excused because of this editorship but I took care not to miss many classes in physics and solid geometry, which did not come easy to me.

In addition to my extra-curricular activities I worked at various jobs to earn money for violin lessons and other extras. My foster parents, Frederick and Theodosia Dyer, were able to provide me with only the barest necessities. We lived under conditions that today are regarded as substandard, yet we were reasonably happy and contented and did not look to outside sources for financial aid. Our house, though large, had no electricity or gas, no bathtub, and no central heating. We used kerosene lamps and wood and coal-burning stoves, and we bathed by means of large bowls of water heated in the kitchen and carried to bedrooms. But our house was spotlessly clean inside and out. Under the simpler conditions of life in those days, poverty was not as degrading and demoralizing as it is today, or at least is believed to be. We did not have the contrasts of affluence and easy living and quick ways to riches that exist today and so we were content with our lot while striving for something better.

COLLEGE AND GRADUATE SCHOOL

Upon graduation from high school I was enabled to enter Bowdoin College in the fall of 1917 owing to the efforts of Mr. Lee T. Gray, sub-master of Bangor High School. He was responsible for getting me a fellowship, contributed chiefly by the Bowdoin Club of Bangor. I also worked as a reporter on the *Bangor Daily Commercial* (now defunct) during the summer after graduation and after my first year at Bowdoin. I earned money playing violin during my second and third years and worked in the summer to supplement scholarships from Bowdoin. During my fourth year my father, with whom I had not had contact for nearly thirteen years, helped me financially and continued to do so during my first two years in graduate school.

By the time I went to Bowdoin I knew I wanted to major in philosophy and psychology because I had read, or tried to read, several works in these areas. However, I could not begin these subjects before my sophomore year as they were not freshman offerings. The courses in psychology did not include laboratory and I had to gain my knowledge of this aspect of psychology largely from Whipple's *Manuals* which encompassed almost the entire range of topics from sensory processes to mental tests, including a set of ink blots which were not then called Rorschach tests. I still have these two volumes and they are remarkably modern in what they cover.

At Bowdoin, I continued my interests in music and debating and worked on the college paper, but I gradually dropped everything except the violin, which I played to earn money for college expenses. Most of the paying jobs required late nights and overnight travel and I was completely worn out by the time Commencement arrived. I managed to deliver one of the two Commencement speeches chosen in classwide competition and went home in a state of complete collapse.

The summer after graduation in 1921 was spent on my back in bed and I dragged myself to Cambridge to begin graduate work at Harvard about as low in body and spirit as one could be and still maintain some semblance of normality. I improved rapidly, as young people are apt to do when there is nothing organically wrong, and my first year of graduate work passed quickly and pleasantly. I carried a double load of classes in order to take as much psychology as philosophy, for I was not certain which way I would eventually travel. Actually, most of the work in philosophy was in logic, which interested me more than history of philosophy, ethics, and epistemology. H. M. S. Sheffer's offerings in mathematical logic appealed to me especially because of the originality and brilliance of his mind, and C. I. Lewis' seminars were equally interesting because of his scientific and naturalistic approach to philosophical problems. Little did I dream when I took L. T. Troland's courses that I would devote the greater part of my scientific life to visual problems, but with a more "perceptual" slant than he gave since he was more interested in classical sensory, Helmholtzian visual science. The moral of this is that one cannot tell which way his interests will eventually develop and one should acquire sound, basic knowledge in a field as preparation for any eventuality. Another important influence in my graduate work was E. G. Boring who came to Harvard from Clark University at the beginning of my second year. His coverage of sensory processes was notable for its range and depth and his emphasis on experimental and quantitative data gave me a new glimpse into psychology as science.

It was through Boring's presentation of the work on apparent movement that I became acquainted with Gestalt psychology and when the time came to choose a thesis topic at the beginning of my third year of graduate work, I proposed a critical review of the Gestalt movement. Boring agreed to act as my adviser and he, Langfeld, and McDougall served as my dissertation committee. My thesis came to nearly five hundred typed pages and made up in volume what it might have lacked in quality! It traced the origins of Gestalt psychology back to the Greeks and covered the voluminous writings of the Gestaltqualität school, the Graz configurationists, and about everything that the Gestalt psychologists and their students had published to date. Most of the literature was experimental and in German. I then had an almost photographic memory and could recall authors, titles, journal references, and specific pages on which specific points were made. The thesis was published in four articles which appeared in the *American Journal of Psychology* (Helson, 1925; 1926). Since these were about the only sources in English dealing with this flourishing movement they were in considerable demand and I became well known among English-speaking psychologists for one so young.

EARLY STUDIES AND CAREER

As is usually the case, my early work was influenced by, if not a continuation of, the Ph.D. dissertation. After the articles on Gestalt psychology appeared both in journal and book form, I published my first and last animal study, appropriately titled: "Insight in the white rat" (1927), which showed that rats, as well as Köhler's chimpanzees, could transfer lightness discriminations on a relative basis. So far as I know, only E. C. Tolman noticed this study and took it very seriously—he had spent a year in Germany and was already acquainted with Gestalt psychology. A number of other studies concerned with various aspects of Gestalt followed, among them an eye-movement study with Guilford (1929) showing that eye movements could not be held responsible for perception of movement from successively exposed stationary stimuli. Although we knew that since movement could be perceived in opposite directions simultaneously, eye movements could not be responsible, the experiment had to be done to lay the ghost of the eye-movement explanation which persisted as "incipient tendencies" and in other hypothetical peripheral explanations. Another study with E. V. Fehrer (1932) was directed against the Gestalt assertion that the circle was the best form because of its simplicity: this experiment involved: (1) determination of absolute thresholds for first perception of light, (2) perceived, though not correct, form, and (3) report of correct form. We found that the circle was not the best form. Deductions from purely phenomenological properties have always seemed to me to be the weakest aspect in an otherwise strong Gestalt approach. Finally, I should mention an article summarizing and codifying 114 laws or descriptive statements concerning the behavior and properties of Gestalten (1933), which Boring (1950) later reduced to six principles. While recognizing the fruitfulness and importance of Gestalt psychology, I believed it needed modification and supplementation to be a really comprehensive theory. I have indicated how the theory of adaptation level seems to me to be a natural and necessary development in the quest for an adequate theory of holistic phenomena without, however, suffering from the defects of the Gestalt approach. I will return to this question later in this paper.

At this point I should mention my early interest in the manifestations of spiritualism, although I have always been skeptical of the phenomena alleged to be due to ESP, spirits, and occult mental or physical powers. In the early 1920s and until World War II practically all funds for support of graduate study were intra-university and were disbursed as scholarships, fellowships, teaching assistantships, and occasionally as research fellowships. During my third year at Harvard I was given a research fellowship from the Hodgson Fund for Psychic Research and was assigned to assist Gardner Murphy, the Hodgson Fellow, who taught also at Columbia. Because I had had considerable acquaintance with mediums at home, owing to the interest of the Dyers in spiritualism, it was not unnatural for me to get this appointment. William McDougall was an avowed dualist and maintained an active interest in telepathy, clairvoyance, and other occult phenomena. Under McDougall's and Murphy's direction, I investigated mediums, among them the famous Margery case, conducted table-tipping sessions in Emerson Hall, where psychology was then housed, and attended seances with various mediums. Occasionally we went to public performances of ESP, clairvoyance, and hypnotism. My contacts with mediums before going to Harvard had made me a complete skeptic regarding phenomena that were produced by professionals, i.e. that were not spontaneous. I adopted as my motto: "Anything that is expected, promised, or produced at will must be *ipso facto* mechanically or knowingly caused, hence, spurious." Several phenomena at home during seances with only the family present have left me puzzled over the years but I could never bring myself to believe in a future life and in disembodied intelligence. My main reason for remaining a skeptic is that spiritualism does not make sense philosophically nor does it fit in with biological life cycles involving birth, maturation, reproduction, and death. Perhaps physics will force us to radically different concepts of space, time, and causality that will make the claims of spiritualism and some religions intelligible, but so far I can make no sense out of individual survival and disincarnate spirits. Philosophically I am an Aristotelian more than anything else and believe with Aristotle that the soul is the form or function of the body and when the body dies there is no further need of a soul.

I have always regretted not having studied enough physics, mathematics, and biology during my undergraduate and graduate training, for it is with such knowledge that one gets the most benefit from subjects that he needs to know later. I took courses in physics, mathematics, chemistry, and neuroanatomy after the Ph.D. degree. These subjects would have been much more useful had they been studied earlier. But at least they enabled me to collaborate with colleagues on problems involving physical, mathematical, and physiological considerations. I am sure I would not have seen and worked on many problems without the late training I received in these subjects. However, let me enter a caveat lest it be thought that I overestimate technical training in subjects outside psychology. Technical competence in physics and mathematics, to take only these as examples, is not enough for the solution of psychological problems. One must have a sense for the basic problems in his own field or else his technical knowledge may be wasted on trivia. One often reads in the literature of physics of the necessity of having a sense of physical reality, something that can be lost sight of quite easily in modern, highly mathematicized physical theories. Similarly, the psychologist needs to have a sense of psychological or behavioral reality or else his work will be of no interest to anyone else in the field. One thinks of elaborate statistical and mathematical studies that do not have psychological substance and have little or no relevance for problems beyond themselves. Ideas are operationally fruitful when they lead back to psychological reality.

Several times during my career I have undertaken studies suggested by individuals in other, related fields. Two of these were in medical or physiological psychology and were meant to answer specific questions raised by practicing neurologists. The first study (Helson, 1932) was made to determine whether the paresthesias reported by patients after sub-total section of the trigeminal nerve to relieve the pain of tic douloureux had a neurological basis or was "mental" in origin. Threshold measurements left no doubt of the objectivity of the phenomena and the work was published in *Brain* with a foreword by the late Dr. Charles H. Frazier. A second study, undertaken at the suggestion of a neurologist, Dr. Theodore Weisenburg, was designed to determine if skin temperature could be raised or lowered as a result of emotional factors. Dr. Weisenburg had found that surface temperature of the skin might be temporarily elevated when there seemed to be no pathology involved. By employing various types of stimuli such as loud sounds, electric shock, or hard slap, it was found that surface temperature in the malar region of the face changed significantly (Helson and Quantius, 1934). Supporting the emotional origin of the temperature changes was the fact that anticipation of shock could cause a higher rise in temperature than did actual administration of the stimulus. These two studies convinced me there is a vast field of "clinical" or medical psychology in which psychologists and medical scientists could collaborate very fruitfully.

Still other programs of investigation were made as a result of external initiation. Shortly after the outbreak of the Second World War, I was asked by Drs. Thornton Fry and Samuel Fernberger if I would be willing to undertake research on anti-aircraft fire controls and allied problems under the auspices of the National Defense Research Committee (NDRC), an offshoot of the Office of Scientific Research and Development that handled most of the developmental research connected with the war effort. Thus was the Foxboro project initiated. There were many reports to the services which were also distributed to scientists and engineers working in other laboratories and in industry. I summarized many of the results from the Foxboro work gained from June 1942 to September 1944 in an article published in the *American Journal of Psychology* (Helson, 1949). In these studies we tried to specify optimal ranges of handwheel variables such as diameter, inertia, and load, and speed of turning. Anything that increased arm motion, whether larger radius of handwheel or higher gear ratios requiring faster turning (within limits), increased accuracy of tracking. I have been told that the Foxboro studies were the most extensive undertaken during the war. Many people were then concerned with optimal design of equipment and a new technology was born that is now generally called "human factors" or "human engineering." I am glad to have had a part in launching this new application of experimental psychology since my work has for the most part been directed toward theoretical issues.

A number of studies undertaken under contract with the Illuminating Engineering Research Institute (IERI) had practical implications. We were asked if it was possible to predict the colors (hue, saturation, and lightness) of objects in passing from daylight to various types of artificial illumination. In the first two studies (Helson and Grove, 1947; Helson, Judd, and Warren, 1952) we found it possible, starting from the C.I.E. specification for daylight colors and taking into account the changed state of adaptation, to predict quantitatively the colors of matt, chromatic papers viewed in incandescent-lamp light. In a third study (Helson, Judd, and Wilson), similar formulae were used to predict the colors of objects in fluorescent sources of illumination, a much harder task because of the uneven spectrum of such sources. By the time the studies of color changes from daylight to indoor sources of illumination were completed, IERI had become interested in the aesthetic (pleasantness) effects of sources. In the huge literature dealing with affective value of colors and combinations of colors, there were practically no studies of the effects of spectral energy differences among sources and backgrounds, most of the studies having been made with some variant of daylight and on neutral backgrounds. By the time we finished with what we thought was a modest design involving 125 Munsell colors on 25 backgrounds (including black, gray, and white), in five sources of illumination, and 10 observers, we found we had over 156,000 observations to deal with (Helson and Lansford, 1970). Owing to the magnitude of this study, it was published in *Applied Optics,* a journal read mostly by physicists and astronomers, so I believe it will be some time before psychologists become acquainted with it.

Finally, other studies were undertaken either at someone's suggestion or because interested collaborators were available. In the early 1950s a number of studies in the field of perception, collectively called the new look approach, were attracting the attention of people in the personality, social, and clinical areas as well as in the area of perception itself. A critical survey of this movement was suggested to me by Dr. Saul B. Sells. While I was not particularly partial to this point of view, my treatment of the literature of this school must have been of interest to many workers, as I was informed by the School of Aviation Medicine, under whose auspices the monograph was published, that more reprints of it had been issued than of any other publication by the school (Helson, 1953). After the completion of this review, R. R. Blake and I, with a number of co-workers, made a number of studies of conforming behavior from the point of view of adaptation-level theory (Helson, Blake, Mouton, and Olmstead, 1955; Blake, Helson, and Mouton, 1958; and others). In these studies we showed that conforming behavior was largely determined by the relative strengths, pro or con, of focal, background, and residual forces.

Our aim was to obtain quantitative data comparable to the functional dependencies, such as learning and sensory processes, found in the older, better-established fields of psychology. We also tried to show that systematic variation in interpersonal conditions could yield lawful dependencies expressible in functional relations as contrasted with the spot checks, and division of persons and social behaviors into dichotomous classes, that are found so often in these areas.

The studies made at Foxboro and Texas, while interesting and important, were not in my main line of interest. They represented applications of techniques, knowledge, or theory to areas then new to me. My main interest was rather in the development of theory in psychophysics, perception, and judgment. I had been strongly influenced by my reading of the Gestalt literature, but as mentioned above, I was not happy with the tendency of Gestalt psychologists to derive laws from purely phenomenological considerations. I was convinced, however, that Gestalt properties could not be accounted for wholly by atomistic approaches, valuable as they are for certain types of information. An accidental observation started me on a long series of studies that culminated in the theory of adaptation level. While developing film under the usual ruby red light, I noticed that the glowing end of my cigarette was a saturated green. There was no physical reason for its change from its daylight orange color since the incandescent tobacco acted like a perfect absorber of the red light while emitting light predominantly in the long-wave end of the spectrum. Nor did I see how the then new method of specifying colors by means of the C.I.E. Standard Observer (which I had learned from Dr. Deane B. Judd) would yield a correct prediction of the color under red illumination. The C.I.E. specification held only for colors seen as film or aperture colors, not necessarily for surface colors subject to contrast effects. So enthused was I over my finding, I contrived a simple demonstration for a meeting of the Optical Society of America; on the face of a large box I mounted a white, matt cardboard and in the center I cut a small hole behind which was another white surface. While the surface inside the box was illuminated with incandescent-lamp light, the front surface was illuminated with strongly chromatic (red) light. Looked at without the chromatic light, the aperture color appeared a fairly good white; looked at with the red surround the aperture color appeared a deep green as in the case of the cigarette tip in the light of the ruby red lamp.

This demonstration was broadened into a systematic experiment by using a series of daylight grays ranging from near-white to near-black on black, gray, and white backgrounds viewed in monochromatic or strongly chromatic illumination (Helson, 1948). The results came out beautifully regular because the problem had been reduced to a unidimensional one through the use of nonselective stimuli: both the focal and background stimuli varied only in reflectance, not in spectral composition. Only those familiar with the large, difficult, and confused literature, practically all in German, dealing with constancy, transformation, and vision in strongly chromatic illumination, can appreciate the simplicity and order enunciated in the principle of color conversion which emerged from this study. It bears repeating here: in every viewing situation there is established an adaptation level such that stimuli with reflectances above adaptation level are more or less tinged with the hue of the illuminant, stimuli below adaptation level are tinged with the hue of the after-image of the hue of the illuminant, and stimuli near adaptation level are achromatic or weakly saturated and often of uncertain hue owing to momentary changes in adaptation as the eyes move or rest. On black background only illuminant hues are seen; on white background complementary hues predominate; and on gray background both illuminant and complementary hues, as well as neutral colors in the vicinity of the adaptation level, appear. We thus were able to account for the breakdown of the C.I.E. specification when the surround was not completely dark as well as its correctness for stimuli viewed on black backgrounds.

The results using strongly chromatic light flooding the whole retina convinced me that much of the work in vision could not give a true picture of visual function because it was based on local, spot stimulation. One or two elementary examples suffice to show that results gained with atomistic procedures may yield completely unrealistic generalizations regarding natural, total field types of situation. Thus, if a spot check is made of retinal sensitivity as is done in perimetry and campimetry, one finds a central zone sensitive to red, green, yellow, and blue, a middle zone sensitive only to yellow and blue, and an outer zone yielding only achromatic colors. But if one looks at a homogeneous red surface near enough to fill the whole eye, one does not find that the red disappears or changes to yellow beyond the central zone: one sees a completely uniform red field as far out as there is any vision. Total field stimulation often yields something different from what one expects from a knowledge of part or spot functions. On the skin, point-like stimulation yields warm and cold spots but simultaneous stimulation of these spots by means of a Dallenbach-type grid evokes perception of a new quality—heat.

Returning to the visual case, it is no longer necessary to use elaborate optical instrumentation and relatively small stimuli to exercise tight control over visual stimuli. Since the "invention" of the Standard Observer of colorimetry, chromatic stimuli of any size which are identical with, or equivalent to, stimuli of known spectral composition can be easily produced, making possible the same control and specification of total field stimulation as was formerly true only of local, point-like stimuli.

All of this may seem recondite and highly specialized but it concerns a fundamental question: can we attain an adequate view of color vision by a piecemeal approach or must we not use total field conditions right from the beginning to obtain correct answers to certain problems? Certainly the piecemeal or atomistic approach may answer certain questions and may serve certain purposes but it has left too many puzzles and yielded too many contradictory results to serve as the only source of information on visual function. But if this is true in the field of vision, it is no less true in other areas, as indeed the example from the skin showed. The differences between spot and field stimulation, between short- and long-lasting stimuli, have not been so readily apparent outside the field of vision because so many perceptual processes are phasic or transient in nature and the influence of contextual stimuli is easily missed if not looked for deliberately. But the loudness of a sound, the heaviness of a weight, the quale of a taste or odor are just as much dependent on previous and environing stimuli as is a patch of color seen against a chromatic ground. Space perception too is subject to contextual effects as shown by the so-called illusions of extent, direction, and perspective. The interactions of space and time in such phenomena as the Tau and Kappa effects also bear witness to the strong interactions among perceptual processes which make necessary a field-theoretical approach.

It is at once apparent from the foregoing that the theory of adaptation level (AL) can be regarded as an extension or species of Gestalt theory. It furnishes a quantitative basis for the study of interaction effects by specifying the neutral or indifferent response as a weighted log mean of focal contextual and residual stimuli. Quality and magnitude of responses (including sensory and perceptual responses) are shown to be a function of their distance above or below level (distance being used here in the sense of interval, ratio, or any other suitable type of scaling). The application of the theory of AL to problems in various areas has been discussed in my book (Helson, 1964), as well as in numerous journal publications, a partial list of which is given in the references.

Much of science is concerned with bringing order into experience and that is one of the reasons why measurement and establishment of functional relations are so important. The order inherent in mathematics, particularly in the "natural" numbers, transfers to scientific data when they are quantified or put into one-to-one relation with a rational, abstract system like the system of numbers. Much of my work has been concerned with bringing order into a number of phenomena that had previously received only verbal, qualitative treatment such as the time-order "error" and its accompanying puzzles in classical psychophysics. Another puzzling phenomenon that has engaged me during the last dozen years or so has been the von Bezold assimilation effect wherein dark surrounds darken instead of lighten, and light surrounds lighten contiguous areas. This reversal of classical lightness contrast had never been subjected to systematic quantitative investigation probably because various workers, following von Bezold's artistic designs, persisted in using stimulus materials difficult or impossible to scale. To obtain stimuli capable of yielding quantitative data, we resorted to ruled white and black lines on gray grounds in place of the patterns used by previous workers (Helson and Rohles, 1959; Helson and Joy, 1962). By varying the width of the lines and the spacing between the lines we were able to establish a steady progression from classical contrast through neutrality, wherein there was neither contrast nor assimilation, to von Bezold assimilation. Later it was shown by Steger (1969) that on near-white and near-black backgrounds only assimilation occurs, a result in accordance with certain suppositions I advanced to explain the contrast-assimilation paradox (Helson, 1963). Most recently Kozaki (1971) has added additional evidence in favor of this hypothesis and in addition he has shown that the reflectance of regions fairly remote from the test fields influence contrast-assimilation relations to a greater extent than we had previously thought possible.

Lest it seem that we are claiming too much, let me point out that many problems in this area still remain to be solved because the simple relations found to hold for straight-line patterns do not necessarily hold when curvilinear figures are used. Contour and other effects occur and must be ordered quantitatively. The fact that the simple line patterns have been shown to be lawful holds hope for bringing complex designs into a rational order.

OTHER ACTIVITIES

Being a psychologist usually involves more than doing research, publishing, teaching, and the usual departmental and university chores. Unfortunately in some respects, the modern scientist-scholar cannot dwell in an ivory tower; he owes a debt to society and his profession for supporting him in his work and he cannot resist all demands of what might be called "good psychological citizenship." While I am not given to involvement in outside activities as much as many of my colleagues, I did concern myself to some extent with matters of more than personal importance. In the late 1920s I suggested to Boring, who was one of the editors of the *American Journal of Psychology*, that date of receipt of articles should be indicated in the published form and he immediately assented with the result that this journal was the first to adopt this practice, soon followed by the APA and other journals.

In the early 1940s when I was secretary-treasurer of the Eastern Psychological Association it was evident to me that there should be some means for getting those looking for academic positions and those wishing to hire psychologists together. I mentioned this to Gardner Murphy who was president of the association that year and we agreed that if EPA had any success in this direction, APA would soon follow. Accordingly, we announced in the program of the annual meeting that such opportunity would be available, allocating time and space for it. Needless to say, the experiment worked and was the forerunner of, perhaps the example for, subsequent similar action by APA that has persisted to the present.

While not a "joiner" I was instrumental in starting two groups that met until the beginning of the Second World War. The first was the Philadelphia area experimentalists which included Bryn Mawr, Swarthmore, Temple, Lehigh, and Pennsylvania. Remembering Benjamin Franklin's advice that if one wants to get something going, one should not present it as one's own idea but say that it was suggested by someone else, I asked S. W. Fernberger at Pennsylvania to issue the initial invitations for the first meeting. We met once a month at each of the institutions and usually at Lehigh for the final spring meeting, where we enjoyed the hospitality of the local psychologists. Usually only one paper was presented by one of the members with an occasional outside speaker. The outbreak of war put an end to our meetings as it did to so much else.

Still another group I was instrumental in founding was the

Philadelphia-Wilmington Color Group paralleling the Baltimore-Washington Color Group, whose meetings I had attended once or twice. These meetings were devoted to a consideration of problems in visual science and in industry and they drew as many from industry as from academia. While I was fairly active in the national association (APA), having served as president of divisions 1 and 10, as a member of council on different occasions, and as one of its representatives on the National Research Council, I regret that I was never asked to serve on any of its important committees that make policy and exert real influence on matters vital to all its members. I doubt if I could have done anything to help stem the change of course of the association from a purely scientific body to one concerned more with professional aspects of psychology and matters of public policy than with its original purposes. While the growing fields of application of psychology probably require some type of organizational activity, I must confess I would have preferred to see another group performing such functions, leaving APA as the body representing scientific psychology.

One final outside activity should be mentioned before closing the account of this life—my editorship of the *Psychological Bulletin,* which is one of the labors of love for one's subject that I took on in 1958. My term as editor began just after I had suffered a coronary thrombosis and my first editorial work for *Bulletin* was begun while convalescing at home. Although I had acted as referee for several journals, I did not realize the enormous amount of work entailed in editing an APA journal. I learned more about writing style through editing, which is really critical reading, than through practice in writing—something I have never seen stated by teachers of English or writing. After several years of critical reading of other people's work I became much more aware of my own stylistic shortcomings and could look at my own writing with almost the same objectivity as I did that of others. The result was that it became much easier to revise and correct my own work than it was before I became an editor. I would advise would-be writers not only to practice writing but to read critically not only the best authors but one's peers, watching out for awkward expressions, unclear statements, abrupt or bad transitions from sentence to sentence, and paragraph to paragraph, and to avoid long sentences like this one!

EPILOGUE

I have tried in this account to delineate the high spots in this psychologist's life without undue egotism or emotionalism. Personal factors play a much larger part in one's career than one often realizes. Probably more important than one's abilities and accomplishments are the friends he makes as he goes about his daily business of being psychologist, teacher, colleague, member of a department and a university, and so on. Some people are naturally good at public relations, some try to cultivate friends, and others go their own way, trusting that their work is what ultimately counts. My deepest and most lasting friendships have arisen out of my work. On the whole, my life has been an agreeable one, both in my profession and in my personal affairs. My appreciation for my co-workers, peers, and students alike, and for my family and friends, is greater than I can ever express in words. It's been a great trip, this life of mine, and I wouldn't mind doing it all over again, the sorrows along with the joys.

PARTIAL LIST OF PUBLICATIONS, INCLUDING THOSE REFERRED TO IN THIS ARTICLE

Boring, E. G. A history of experimental psychology. (2nd ed.) New York: Appleton-Century-Crofts, 1950. Pp. 611-12.

The psychology of *Gestalt. American Journal of Psychology,* 1925, *36,* 342-70, 494-526.

The psychology of *Gestalt. American Journal of Psychology,* 1926, *37,* 25-62, 189-223.

Insight in the white rat. *Journal of Experimental Psychology,* 1927, *10,* 378-96.

The effects of direct stimulation of the blind-spot. *American Journal of Psychology,* 1929, *41,* 345-97.

With J. P. Guilford. Eye-movements and the phi-phenomenon. *American Journal of Psychology*, 1929, *41*, 595-606.

A new visual phenomenon—the cigarette illusion. *Psychological Review*, 1930, *37*, 273-75.

With S. M. King. The *Tau* effect: An example of psychological relativity. *Journal of Experimental Psychology*, 1931, *14*, 202-17.

With E. V. Fehrer. The role of form in perception. *American Journal of Psychology*, 1932, *44*, 79-102.

With D. B. Judd. A study in photopic adaptation. *Journal of Experimental Psychology*, 1932, *15*, 380-98.

The part played by the sympathetic system as an afferent mechanism in the region of the trigeminus. *Brain*, 1932, *55*, 114-21.

The fundamental propositions of Gestalt psychology. *Psychological Review*, 1933, *40*, 13-32.

With J. P. Guilford. The relation of visual sensitivity to the amount of retinal pigmentation. *Journal of General Psychology*, 1933, *9*, 58-76.

With L. Quantius. Changes in skin temperature following intense stimulation. *Journal of Experimental Psychology*, 1934, *17*, 20-35.

With R. H. Burgert. Prediction and control of judgments from tactual single-point stimulation. *American Journal of Psychology*, 1936, *48*, 609-16.

Size-constancy of the projected after-image. *American Journal of Psychology*, 1936, *48*, 638-42.

Fundamental problems in color vision. I. The principle governing changes in hue, saturation, and lightness of non-selective samples in chromatic illumination. *Journal of Experimental Psychology*, 1938, *23*, 439-76.

With V. B. Jeffers. Fundamental problems in color vision. II. Hue, lightness, and saturation of selective samples in chromatic illumination. *Journal of Experimental Psychology*, 1940, *26*, 1-27.

Some factors and implications of color constancy. *Journal of the Optical Society of America*, 1943, *33*, 555-67.

Adaptation-level as frame of reference for prediction of psychophysical data. *American Journal of Psychology*, 1947, *60*, 1-29.

With J. Grove. Changes in hue, lightness, and saturation of surface colors in passing from daylight to incandescent-lamp light. *Journal of the Optical Society of America*, 1947, *37*, 387-95.

With W. C. Michels. The effect of chromatic adaptation on achromaticity. *Journal of the Optical Society of America*, 1948, *38*, 1025-32.

Adaptation-level as a basis for a quantitative theory of frames of reference. *Psychological Review*, 1948, *55*, 297-313.

With W. C. Michels. A reformulation of the Fechner law in terms of adaptation-level applied to rating scale data. *American Journal of Psychology*, 1949, *62*, 355-68.

Design of equipment and optimal human operation. *American Journal of Psychology*, 1949, *62*, 473-97.

With D. B. Judd and M. H. Warren. Object-color changes from daylight to incandescent-filament illumination. *Illuminating Engineering*, 1952, *47*, 221-33.

Perception and personality—a critique of recent experimental literature. *United States Air Force School of Aviation Medical Reports*, Proj. no. 21-0202-0007, Report no. 1, 1953.

With W. C. Michels and A. Sturgeon. The use of comparative rating scales for the evaluation of psychophysical data. *American Journal of Psychology*, 1954, *67*, 321-26.

With W. C. Michels. A quantitative theory of time-order effects. *American Journal of Psychology*, 1954, *67*, 327-34.

With W. C. Michels. A reconciliation of the VEG scale with Fechner's law. *American Journal of Psychology*, 1954, *67*, 677-83.

With D. B. Judd and Martha Wilson. Color rendition with fluorescent sources of illumination. *Illuminating Engineering*, 1956, *51*, 329-46.

With R. R. Blake, J. S. Mouton, and J. A. Olmstead. Attitudes as adjustments to stimulus, background, and residual factors. *Journal of Abnormal and Social Psychology*, 1955, *52*, 314-22.

With R. S. Dworkin and W. C. Michels. Quantitative denotations of common terms as a function of background. *American Journal of Psychology*, 1956, *69*, 194-208.

With R. R. Blake and J. S. Mouton. The generality of conformity behavior as a function of factual anchorage, difficulty of task, and amount of social pressure. *Journal of Personality*, 1957, *25*, 294-305.

With R. R. Blake and J. S. Mouton. An experimental investigation of the effectiveness of the "big lie" in shifting attitudes. *Journal of Social Psychology*, 1958, *48*, 51-60.

With R. R. Blake and J. S. Mouton. Petition-signing as adjustment to situational and personal factors. *Journal of Social Psychology*, 1958, *48*, 3-10.

Adaptation-level theory. In S. Koch (Ed.), *Psychology: A study of a science*. Vol. I. New York: McGraw-Hill, 1959. Pp. 565-621.

With F. H. Rohles, Jr. A quantitative study of reversal of classical lightness-contrast. *American Journal of Psychology*, 1959, *72*, 530-38.

With M. C. Nash. Anchor, contrast, and paradoxical distance effects. *Journal of Experimental Psychology*, 1960, *59*, 113-21.

With V. L. Joy. Domains of lightness assimilation and contrast. *Psychologische Beiträge*, 1962, *6*, 405-15.

Studies of anomalous contrast and assimilation. *Journal of the Optical Society of America*, 1963, *53*, 179-84.

Current trends and issues in adaptation-level theory. *American Psychologist*, 1964, *19*, 26-38.

Adaptation-level theory: An experimental and systematic approach to behavior. New York: Harper & Row, 1964.

With W. Bevan and H. G. Masters. A quantitative study of relevance in the formation of adaptation levels. *Perceptual and Motor Skills*, 1966, *22*, 743-49.

With H. G. Masters. A study of inflection-points in the locus of adaptation-levels as a function of anchor-stimuli. *American Journal of Psychology*, 1966, *79*, 400-408.

Some problems in motivation from the point of view of the theory of adaptation level. In D. Levine (Ed.), *Nebraska Symposium on Motivation, 1966.* Lincoln: University of Nebraska Press, 1966. Pp. 137-82.

With L. Avant. Stimulus generalization as a function of contextual stimuli. *Journal of Experimental Psychology*, 1967, *73*, 565-67.

With T. Kozaki. Effects of duration of series and anchor-stimuli on judgments of perceived size. *American Journal of Psychology*, 1968, *81*, 291-302.

With T. Kozaki. A study of visual temporal size contrast. *Perception and Psychophysics*, 1969, *5*, 239-40.

Why did their precursors fail and the Gestalt psychologists succeed? Reflections on theories and theorists. *American Psychologist*, 1969, *24*, 1006-11.

With T. Lansford. The role of spectral energy of source and background color in the pleasantness of object colors. *Applied Optics*, 1970, *9*, 1513-62.

The perception of Gestalt—1969. *Annals of the New York Academy of Sciences*, 1970, *169*, 654-63.

With L. Avant. Theories of perception. In B. J. Wolman (Ed.), *Handbook of general psychology.* Englewood Cliffs, N. J.: Prentice-Hall. In press.

5

To Live with Judgment

WILLIAM A. HUNT

In going over some old papers after the death of my mother, I came across an essay I had written for my own amusement when I was a junior in high school. It was entitled "The Brain," and in it I developed the functional role of the mind as mediator between the body and its environment. At nineteen when I wrote it I had not yet read Freud, but I had provided myself with the basic idea of ego and id and from my Unitarian upbringing I had the equivalent of superego in the form of "conscience." This last I identified as a creation of the brain as reason interacted with experience. I suppose this establishes me as a "cognitive" psychologist, although in my graduate days at Harvard "conscience" was "higher mental processes." In any case, an interest in cognition has been a major motivating force in all my subsequent work. Even in my early work on affectivity and emotion I tended to stress the importance of cognitive content as a major element in feeling.

I mention this for two reasons. In the first place, I have been impressed all through my personal and professional life with the relative permanence of the basic attributes of personality. In the second place, in striving for a balance between body and mind, I have sought full expression for each. This results in a diverse range of interests and activities that sometimes puzzles my acquaintances.

My heredity is equally mixed. On my father's side I have some Mohegan Indian blood from around 1680. On my mother's side Cornet Stetson led several charges in battles against the Indians threatening the Massachusetts Bay Colony. Her family was tangentially related to both Adamses—Sam, the tavern keeper, and John, the President, both in their diverse ways effective citizens.

This has given me some personal sense of the span and continuity of history, and particularly of the amazing diversity, complexity, and varied potential of the people whose lives have made it. It also has given me a deep and abiding love for my country, not chauvinistically but with the sympathy and understanding one accords a child of one's own, no matter how wayward she may be at times.

Socioeconomically and culturally as well, my family would be categorized as upper middle class by most indices. My education was typical. As I remember my elementary education, it was average. I was fortunate in attending Hartford Public High School, however, as its curriculum was excellent. There were several outstanding teachers to encourage me, and I received an excellent grounding for my subsequent career at Dartmouth which I entered in the fall of 1923 at the age of twenty.

At Dartmouth College I had trouble selecting a major. It was not a problem of finding myself. I had done that in high school. The problem was where did *I* fit in. Where best could I study and come to understand this "brain" which mediated between body and environment? People seemed to be the answer, but what discipline led most directly to their study?

In psychology I finally found an area that offered not only direct interaction with people but the added inducement of an intellectual intervention directed toward their further understanding. Science as applied to human behavior fascinates me, but throughout my life I have always cherished the direct interaction with living people which is the very guts of what we call clinical psychology. So as a clinical psychologist I help people in their efforts to modify their behavior and fit it to the demands of living, but as an experimental psychologist, I subject their efforts *and my own* to experimental investigation. The roles of practitioner and scientist are complementary, and I have never felt any conflict (Hunt, 1951).

At Dartmouth I became a behaviorist. Pavlov and the conditioned reflex under the salesmanship of John B. Watson offered me the same promise for modifying human behavior that the present generation sees in Skinner and operant behavior, and my Commencement address of 1928 was a behavioristic elaboration of my high school essay of 1922. Fortunately the late Gordon Allport was teaching at Dartmouth, and I had his courses in personality and in social psychology. He was back from Germany with its stress on the cultural, subjective, and idiomorphic; and the peculiar blending of the intuitive and scientific approaches which was to distinguish all his work left a deep impression on me and leavened my somewhat naïve behaviorism. At his suggestion I entered graduate school at Harvard in the fall of 1928.

At Harvard I was able to keep my clinical and experimental leanings both satisfied and working in tandem. For one I had Henry Murray and work at the Psychological Clinic; for the other there were E. G. Boring's famous four courses in sensation, perception, the higher mental processes, and systems and theories supported by Leonard Troland, Carol Pratt, and my adviser, J. G. Beebe-Center. Harvard was fun (and hard work). Each student had his own room, proudly labeled his "laboratory," and there were apparatus, intellectual stimulation, and ourselves as subjects. I learned the intellectual delights of curiosity, the usefulness of scientific methodology in formulating a way in which questions could be answered, and the sense of mastery when an answer was finally forthcoming.

Everyone was busy with something. Irrespective of a formal dissertation, one always had several things going informally. Today I would call them pilot studies. They were somewhat informal probings into an area of interest. If the problem still seemed promising and interesting once you got the feel of it, you could back up, rethink it thoroughly, and design an adequate formal experiment. Today it seems to me that much less of this stimulating "monkeying around" goes on, and I think it is the students' loss. The techniques of experimental design have become so elaborate and sophisticated (and at the same time so cumbersome and restrictive), and our determination to avoid any effort that will not be immediately productive of publication has become so great that they place formidable barriers in the way of that natural curiosity which is the basic motivation of science.

Emotional behavior and its conditioning played a large part in Watsonian behaviorism, and I shortly found myself involved in two projects which combined my behavioristic interest in emotion with a new-found fascination in the methodological use of introspection: the analysis and reporting of conscious states or experiences. The introspective technique as developed by E. B. Titchener at Cornell was unfamiliar to me until I reached Harvard, but I had never been completely comfortable with the behaviorist ruling that consciousness and introspection must be excluded from the science of psychology as a thoroughly unreliable source of data. On the other hand, I never could agree with Titchener's structuralistic position that the sole task of psychology was the analyzing and charting of the elements of consciousness to provide a descriptive picture of the mind. In my eyes, physiology provided the ultimate frame of reference for psychology, and conscious states were merely concomitants of underlying physiological processes. When these physiological processes were not available for direct objective measurement, they might be charted through the accompanying changes in consciousness. For me, introspection was basically a search through the window of consciousness for some cue or index which could be used in tracking down the fundamental neurophysiology involved. Titchener himself admitted that a strictly descriptive psychology could not attain unity and coherence without a reference to the nervous system.

While at Dartmouth I had been influenced by the English utilitarians, James Mill and Jeremy Bentham, with their doctrine of promoting the greatest happiness of the greatest number of people as a social goal. In a crude way one could hope to use feelings of pleasantness and unpleasantness as evaluative indices of happiness and unhappiness and thus I became involved with hedonic tone as an offshoot of my interest in hedonism and the utilitarian philosophy.

In the Titchenerian system pleasantness and unpleasantness were identified as bright and dull pressures, or sensory contents of brightness and expansiveness on the one hand, and of heaviness, dullness, and contraction on the other. If we could verify this and learn more about the underlying physiology involved we might learn more about the motivational nature of pleasantness and unpleasantness. So I plunged into the study of bright and dull pressures.

We forget today how crude and simplistic laboratory procedures were in 1930. My thesis had three parts. I suppose the first might be called a validity study since it dealt with the relationship of pleasantness and unpleasantness to bright and dull pressures. My subjects gave me reports on the pleasantness and unpleasantness of a series of color stimuli and at another sitting reported on the presence of pressures, the order of presentation being of course balanced among observers to avoid any sequence effect. In what was then considered an ingenious use of the measure of correlation, I compared the judgments of affect and of pressure and established their concomitance (Hunt, 1931a). The second part investigated the pressure components of emotion (Hunt, 1931b), and the third section dealt with bodily localization, placing bright pressure in the chest and dull pressure lower down toward the abdomen (Hunt, 1932). The stress on localization pointed up my preoccupation with the physiological explanation of these conscious contents. I wish I had had the later work of Olds and others on "pleasure centers" in the brain to guide me!

All of this involved me more and more in the phenomenology of emotion and I became deeply interested in the James-Lange theory of emotion, which identifies the feeling of emotion as a conscious reflection of the bodily responses occurring in the emotion. If this were so, then reproducing the bodily responses typical of emotion should elicit introspective reports of emotion. The late Hadley Cantril and I decided to test this by the subcutaneous injection of adrenalin with a group of human subjects. The resulting state of arousal in the autonomic nervous system should produce a conscious state recognized by our subjects as emotion. The results, I believe, showed the semantic trap inherent in the James-Lange controversy. Some subjects did report feeling a genuine emotion, others reported feeling "as if" they had an emotion, but said it was not a real emotion because it had no meaningful object, no situational reference. A few medical students even overlooked any reference to emotion whatsoever and merely reported (in the true medical tradition) their physiological symptoms such as heightened blood pressure, increased pulse rate, tremor, etc. It seemed that whether or not a subject felt emotion depended on how he defined emotion, and these definitions obviously were different for different people (Cantril and Hunt, 1932).

It was obvious from the above that emotion was not a mere reflection of sensory process. Something of a cognitive nature was being added in the brain. For many people an emotion to be genuine had to have some meaningful content, to refer to a real situation. Both Cantril and I followed this for a bit but the field lay largely fallow until the recent work of Stanley Schacter.

In my work with pleasantness and unpleasantness as well, it was becoming obvious that something cognitive was being added to the sensory picture. I was finding further evidence of the intrusion of judgmental phenomena into what was previously accepted at Harvard as a sensory world (Hunt, 1933). It is difficult today to comprehend the dominant position of sensory physiology in early psychology. I am sure that this interest in the physiology of the sensory processes was as fundamental in leading Titchener to a structuralist interpretation of consciousness as being constructed from the building blocks of sensation as were the empirical results of actual introspection.

Some of us who were fellow graduate students at Harvard then, and I think particularly of John Volkmann, Hadley Cantril,

Muzafer Sherif, and myself, began to question the dominance of sensation and to turn more and more to central processes as an underlying basis for the complicated phenomena we now investigate as human judgment. It was thrilling to us because it meant that if judgment were a central process, then it should be responsible for a common set of phenomena running through all the separate areas each of us was investigating. This has been an important motivating concept for the subsequent work of all of us, but particularly for Volkmann, Sherif, and myself.

Subsequently, John Volkmann and I reasoned more specifically that if judgment were a central phenomenon then some of the characteristics of the classical psychophysical judgment should be found in other areas of judgment. If judgments of lifted weights could be moved around by shifting the contexts in which they were presented, then one should find the same effects in judgments of pleasantness and unpleasantness. Volkmann had been studying the effects of anchoring values using a classical psychophysical setting. Now we proceeded to duplicate these anchoring phenomena using an affective scale (Volkmann and Hunt, 1937). This started me on a series of studies using judgments of aesthetic value (Hunt, 1941), and eventually, as part of our investigation of psychiatric selection in World War II, I was able to extend the analogy with psychophysics to the processes of clinical judgment involved in diagnosis and the evaluation of maladaptive behavior.

My interest in central processes even involved me in a sensory problem, the phenomenon of "cortical yellow," now largely forgotten but in the thirties attracting some attention. Classically, color vision and color mixing had been a retinal matter, but there were reports that when red was presented to one eye and green to the other a sensation of yellow sometimes resulted. Obviously the mixing must be in the cortex rather than the retina. Unfortunately there were some technical problems of stimulus control which cast doubt over the findings. Edwin Land of Polaroid, a life-long friend, lent his innovative genius to the problem and we worked out a technique for using polarized light for the simultaneous comparison of retinally and cortically fused colors, which we published in *Science* (Land and Hunt, 1936). Unfortunately, cortical yellow proved elusive. The usual phenomenon was dominance of one or the other color with alternation as fatigue set in. When "yellow" did appear it was a muddy, degenerate yellow that no Titchenerian could rightly accept as an adequate sensation. We realized that we were beyond our depth, and in a great exercise of rational discretion dropped the problem. But where and why our muddy yellow, bastard sensation though it might have been?

In the winter of 1931 during my last year at Harvard I had dropped in to visit with Carney Landis at the New York Psychiatric Institute in New York City. We discussed the problems of emotion and the attempts to mimic it through the use of sympathetico- and parasympathetico-mimetic drugs, and as a result I received an offer to spend the summer of 1931 at the institute. It was the beginning of a stimulating cooperative relationship that was fruitful for both of us for many years.

That last winter at Harvard also marked my first interest in the startle pattern that Landis and I subsequently researched extensively. Beebe-Center had decided to visit the barber one afternoon, and in the best scholarly tradition took something along to read in order that his time would not be wasted. It happened to be a German journal devoted to psychology and neurology in which a German neurologist, Hans Strauss, discussed a "shrinking together" (Das Zusammenschrecken) which he found as a universal postural response to sudden loud sounds (Strauss, 1929). At the time, however, we had no idea of our subsequent interest in it as the Startle Pattern. As I have said, I had no interest in bright and dull pressures per se as elements in a formal Titchenerian system, but hoped to use them as indices of whatever physiological processes I felt must underlie and be responsible for pleasantness and unpleasantness. Beebe-Center returned from the barber shop in a state of high excitement. Perhaps this response which Strauss had discovered was the basis of the pressures I was studying. It turned out not to be so, and "Das Zusammenschrecken" was tucked away in memory until a continuing curiosity and a heightened interest in emotion led me back to it two years later.

That summer of 1931 at the Psychiatric Institute, Landis and I repeated the Cantril and Hunt adrenalin study with a patient population (Landis and Hunt, 1932). It added much supportive detail but little in the way of any new basic insights. It did teach me the deadening effect of routine custodial care upon the behavior of the psychiatric hospital patient. Any interest you take in a chronic schizophrenic, any novelty you introduce into the usual hospital routine will improve his contact with you, at least for a while. Among our subjects were a group of mute, regressed schizophrenics who improved with a daily subcutaneous injection of adrenalin. Landis and I thought that through sheer serendipity we had stumbled across a new "cure" for schizophrenia. But, alas, when the novelty wore off, the improvement disappeared and our patients went out of contact once more and resumed their previous picture of typical regressed ward behavior.

Among the many Landis-Hunt collaborations in this period one in particular should be mentioned as another example of the relatively primitive state of the experimental methodology of the early thirties. "The Conscious Correlates of the Galvanic Skin Response" was well received when it was published in the *Journal of Experimental Psychology* (Landis and Hunt, 1935). I wonder how the present editors would treat it today?

Landis always had maintained an intense interest in electrophysiology and the GSR at that time was the center of an involved and bitter controversy. With what was it correlated? Was it the concomitant of an emotional response, or possibly an indicator of hedonic tone; or did it have some cognitive significance, say as an indicator of intellectual effort? The British had their own particular problems with it. Was it conative in nature, the resultant of an act of will, or was it broader in nature indicating orexis or some appetitive drive? These words sound strange and archaic today, but they were battle cries in 1935 and ink flowed freely in the conflict.

Historically speaking, sophisticated use of the control group technique is relatively recent in the experimental armamentarium, and this was the source of the problem. If you believed that the GSR accompanied emotion, you presented emotional stimuli to your subjects and recorded the resulting deflections on your galvanometer. If you were conatively inclined you presented conative stimuli, and there were *your* deflections. Surely the other fellow must be lying; they could not appear in both situations.

The solution of course is obvious, the GSR was a ubiquitous phenomenon appearing everywhere. But how to convince the embittered contestants? Landis and I performed a shotgun experiment with our controls built in by the inclusion in our stimulus series of stimuli of every variety: emotional, affective, conative, orectic, etc. We even selected our subjects to represent every variety of systematic bias we could lay our hands on, ranging from hard-core behaviorists to the most introspective of Titchenerian structuralists. And they all deflected to all our stimuli, and that was that. Our colleagues national and international then found something else to fight about.

Hans Strauss' work on the Startle Pattern continued to bother me, however. The idea of a fixed inviolable bodily response pattern to a sudden loud sound was intriguing. Strauss had taken his "slow motion" pictures by running the camera at top speed (64 frames per second) and projecting them at normal speed (16 frames per second). The institute had a camera good for the 64-frame speed and Landis provided some film. During the summer of the GSR study I spent what spare time I had checking on Strauss' work. Every willing visitor to the laboratory was recruited as a subject, and we ended the summer with a choice collection of films depicting some of America's leading psychologists being "startled" while stripped down to their shorts. We were willing to give our all for science in those days.

The bodily pattern was there just as Strauss had described it—eye blink, head movement, facial grimace, a raising and drawing back of the shoulders, abduction of the upper arms, bending of the elbows, pronation of the lower arms, flexion of the fingers, forward movement of the trunk, contraction of the abdomen, and bending of the knees—and it appeared in all of our subjects. The idea of a fixed, identifiable response pattern in the general area of emotion was something everyone had been looking for. Landis was particularly excited because he had developed quite a critical reputation for negativism because of his success in refuting the work of many of his colleagues in the field of emotion. He was unhappy about this, so now was overjoyed that we had confirmed Strauss' findings and at last he had something "positive" to offer. I was less sanguine about its significance for emotion, but intrigued by the idea of the pattern's universality and constancy which suggested its use as a probe in various areas. When one has a constant, predictable response like this, it can be used as a measuring stick by subjecting it to different stimulus conditions and noting any resulting changes. Thus we eventually did look into what happened to it in schizophrenia, in hypnosis, under voluntary attempts at suppression, etc.

Landis decided to go all out for a thorough investigation involving the latest equipment for ultra-rapid photography which at that time was being developed as a technique for photographing the finish at some of our bigger horse-racing tracks. The Markle Foundation backed us and we were off. The cameras we used enabled us to photograph at from 300 frames per second up to 3,000 by the use of cameras with a motor-driven rotating prism instead of an ordinary shutter device. The lighting demands at such speeds are fantastic and at our fastest we used photoflood lamps with a power requirement of more than 10,000 watts, which involved us in many amusing battles with the New York Consolidated Edison Company: electric power all over Washington Heights dropped when our lights went on for the few seconds we ran at 3,000 frames per second. If you realize we were burning film at some 150 to 200 times the usual photographic speeds you can realize the expense involved. (Our troubles with the institute's budget are best unmentioned.)

So we studied the startle pattern in man and in animals, in child and adult, in sickness and in health. In the course of all this

I became something of an authority on reflexes in the human infant, even publishing with Kurt Goldstein on the Moro reflex (Goldstein, Landis, Hunt, and Clarke, 1938). our researches were finally pulled together in a book, *The Startle Pattern,* published in 1939. Both Landis and I were impressed with the potentialities of ultrarapid photography for the investigation of motor phenomena and had begun exploring its use in studying various neurological disorders with attendant tremors, in epilepsy, and even in the analysis of ordinary normal motor responses. The motor side of psychology has long been neglected and here was a direct approach to it, as we pointed out in *Science* in discussing the magnification of time as a research technique in the study of behavior (Landis and Hunt, 1937).

Sometimes books are dangerous, however. They serve as markers, round out periods of time and development, and give one a sense of completion. Publication of *The Startle Pattern* had some of this effect. In addition the war was looming closer and closer, I ran into some employment difficulties, and for one reason or another, we never did get back to ultra-rapid photography.

In my earlier days I was interested in Rorschach's test and even could score it in conventional fashion. Piotrowski was the first to give me the test in 1931 and his analysis of my personality was very perceptive. But I was never sure whether it was Rorschach's test of Piotrowski's sensitivity that was responsible. It was, he said, essentially a schizoid personality with a heavy defensive manic overlay.

A study of the repeat reliability of the Rorschach that I carried out involving ten retestings at two-week intervals of twenty subjects was never submitted for publication. By the time I had finished it, it did not seem important enough to share with an audience. New responses came in with repeated testing, they did not upset the balance, and there was some increase in unusual detail. Piotrowski altered his original organic signs somewhat on the basis of findings of mine at the Institute for Living in Hartford. Later I again involved Edwin Land in my problems with a resultant apparatus note in the *American Journal of Psychology*

(Hunt, 1939) on a means for presenting Rorschach-like stimuli with color, depth, and motion. It came to naught as the combination of meaningless color, depth, and movement apparently was too complex and confusing for meaningful integration, and inhibited rather than stimulated any projective productivity.

I mention these matters to show that I was maintaining a clinical interest in people as well as in psychopathology. In my day there were no training programs in clinical psychology. One had a few formal courses in testing, personality, and psychopathology and carried on from there, learning from personal experience. As a psychologist working in the area of psychopathology, it was taken for granted by the college administration that I would accept and execute any diagnostic or therapeutic duties that might arise. At Connecticut College, for instance, I received mental hygiene referrals from the Dean, and was supervised by a visiting lady psychiatrist who graced the campus one afternoon every two weeks. It was an amicable arrangement based on mutual respect, and in the four years I was there we had no suicides, serious psychotic breaks, or any untoward incidents we could not handle.

This continuing involvement with both clinical practice and research ultimately led to the most intense, strenuous, demanding, and yet satisfying five years of my life: my active duty with the Navy during World War II. I have never approved of aggressive war as an instrument of national policy, but there are times, I feel, when a defensive war may be forced on a people. I doubt the ultimate wisdom of such wars, but I accept their social inevitability. Such seemed to be the case in 1940. For several years the United States had been offering a relative haven to many refugees from fascist suppression. If we fell under totalitarian domination (of any sort) where would they go? And where would I go, for my reading of history has convinced me that college professors who are among the first to advocate and defend freedom of speech and inquiry are among the first to be denied it under a totalitarian regime?

Anticipating an inevitable large increase in manpower, irrespective of the advent of a shooting war, the Navy decided to benefit from the lessons of World War I and make some provision for a program of psychiatric selection at the naval training centers. The original concept was for three-man teams consisting of a psychiatrist, a neurologist, and a clinical psychologist. I was recruited through district headquarters in the fall of 1940, and on April 28, 1941 (nine months before the advent of hostilities), I reported for duty at the Newport Naval Training Center as a lieutenant in what is now the Medical Service Corps. Cecil L. Wittson, the psychiatrist, and Herbert I. Harris, the neurologist, were already on board when I joined them. We were the first training-station psychiatric unit on duty.

We were a congenial team, both personally and professionally. There was little specific direction from Washington which we seized upon as an opportunity, and by Pearl Harbor we had mapped out the main details of a workable selection procedure. Our main purposes were three: (1) to improve the efficiency of the Navy by removing at the training-station level those neuropsychiatric high-risk cases who were potential psychiatric casualties in the military service; (2) by such removal to save these men the disastrous experience of subsequent breakdown during service, and (3) thus to lighten the subsequent drain upon public funds by lessening the demands for post-war medical treatment for veterans.

The major selection process involved an individual interview with each recruit as part of his medical examination upon reaching the training station. Brief testing procedures were available at this time. As a result of this screening the new recruit was either cleared for further duty without qualification, noted as a possible risk and entered for further follow-up during training, or sent immediately to the psychiatric unit for a complete psychiatric, neurological, and/or psychological examination as indicated. Selection is usually viewed as an elimination procedure, but we saved or "screened in" more people than we discharged. Of the recruits admitted to the unit for study approximately two-thirds were returned to duty. Without this further study these men would have been lost to the service (Wittson and Hunt, 1945).

The actual execution of our program left little time for any formal research, but we did commit ourselves to a policy of keeping as complete and accurate records as possible. During the war any follow-up of our procedures was limited to the six weeks of recruit training, but we were able to demonstrate an inverse ratio between the psychiatric discharge rate and such station problems as disciplinary rate, hospitalizations, and attendance at sick call. As the discharge rate went up, the others went down.

After the war the Office of Naval Research had all our Newport records (two tons of them) moved to Northwestern University where we started an extensive study of our wartime selection procedures. We first compared differing selection rates at various training stations with the subsequent psychiatric attrition among their recruits. As predicted, the more men screened out at the training level, the less attrition during subsequent service, but somewhere around a selection rate of 4 per cent diminishing returns set in. Apparently, psychiatric selection works but it can be overdone.

We did a number of studies focussed on the cost of using marginal men, illiterates, the mentally retarded, neurotics, etc. Such men render less efficient service than the non-handicapped, but their use may be necessary in a manpower emergency. Our hope was the development of a computer program that would automatically adjust selection standards to the manpower needs of the moment. Like many computer projects it died aborning because of the difficulty of attaining data for establishing the basic risk values necessary for any computer decision (Hunt, 1955).

Since longitudinal studies of high-risk psychiatric cases are relatively rare in the literature, one study deserves particular mention. We selected groups of approximately a hundred recruits each from among our neurotics, schizoid personalities, alcoholics, mentally retarded, and asocial psychopaths, and added a control group of normal recruits. Each (including the controls) met the following criteria: he had been intensively studied on the ward, two or more clinicians had seen him, the diagnosis was unanimous, and his condition was not considered serious enough to pre-

vent his being sent to duty. His hospital and disciplinary records
were then examined after a three-year period of service.

The findings confirmed the classical picture of these categories
and evidenced their potentiality for predicting future behavior.
All the marginal cases had higher rates of hospitalization than the
controls and had a greater number of disciplinary infractions except for the neurotics who were less trouble than the normals.
When they did get in trouble, however, their outstanding difficulty was with alcohol. The alcoholics distributed themselves over
the complete range of disciplinary infractions, as did the retarded
in a lesser way. The schizoid personalities had no case involving
misuse of alcohol. The asocial personalities, as would be predicted, excelled in all infractions, but their outstanding characteristic was the preponderance of insubordination. A subsequent
study replicated our findings (Hunt, Wittson, and Hunt, 1952,
1954).

These results plus other studies of ours directed specifically toward the diagnostic process and the categorical schemata typically
used for purposes of classification (Hunt, Wittson, and Hunt,
1953; Caveny, Wittson, Herman, and Hunt, 1955) have convinced
me that there is more value in diagnosis than its critics are willing to admit, particularly when it is executed by knowledgeable
persons trained for the task. Basically, diagnosis is a taxonomic
process wherein a name is attached to a phenomenon to indicate
its membership in a class of phenomena possessing certain characteristics in common. On the basis of this class membership one
can then infer things about the phenomenon which are not immediately apparent from the original observation. Thus, to identify a four-legged animal as a horse enables you immediately without further observation to know that he is herbivorous, can be
domesticated, and can be used for transportation. The purpose of
taxonomy or diagnosis then is to furnish information.

In biology, taxonomy stresses information bearing mainly upon
understanding the present and historical aspects of the animal
and its relation to other animals; while in psychiatry the stress is
largely upon the prediction of future developments, the future

course of behavior, later symptomatology to be expected, and the delineation of a therapeutic program to be followed. Seen in this light diagnosis becomes an orderly and necessary scientific process.

If diagnosis is to provide adequate information, however, the classification system involved must be valid, there must exist an extensive background of knowledge about the phenomena in question, and there must be a choice of demonstrably efficient therapeutic tactics from which a suitable selection may be made. Admittedly, this is not the situation. Our neo-Kraepelinian categories are far from perfect, our knowledge of the psychopathology involved is by no means extensive, and our therapeutic procedures still relatively experimental. The difficulty, however, lies in the immature state of the art in psychiatry, not in any inherent deficiency in the diagnostic process per se. Most critics of contemporary diagnostic practices realize this (Thorne and Nathan, 1970), but some continue to advocate the abandonment of any sort of diagnostic procedure as unnecessary in the treatment of maladjustive behavior.

There are two aspects involved in the application of scientific knowledge to the solution of a practical problem. One is research, obtaining the basic data necessary for understanding the potential solution of the problem. The other is development, the adaptation of this knowledge to a specific and workable procedure, and its subsequent field testing under service conditions. We felt that in working out our various screening procedures we already had accomplished the major portion of the developmental work and that the greatest hope for future improvement lay in further basic research on the processes involved.

At the very heart of our selection procedures was the exercise of clinical judgment, the decision-making process whereby the clinician evaluates human behavior and renders a qualitative and/or quantitative judgment of its significance. Here were the omnipresent phenomena of judgment which I had been studying in psychophysics, affectivity, aesthetics, and ethics for some twenty years. Is the clinician making decisions in a psychiatric interview basically acting any differently than an experimental subject estimating lifted weights, or judging the length of lines? I felt not.

If, then, clinical decision-making *is* analogous to psychophysics, it should be possible to demonstrate the phenomena of classical psychophysics when the exercise of clinical judgment is involved. This reasoning seems straightforward and logical, but it must be remembered that in applying psychophysical analogies to clinical judgment we were opposing a well-entrenched professional attitude which viewed this clinical judgmental process as intuitive, unique, and outside the possibility of any objective, experimental approach. In short, we were challenging a whole psychiatric mystique (Hunt, 1959).

For our investigation we needed an experimental procedure which would duplicate a typical clinical situation. In addition, it must be easy, economical, capable of replication in other laboratories, and relatively foolproof to administer. Obviously, interviewing patients was ruled out! We found the answer as a by-product of some of our other research involving the development of abbreviated intelligence tests. We selected lists of test responses obtained from patients, and our clinicians were then asked to rate them. Originally we started with vocabulary items such as this definition of a guillotine, "a legal matter pertaining only to those with no call to remain further on earth." The clinicians were asked to rate this response for evidence of schizophrenic confusion, using a seven-point scale. Later we used verbal responses from other types of tests such as information and comprehension, and ratings were called for on intelligence, concreteness, etc. In some studies diagnostic categories, rather than quantitative ratings, were called for. The above example, for instance, is clearly schizophrenic. Thus our clinicians were given a congenial task, and one they had had experience with before—the interpretation of test responses.

Using trained clinicians (Ph.D. and five years' experience) we were able to demonstrate satisfactory reliability (inter-judge agreement) and validity as well since we found our clinicians able to match diagnostic judgment from test response with actual case diagnosis well above chance levels. We also were able to show satisfactory correlations between scale ratings for intelligence and actual test results, as well as between ratings for the severity of confusion in thinking and subsequent clinical progress. Interestingly enough, graduate students performed almost as well as trained clinicians, and even schizophrenic patients showed good agreement in judging the amount of confusion exhibited in other schizophrenics' test responses.

At a more basic level again using an analogy with psychophysics we investigated the distortions of judgment produced by altering the context within which the stimuli were presented. Thus when test responses showing a medium amount of confused thinking were presented with a series of other responses all of lesser confusion, the medium responses were adjudged more confused than was usual; and conversely when presented against a background of more severe stimuli they were judged less severe than usual. We roamed through the classical field of the relative versus the absolute judgment in psychophysics, finding the familiar contrast effects, and occasionally assimilation as well.

Manifest anxiety seemed to increase the unreliability of our judgments, and the effect appeared only when our subjects were working individually and alone. When their judgments were made in a group, this effect disappeared. We were intrigued for a while, but the effect was weak and evanescent, and finally it seemed of no profit to pursue it further. Our current interest lies in applying analogies from the field of learning and in investigating the age and developmental aspects of this universal human attribute of using quantitative scales (Hunt, W. A., and Jones, N. F., 1961).

All of this time I had of course been teaching, and I enjoyed it thoroughly (Hunt, 1950, 1958, 1968). I have had several experimental forays into the educational process and for several years edited *Psychology in the Schools*. The diversity of my interests is explained in part by the fact that in the twenties and thirties psychology was much less specialized than it is today, and I sometimes bill myself as "the last of the generalists."

During the last year of the war I had been moved to Washington to take charge of the Navy's clinical psychology program (Hunt, 1945). Washington was particularly exciting then. With the end of the war in sight professional psychology was laying plans for an inevitable expansion. As the Bureau of Medicine and Surgery was housed in the old naval hospital, I was one of the few government psychologists in Washington at that time with a private office equipped with a door that could be closed for confidentiality. It became a popular meeting place.

This was the year in which the American Association for Applied Psychology (AAAP) was maneuvering to amalgamate with the American Psychological Association (APA). As Secretary of the Military Division of the AAAP, a Fellow of the Experimental Division of the APA, and a member of the Society of Experimental Psychologists, I furnished one of the ameliorating bridges between the practical clinical interests and the experimental ones when their mutual paranoia ran too high.

The amalgamation was finally accomplished, and I found myself on the first board of directors of the new APA. Since then I have served it as President of the Clinical Division and then as President of the Division on the Teaching of Psychology, with numerous other committee appointments and task force assignments.

These activities plus my administrative experience in the Bureau of Medicine and Surgery resulted in my being used as a consultant in several government bureaus. Naturally I continued as a consultant on psychiatric matters to the Surgeon General of the Navy. I served the Army Surgeon General as a member of his committee on clinical psychology and on psychophysiology and had six years on the Army Scientific Advisory Panel as a consultant on human factors research. I was the first psychologist appointed to the Medical Advisory Group to the Administrator of the Veterans Affairs and served there for eight years, subsequently helping the V.A. from time to time in various consulting capacities. I had three years on the old Community Research and Resources Panel of the National Institute of Mental Health, and have acted as consultant to several divisions of the Office of Education. In 1954 I gave the Salmon Lectures at the New York Academy of Medicine, the first psychologist invited to do so (Hunt, 1956).

In all these activities I had a chance for the practical exercise of those judgmental processes I have so often researched in others. My government work has given me a wealth of administrative experiences (Hunt, 1965). It left me ambivalent to bureaucracy and somewhat cynical about the motivation and planning capacity of politicians, but it did give me a healthy respect and admiration for those dedicated administrators who labor to bring some social benefit out of politically imposed chaos.

All these experiences were an invaluable resource for me in my fifteen years as chairman of the Psychology Department at Northwestern University. I have always been a "team" man and my conception of the chairman's role was 25 per cent quarterback and 75 per cent blocking back. I enjoyed it, but eventually one tires of the organizational responsibilities inherent in an administrative position and desires a bit more independence, perhaps even the selfishness of anonymity. The logical thing might have been to resign the chairmanship and remain on in a professorial role. Experience has taught me, however, that the administrator who sheds his authority but remains on in the organization is often an unwitting albatross around the neck of his successor.

So I resigned my position at Northwestern and moved to Loyola University of Chicago where I find it exciting to be involved in the challenging problems of Catholic higher education and to have time for study uninterrupted by administrative chores. My interest in the part learning plays in judgment, particularly as it is revealed in diagnostic bias (Hunt, Schwartz, and Walker, 1964, 1965) has led me to an interest in habit mechanisms in general, currently with special reference to the control of smoking and other drug behaviors (Hunt and Matarazzo, 1970; Hunt, Barnett, and Branch, 1972). We academicians, once we achieve the security of rank and tenure, often lose our sense of adventure and forget the intellectual and emotional renewal attendant upon a change of scenery. I have found these at Loyola.

REFERENCES

Cantril, H., and Hunt, W. A. Emotional effects produced by the injection of adrenalin. *American Journal of Psychology*, 1932, *44*, 300-307.

Caveny, E. L., Wittson, C. L., Hermann, R. S., and Hunt, W. A. Psychiatric diagnosis: Its nature and function. *Journal of Nervous and Mental Diseases*, 1955, *121*, 367-73.

Goldstein, K., Landis, C., Hunt, W. A., and Clarke, F. M. *Archives of Neurology and Psychiatry*, 1938, *40*, 322-27.

Hunt, W. A. The relation of bright and dull pressure to affectivity. *American Journal of Psychology*, 1931a, *43*, 87-92.

———— The pressure correlate of emotion. *American Journal of Psycology*, 1931b, *43*, 600-605.

———— Localization of bright and dull pressure. *American Journal of Psychology*, 1932, *44*, 308-13.

———— The meaning of pleasantness and unpleasantness. *American Journal of Psychology*, 1933, *45*, 345-48.

———— Rorschach interpretation for color, depth, and movement. *American Journal of Psychology*, 1939, *52*, 640-41.

———— Anchoring effects in judgment. *American Journal of Psychology*, 1941, *54*, 395-403.

———— Clinical psychology in the Navy. *Journal of Clinical Psychology*, 1945, *1*, 99-104.

———— On the teaching of clinical psychology. *Journal of Clinical Psychology*, 1950, *6*, 143-48.

———— Clinical psychology—science or superstition. *American Psychologist*, 1951, *6*, 683-87.

———— Wittson, C. L., and Hunt, E. B. Military performance of a group of marginal neuropsychiatric cases. *American Journal of Psychiatry*, 1952, *109*, 168-71.

———— Wittson, C. O., and Hunt, E. B. Theoretical and practical analysis of the diagnostic process. In P. H. Hoch and J. Zubin (Eds.), *Diagnosis and etiology of mental disorders as perceived in our time*. New York: Grune and Stratton, 1953.

———— Wittson, C. L., and Hunt, E. B. Hidden costs in the utilization of the psychiatrically marginal man. *Journal of Clinical Psychology*, 1954, *10*, 91-92.

———— A rationale for psychiatric selection. *American Psychologist*, 1955, *10*, 199-204.

———— Education—the dream and the reality. *Nursing World*, 1958, *132*, 26-30.

———— An actuarial approach to clinical judgment. In B. M. Bass, and I. A. Berg, (Eds.), *Objective approaches to personality assessment.* New York: Van Nostrand, 1959.

———— and Jones, N. F. The experimental approach to clinical judgment. In A. J. Bachrach (Ed.), *Experimental foundations of clinical psychology.* New York: Basic Books, 1961.

———— Relations with other professions. In B. B. Wolman (Ed.), *Handbook of clinical psychology.* New York: McGraw-Hill, 1965.

———— The American school system, a possible locus for a universal mental health program. *Psychology in the Schools,* 1968, *5,* 35-40.

———— and Matarrazo, J. Habit mechanisms in smoking. In W. A. Hunt (Ed)., *Learning mechanisms in smoking.* Chicago: Aldine, 1970.

———— Barnett, L. W., and Branch, L. G. Relapse rates in addiction programs. *Journal of Clinical Psychology,* October 1971, *27*(4), 455-56.

Land, E. H., and Hunt, W. A. The use of polarized light in the simultaneous comparison of retinally and cortically fused colors. *Science,* 1936, *83,* 309.

Landis, C., and Hunt, W. A. Adrenalin and emotion. *Psychological Review,* 1932, *39,* 467-85.

Landis, C., and Hunt, W. A. The conscious correlates of the galvanic skin response. *Journal of Experimental Psychology,* 1935, *18,* 505-29.

Landis, C., and Hunt, W. A. Magnification of time as a research technique in the study of behavior. *Science,* 1937, *85,* 384-85.

Landis, C., and Hunt, W. A. *The startle pattern.* New York: Farrar and Rinehart, 1939.

Strauss, H., Das Zusammenschrecken. *Journal für Psychologie und Neurologie,* 1929, *39,* 111-231.

Thorne, F. C., and Nathan, P. E. Systems analysis methods for integrative diagnosis. *Journal of Clinical Psychology,* 1970, *26,* 3-17.

Volkmann, J., and Hunt, W. A. The anchoring of an affective scale. *American Journal of Psychology,* 1937, *49,* 88-92.

Wittson, C. L., and Hunt, W. A. Three years of naval selection—a retrospect. *War Medicine,* 1945, *7,* 218-21.

6

A Psychologist's Account at Mid-Career

JEROME KAGAN

An autobiographical statement is under severe pressure to depart from the fidelity of the facts, for the reader expects and the writer believes that a career has both a logic and continuity, and the former is as eager to learn of it as the latter is to discover it. The statement most faithful to history is probably the least interesting to read and the most distressing to compose. Although I have tried to be objective, this essay should be read as a story, for repression, forgetting, and the continual need to see decisions as sensible make the degree of resemblance between what happened and what I think happened range from fair to hopelessly distorted. Kurt Vonnegut's Tralfamadorians see the issue more clearly in *Slaughter House Five*.

There are no telegrams in Tralfamadore. But you're right; each clump of symbols is a brief urgent message—describing a situation, a scene. We Tralfamadorians read them all at once, not one after the other. There isn't any particular relationship between all the messages, except that the author has chosen carefully, so that, when seen all at once, they produce an image of life that is beautiful and surprising and deep. There is no beginning, no middle, no end, no suspense, no moral, no causes, no effects. What we love in our books are the depths of many marvelous moments seen all at one time.

This statement tries to answer three questions, and even if crisp answers are not forthcoming, their posing at least puts some order into the tale. Why was science chosen—as a strategy of gratifying the continual need for love and work? Why was psychology selected? Why the specific problems pursued during the past twenty years? Answers to the first two questions are more convincing and more easily set down than resolutions of the third, for the latter is too much the slave of chance and context. Had different telephone calls or letters arrived, my bibliography would contain a different set of titles.

I was the first-born son of a doting and excessively protective mother, and a father whose crippling arthritis, first noted in his thirties, bred a premature bitterness toward his existence. Fortunately, he was zealously protective of his personal freedom and autonomy, not out of philosophical reflection but simply because it was necessary for his equilibrium. Hence he reflexively awarded to me this autonomy and defended my freedom of decision, especially during adolescence, against his wife's nervous apprehensions.

My mother viewed knowledge as a sacrament and must have reminded me hundreds of times that her father, whom I had never known and to whom she felt strong affection, died quietly in a stuffed living-room chair with an open book on his chest. This image, which never had the opportunity to become tarnished, exerted its strong influence years later when I began to brood about a vocation. I loved her and she loved a wise, gentle, tolerant, reflective scholar who was full of insights about man. The incentive provided by this idealized hero was complemented by the good fortune that delivered me into a public school system where I perceived myself to be among the most proficient in my primary grade classes. I stress the role of chance not out of a dishonest desire to appear modest, but because I believe that my own sense of competence was enhanced by the structure of the community in which I was raised. I spent my first seventeen years in the same New Jersey town of about 20,000 people. It was located about twenty-five miles south of New York City and was an industrial town when I lived there. My father owned a small business on one of the three main streets. Many of the children came from working-class families and did not have strong motivation to master the arbitrary requirements of the school. Furthermore, the classrooms were still managed by that rare caste of woman totally devoted to teaching. The composite memory of my first six teachers is overwhelmingly positive— endomorphic, middle-aged, unmarried women who liked children and enjoyed showering praise on the tiniest intellectual victory displayed by any member of their temporary family. With their help I and several others assumed the role of class scholars—a role I have probably tried to maintain ever since.

There were also more specific circumstances that made academic life a probable choice. The economic depression was acute during my early school years. My father's unhappiness with his own fate in the arena of commerce, continually affirmed by my mother, turned me from this avenue. The possibility of choosing a business career was never seriously considered. The popular professional options of law and medicine, so natural to my reference group, were considered for a while. My uncle was a lawyer in the town and hinted about future collaboration. But I felt a deep uneasiness with the law. Man's statements about how men should behave seemed so arbitrary and fragile. I wanted laws that were permanent and was ingenuous enough to believe that only science had privy to these precious statements. How ironic that twenty years later, in the essay "On the Need for Relativism," I should plead for partial desertion of the view that initially attracted me to science. Although it is probably of minimal consequence, I remember a movie called *Goodbye, Mr. Chips* which opened my adolescent eyes to the quiet, reflective life of the teacher and complemented the holy image of my grandfather with the open book. I began to think more seriously of being a professor of something. I don't think I knew there were such things as professors of psychology.

The decision to choose an intellectual career seems to make some sense, and it is the most reasonable part of the narrative. Answers to the last two questions are more speculative. I was attracted to the natural sciences for the obvious reasons and took many biology and chemistry courses as an undergraduate. Chemistry became particularly appealing and I decided in my senior year to become a biochemist. There was some ambivalence about that choice, for my chemistry professors persuaded me that a creative career required a natural ingenuity in the laboratory. I felt at ease with theoretical ideas, but less sure during the six-hour laboratory sessions. One event is memorable. The laboratory assignment in the course on quantitative analysis was the determination of barium sulphate. We began after lunch and at six-thirty that evening I was ready to take my crucible to the balance to weigh the few milligrams of white precipitate. Moments later a classmate followed and halfway to the balance dropped his crucible and its precious contents on the floor. There were probably eight of us left in the laboratory at that late hour, and he asked each of us for an estimate of how many milligrams of barium sulphate lay spilled on the concrete. He computed the mean and submitted it as his answer. I was peeved and skeptical when he received an A— and I a B+.

My commitment to chemistry was also weakened by a psychology professor's idle comment in the introductory psychology course. He had posed a question I cannot remember, but to which I apparently gave a good answer. He asked me to stay and as we walked across the campus he said I had an apperceptive feeling for psychology and added, "You would probably be a good psychologist." The sentence rings as clearly now as it did that afternoon twenty-two years ago. I began to think about psychology more seriously. The self strives to be generative; the content of the commitment is secondary to that prize. The task is to find, amid the confusion of distorted feedback and the devilish temptation of power, where the blend of temperament and expertise is best exploited in the service of creativity. I had a gnawing doubt that chemistry was not the best solution for my profile, and so the professor's evaluation—probably given with the casualness that one describes the weather—was seized upon as a seriously considered prediction of my future. I acted on it and took more psychology courses. They were moderately interesting but not sufficiently challenging, and my motivation wavered.

The next important event occurred during Christmas vacation of my senior year. I had applied to graduate school in biochemistry but had written to Yale for an application in psychology. The chairman of the Rutger's Psychology Department, who was more dogmatic than he had a right to be, advised that Yale was the only outstanding graduate school in psychology and I should not consider any other university. I sent for the application but had not completed it because of insufficient enthusiasm. Psychology did not have the elegant methods and powerful principles I had become accustomed to in my natural science courses. Moreover, the ten-dollar application fee required more motivation than I had at the moment. The deadline for the application was a few days off and it still lay in my desk. A snowstorm forced me to cancel a date during that pre-New Year's week and I filled the empty evening by completing the application. I believe that had the storm not canceled the evening's fun I would not have applied to Yale.

The next critical event occurred four months later. I had been offered a fellowship in biochemistry at the University of Texas in late March and was leaning in that direction. I had not yet heard from Yale and in order to acquire more information about the impending decision, I borrowed a book from the local library whose author was unknown to me, but whose title seemed interesting. It was Donald Hebb's *Organization of Behavior,* published less than a year earlier. I was reading Hebb with interest when a letter from Professor Frank A. Beach informed me that I had been accepted by Yale, and he was offering me a research assistantship to work with him on problems of mating behavior in animals. I turned to the bibliography of Hebb's book and noted with pleasure that Hebb regarded Beach as an exceptionally good scientist, for Beach's papers occupied most of the first two pages. My fate was sealed. Hebb was clearly an outstanding psychologist; he regarded Beach similarly and the latter wanted me to work with him. I wrote a polite letter to Texas and prepared for New Haven. Nineteen years later, at a cocktail party at my home following a colloquium, I told Hebb this story and thanked him for publishing at the proper time.

Although I almost abandoned psychology for psychiatry during my first year at Yale, I stayed for several reasons. Frank Beach was a good model. I was energetic and curious and my undergraduate work in biology made me friendly toward biologically phrased problems. Beach had three students working with him and he made each of us feel that each day we might discover a new phenomenon. Frank believed in the excitement of inductive empiricism; and his style was exquisitely tailored to my temperament. Moreover, sexual behavior was a more interesting subject than maze-running. Neal Miller's commitment to science and his attitude toward theory was a second magnet. Although he defended stimulus reduction as the sole explanation of reinforcement in his more public appearances, his attitude in our small learning seminar was altogether more reasonable and utilitarian. A hypothesis was something to pursue until it had lost its glamour and was to be laid aside when a more attractive idea appeared. One afternoon a visiting British student asked Miller why he did not hedge the issue in his writing; why was he always so dogmatic about the principle that stimulus reduction was the only mechanism of reinforcement? Miller replied in his wonderful Washington twang, "There is only one thing you find in the middle of the road."

There was, moreover, an evangelical mood among the graduate students in the early 1950s. The senior faculty created the illusion that the students were the most talented young scholars in the most enlightened department, and that each of us had the obligation to move psychology forward. Frank Beach gave a final examination during my first year that probably influenced my attitude toward psychology and my expectation of contributing to it. The examination consisted of reading several current issues of the *Journal of Comparative and Physiological Psychology* and criticizing the papers. The initial feeling was despair. How could a first year graduate student find any serious defects in the methodology or interpretation of papers that had passed professional judgment. But when I quieted my fear and began the task, I was alternately delighted and appalled by how easy the assignment was to complete. The message Beach intended had been assimilated. When I came to Harvard in 1964 to direct the graduate training program in developmental psychology I self-consciously tried to create the same heady atmosphere that so effectively caught me in 1950. It is unlikely that I will be as successful as the Yale department was twenty years ago. For the group that was in New Haven during those good years included Byron Campbell, William Kessen, Martin Kohn, Gerald Lesser, George Mandler, Allen Mirsky, Lloyd Morrisett, Edward Murray, and Roger Shepard.

A final force that held me in New Haven were three students with whom I regularly had dinner. Our conversations at the end of each day were exhilarating. Edward Murray, Byron Campbell, Martin Kohn, and I would talk psychology continually on our way to, during, and from dinner. Occasionally Bill Kessen, who was the married one among us, would join us or invite us to dinner at his apartment where discussions about learning, reinforcement, and motivation dominated the long, pleasant evenings. I told my future wife that the strictest test of my love was that our marriage would mean no more dinners on Chapel Street. We married at the end of my first year after I had decided to become a psychologist.

The remainder of this essay is devoted to the last question; what influenced the selection of problems and the style of the work that implemented those ideas. I can easily account for the shift of interest from comparative psychology to human motivation and thought. I have always felt the tension of two loyalties. The aesthetic satisfaction of an elegantly designed experiment and the subsequent plotting of orderly curves have always competed with a desire to understand more about man. The wish to enter man's mind is less in the service of placating conscience's demand for socially relevant inquiry, although that is a small factor, than it is an insatiable desire to covet the principles that permit a rational construction of this inscrutable mammal. The depth of the motive suggests that it must serve self-understanding in a serious way; and make my addiction something like a religious search. Alfred Kazin, in a recent review of Saul Bellow's writing, perceptively notes that, for Bellow, knowledge is synonymous with virtue. This sentence released a surge of affect as I realized the spirituality of my own efforts. I am fortunate to have picked a goal that, although never attainable, permits me to relate all of experience to a single theme. It provides unity of purpose and maximal variety of action when boredom, worry, or anger surreptitiously sneaks up behind me and attempts to subdue the clarity of awareness that is difficult to maintain, but necessary for taming the day. I am currently more involved in psychology than ever in the past, save perhaps for those precious years at Yale.

I decided early in graduate work that the questions to be put to nature would be about man. I continued to work with Frank Beach and did my dissertation on mating behavior in the albino rat because Frank's friendship was assuring, and the questions were interesting. But there was no doubt in my mind that my first independent investigation would be with children. Although I have been identified with developmental psychology for all of my career, I am least certain of why I selected the child, and the reasons I am about to set down do not have the ring of phenomenological authenticity.

I had been attracted to psychoanalytic theory at Yale because of lectures by Irving Janis, Katherine Wolf, Sybille Escalona, and Seymour Sarason, and the most intriguing empirical questions implied by the theory involved the genesis of personality. I managed to fulfill the requirements for both clinical as well as physiological psychology and spent an internship year at the Clifford Beers Guidance Clinic for Children in New Haven, succeeding George Mandler, with whom I had many good talks. The year's experiences with diagnosis and therapy nudged me toward a cognitive view of psychopathology. The children's private confessions suggested that the demons that distorted their lives were false beliefs about themselves. I remember on several occasions saying to myself—as if I were giving a speech—"If only man didn't think so much," my version of the Buddhist maxim "Beings are defiled through the defilement of thought." This toxic view of cognition as an etiological agent in unhappiness produced considerable intellectual resistance when I studied Piaget seriously a decade later. Initially, I found the theory obtuse and was irrationally harsh with the author. I suspect that the intolerance rose from Piaget's often repeated phrase, "intelligence is adaptive." This constructive view of thought slammed against the judgment of a decade earlier. As I became aware of this prejudice, Piaget became more palatable.

The experience at Clifford Beers also persuaded me that the special talent my undergraduate professor saw was perhaps best exploited with children. A creative idea requires a penetrating appreciation of the agent responsible for an intriguing behavior; an appreciation that is neither easily verbalized nor assigned to neat conceptual categories.

One must be able to empathize with the organism under study in order to generate good guesses as to the forces activated when that organism is placed in an experimental context. It is said that Edward Tolman could do this for rats. The possibility of generating a good idea or uncovering a significant fact was the major determinant of my choice of the child, not my didactic training or identification with individual professors. Thus when it was time to declare myself and take an academic job in 1954, I decided that I was a child psychologist, and have taught a course in child psychology every year since, with the exception of the two years in the Army and 1967-68, when I had a leave of absence.

The problem that was most attractive when I arrived at Ohio State in 1954 was the child's perception of his parents. The child's view of himself and his profile of behaviors were given form not by how he was treated, but by how he believed he was treated. That theme became the central issue in the essay on relativism written a dozen years later. The first study involved interviewing elementary school children several afternoons a week. I learned three things from that first postgraduate investigation. No matter how sensitive the interview technique there were serious constraints on what the child could tell you, even if he was willing. Piaget recently wrote in a foreword to a colleague's book that he stopped asking children questions about animism and morality for the same reasons. This view has always biased me against questionnaire methods with children or adults. I also learned how important it was to make one's own observations and not rely completely on assistants. The first insights, therefore, were methodological and not very illuminating substantively.

My career at Ohio State was interrupted by a draft call in March of 1955 and subsequent induction into the Army. Fortunately I was stationed at West Point and assigned to a research project investigating the high rate of attrition during the first year. The team consisted of a psychiatrist, a social worker, and a psychologist—all career officers—and myself, a private first class. The lessons learned here complemented those acquired in Columbus. Long interviews and questionnaires were useful, but not powerful enough alone to probe the essence of human personality. The substantive gain was a firmer conviction that the child's experiences, most of which the young adult was unaware of, controlled adult personality structure, for it seemed that the men who left the academy before the first year was over had had estranged relationships with their fathers during childhood. Hence I set for myself the oldest question ever asked about man— how does the past constrain the present. I was eager for an opportunity to commit myself to that theme. The opportunity to make that commitment came soon and was as unpredictable and improbable as the December snowstorm that permitted the Yale application to go forward. I was four months from discharge and ready to return to Ohio State when Lester W. Sontag, director of the Fels Research Institute in Yellow Springs, Ohio, invited me to be interviewed for a research position. He had offered me a job in New Haven two years earlier, but faculty friends advised me to go to a university rather than risk the isolation of Yellow Springs.

I took the sooty overnight train from New York City and arrived in Xenia, Ohio, on a cold gray morning in late November. It was the first time I had been west of Philadelphia. The scene at 7:00 a.m. at the Xenia depot shall always remain clear, down to the ache in my back developed in a cruelly small roomette. The institute had just received a grant from the National Institute of Mental Health to study the personality of a group of adults on whom longitudinal data had been gathered since their birth in the 1930s. Sontag wanted me to direct the project and promised complete independence and generous support. I spent the next two days alone in the library of the institute reading excerpts from individual records. The success of the project depended on the quality of the historical data. One could invest five years of honest effort, and if no meaningful relations between the child and adult corpuses emerged, which was possible, the most reasonable interpretation was that the quality of the childhood information was poor. The protocols consisted of lengthy descriptive reports of naturalistic observations on the child at home, in the nursery school at the institute (where the child came for six to ten weeks a year), and in his public school. The more I read, the lighter my mood became for there were so many instances of exquisitely detailed descriptions of fear, passive withdrawal, anger, aggression, and mastery that I was persuaded the risk was worthwhile. I was more certain than I had a right to be that there was no other setting that could provide as good a start at understanding the genesis of personality than the institute. I brought my wife and three-year-old daughter to Yellow Springs on a snowy day in January of 1957 to begin an unusually rich seven years. I threw myself into the work with a vigor that surpassed the days at Yale. There was nothing to distract me—no committees, only a little teaching, and minimal traveling. I usually arose between 5:30 and 6:00, arrived at the institute by 6:30 —or 7:00 if I walked the mile of lovely rural road—left at 6:00 p.m. for dinner and usually worked at home until exhaustion sent me stumbling off to bed.

The design of the study was simple. The historical data would have to be analyzed by someone unfamiliar with the adult information. Unfortunately, rating scales were the most valid way to quantify the childhood protocols. Howard Moss, who had just recently received his Ph.D. from Ohio State, took responsibility for this phase of the project. The assessment of the adult's personality would be based on lengthy interviews over several days, complemented by experimental procedures. The theoretical basis for the selection of variables had to be accommodated to the historical data. The information on the children emphasized aggression, dependency, passivity, school achievement, and sex typing, as well as conflicts in these areas. We used the interview to explore each of these areas and created special procedures to assess conflict. In a moment we shall see how that strategy led to an accidental discovery that, in turn, led to a new problem for study. Howard Moss rated the childhood data while I interviewed each of the adults, who were between nineteen and twenty-nine years of age. It took over two and a half years to talk with and test the adults and quantify the historical data. The analysis was pure fun and Howard and I extracted three major generalizations from the pounds of computer printout. As I have said publicly many times, these three inferences have influenced, directly or indirectly, all of my subsequent work.

There were selected instances of stability in behavior from childhood to adulthood and the vitality of those continuities depended on their congruence with societal standards, especially sex role standards. The data also yielded a related methodological caution that I have heeded since and have urged, with only moderate success, on others. Many of the variables yielded no sex differences in means or variances, but the patterns of correlates of a specific variable were dramatically different for the men and women. The obvious corollary was that a specific action, or a specific magnitude on a test variable, does not have a fixed meaning. All behaviors are ambiguous as to cause, and deciphering the significance of a response always requires additional information.

Second, there were a few very young children whose temperamental passivity during infancy seemed to persist throughout childhood and adolescence. This observation prompted the work with infants that began at Fels in 1962 and has continued at Harvard.

The last result suggested a new dimension that culminated five years later in the delineation of the construct reflection-impulsivity. That discovery contains all the elements of the classic plot which has the bumbling but energetic scientist fall upon a good idea following careful analysis of a set of data that did not verify an initial hypothesis.

As part of the adult assessment battery, Moss and I devised a conceptual sorting task. The idea behind the task made good sense in 1957, it makes less sense today. We wanted to measure degree of conflict over aggression, dependence, and sexuality, and we constructed some human figures whose postures and dress suggested those motive dispositions. The subject was shown the array of figures and asked to sort the array into conceptual groups. We assumed that the subjects who did not create groups based on the motive areas implied by the figures did not activate those ideas and were more conflicted about that motive than those who did. This hypothesis has apparently remained in the back of my mind for it was the theme of a recent essay on motives. The content of conceptual groupings showed no relation with independent indexes of conflict derived from the interviews, the subject's performance on various tests, or behavior during childhood. We were disappointed and frustrated and I spent weeks examining each subject's protocol, trying to determine why such a good idea failed. After hours of pouring over hundreds of conceptual groupings I noted that there was a small group of adults who preferred concepts based on physical aspects of the stimulus—a tendency we later called analytic. The adults who produced these concepts were distinguished from others, not on the basis of conflict, but because they were more concerned with the quality of their intellectual products. We quickly shifted our orientation and examined the protocols for other formal dimensions in the conceptual material, and generated the three basic categories: analytic—categorical—relational. We initiated a set of studies on children that asked three questions. Could we duplicate the tripartite arrangement of concepts seen in adults, what were the developmental changes in these variables, and, most important, could we learn something of the basic determinants of differential preference for these dispositions? After two years we were ready for the next empirical foray which led to the more definitive work on reflection-impulsivity. We replicated the adult findings. Some children preferred analytic concepts, some relational, and some categorical. But we still did not know why. For reasons I cannot recall at the moment, we recorded the subject's latency to produce each of the concepts. While leafing through the data, I noted that production of analytic concepts tended to be preceded by slightly longer response times than the other two categories. The obvious association was that an analytic concept required a more detailed analysis of the stimulus, and children who took the extra time to examine the material might be predisposed to produce analytic categories. We had a clue as to process; now we had to explain why a child took the extra few seconds before reporting his concept. The notion of a reflective child was invented that week. The next few years were devoted to understanding why some children were reflective and some impulsive. The history of that work is well documented.

One evening that was part of the adventure occurred soon after we had invented the analytic, relational, categorical ideas, but before we were aware of the reflection-impulsivity dimension.

Irving Sigel and I had met in the spring of 1957 in Iowa City at a meeting of the Society for Research in Child Development. We were attracted to each other's fondness for debate and child psychology, and a strong friendship was established. Irv was responsible for my being invited to the Merrill Palmer Institute to attend a workshop on identification, a meeting that provided the incentive for the theoretical paper on identification published in the *Psychological Review* in 1959. Irv visited Yellow Springs and after dinner we sat and talked about cognition. Irv was attracted to the older abstract-concrete classification promoted by Kurt Goldstein and I suggested that the analytic-relational-categorical dimensions might be more productive, especially with children. When we turned off the lights a few hours before dawn, the mood contained the tension of a treasure hunt. We decided to cooperate on a series of studies in Detroit and Yellow Springs on the significance of the analytic-categorical-relational categories. We talked on the phone, visited back and forth, and supported each other's work for several years.

One investigation forms the link between the work at Fels and the infant research in Cambridge. We had demonstrated that reflection-impulsivity was stable, reliable, and of psychological significance. As a result, we administered the test of reflection-impulsivity to school-age children who were members of the Fels longitudinal population and on whom we had excellent data from infancy. The reflective children, in contrast to the impulsive ones, were described during infancy and early childhood as more passive, gentler, and less active. My curiosity was piqued. The possibility that we might see analage of reflection-impulsivity during infancy made this issue paramount and led to our first studies of early cognitive development; the sequellae of which are still being written.

Another set of functional relations that recruited my interest to infants involved social class differences during this early period. We knew that infant intelligence tests did not predict quality of cognitive functioning during childhood, but resisted the implication that no pattern of behavior during the first year was related to psychological functioning at age four. This resistance was based on two prior prejudices. I had a dogmatic faith in the continuity of psychological functions. Since the four-year-old middle-class child was different from the four-year-old working-class child, we should see some preview of this at age three, and if at age three then at age two, and if at age two then at age one, and if at age one then perhaps even before the first birthday.

Still another reason for examining the infant resulted from a chapter on sex differences prepared for the Hoffman and Hoffman volume *Review of Child Development Research*. This assignment forced me to read the literature on sex differences in infancy and childhood and persuaded me of the inherent interest of the problem. I was motivated to look with a fresh perspective for different behavioral profiles for the sexes. Finally, I wanted to learn more about infants qua infants, for the larger prize had not lost its glitter. I did not understand the human infant very well and wanted to enrich my appreciation for this epoch of development.

Hence, soon after settling in at Harvard, we initiated a longitudinal study that asked about the prolegomena of cognitive tempo, and sex and social class differences during the first two years of life, as part of a more general investigation of psychological continuity. The theoretical focus was on patterns of attention distribution to interesting events, rather than maturation of motor skills, sensory motor schemes, or ease of conditioning, because I believed then, and continue to believe now, that the development of purely cognitive representations of experience is a central issue in development. If we knew how the infant represented events we would possess a profound insight. It seemed reasonable that study of the infant's distribution of attention to normal and distorted auditory and visual stimuli was a good way to approach this problem. Moreover, this strategy implied that the primary variables to quantify should be naturally occurring, frequent reactions like distribution of attention, babbling, smiling, and heart-rate change. Frank Beach had recently written a paper on the value of studying species specific patterns, and ethological theory, which was congruent with Beach's plea, was slowly being introduced into lecture halls and brown bag discussions. So Michael Lewis and I, while still at Fels, spent two years exploring attentional phenomena in infants. We constructed some interesting representations of human faces and forms and showed them to infants six months of age to see what would happen.

One more factor prompted us to design these rather simple experiments with infants. John and Beatrice Lacey had demonstrated convincingly that when an adult attended to an event, his heart slowed down. Bernice Rosman and I replicated this important phenomenon with six-year-old children. The implication was crisp and clear. If infants also showed cardiac deceleration when they were interested in an external stimulus, we might be able to use changes in heart rate to determine what attracted the infant. One could touch the tension in the laboratory the first day we presented our slides to a six month old and watched the needle-like pen trace the meandering of his heart on John Lacey's Brush recorder. Six-month infants did slow their heart to certain events. We soon became persuaded that discrepant stimuli had the greatest power over their hearts.

Hence the decision to initiate the longitudinal study of infants at Harvard was based on several independent factors. But it was also, in part, a Darwinian expedition into the world of the non-verbal human. The procedures chosen for the Harvard study focused on patterns of attention distribution to visual and auditory stimuli, as well as tempo of play across the period four through twenty-seven months. We believed these behaviors would reveal the mysterious cognitive processes we wanted to understand. Five years later we had extracted three new generalizations. We were able to predict reflection-impulsivity at twenty-seven months from play behavior at eight months and rate of habituation to visual stimuli at sixteen weeks. The degree of predictive continuity was fragile, but palpable. The initial justification for the study had been vindicated.

There were no strong social class differences at four and eight months of age, but by one and two years, the differences were un-equivocal. Lower-middle-class one year olds were less attentive to faces and forms than middle-class children. Accommodation to this fact led to the hypothesis that an important change in cognitive functioning occurs toward the end of the first year, when the child begins to interpret transformations of what he knows, rather than merely assimilate the unusual to existing schemata. He attempts to transform the odd event to the one with which he is familiar. He has become a thinking creature. And this process seems to have no obvious representation in his gross motor action patterns. Long before the sensory-motor period is over, the child appears to be conceptually operational, albeit at a primitive level. The nicest set of curves we have ever generated came from independent replications of a U-shaped relation between age and duration of attention to human faces in Cambridge, and Guatemalan Indian children, with the trough at twelve months.

This hypothesis has provoked a series of studies, each of which affirms the likelihood of a serious maturational change in cognitive functioning between nine and twelve months. We are now actively involved in experiments directed at deeper understanding of this intriguing phenomenon.

The last part of the story describes a return to the problem of motivation. The major goal of the first longitudinal study at Fels was to study continuity of behavioral indexes of motivation and conflict, but we were continually frustrated by frail methodology. The test protocols on the adult subjects were of minimal help in providing insights into hidden wishes. When this fact became obvious, we implemented a study at Fels that demonstrated that the production of aggressive imagery to Rorschach ink blots, which were then believed to index unconscious hostility, was merely a reflection of available aggressive ideation.

We created a concept induction task in which one of the five concepts was hostility-anger, and we had the subjects, who were college students, produce interpretations to ink blots. The more aggressive imagery a subject reported to the ink blots, the easier it was for him to attain the concept of hostility-anger relative to the other concepts in the task. The paper was published in the *Journal of Personality* and, to my disappointment, received very few reprint requests. I rationalized the mass indifference to the report by scapegoating the clinicians as uninterested in data that did not corroborate their biases. It was the last work I ever did with projective tests, save for summarizing the Rorschach and TAT data on our longitudinal subjects in the book, *Birth to Maturity*.

But the experiment on concept induction had a more constructive effect. It reinforced the cognitive view of motives that lay latent for eight more years. It was revived by a year of theoretical analysis and data emerging from the infant study that implied a relation between stranger and separation anxiety, on the one hand, and motivation, on the other. Infant, child, and adult are goaded by the wish to resolve uncertainty, and that deep need seems to fuel the long list of motives that occupy the first lines of the titles that fill our journals. The cognitive basis of motivation was becoming clearer in my mind and I began to set down thoughts, a paragraph at a time, that two years later resulted in a theoretical paper on motivation. That essay was shaped by many influences over many years. The experiences at Clifford Beers and West Point initially suggested the cognitive character of motives. The ink blot-concept acquisition experiment supported that view. The theoretical paper on identification defined this popular construct as a cognitive belief. And Schachter's intriguing work on affect, complemented by the cognitive interpretation of infant anxiety, added support to the total structure. The experiments of the next half-decade, which are still in their formative stages, will try to test these ideas in the harsh empirical arena.

EPILOGUE

I have become impatient with contemporary psychology's barbaric empiricism and saddened by its primitive methodology. We need more thoughtful analyses of mind and a richer appreciation of belief structures across cultures and time if we are to gain a more profound understanding of man. I thought I would be nearer that goal by now but continue to have the illusion of correct direction.

I have been an empirical opportunist—often just following my nose from experiment to experiment—because curiosity and the plain fun of new observations have been easy temptresses. But I have recently begun to look to anthropology, history, and plain reflection for answers I believed could be found only in the psychology laboratory. On a summer afternoon two years ago I sat in an isolated wooded grove on Martha's Vineyard thinking about memory. In the minutes before lunch I saw the possibility of defining certain motives simply as a specific class of cognitive structures that became linked to the uncertain anticipation of specific affects. The cognitive structure was permanent, but depending on changing experience, it might or might not be a motive. I could not suppress the smile that trailed the realization that a morning's quiet thought was such a rich source of pleasure. Perhaps all of the earlier research had been an attempt to generate data that would allow the greatest interpretive challenge; perhaps I generated 50 $\times$ 50 correlation matrices in order to set myself deliciously complicated puzzles to solve. This interpretation has the texture of truth for the three papers toward which I feel the greatest pride are the theoretical essays on identification, relativism, and motivation. None is primarily an empirical effort. The empirical reports bear the mark of obsolescence, for newer findings have shortened the half-life of their conclusions. There is, therefore, a paradox in the fact that I have always regarded myself primarily as an empiricist, yet reserve my private satisfaction for three theoretical pieces. This bothersome inconsistency is part of a larger tension produced by a vector that strains toward ideological unification but is opposed by one that reaches toward the excitement of new phenomena. Perhaps the common aim has been aesthetic. Although I have never been drawn to the experiment that proves—with the sole exception of the study with Robert McCall that indicated that contour, not complexity, seemed to control duration of attention in the four-month infant —it is precisely that form of science that most often provides the greatest satisfaction. The searching empirical foray lacks the beauty of design and data analysis. It gives its joy in the planning and the doing. The reasoned theoretical argument, on the other hand, can satisfy the aesthetic requirement and, as a dividend, create the illusion of deeper insight than current psychological methods permit.

The questions that presently seize my interest have a link to that first study at Ohio State that inquired into the child's conception of his parents. But now the intrigue centers not on lawful variability in a specific belief, but on the nature of belief itself. In greener days I accepted the simple fact of belief and thought the puzzle was in the variety. That simple assumption has lost its earlier clarity, and has become the question.

The point of philosophy is to start with something so simple as not to seem worth stating and end with something so paradoxical that no one can believe it (Bertrand Russell, *The Monist*, 1918).

How should psychology characterize the representation of a face, the concept of justice, or the subtle state created when one recognizes inconsistency? Why is Western man troubled when he discovers that he harbors incompatible views toward the same object? Why can not anger be both good and bad? It has taken seventeen years to arrive at the question of belief. Man's beliefs about himself and others seem to be not only at the core of his conflicts, but also the means by which he rights himself when the intrusion of doubt, disbelief, or deprivation throw him off balance. The present aim is to understand how a mind transduces raw experience into patterns of ideas that are continually transformed to serve an executive that has an insatiable need for harmony among its constituents.

PUBLICATIONS

1. Kagan, J., and Beach, F. A. Effects of early experience on mating behavior in male rats. *Journal of Comparative and Physiological Psychology*, 1953, *46*, 204-8.
2. Kagan, J., and Berkun, M. The reward value of running activity. *Journal of Comparative and Physiological Psychology*, 1954, *47*, 108.
3. Kagan, J. Differential reward value of incomplete and complete sexual behavior. *Journal of Comparative and Physiological Psychology*, 1955, *48*, 59-64.
4. Kagan, J., and Mussen, P. H. Dependency themes on the TAT and group conformity. *Journal of Consulting Psychology*, 1956, *32*, 20-29.
5. Kagan, J. Psychological study of a school phobia in one of a pair of identical twins. *Journal of Projective Techniques*, 1956, *20*, 78-87.

6. Kagan, J. The measurement of overt aggression from fantasy. *Journal of Abnormal and Social Psychology,* 1956, *52,* 390-93.

7. Kagan, J. The child's perception of the parent. *Journal of Abnormal and Social Psychology,* 1956, *53,* 257-58.

8. Mussen, P. H., and Kagan, J. Group conformity and perceptions of parents. *Child Development,* 1958, *29,* 57-60.

9. Kagan, J., Sontag, L. W., Baker, C. T., and Nelson, Virginia L. Personality and IQ change. *Journal of Abnormal and Social Psychology,* 1958, *56,* 261-66.

10. Kagan, J. Socialization of aggression and perception of parents in fantasy. *Child Development,* 1958, *29,* 311-20.

11. Kagan, J., and Moss, H. A. Stability and validity of achievement fantasy. *Journal of Abnormal and Social Psychology,* 1959, *58,* 357-64.

12. Kagan, J. The concept of identification. *Psychological Review,* 1958, *65,* 296-305.

13. Kagan, J. The stability of TAT fantasy and stimulus ambiguity. *Journal of Consulting Psychology,* 1959, *23,* 266-71.

14. Kagan, J., and Moss, H. A. Parental correlates of child's IQ and height: A cross-validation of the Berkeley Growth Study results. *Child Development,* 1959, *30,* 325-32.

15. Moss, H. A., and Kagan, J. Maternal influences on early IQ scores. *Psychological Reports,* 1958, *4,* 655-61.

16. Kagan, J. Thematic apperceptive techniques with children. In A. I. Rabin and Mary R. Haworth (Eds.), *Projective techniques with children.* New York: Grune and Stratton, 1960. Pp. 105-29.

17. Kagan, J. The long term stability of selected Rorschach responses. *Journal of Consulting Psychology,* 1960, *24,* 67-73.

18. Kagan, J., and Moss, H. A. The stability of passive and dependent behavior from childhood through adulthood. *Child Development,* 1960, *31,* 577-91.

19. Kagan, J., and Lesser, G. S. (Eds.). *Contemporary issues in thematic apperceptive methods.* Springfield, Ill.: C. C Thomas, 1961.

20. Mussen, P. H., Conger, J. J., and Kagan, J. *Child development and personality* (2nd ed.). New York: Harper & Row, 1963.

21. Kagan, J., and Lemkin, Judith. The child's differential perception of parental attributes. *Journal of Abnormal and Social Psychology,* 1960, *61,* 440-47.

22. Kagan, J., and Lemkin, Judith. Form, color, and size in children's conceptual behavior. *Child Development,* 1961, *32,* 25-28.

23. Kagan, J. The ontogeny of behavior. In *Encyclopedia of science and technology.* New York: McGraw-Hill, 1960, pp. 132-33.

24. Lansky, L. M., Crandall, V. J., Kagan, J., and Baker, C. T. Sex differences in aggression and its correlates in middle class adolescents. *Child Development,* 1961, *32,* 45-58.

25. Kagan, J. Stylistic variables in fantasy behavior. In Kagan, J., and Lesser, G. S. (Eds.), *Contemporary issues in thematic apperceptive methods.* Springfield, Ill.: C. C Thomas, 1961, pp. 196-220.

26. Moss, H. A., and Kagan, J. The stability of achievement and recognition seeking behaviors. *Journal of Abnormal and Social Psychology,* 1961, *62,* 504-13.

27. Kagan, J. Review of Sibylle Escalona and Grace M. Heider, Prediction and outcome: A study in child development. *Contemporary Psychology,* 1961, *6,* 78-80.

28. Kagan, J., Moss, H. A., and Sigel, I. E. Conceptual style and the use of affect labels. *Merrill-Palmer Quarterly of Behavior and Development,* 1960, *4,* 261-78.

29. Kagan, J., and Garn, S. M. A constitutional correlate of early intellective functioning. *Journal of Genetic Psychology,* 1963, *102,* 83-89.

30. Kagan, J., Hosken, Barbara, and Watson, Sara. The child's symbolic conceptualization of the parents. *Child Development,* 1961, *32,* 625-36.

31. Kagan, J., and Moss, H. A. *Birth to maturity: A study in psychological development.* New York: John Wiley, 1962.

32. Kagan, J., and Moss, H. A. The availability of aggressive ideas: A neglected parameter in assessing projective test responses. *Journal of Personality,* 1961, *29,* 217-34.

33. Kagan, J., and Moss, H. A. Personality and social development: Family and peer influences. *Review of Educational Research,* 1961, *31*(5), 463-74.

34. Kagan, J., Moss, H. A., and Sigel, I. E. Psychological significance of styles of conceptualization in basic cognitive processes in children. In J. C. Wright and J. Kagan (Eds.), *Monographs on Social Research and Child Development,* 1963, *28*(2, Whole No. 86), 73-112.

35. Lee, Lee C., Kagan, J., and Rabson, Alice. Influence of a preference for analytic categorization upon concept acquisition. *Child Development,* 1963, *34,* 433-42.

36. Lacey, J. I., Kagan, J., Lacey, Beatrice C., and Moss, H. A. The visceral level: Situational determinants and behavioral correlates of autonomic response patterns. In P. H. Knapp (Ed.), *Expression of the emotions in man.* New York: International University Press, 1963. Pp. 161-96.

37. Kagan, J., and Freeman, Marian. Relation of childhood intelligence, maternal behaviors and social class to behavior during adolescence. *Child Development,* 1963, *34,* 899-911.
38. Kagan, J. The acquisition and significance of sex typing and sex role identity. In Martin and Lois Hoffman (Eds.), *Review of child development research.* Vol. 1, New York: Russell Sage, 1964. Pp. 137-67.
39. Kagan, J. The choice of models: A developmental analysis of conflict and continuity in human behavior. In Esther Lloyd-Jones and Esther M. Westervelt (Eds.), *Behavioral science and guidance: Proposals and perspectives.* New York: Bureau of Publications, Columbia University Press, 1963. Pp. 63-85.
40. Kagan, J., Rosman, Bernice L., Day, Deborah, Albert, J., and Phillips, W. Information processing in the child: Significance of analytic and reflective attitudes. *Psychological Monographs,* 1964, *78* (1, Whole No. 578).
41. Kagan, J., and Rosman, Bernice L. Cardiac and respiratory correlates of attention and an analytic attitude. *Journal of Experimental Child Psychology,* 1964, *1,* 50-53.
42. Kagan, J. and Phillips, W. The measurement of identification: A methodological note. *Journal of Abnormal and Social Psychology,* 1964, *69,* 442-43.
43. Kagan, J. Human perception or machine perception: The problem of cognition. Discussion of paper by Leonard Uhr. In S. Tomkins and S. Messick (Eds.), *Computer Simulation of Personality.* New York: John Wiley, 1963. Pp. 267-71.
44. Kagan, J. Review of Sally Provence and Rose C. Lipton, Infants in Institutions. In *Journal of Nervous and Mental Disease,* 1964, *138,* 405-7.
45. Kagan, J. Developmental studies in reflection and analysis. In A. H. Kidd and J. L. Rivoire (Eds.), *Perceptual development in children.* New York: International University Press, 1966. Pp. 487-522.
46. Kagan, J. American longitudinal research on psychological development. *Child Development,* 1964, *35,* 1-32.
47. Kagan, J. Personality, behavior and temperament. In Frank Falkner (Ed.), *Human development.* Philadelphia: W. B. Saunders, 1966. Pp. 326-67.
48. Kagan, J., and Mussen, P. H. Personality development. In *International encyclopedia of the social sciences,* Vol. II, edited by David L. Sills. New York: The Free Press, 1968. Pp. 606-14.
49. Kagan, J. On measurement: Suggestions for the future. *Journal of Projective Techniques and Personality Assessment,* 1964, *28,* 151-55.

50. Moss, H. A., and Kagan, J. The Fels longitudinal study. *Vita Humana*, 1964, *7*, 127-38.
51. Kagan, J. Change and continuity in development (Ch. 9). In J. E. Birren (Ed.), *Relations of development and aging*. Springfield, Ill.: C. C Thomas, 1964. Pp. 139-47.
52. Kagan, J. The child's sex role classification of school objects. *Child Development*, 1964, *35*, 1051-56.
53. Kagan, J. Individual differences in the resolution of response uncertainty. *Journal of Personality and Social Psychology*, 1965, *2*, 154-60.
54. Kagan, J. Personality development. In P. London and D. Rosenhan (Eds.), *Foundation of Abnormal Psychology*. New York: Holt, Rinehart and Winston, 1968. Pp. 117-73.
55. Kagan, J., and Lewis, M. Studies of attention in the human infant. *Merrill-Palmer Quarterly of Behavior and Development*, 1965, *11*, 95-127.
56. Kagan, J. Information processing in the child. In P. H. Mussen, J. J. Conger, and J. Kagan, *Readings in Child Development and Personality*. New York: Harper & Row, 1965. Pp. 313-23.
57. Kagan, J. Impulsive and reflective children: Significance of conceptual tempo. In J. D. Krumboltz (Ed.), *Learning and the educational process*. Chicago: Rand McNally, 1965. Pp. 133-61.
58. Lewis, M., Kagan, J., Campbell, H., and Kalafat, J. The cardiac response as a correlate of attention in infants. *Child Development*, 1966, *37*, 63-72.
59. Kagan, J. Reflection-impulsivity and reading ability in primary grade children. *Child Development*, 1965, *36*, 609-28.
60. Mussen, P. H., Conger, J. J., and Kagan, J. *Readings in child development and personality*. New York: Harper & Row, 1965.
61. Kagan, J. Reflection-impulsivity: The generality and dynamics of conceptual tempo. *Journal of Abnormal Psychology*, 1966, *71*, 17-24.
62. Kagan, J. The three faces of continuity in human development. In D. A. Goslin (Ed.), *Handbook of socialization theory and research*. Chicago: Rand McNally, 1969. Pp. 983-1002.
63. Kagan, J. Answers in Errors. Review of Margaret Donaldson, A Study of Children's Thinking. *Contemporary Psychology*, 1965, *10*, 470-71.
64. Kagan, J., and Henker, B. A. Developmental psychology (Ch. 1). *Annual Review of Psychology*, 1966, *17*, 1-50.
65. Kagan, J. Personality and the learning process. *Daedalus*, 1965, *94*, 553-63.

66. Kagan, J. Body build and conceptual impulsivity in children. *Journal of Personality*, 1966, *34*, 118-28.
67. Kagan, J. Understanding the psychology of mental growth. *Grade Teacher*, 1966, *83*(7).
68. Kagan, J. Personality development. In I. J. Janis (Ed.), *Personality: Dynamics, development and assessment*. New York: Harcourt, Brace & World, 1969. Pp. 407-575.
69. Kagan, J. Learning, attention and the issue of discovery. In Lee S. Shulman and Evan R. Keislar (Eds.), *Learning by discovery*. Chicago: Rand McNally, 1966. Pp. 151-61.
70. Kagan, J. The new marriage: Pediatrics and psychology. *American Journal of Diseases of Children*, 1965, *110*, 272-78.
71. Kagan, J., Pearson, L., and Welch, L. Conceptual impulsivity and inductive reasoning. *Child Development*, 1966, *37*, 583-94.
72. Kagan, J., Pearson, L., Welch, L. The modifiability of an impulsive tempo. *Journal of Educational Psychology*, 1966, *57*, 359-65.
73. Kagan, J., Henker, B. A., Hen-tov, A., Levine, J., and Lewis, M. Infants' differential reactions to familiar and distorted faces. *Child Development*, 1966, *37*, 519-32.
74. Kagan, J. The growth of personality: Theory and research. In J. I. Goodlad (Ed.), *Blackiston*. In press.
75. Kagan, J. The role of theory in human development. In T. Stephens (Ed.), *Lectures in child psychology*, 1967.
76. Lewis, M., Kagan, J., and Kalafat, J. Patterns of fixation in the young infant. *Child Development*, 1966, *37*, 331-42.
77. Kagan, J. A developmental approach to conceptual growth. In H. J. Klausmeier and C. W. Harris (Eds.), *Analyses of concept learning*. New York: Academic Press, 1966. Pp. 97-115.
78. Kagan, J. On the need for relativism. *American Psychologist*, 1967, *22*, 131-42.
79. Yando, R. M., and Kagan, J. The effect of teacher tempo on the child. *Child Development*, 1968, *39*, 27-34.
80. McCall, R. B., and Kagan, J. Attention in the infant: Effects of complexity, contour, perimeter and familiarity. *Child Development*, 1967, *38*, 939-52.
81. McCall, R. B., and Kagan, J. Stimulus-schema discrepancy and attention in the infant. *Journal of Experimental Child Psychology*, 1967, *5*, 381-90.
82. Kagan, J. Review of E. E. Maccoby (Ed.), The Development of sex differences. *Science*, 1967, *156*, 371.
83. Kagan, J. (Ed.). *Creativity and learning*. Boston: Houghton Mifflin, 1967.

84. Kagan, J. On cultural deprivation. In D. C. Glass (Ed.), *Biology and behavior: Environmental influences.* New York: Rockefeller University Press, 1968. Pp. 211-50.

85. Kagan, J., and Havemann, E. *Psychology: An introduction.* New York: Harcourt, Brace & World, 1968.

86. Kagan, J. Biological aspects of inhibition systems. *American Journal Diseases of Children,* 1967, *114,* 507-72.

87. Yando, R., and Kagan, J. Differential reactions to increasing response uncertainty. *Cognitive Psychology,* 1970, *1,* 192-200.

88. Kagan, J. The growth of the face schema: Theoretical significance and methodological issues. In J. Hellmuth (Ed.), *Exceptional infant,* Vol. I, *Special Child Publications.* Seattle, Washington, 1966. Pp. 336-48.

89. Kagan, J. The many faces of response. *Psychology Today,* January 1968, *2,* 22-27.

90. McCall, R. B., and Kagan, J. Individual differences in the infant's distribution of attention to stimulus discrepancy. *Developmental Psychology,* 1970, *2,* 90-98.

91. Kagan, J. Continuity in cognitive development during the first year. *Merrill-Palmer Quarterly of Behavior and Development,* 1969, *15,* 101-20.

92. Kagan, J., and Kogan, N. Individual variation in cognitive processes. In P. H. Mussen (Ed.), Carmichael's *Manual of child psychology.* (3rd. ed.) New York: John Wiley, 1970, Vol. I. Pp. 1273-1365.

93. Kagan, J. On the meaning of behavior: Illustrations from the infant. *Child Development,* 1969, *40,* 1121-34.

94. Henker, B. A., Asano, S., and Kagan, J. An observation system for studying visual attention in the infant. *Journal of Experimental Child Psychology,* 1968, *6,* 391-93.

95. Kagan, J. His struggle for identity. *Saturday Review,* December 7, 1968, 80-88.

96. Kagan, J. On children and learning. *Today's Education,* 1968, *57*(9), 23.

97. Kagan, J. An essay for teachers. *Young Children,* 1969, *24*(3), 132-42.

98. Mussen, P. H., Conger, J. J., and Kagan, J. *Child development and personality.* (3rd ed.) New York: Harper & Row, 1969.

99. Janis, I. J., Mahl, G. M., Kagan, J., and Holt, R. R. Personality development. *Personality: Dynamics, development and assessment.* New York: Harcourt, Brace & World, 1969, Pp. 407-575.

100. Whitten, P., and Kagan, J. Jensen's dangerous half-truth. *Psychology Today,* August 1969, *3,* 8.

101. Kagan, J. Check one: Male-female. *Psychology Today*, July 1969, *3*, 39-41.
102. Mussen, P. H., Conger, J. J., and Kagan, J. *Readings in child development and personality*. (2nd ed.) New York: Harper & Row, 1970.
103. Kagan, J. Human development. *Encyclopedia brittanica*.
104. Tulkin, S., Littenberg, R., and Kagan, J. Cognitive components of separation anxiety. *Developmental Psychology*, 1971,
105. Kagan, J. Who is the beneficiary? Paper presented at J. P. Kennedy Symposium, October 16, 1971, Washington, D.C.
106. Kagan, J. The maturation of cognitive development. *Scientific American*, 1972,
107. Kagan, J., and Tulkin, S. Social class differences in child rearing practices. CASDS-CIBA Symposium ed. by H. R. Schaffer. Academic Press, 1970.
108. Kagan, J. On class differences and early development. In V. Denenberg (Ed.), *Education of the infant and young child*. New York: Academic Press, 1970, 5-24.
109. Kagan, J. Student unrest: The university dilemma. *Radcliffe Quarterly*, December 1969, *53*(4), 2-4.
110. Kagan, J. How much can we boost IQ and scholastic achievement? or, Inadequate evidence and illogical conclusions. *Harvard Educational Review*, Spring 1969, *39*(2), 274-77.
111. Kagan, J. The determinants of attention in the infant. *American Scientist*, May-June 1970, *58*, 298-306.
112. Kagan, J. *Change and continuity in infancy*. New York: John Wiley, 1971.
113. Kagan, J. Attention and psychological change in the young child. *Science*, 1970, *170*, 826-32.
114. Kagan, J. A rationale for day care. *Medical Insight*, December 1970.
115. Super, C. M., Kagan, J., Morrison, F., Haith, M. M., and Weiffenbach, J. Stimulus-schema discrepancy in five-month-old infants. *Journal of Genetic Psychology*. In press.
116. Kagan, J. The distribution of attention in infancy. In D. H. Hamburg (Ed.), *Perception and its disorders*. Res. Publ. ARNMD. Vol. XLVIII. Baltimore: Williams & Wilkins, 1970, 214-37.
117. Kagan, J. Day care can be dangerous. *Psychology Today*, December 1970, *4*, 36-39.
118. Kagan, J. A sexual dimorphism in vocal behavior in infants. In *Enviromental influences on genetic expression*. Fogarty International Center Proceedings, ed. by N. Kretchmer, and D. N. Walcher. Bethesda, Maryland: 1969. Pp. 155-63.

119. Kagan, J. *Understanding children.* New York: Harcourt Brace Jovanovich, 1971.

120. Kagan, J., Haith, M. M., and Caldwell, C. *Psychology: Adapted readings.* New York: Harcourt Brace Jovanovich, 1971.

121. Messer, S. M., Kagan, J., and McCall, R. B. Fixation time and tempo of play in infants. *Developmental Psychology,* 1970, *3,* 406.

122. Minton, C., Kagan, J., and Levine, J. A. Mother-child interaction in the two year old. *Child Development.* In press.

123. Kagan, J. The concept of motivation. *Journal of Personality and Social Psychology.* In press.

124. Finley, G. E., Kagan, J., and Layne, O. The development of young children's attention to normal and distorted stimuli. *Developmental Psychology.* In press.

125. Kagan, J. A conception of early adolescence. *Daedalus,* Fall 1971, *100,* 997-1012.

126. Sellers, M. J., Klein, R. E., Kagan, J., and Minton, C. Developmental determinants of attention: A cross cultural replication. *Developmental psychology.* In press.

127. Kagan, J. The psychology of sex differences. In F. A. Beach (Ed.), *Human sexual behavior.* New York: McGraw-Hill, 1972.

128. Kagan, J. The role of evaluation in problem solving. J. Hellmuth (Ed.), *Cognitive studies,* Vol. 2. *Deficits in cognition.* New York: Brunner-Mazel, 1971. Pp. 109-26.

129. Kagan, J. Personality development. In N. B. Talbot, L. E. Eisenberg, and J. Kagan (Eds.), *Behavioral sciences in pediatrics.* Philadelphia: Saunders, 1972.

130. Kagan, J. A psychologist's account at mid-career. In T. S. Krawiec (Ed.), *The Psychologists.* New York: Oxford University Press, 1972.

7

A Tale of a Teacher

W. P. McKEACHIE

In 1935 I was fourteen years old, an ardent baseball player, a dedicated Presbyterian, and secretary-treasurer of the Sunday school of the small rural church near my home in White Lake Township, Oakland County, Michigan. Each Sunday afternoon I counted the collection (average per Sunday, 77 cents), checked the date on each penny for my penny collection, and read the Sunday school paper, *Young People*. It was on a Sunday afternoon that I read a half-page article on psychology as a vocation, and from that day to this, psychology has seemed to me the most fascinating field in which one could work.

A year after first reading about psychology I was operated on for a mastoid infection and during my convalescence read a paperback book, *The Return to Religion* by Henry C. Link of the Psychological Corporation. The book, as I recall it, was sprinkled with case histories illustrating the favorable psychological functions of religion. I suspect that I would now be critical of the book both from religious and psychological perspectives, but to a fifteen year old, the book represented ideas that were new and gripping. It is significant that both early contexts for encountering psychology were religious, for religion was at that time and continues to be, an important part of my life.

What fascinated me was the sense of new ways of understanding myself and other people and thereby helping to achieve a better life. We psychology teachers are likely to attempt to disabuse our students of the notion that our courses will help them understand themselves or others better, but I suspect that part of the vigor of our iconoclasm comes from our own primitive hopes that psychology would help us. In any case remembering my own hopes and enthusiasm, I have always been gentle with students who describe this as their goal in electing introductory psychology. (In fact I still believe that psychology really *is* helpful in understanding people!)

I dreamed of becoming a psychologist, but the notion that the son of a teacher of a one-room country school earning $70 a month could aspire to such a vocation was patently unrealistic and I still worried about what I should do. In our rural community the notion of a liberal arts education was almost unknown. Education beyond the eighth grade had vocational purposes, and if I were to go to college, I needed to decide what field I was going to college for. This led to my next encounter with psychology. Toward the end of my senior year in high school when I became interested in trying to choose from a number of different vocations that seemed possible, my father located a personnel psychologist in a local business who agreed to give me the Strong Vocational Interest Blank. I was very impressed that a psychologist could help people who didn't know what vocation to enter. Having always liked tests of all sorts, I became even more interested in the possibility that I might go into vocational counseling and help other young people who faced the same decision problems that I did. While I didn't think of it at the time, the fact that my father thought psychologists could help was probably an unusual attitude for our area and times. Certainly I had no sense of restriction from my parents in the freedom of my choice.

Simply going to college was an achievement in the late 1930's. It never occurred to me to inquire about the curricula offered. When I won a scholarship for $30 a semester tuition at Michigan State Normal College and found that I could ride back and forth weekends with a cousin, I felt lucky. I don't recall that at any time during my college career did I regard it as unusual that Michigan State Normal did not offer an undergraduate major in psychology. I did take all three courses offered in psychology. My introductory course used the first edition of Floyd Ruch's *Psychology and Life,* and I enjoyed the whole course. My professor, Dr. Everett Marshall, gave us a group intelligence test and I remember being very pleased that I scored at the top of the scale. This probably reinforced my strong interest in psychological testing. My interest even endured through a course in intelligence testing where I was the only student in class and sat every day trying to stay awake through a lecture delivered to me alone, and read from aging notes by one of the senior professors.

I still had in the back of my mind the hope that someday I might study psychology more seriously. But my immediate vocational aspiration was high school teaching, and because I was a voracious reader I went with enthusiasm into English and history as my fields of specialization. At the same time I began taking mathematics, which at least at this level, was not easy but fun. I kept electing one more mathematics course each term simply out of curiosity to see what would come next, as well as to try to get a better understanding of what I had been doing in solving the problems of the previous course. By the time I reached the senior year, I had more credits in mathematics than I had in history and English, and therefore switched my major to mathematics with minors in history and English.

From the age of twelve I took it for granted that I would earn the money for my clothes and personal expenses although I knew that I could rely on my parents for a loan for major expenses like college. My work experiences gave me a feeling that I could always make a living in a number of ways and at least two experiences increased my interest in human nature. One of these was a summer spent working on an assembly line at General Motors Truck and Coach, where I had the opportunity to work with long-time factory workers, newly immigrated "hillbillies" from Kentucky and Tennessee, second-generation Poles, Italians, and

Armenians, and others. The other curiosity-arousing experience was a series of jobs playing piano and singing with small, non-union bands in bars. Not only was the behavior of patrons, bartenders, and my fellow musicians sometimes bizarre, but their experiences, daily lives, and aspirations were eye-opening to me. The managements always liked long breaks between sets to give the customers more time to drink, so that I had lots of time to talk to the people in the floor show and learn about life in old-time vaudeville from a magician or about how an exotic dancer kept her husband from learning about her infidelities.

Each weekend I rode home on Friday night with my cousin, gave violin, piano, and cello lessons for 50 cents an hour on Saturday, sang and played piano in a bar Saturday night, sang in the church choir Sunday, and rode back to college Sunday night. When I arrived at the house on one such Sunday night I found my roommates gathered around the radio listening to a report that the Japanese had attacked Pearl Harbor.

The war in Europe and the draft had already colored our college years, and the actual declaration of war had little additional direct impact on my senior year. But it did affect planning for the future. I had assumed that after graduation I would go to some small town to teach high school mathematics, but since I would be eligible for the draft only a few months after graduation (the draft age was then twenty-one), teaching was no longer an option. About the only choice was what branch of the armed forces to join. But I wasn't willing to accept that limitation.

I had little doubt that the Nazis and Japanese were the bad guys, but I was not convinced that war was morally justifiable, and I wrestled a good deal with the question of whether or not I was a conscientious objector. (The decision would have been much easier for me in the 1960s.) To complicate matters further, in May of my senior year I fell in love with Virginia Mack, a beautiful blonde whom I'd admired from a distance for years and now actually asked for a date. The last month of my senior year was idyllic—seeing Ginny almost every night and getting our quartet together to serenade her after closing hours at the dormitory.

And it was partly through the quartet that another option emerged. My best friend, Ed Bowles, was a Methodist and an excellent singer. He had formed the quartet to sing at some Methodist youth programs, and in connection with one or more of these I'd been asked to give a brief inspirational talk. Ever since high school days our minister and others had suggested that I consider the ministry, and with my doubts about entering the service I began considering entering seminary. A college friend, Asa Compton, had entered Garrett Seminary in the fall of 1941. When he came back to Michigan Normal to visit in May 1942, I mentioned our quartet's religious programs and my quandary about what to do. He said, "Why don't you try it out? I have seven churches to serve, and I just can't cover them all commuting from Chicago to the Upper Peninsula of Michigan. You could take a couple for a year and then go on to seminary if you feel called to the ministry."

Thus it was that I asked Ginny if she'd like to become a minister's wife. She was so shocked and speechless that she didn't say "No," and this confirmed my decision to become a minister. Shortly after graduation I drove my 1936 Ford to the upper peninsula of Michigan to begin my career as minister of the Trout Lake and Hulbert Methodist Churches. To supplement my $500 a year ministerial salary, I taught mathematics, geography, English, history, and science in the Trout Lake School. Every night I wrote a letter to Ginny.

My experience in the small logging and railroad communities in which I worked was interesting and frustrating. As a teacher I found that playing softball with the students and being friendly and helpful did not prevent disruptive behavior and that my students took paddling for granted as the appropriate device for controlling behavior. Moreover while teaching was generally fun, there were some students who just couldn't understand algebra or geometry no matter how I tried to vary my approach. As a minister I made calls in homes quite different from my own; I baptized babies; I performed a marriage; I prayed with a woman dying of cancer, and conducted a funeral. I became more and more convinced that if I were to be successful in helping people,

I needed to understand people better, and I thought psychology offered the sort of wisdom I needed.

My draft board, however, felt that my decision to enter the ministry had come rather late and did not accept my plea for deferment as a minister. The result was that after two months of teaching and five months of preaching, I called my future mother-in-law one weekend to ask "Can Ginny and I get married next Friday? I'm going to enlist in the Navy and I can't get married once I enter training." My future mother-in-law agreed and within the next week I was not only married but had signed the papers for officers' training in the Navy.

I spent most of World War II as a radar and communications officer on a destroyer in the Pacific. I liked the sea. I enjoyed skin-diving in the Solomon Islands. I enjoyed ship handling and maneuvering and I enjoyed solving the problems of computing the speed and course of enemy aircraft or ships. But I hated the Navy. The authoritarian system of military life ran directly counter to my whole way of life. Time and again I was castigated by my captain for being too sympathetic toward the enlisted men. Over and over he said, "If you like enlisted men, you should be an enlisted man." I kept applying for various kinds of hazardous duty in the hopes that I could get a transfer off the ship, but the captain would never transmit my applications, saying, "The only transfer I'll approve for you is a resignation of your commission and a request to be a chaplain's assistant." Much as I disliked him, I suppose I should thank him for my survival.

The captain did permit me to hold religious services and I was an unofficial chaplain aboard the ship. The men were a very interesting crew. Once again I felt the need for greater understanding of such varied people as southern plantation owners, blacks from northern ghettos, California grape workers, and southern sharecropper's sons.

As the war wore on, and particularly as the Japanese began their suicide plane attacks, I had little optimism that I would survive the war, but I began writing to my wife about going to graduate school when and if the war ended. Sometime during

1 arrived at the conclusion that if I survived the war,
uld try to enter psychology as a graduate student.

Even then I had little conception that I would study for a
h.D. I continued to think of a master's degree in vocational
counseling or clinical psychology as my vocational aspiration.
When I received a leave during the time our ship was in San
Francisco for repairs, I went to the Psychology Department at
the University of Michigan and was told by Dr. Shepard, the acting chairman, that Michigan offered a Master of Clinical Psychology Program that seemed to fit my interests. He assured me
that Michigan had a strong department and would be a good
choice for my graduate work.

Thus when the war ended, I immediately applied for graduate
work at Michigan. Since the government had a discharge system
which gave preference to those with a good deal of combat experience, I was one of the first returning veterans to come back
to the university and had no problems in obtaining admission in
the fall of 1945. The months after my return were great! Life was
a honeymoon. Ginny and I lived in a two-room apartment with
a dirty, coal, cooking-heating stove, but we were together. At
school I was in an atmosphere where I didn't have to cringe
every time I heard the voice of my commanding officer. I retained
my well-learned Navy habit of going to sleep almost as soon as a
lecture began, but I found my courses in experimental psychology, individual differences, genetic psychology, and comparative
psychology fascinating.

I remember talking with other students after we received our
first test papers back. One of the undergraduates was saying
"Well, even one of the graduate students got a D on his test" and
I blushed and admitted that I was that graduate student. Nevertheless, by the end of the year I had made up the required undergraduate work and was awarded the Master's degree. By the
middle of the first year I knew that the G.I. Bill would provide
enough financial help to complete a Ph.D. and it seemed silly not
to learn more while I had the chance. Since every course was interesting, I fully intended to take all the graduate courses offered

(which was probably no more than a dozen). In fact, a
dent, Don Lauer, and I even persuaded the department to o
a new course, Learning, which had previously only been covere
as part of the major course in Systematic Psychology.

Probably the most significant thing influencing my career in
psychology occurred in the summer of 1946 when one of the assistant professors, Harold Guetzkow, asked me if I would like to
become a teaching fellow in the introductory course. There was
a persistent rumor that the decision to appoint me as a teaching
fellow came when I pitched the students to victory over the faculty in the annual faculty-student softball game. While I don't
believe the rumor to be valid, it is true that as a teaching fellow
the next year I pitched for the faculty and the faculty was never
thereafter defeated by the students.

In any case I enjoyed teaching and formed warm friendships
with Roger Heyns, Herb Meyer, Ralph Gibson, Ted Hariton,
Phil Sperling, Lee Danielson, Jerry Gurin, Libby Douvan, Marty
Hoffman, Lloyd Barenblatt, Elliott Mishler, Barbara Cook Pott-
harst, and the other teaching fellows. Harold established a weekly
dinner meeting of the teaching fellows in which we argued
about goals of the introductory course, worked out the administrative details of the course, and discussed teaching methods.
He pushed us toward empirical answers to our questions and
before the end of the first term we had designed a research study
and had begun work on various measures of attitudes and thinking which we could use as criteria for comparing the effectiveness
of three different methods of teaching. I was asked to act as research coordinator for the project and my $350 half-time teach-
ing fellowship was supplemented by $100 for coordinating the
research effort.

The research coordinator job was mostly administrative, but
it got me involved in research, and the fascination of research design, construction of measures, and especially data analysis really
hooked me. That year made me sure that I wanted a career in
teaching and research.

My interest in clinical psychology and personality theory continued to be strong and I took courses in personality theory, psychoanalytic theory, and psychiatry from Urie Bronfenbrenner, Dan Miller, Max Hutt, and Fred Wyatt, in our department as well as completing all the formal courses in psychiatry offered by the Psychiatry Department, but I also continued even after my Ph.D. to take each new course in statistics and mathematical psychology offered by Clyde Coombs, Leon Festinger, and others.

The research in the introductory course turned out to be my first experience in what has continued to be my major research interest—effective college teaching and the interactions of teaching methods and student characteristics in affecting student learning.

My doctoral research, another study of social psychological factors in college classrooms, was carried out during my third year of graduate work, 1947-48. Since the end of my graduate study seemed in view, I went to see Professor Marquis, the chairman of the department and chairman of my doctoral committee. He said, "Where do you want to go?" I said, "What kind of choices are there?" He replied, "You can pick any college or university in the country and I'll get you a job there!" What a contrast between the job market in 1948 and that in the 1970s!

In any case I told Dr. Marquis that I thought I'd like an innovative college, like Bennington or Sarah Lawrence where I could try new things in teaching and do research on them. A few days later he asked whether I would like to stay at Michigan to take Harold Guetzkow's place as coordinator of the introductory course and supervisor of the training of teaching fellows. This opportunity to make a career in what I was finding to be one of the most interesting parts of my graduate study was attractive at the time and continued to be a very satisfying way of life for me. Of the many lucky breaks that affected my career, being at Michigan at this time was probably most important, for few other departments and few chairmen other than Marquis would have supported a career in teaching and research on the teaching of psychology.

By this time my religious and intellectual interests were moving toward integration. During our first year and a half at Michigan, Ginny and I had visited forty-two different churches in the Ann Arbor-Ypsilanti area and had joined with sympathetic interest in the worship services of Pilgrim Holiness, Wesleyan Methodist (the shouting Christians), Unity, and all of the main line churches. I still thought of myself as a middle-of-the-road Presbyterian but when the Baptists asked me to pitch for their softball team, I was glad to accept and began forming friendships in the church. This alone might have induced us to join the Baptist Church but two more fundamental bases were influential. One was that the Baptists seemed to be the only campus church with Negro members; the other was the Baptist belief in the freedom of the individual to determine his own belief without conformity to creed. Since our beliefs were becoming humanistic rather than deistic, the fact that we did not have to accept a traditional creed was important. Even more important was the fact that the church seemed in its membership practices to implement what we believed to be the fundamental of Christianity— the brotherhood of man.

My religious commitment thus remained strong, but in many respects psychology became the vehicle for the expression of my commitment. I arranged to review psychology books for the *Christian Century;* I wrote a couple of articles for religious journals; I began teaching the course, "Psychology and Religion." But in addition to these formal attempts to bring psychology and religion together I brought to the teaching of psychology an evangelism for psychology as a force for social good, which I now view with some skepticism but sympathy as I see it in teaching assistants of the present generation.

Like many current graduate students I saw in psychology a potential for changing people and society. I believed that if individuals took a scientific approach they would be more skeptical of stereotypes, and if they had greater understanding of human behavior, they would be more tolerant and more humane in their interactions with other individuals and groups. One of the measures in my doctoral research was a scale of attitude toward

Negroes, and I saw this as a legitimate criterion of our ability to get across psychology's way of thinking in a manner that would lead it to have meaning for the individual beyond answering final examination questions.

Trite as it may be I still have much of my original naïve faith in the potential value of psychological research and teaching. I now have a greater awareness of the pitfalls and complexities; I still remain convinced that each individual must determine his own values and that as a teacher I have an obligation to protect his freedom by exposing my own values and differentiating so far as I can when I am expressing a personal value and when talking psychological fact or theory. Nevertheless psychology offers me a unique way of combining the great aesthetic pleasure of problem-solving and research with the religious value of promoting more humane relationships.

RESEARCH

My years as an assistant professor were marked by rich experiences with the graduate students who were teaching fellows in the introductory course, with increasing involvement with university and professional affairs, and with continued activity in research.

In graduate school one course stood out above all others—a course in research design taught by Don Marquis. Marquis introduced us to analysis of variance, whose elegance excited the almost aesthetic pleasure which mathematics has always given me and also met my needs for a statistical tool which would enable me to deal with more than one variable at a time. The concept of interaction between variables had great intuitive appeal to me, and even in my doctoral dissertation in 1948 I was looking for possible interactions in a complex double Latin square research design.

By this time I had chosen social psychology as my major field, and group dynamics was the big thing in social psychology in the post-World War II era. The Research Center for Group Dynamics had just moved to Michigan and its approach of integrating laboratory and field experiments was one which had enormous appeal for me. But to members of the Research Center for Group Dynamics staff at that time, groups were diagramed with empty circles representing group members. I can still remember heated arguments with one of the young assistant professors, Leon Festinger, in which I insisted that it made a difference what persons were inside each of these circles, while he argued that in a true science of social psychology, personal characteristics of group members would be irrelevant.

I guess that I've never given up trying to win that argument. The interest I expressed then has characterized my research for the last twenty years. I've always been concerned about individual characteristics as they interact with social psychological group characteristics and group variables. I can still remember my delight as I listened to Lee Cronbach's presidential address to the APA, "The Two Disciplines of Scientific Psychology," and I was enormously pleased when he sent me a reprint with the inscription, "This should have been dedicated to you as the guy who *works* on interactions."

The interaction hypothesis seemed an obvious one; yet the evidence supporting it is still rather scanty. Within the last couple of years Cronbach and Snow (1969) and Goldberg (1969) have written long monographs concluding that the hypothesis is still plausible but unproven. That is a conclusion whose validity I can't quite concede, even though I'd grant that results of research are less spectacular than I would have hoped for.

The problem is one of identifying appropriate individual difference variables linked to treatment variables and to appropriate criterion measures. I suspect that some of the difficulty in getting results has been in inadequacies in measures of each of these three sets of variables. But even more important have been the inadequacies in our theories about which variables should interact with which.

As I started work in this field and had to decide whether to start in terms of treatment variables or individual difference variables, it seemed to me that we had better theories and measures of individual differences than of the educational or social situation. So I started from the individual difference end and tried to think of what educational variables would interact with important individual differences. Jack Atkinson and Roger Heyns, two of my closest friends, were working on the projective measures for Achievement, need for Affiliation and need for Power, so it was no accident that I began with these needs. My students and I tried to categorize classroom situations in terms of cues to these needs. For example, we thought a person high in the need for Affiliation would be affected by the friendliness of his teacher and his classmates and by the personal interest taken by the teacher in students as exemplified by the teacher's knowing and calling on students by name. The result of our research studies came out fairly well for need for Affiliation—at least well enough to give us some sense of satisfaction—but with need for Achievement and need for Power, I was not very successful in identifying the sort of interactions I expected. At this point I think that there simply are so many variables involved in most natural situations that even with fairly firm theoretical notions one has difficulty tying down very much variance. Nevertheless, Dr. Yi Guang Lin, my long-time research associate, and I are still trying to identify interactions and reduce the amount of unknown identified variation little by little. Year by year we make some progress even though we've made no revolutionary discoveries.

Although much of my graduate training was in Hullian S-R theory and psychoanalytic theory, my own bias has increasingly been toward a more cognitive, expectancy orientation. This has meant that in our research we have always put heavy emphasis on student perceptions of teaching, which in turn has led us in two directions. The first was involvement in research on student ratings of teaching. I've always enjoyed using multivariate statistics, and the work on student ratings gave me the chance to use factor analysis (which I liked even when we did everything by hand) and multiple discriminant analysis to try to get at the dimensions which differentiate teachers.

The second direction in which emphasis on student perceptions led was to the study of student feelings. Clearly students had strong feelings about teaching. My interest in student feelings was greatly stimulated by association with Dick Mann, whose detailed studies of psychology classrooms gave me some of the same sense of revelation of new worlds as Leeuwenhoek's first observations with his microscope. The rich clinical detail of Dick's work struck the old chord of my continuing interest in personality and clinical psychology.

THE LIFE OF A YOUNG FACULTY MEMBER

Rather than being born "thirty years too soon," I've always felt that I was extremely fortunate in being at the right place at the right time. The University of Michigan during Marquis' tenure as chairman was an exciting place. The Psychology Department was young and vigorous; young people had unusual opportunities to participate in and influence the direction in which the department went. Marguis was quite willing to take chances on assigning responsibilities to his younger staff members and Jack Atkinson, Roger Heyns, Ed Walker, and I, who were among the younger staff, worked together on several fascinating projects. One of these was revision of the undergraduate curriculum.

The year before I received my doctorate I was placed in charge of the introductory psychology course and the training of the graduate students who were assisting in the teaching of the course. Shortly after that Marquis established the Committee on the Undergraduate Curriculum with Walker as chairman and we began to devise a curriculum which would make sense in terms of the goals of post-war psychology. Early in 1950 Marquis told me that the University of Michigan was to receive a grant from the Grant Foundation and the Carnegie Corporation to study the undergraduate curriculum. The funds had been obtained by Dael Wolfle, who at that time was executive officer of the American Psychological Association. Walker was not able to attend, and Marquis asked if I would be interested in participating.

When I expressed enthusiasm, he recommended me to Wolfle, and my wife and I spent the summer of 1951 at Cornell University with the Wolfles, Buxtons, Cofers, Gustads, and MacLeods—fine psychologists with nice families.

Cornell is a beautiful place in the summer and we had a wonderful time together. Before going to Cornell I had written to Robbie MacLeod asking if he could locate a class B or C softball team that needed a pitcher. Mrs. MacLeod called the local sports announcer, who put me in touch with the team from Varna. So two nights a week I played softball, with the MacLeods, Wolfles, Cofers, Gustads, and Buxtons cheering our team on. We won the league championship, but after the last game the manager of the Lehigh Valley Railroad team, our chief rival, called a special league meeting, which ruled that as an outsider I was ineligible to pitch and that our team must replay all the games I had pitched with me restricted to playing outfield. Our victories in these replayed games were especially satisfying to us and frustrating to our opponents and the final victory over Lehigh Valley narrowly missed turning into a melee.

It was during this summer that I realized that I was a thoroughgoing functionalist. Michigan, when I entered the department, was largely Gestalt in orientation. Marquis began bringing in representatives of S-R and psychoanalytic points of view. In our learning seminar Eleanor Maccoby vigorously presented Guthrie's position, so that I perceived myself as having a fairly eclectic knowledge of major viewpoints of psychology. When I bumped up against Robbie MacLeod, however, I found that there was a whole way of looking at psychology that I had largely missed and which I found tremendously interesting. His phenomenalist approach to psychology stimulated me to think through a number of issues that I had previously taken for granted, and the summer was valuable not only for lasting friendships with the other members of the group but also for the intellectual stimulation it provided.

The curriculum upon which our Cornell group finally reached agreement was much like the one Walker, Heyns, and I had been putting together at Michigan. Upon my return, I became chairman of the Committee on Undergraduate Curriculum and we worked out a curriculum based on that recommended by the conference (see Wolfle *et al., Improving Undergraduate Instruction in Psychology.* New York: The Macmillan Co., 1952). This curriculum worked well for almost a decade. By 1960 John Milholland had become chairman of the Committee on Undergraduate Studies in the department and when the curriculum began showing some signs of age, John and I organized another study of the curriculum. Lawrence Cole of Oberlin, William Hunt of Northwestern, Robert Leeper of Oregon, and Wilbert Ray of Bethany, joined Bob Isaacson, Jim McConnell, Ed Walker, John Milholland, and me in Ann Arbor and we spent the summer of 1961 re-debating the old issues, reviewing the results of a national survey of psychology curricula John and I had conducted, and devising new alternatives to the traditional curricular pattern (see McKeachie, W., Milholland, J. *et al., Undergraduate Curricula in Psychology.* Chicago, Scott, Foresman, 1961).

Marquis, Walker, Heyns, Atkinson, and I worked on other projects as well. All of us were deeply concerned about how peace might be maintained, and we spent some time developing a proposal for research on peace, which Marquis and I presented to a group of Harvard and MIT professors who were working with the State Department. We also developed a joint research project, funded by Ford Foundation money around the theme of conformity. While I carried out only one study in that program myself, we had many stimulating discussions and Roger Heyns and Ed Walker eventually wrote up the major substance of the project in their book, *The Anatomy of Conformity* (Englewood Cliffs, New Jersey: Prentice-Hall, 1962). Roger Heyns, Ted Newcomb, Dan Katz, Helen Peak, and I were also involved in an attitude change research project which provided many fascinating hours of discussion as well as some good doctoral dissertations by Milt Rosenburg, Earl Carlson, and others. My early years on the faculty at Michigan thus were ones in which I had an ideal environment in which to grow and develop.

My major role at this time was that of coordinator of the introductory psychology course and supervisor of the graduate students who conducted the discussion sections which accompanied the large lectures. I gave the lectures myself for one or two hours a week and the graduate students led discussion sections for two hours a week, meeting with me twice a week to discuss problems of teaching and the general administration of the course.

The graduate student teaching fellows were outstanding people. Many are now prominent researchers and teachers of psychology; several have since become chairmen. We argued about the objectives of the course; we compared notes on techniques of teaching; we supported one another during times of discouragement. Marquis gave us strong backing in the department. He contributed to the sense that doing an excellent job of teaching the introductory course was important and valued by the department.

As I worked with the graduate students year after year, I found that some problems came up again and again and I began to mimeograph the advice I generally gave. These mimeographed notes gradually grew in volume, and I began to gather and distribute them at the beginning of the year. As the teaching fellows took their own degrees and went to other universities, they began writing back for additional copies, and before long the requests became so numerous that I decided that I should lithoprint the notes and ask one of the local bookstores to distribute them. This was the genesis of my book *Teaching Tips,* which has probably given me the most satisfaction of anything I have written. It was never intended to be a major publication; in fact for many years I paid the printing costs and set a price only sufficient to return the money I had invested. Yet knowledge of the book spread by word of mouth so that over the years thousands of copies were distributed as people wrote in for copies. It spread beyond the boundaries of the United States to Europe and other continents and eventually D. C. Heath and Company asked to publish it commercially. Its sale has continued under their auspices in a sixth edition.

Teaching Tips represents two of the fundamental beliefs I developed in my years of helping graduate students learn how to teach psychology—that almost everyone can become a good teacher if he enjoys teaching and that almost everyone will enjoy teaching if he can be given some basic skills, tricks of the trade, or alternatives to try when his class isn't going well.

I liked the introductory course also because its content covered the whole range of psychology. John Shepard had imprinted me with a permanent interest in comparative, physiological, and sensory psychology and Don Marquis and Ed Walker continued to keep glowing my warm interest in learning and behavior theory. The teaching fellows represented all of the areas of psychology and I liked the way they kept me up to date with the latest developments. I delighted in insights we achieved of new ways of integrating laboratory findings in experimental psychology with observations and concepts used in personality and social psychology.

In 1950 Marquis asked if I would join him in revising Woodworth's classic introductory textbook. Selecting, thinking through, and writing in understandable prose what will be the most useful foundation for a student's life-long learning about behavior and experience was a major intellectual challenge in which over the next twenty years first Marquis and then Charlotte Doyle contributed to my intellectual development.

SPORTS

No account of my life in the Michigan Psychology Department would be complete without a section on athletics. For years a standard element of the graduate students' skit on faculty foibles was a Charlie Brown type of character with baseball hat and glove leading his psychology team out on the field to conquer their rivals from Mathematics, Physics, or Physical Education. While my own competitiveness and dedication to sports has no doubt been a factor in our department's preeminence in university athletics, a more fundamental reason is that Marquis, Melton, and others selecting staff and graduate students have believed that beyond a certain level of intelligence, an individual's contribution to psychology depended much more upon his energy output and work habits than upon additional points on the Miller Analogies test of ability. Thus both students and faculty at Michigan have been characterized by high energy levels—a quality likely to be associated with active participation in sports.

In any case I like the fact that my office has almost as much space for volleyball and softball trophies as for books. I wouldn't trade my thirty-one no-hit games for thirty-one more publications and when the Intramural Department began an annual award for outstanding faculty athletes, I was delighted to be the first recipient. In fact I can't resist adding that our team has just won once again the all-University student and faculty softball championship, and I pitched a two-hitter in the final play-off game.

ADMINISTRATION

After I had conducted the introductory course and chaired the Committee on Undergraduate Curriculum for several years, it seemed time for a change, and I was asked to become chairman of Graduate Studies. This provided a new challenge and I plunged into the task of reorganizing the graduate curriculum and working on recruitment of outstanding students. I found that recruitment was particularly enjoyable. I liked trying to identify the most promising potential psychologists and the challenge of attracting them to Michigan. I arranged to talk to prospective graduate students whenever I visited another college. The fact that I firmly believed that we offered the best graduate training in the country helped in the sincerity of the letters I wrote about Michigan, and I was very pleased when the rate of acceptance of our admissions rose by almost 50 per cent during the time I was chairman of Graduate Studies.

In the early fall of 1960 John F. Kennedy arrived in Ann Arbor on his campaign tour for the Presidency. Waiting until 2:00 a.m. around the steps of the Michigan Student Union Building were some 8,000 students. "How many of you would be willing to spend time in Africa and other areas working for the development of emerging nations in the cause of world peace?" he asked. The response was one not only of immediate enthusiasm but sustained commitment. In the days following, Alan Guskin, one of our graduate students, organized mass meetings of interested students and relayed to the Kennedy entourage the vigor of the student response to his challenge. While the Peace Corps also has other antecedents, University of Michigan students and faculty from the beginning felt a special responsibility. Thus it was that when Lowell Kelly, our departmental chairman, was asked to go to Washington to direct the selection of Peace Corps Works, he accepted. I was named acting chairman for the year he expected to be gone.

I entered into the work with great enthusiasm, feeling that I'd like to make that year a significant one in the history of the department rather than simply holding the line until Lowell returned. But by the middle of the year we learned that Lowell would not be able to return for still another year and that we must therefore choose a chairman for the next five-year term. For me this was bad news. It seemed likely that I would be one of those considered for the position since I was already doing it. But this was not something I had bargained for. I had in fact just the previous summer turned down offers to become vice president of another big ten university or to become president of a new college just being formed and had come to a firm conclusion that my career lay in teaching, training graduate students in college teaching, and research, rather than in administration.

As it turned out, I was nominated by the staff for the chairmanship, and since the dean of our college, Roger Heyns, was one of my best friends, he soon was able to convince me that I should take a five-year term. As I now conclude my tenth year as chairman and look forward once again to returning to full-time work in teaching and research, I have no regrets for the decision to accept the chairmanship. The ten years have often been frustrating but also frequently satisfying. Undoubtedly much that I did as chairman was based on my admiration for my predecessors, Donald Marquis and E. Lowell Kelly. They had built the Psychology Department at Michigan into one of the larger departments in the country, yet one in which there were high standards of quality, tolerance of differing points of view, and supportive interpersonal relationships.

The years 1946-60 had been golden years for our department. Marquis had during the war years been in charge of psychological personnel and thus had a good knowledge of who the most promising young psychologists were. During his tenure as chairman he brought in an outstanding group of bright, hard-working staff members. His ability to listen to each person's problems and aspirations and to apply his great intelligence to solving each problem gave us a sense of personal support of our own goals and identification with an outstanding group. We were convinced that we were good and that anything worth doing we could do, if not that year, in the years ahead. Moreover, because of the support for our own individual work there was little need to attack our colleagues' work and the department had an unusual openness and tolerance for diversity.

During Lowell Kelly's term as department chairman, we had had an opportunity to consolidate the period of growth and development that had occurred under Marquis, and as I assumed the chairmanship it seemed to me that there were new opportunities requiring expansion once again. I had some specific goals in mind. Michigan was known as being outstanding in clinical psychology and social psychology but our excellence in experimental psychology was not yet recognized, and I hoped to be able to build experimental psychology to the level of national prestige of our other major areas. I hoped to strengthen clinical psychology by establishing better relationships with the Department of Psychiatry, which at that time had very little representation of our regular clinical psychology staff, provided few opportunities for the training of clinical psychology interns in the Neuropsychiatric Institute, and gave psychiatric residents little opportunity to observe the potential contributions of first-rate clinical psychologists.

In addition to these specific goals I had some general objectives.

I obviously had strong interests in maintaining and increasing the quality of our teaching in both the undergraduate and graduate levels. I saw Michigan as a department in which new areas of research could develop and graduate students could be trained to carry these new developments into other departments. I hoped that along with their intellectual excitement they would transmit the humane patterns of interaction which were valued at Michigan with students and colleagues.

We had already pioneered in social psychology, mathematical psychology, and clinical psychology. During my years as chairman we continued to produce outstanding students in these fields and built on the foundations laid by Marquis and Kelly in human information processing, brain and behavior, organizational psychology, and school psychology. We developed new programs in developmental psychology, community psychology, psychopharmacology, and psycholinguistics.

Our attitude was typified when we considered whether to pursue computer simulation as a field of research and training. I was impressed by the publications of Herb Simon, Al Newell, Walt Reitman, and the enthusiastic group of computer simulation experts, but I wasn't sure whether they were simply talking to one another or could make a significant contribution to psychology as a whole. One psychologist who seemed to me in a position to understand and evaluate this was George Miller, who was then department chairman at Harvard. I called him and asked his advice. "Go ahead," he said. "With only four tenure positions in psychology Harvard can't take a chance. We have to stay in the traditional central areas. But Michigan is big, strong, and prestigious. You can afford to gamble. Someone needs to find out what computer simulation can do. Only a department with strong experimental psychology as well as the willingness to take risks on new approaches can give it a fair chance." We did.

But not all my goals were in terms of strengthening areas of teaching and research. One of the most satisfying achievements of the department during the years of my chairmanship was our leadership in training black psychologists.

This was not in my mind when I became chairman. Like most liberals I had always been committed to the goals of racial equality and integration. Ralph Gibson had been a friend in graduate student days. As teaching fellow coordinator I had hired Bob Davage as a teaching fellow, suffered with his efforts to find landlords who would rent to Negroes, and chaired his doctoral committee. As graduate chairman I had spent an evening in Yellow Springs recruiting Del Jenkins for graduate work at Michigan and I had worked to get grants for summer institutes to bring black students and faculty from the South to study in our department. But it took Roger Heyns, Pat Gurin, Dan Katz, Herb Kelman, Dick Mann, and other colleagues to help me see that we were never going to solve the problem of under-representation of blacks in psychology by passive, well-intentioned non-discrimination. We began recruiting able black students more nearly like our coaching staff recruits football players and thus we were a little bit ahead of the social changes that led to widespread active recruitment of black students. Once a critical mass of bright, committed black students had gathered in our department, they provided able leadership in recruiting more black students and faculty. Not that there have been no problems. There have, and there will no doubt be more. But I am confident that our Michigan black Ph.D.'s will be making contributions to society in the years ahead that would be impossible for a white psychologist.

At the end of five years, my own enjoyment of the position and my sense that there were still jobs to be done persuaded me to accept another term as chairman. My wish was to take the chairmanship for a second term of only three years, but our dean, William Haber, persuaded me to agree to another full term of five years with the option of resigning before the end of that period if I felt that this were appropriate. The eighth year was a sabbatical year for me. During the year I kept thinking of problems I would like to work on when I returned to the chairmanship, so it wasn't difficult for him to persuade me to stay on for the last two years.

The job of department chairman is, I think, particularly fascinating to a psychologist, especially one with my enjoyment of problem solving and of helping other people achieve their goals. When I took the position I had some doubts about my ability to be tough enough to maintain the high standards Marquis and Kelly had set, and I knew that Clyde Coombs and other colleagues thought I was too nice a guy to be chairman. But even though I find it difficult to be aggressive to another person in behalf of my own interests, I can press very hard for a group which I represent. (I suspect that this is one of the reasons I've always preferred team sports to individual sports.) The mythology that developed about my forcefulness and craft in getting resources for the department from deans and vice presidents was only occasionally supported by empirical success, but it is certainly true that I tried hard.

And the inevitably difficult decisions to let friends and colleagues leave the staff are also made. Here my Calvinist sense of duty proves to be pretty deeply ingrained. Much as I dislike moralistic justifications for one's behavior, there is no doubt that the pain I feel when I must give terminal notice to a fine person who is good but not outstanding is balanced by a sense that I have done my duty. In fact there is probably still a little bit of my Scotch grandfather's dour feeling that duty should not be easy.

I learned early that one of the easiest mistakes in administration is to write a memo or letter whenever one dreads telling someone bad news in person. I still have trouble in taking responsibility for an adverse decision myself rather than speaking ambiguously about departmental policies or the "consensus of the Executive Committee." It seems to me that everyone deserves the chance to confront a person and argue against those decisions that affect him. The more the decision is depersonalized by letters, committees, abstract policies, and a bureaucracy, the more frustrating and damaging for the individual.

Department organization and management was a continuing intellectual challenge. During my tenure the staff of the department increased in size from ninety to two hundred. Healthy organisms grow, and I was keenly aware of the great advantages in morale and avoidance of conflict when staff members can see their areas of interest growing stronger and larger. But at the same time, size threatens the individual's sense of personal identity and of his ability to have personal influence on the direction in which the department is going. As Art Melton once said, "When I was a young man at Missouri the president of the university consulted me whenever decisions with respect to psychology were made; here as one of seventy full professors of psychology I know I can't have the same influence, but I miss it."

I tried to maximize the advantages of size while preserving individual participation by decentralization of much authority. I think this helped, but I was never satisfied with my ability to monitor the performance of each of the subunits. I think some of the sense of identification with the department as a whole depends upon personal knowledge and trust of the key figures in administration. Thus I tried hard to keep up with each staff member's activities and to talk with him or her personally as often as possible—which may not be very often with almost two hundred staff members scattered in twenty-five buildings. As an administrator I liked working with the Executive Committee and each year was impressed by their creativity and good judgment; I enjoyed our staff meetings and the vigorous debate coupled with mutual respect; I liked interacting with individual staff members, and it was this that I missed as my role shifted to greater functioning in reviewing and monitoring the work of an intermediate level of organization and administration.

Growth has, as I've indicated, many advantages in reducing conflict and competition for scarce resources. Priority decisions are not difficult when the decision is between those plans to implement now versus those to be done next year. Yet, again, largeness has many disadvantages. In coping with these our department was fortunate in having a large corps of cooperative secure permanent staff whose broad interests helped to maintain a sense of community even as it became impossible for every member of the department to know all his colleagues personally. The department was also fortunate in having a structure in which the key committee, the Executive Committee, was elected in a manner which gave most staff members trust in the fairness and wisdom of those elected. The norms of tolerance and pluralism persisted despite the lack of interpersonal interaction and liking which had supported them when the department was smaller.

Although there were many kind and thoughtful statements of appreciation and urgings to continue as chairman during the last year of my second term as chairman, I became more and more convinced that it was time for a change. While I saw more to do, I thought that a new chairman with different strengths and weaknesses would correct my errors before they became crippling to the department. In addition to feeling that a change would be good for the department, I thought that a change would be good for me.

Some of the characteristics I was developing as department chairman were not ones I liked. I like to think of reason and evidence as the primary determiner of university decisions, and while I recognized and enjoyed the power of the department chairman, I rarely let issues get to the point where the resolution was simply dependent on who had the greatest power. But I found that I was growing increasingly impatient and tempted to threaten resolution of issues by the use of power. When the members of the clinical psychology staff were slow to accept and provide support for community psychology, I reminded them that I had delegated to them the administration of the training grant in clinical psychology and that I was quite ready to reassume its control if they didn't shape up. As soon as I said it, I felt like a blustering childish bully.

Similarly I threatened the use of power against administrators above me. Our budget for supplies was never enough to last the year. When I heard that chemistry stores had been told not to accept orders from psychology I called the controller to tell him that the day a "stop" order was placed on psychology requisitions he should be prepared to explain to 8,000 psychology students why their classes could no longer be taught. We kept on buying animal food and mimeograph paper.

Just as I disliked my growing tendency to think in terms of power, I disliked my increasing sense of status and self-importance. Before becoming chairman I had revelled in the role of bright young man. I enjoyed popping up in meetings with new ideas. Some of the ideas were good, some bad, but the bad ones were quickly rejected and no harm was done. Soon after becoming chairman I was disturbed to find that my ideas were being taken too seriously. I could no longer say something stupid and have it ignored. People assumed that when I tossed out a suggestion I was promulgating a policy.

While I developed some control over my utterances, I still utter too many unhelpful ideas, and I discovered that not only did others take them seriously, but as time wore on I was beginning to take them seriously myself.

This, as much as anything, persuaded me that I should get back into a position where I had to stand on my own rather than rely on the status and power of my position.

An academic man is not supposed to enjoy the role of department chairman. It is often perceived as being onerous and unrewarding. For me, however, it was a real opportunity to feel that I could have some impact upon the field to which I am dedicated not only in terms of the training of our own students, but in the impact Michigan, as a leading department in the country, could have upon psychology nationally and in other universities. Moreover the department chairmanship met my personal needs. I really enjoyed the chance to talk to psychologists in all areas of the field. Through recruiting staff, reviewing research and training grant proposals, talking to site visitors and reading the publications of our staff, I had opportunities to hear of the new findings and the hot ideas long before they were generally known. I liked the feeling of being a real general psychologist.

UNIVERSITY AFFAIRS

Anyone interested in effective teaching is inevitably drawn into involvement in the affairs of the college or university where he teaches. I was an academic counselor, chairman of the Committee on Student Opinion of Courses and Teaching, member of the

Committee on the Program in Religion, member of the Honors Council, chairman of the College Committee on Curriculum, and along with service on many other committees was elected chairman of the University Faculty Senate.

Any faculty member who is reasonably conscientious and thoughtful can make a real contribution to the intellectual climate of his campus through involvement in university policymaking; he can also waste a great many hours. While a lot of committee work could be avoided if faculty members were more willing to trust deans and other administrators, I think active faculty participation is valuable and I believe psychologists have particular contributions to make. In my experience psychologists more than other professors are likely to question assumptions and ask for evidence, a quality we share with law professors, who are delightful associates on committees; but linked with our rather hard-headed empiricism is a concern for individuals, not always shared by the lawyers. This doesn't mean that psychologists do not come in all shapes and sizes of irrationality and prejudice, but I can't help believing psychologists are something special.

The achievement in which I took most pride as a committee member was the creation of Michigan's Residential College, a small liberal arts college within the larger university. When I became chairman of the College Curriculum Committee, I asked Roger Heyns, who had become our dean, to come to a meeting to discuss some major problems of the college which might provide a focus for our ideas. One of the problems was that of the size of the college and the resulting loss of continuing personal intellectual interaction between students and between students and faculty. He suggested that one possible solution might be the organization of small residential colleges within the larger college. This idea excited us and we spent the year developing plans for the college. Our proposal was passed on to other committees and eventually the faculty voted to approve the creation of the new college. The first class has now graduated and although I have had little direct involvement in the college's development I take paternal interest in its troubles and achievements.

APA

Another source of interest and satisfaction for me has been the American Psychological Association. I have been on almost every major board and committee of APA. I'm not exactly sure how I first came to be involved. I suspect that Claude Buxton had something to do with it, for even while I was a graduate student, I knew of Claude and his work in training graduate students as teachers of psychology at Northwestern University and corresponded with him about what we were trying to do at Michigan.

In any case, I was invited to present a paper on our research on the teaching of psychology at the APA Convention at Pennsylvania State University in 1950. The Division on the Teaching of Psychology was a natural home for me and since attendance at business meetings of the division was sparse in those days (as it still is), I soon became known as someone interested and willing to work and was appointed chairman of the Committee on Research in the Teaching of Psychology.

I also served as program chairman for the division and expanded the program from approximately four hours to twenty hours by virtue of recruiting a number of papers from friends and others who were active in research on the teaching of psychology. When I was elected president of the division in 1956, I was told that I was the youngest divisional president in history.

When APA developed its new structure of boards, the Educational and Training Board established a committee on undergraduate teaching, which Claude Buxton chaired. Our committee developed a series of analyses of issues in college teaching which form part of the substance of Claude's book *College Teaching, A Psychologist's View* (New York, Harcourt, Brace, 1956). A little later I became a member of the Education and Training Board itself and have maintained almost continual involvement with one or another committee or board of APA ever since.

My interests in professional affairs of psychologists developed not only from involvement in committees and in groups concerned with the teaching of psychology and appropriate curricula for psychology but also from concerns with the practice of psychology, particularly the private practice of psychotherapy. This concern was truly adventitious. I might well have maintained a traditional academic life secluded from the life of professional psychologists had it not been for a sequence of events beginning the year after I completed my Ph.D., when the University of Michigan began a series of television courses on Station WWJ, Detroit.

The university's Television Center felt that one area of much interest to the public was psychology and asked Don Marquis if it would be possible to develop a psychology course for television. Don asked me to do it and relieved me of lecturing in the introductory psychology course in order that I might prepare a series of fourteen programs on psychology.

Since television was a new and an exciting educational tool, I jumped at the chance and began working with Hazen Schumacher, Robert Newman, and other members of the university's Television Center on the preparation of the series.

Television teaching was hard work. The preparation was much more demanding than that for regular classroom lectures. The television staff kept reminding me that people could tune me out very rapidly if they lost interest and that if I were to use television as a medium, I needed to be much more concerned about the visual aspects of my teaching than I had ever been before. So we developed outlines of the program, worked out ideas for visual aids, rehearsed short dramas illustrating points, and each week drove into Detroit on Sunday morning for a run through with the director and camera man before presentation of the show live at noon.

The audience response was remarkably good. Many people sent in for a set of reading materials we developed to go with the televised presentation. Polling techniques indicated that we were drawing a large portion of the television audience. I discovered that while I had conceived of my audience as being a very heterogeneous group of laymen, most of my colleagues and many of the psychologists in the state were also interested observers. Moreover since this was probably the first telecourse in psychology in the United States, I became known as an expert on television all across the country.

The course's unexpected impact on my professional reputation was probably a major reason that I was elected president-elect of the Michigan Psychological Association the following year. And it was during my year as president-elect (1953) that the attorney general of the state of Michigan ruled that psychotherapy was a medical technique and that psychotherapists must thus be medical doctors.

While there were relatively few psychologists in private practice in psychology in Michigan at the time, the ruling aroused psychologists in all fields. The Michigan Psychological Association, which had been a relatively small and quiet organization, suddenly boomed in membership and we immediately formed a committee to seek legal recognition of psychology. Orlo Crissey of General Motors was the first chairman of the committee, but when his duties prevented him from continuing, I became the chairman of the Committee on Certification as well as president of the State Association, being persuaded by the past president, Marie Skodak, and my other fellow officers that this was the highest priority concern of the association. Our committee represented all types of psychologists from all parts of the state and worked hard and long in developing a proposal for certification of psychologists, which would be a model for such legislation. With the help of the Bureau of Legal Research of the university and Jane Hildreth of the central office of APA, we developed a good deal of expertise on various issues involved in certification and licensing. Eventually we submitted a proposal which was adopted by the Michigan Psychological Association and was the basis for the law passed by the Michigan legislature, albeit after amendments and alterations which made the final law considerably less of a model than we had hoped it would be.

As a result of this heavy involvement with the state association, I became active in the Conference of State Psychological Associations. The Conference of State Psychological Associations was a semi-autonomous organization, meeting at the time of the American Psychological Association and having representation on the APA Council, but with its own independent budget and its own officers. Before long I was elected chairman of CSPA, but by that time those of us active in state associations felt that the states must play a more vital and direct role in APA affairs. We worked to have direct state representation on APA Council. When this change was made, we disbanded CSPA and turned our funds over to APA to be used as loan funds for any state associations experiencing difficulty with their legislative efforts.

It was ironic that only a decade or so later, as a member of the Board of Directors of APA, I participated in Council meetings in which the recommendation was passed that states should be taken off APA Council and the Division of State and Professional Affairs be formed to represent the interests of the state associations. While I pleaded that this was simply going back to a system which had been given up for good reasons, the new division was formed. Fortunately the idea of state representation was not abandoned and by-law changes preserving state representation on APA Council were approved. Thus the cycle is completed.

Why have I devoted so much time to APA? One reason certainly is my continual sense of awe that I should be interacting as a peer with the great names of contemporary psychology. I can remember how impressed I was at seeing the Board of Directors march into the annual meeting at early APA conventions I attended. We're not now as impressive a group, but I still have a sense of wonder that I should be on a first name basis with the men and women who are shaping contemporary psychology.

But there is more to it. I was not facetious when I suggested at a recent APA Board of Directors meeting that for me, and perhaps for others as well, one of the functions of APA is to serve as the organized expression of our major value commitment. Just as I remain active in the Baptist Church, so too I work in APA to help achieve some of the goals of scientific and professional contributions to mankind which I believe psychology can make.

This has brought my story up to date. The life of a psychologist is a good life. In each of the past twenty years I've received several inquiries about my interest in a deanship, presidency, or some other administrative position. Invariably I've replied that I was happy in my present position. One of the major reasons for my lack of interest in "higher" administration is my identification with psychology and my feeling that to move into a higher administrative position would threaten my identity as a psychologist. Being a psychologist is an important part of "me." Now after ten years as a department chairman, I'm looking forward to returning to full-time teaching and research in psychology. I look forward to this with mingled anxiety and eagerness. I know that as a fifty-year-old full professor, I cannot achieve the same rapport with my students that I had as a twenty-five-year-old teaching fellow. Can I still make learning exciting? I'm not sure, but I feel that this is where my roots are and that I need to get firmly and deeply into the reality of the classroom.

BIBLIOGRAPHY

1939 Holly High School (Holly, Michigan) "Fight song," with Robert Bravender, first performed in 1939.

1950 Anxiety in the college classroom. *Papers Michigan Academy,* 1950, *36,* 343-49.

Summary of Second Annual Conference on Research in the Teaching of Psychology. *Newsletter Committee on Teaching Social Psychology,* SPSSI, 1950.

What about the Church? *Young People,* January 22, 1950, 4-6.

1951 Anxiety in the college classroom. *Journal of Educational Research,* 1951, *45,* 135-60.

REPRINTED IN:

J. Seidman (Ed.), *The Adolescent.* New York: Dryden Press, 1953. Pp. 576-83.

A. P. Colodarcci (Ed.), *Readings in Educational Psychology.* New York: Dryden Press, 1953.

Readings in introductory psychology. With D. Beardslee, D. Dulany and others (Eds.) Ann Arbor: George Wahr, 1951. Pp. xiii-347.

A Review Outline of General Psychology. (Ed.) Ann Arbor:

George Wahr, 1951. (2nd ed.) Ann Arbor: George Wahr, 1955.
The Church can use science. *The Churchman,* August 1951.

Personality and independent study. With Kathryn Koenig. *Journal of Educational Psychology,* 1951, *50,* 132-34.

A program for training teachers of psychology. *American Psychologist,* 1951, *6,* 119-21.

Teaching tips: A guidebook for the teaching of general psychology. With G. Kimble. Ann Arbor: Author, 1951. Pp. 105.

1952 *Improving undergraduate instruction in psychology.* With C. E. Buxton and others. New York: Macmillan, 1952. Pp. vii-60.

Man in his world: Human behavior. Ann Arbor: University of Michigan Extension Service, 1952.

Teaching psychology on television. *American Psychologist,* 1952, *7,* 503-6.

Lipstick as a determiner of first impressions of personality. *Journal of Social Psychology,* 1952, *47,* 25-27.

A rating-ranking scale for goals of life. With H. Guetzkow. *Religious Education,* 1952, *47,* 25-27.

Review of H. A. Overstreet, The great enterprise. *The Christian Century,* September 24, 1952, 1097.

Review of H. J. Eysenck, Dimensions of personality, The scientific study of personality, and The structure of human personality. *The Christian Century,* January 26, 1952, 112.

Review of Swami Akhilananda, Mental health and Hindu psychology. *The Christian Century,* February 6, 1952, 162.

Review of A. A. Roback, History of American psychology. *The Christian Century,* December 3, 1952, 1408.

1953 Effects of different instructions in multiple choice examinations. With R. C. Teevan. *Papers Michigan Academy,* 1953, 39.

Teaching tips: A guidebook for the beginning college teacher. With G. Kimble. (2nd ed.) Ann Arbor: George Wahr, 1953. Pp. 107.

1954 An experimental comparison of recitation. Discussion and tutorial methods in college teaching. With H. Guetzkow and E. L. Kelly. *Journal of Educational Psychology,* 1954, *54,* 193-207.

Individual conformity to attitudes of classroom groups. *Journal of Abnormal and Social Psychology,* 1954, *49,* 282-89.

The problem-oriented approach to teaching psychology. With W. Hiler. *Journal of Educational Psychology,* 1954, *45,* 224-32.

Student-centered vs. instructor-centered instruction. *Journal of Educational Psychology,* 1954, *45,* 143-50.

REPRINTED IN:

J. P. DeCecco (Ed.), *Educational technology: Readings in programmed instruction.* New York: Holt, Rinehart and Winston, 1964.

G. J. Mouly. *Handbook in Educational Psychology.* In Press.

Church groups and mental health. *Pulput,* 1954, *25,* 342-43.

College teaching and student motivation. *Improving college and university teaching,* 1954, *2,* 39-41.

Objectives of the general psychology course. With R. DeValois and others. *American Psychologist,* 1954, *9,* 140-42.

The structure of the state psychological association. *American psychologist,* 1954, *9,* 810.

Past, present, and future in the relation of psychology to general education. Galesburg, Illinois: Knox College, 1954.

1955 Relieving anxiety in classroom examination. With D. Pollie and J. Speisman. *Journal of Abnormal and Social Psychology,* 1955, *50,* 93-98.

REPRINTED IN:

F. A. McGuigan and A. D. Calvin (Eds.), *Current studies in psychology.* New York: Appleton-Century-Crofts, 1958. Pp. 53-59.

The teaching of psychology: A survey of research since 1942. With R. Birney. *Psychological Bulletin,* 1955, *51,* 51-68.

Current enrollment trends and college teaching. *Improving College and University Teaching,* 1955, *3,* 87-88.

Improving your teaching. *Adult Leadership,* 1955, *3,* 14-16.

REPRINTED IN:

How to teach adults. Chicago: Adult Education Association of U. S. A., 1955.

Religion and social science. *Religious Education,* 1955, *50,* 306-7.

Three problems of general education. *Improving College and University Teaching,* 1955, *3,* 42.

1956 Group dynamics: Implications from research for instruction and for institutional programs. In G. Kerry Smith (Ed.), *Current issues for higher education.* Washington, D.C.: Washington Association for Higher Education, 1956.

Mental health and ministers. With W. Allinsmith and L. Berman. *The Pulpit,* 1956, *27,* 4-17.

Teaching tips: A guidebook for the beginning college teacher. (3rd ed.) Ann Arbor: George Wahr, 1956.

Review of E. S. Bordin, Psychological counseling. *Michigan Alumnus Quarterly Review,* 1956, *62,* 181.

1957 The joy of teaching. In D. Louise Sharp (Ed.), *Why Teach?* New York: Henry Holt, 1957.

Retention of general psychology. With D. Solomon. *Journal of Educational Psychology,* 1957, *48,* 110-12.

Student ratings of faculty: A research review. *Improving College & University Teaching,* 1957, *5,* 4-8.

1958 How do students learn? In R. Cooper (Ed.), *The two ends of a log.* Minneapolis: The University of Minnesota, 1958.

Motivating students' interest. In R. Cooper (Ed.), *The two ends of a log.* Minneapolis: The University of Minnesota, 1958.

Students, groups, and teaching methods. *American Psychologist,* 1958, *13,* 580-84.

REPRINTED IN:

Newsletter, Educational Psychology Division, National Society of College Teachers of Education, Spring, 1958, 1-3.

W. Morse and M. Wingo, *Psychology and teaching.* (2nd ed.) Chicago: Scott-Foresman, 1962.

J. B. Murray (Ed.), *Readings in educational psychology.* Jamaica, New York: St. Johns University Press, 1963.

The Bobbs-Merrill Reprint Series in the Social Sciences.

Hamachek, D. E. (Ed.), *Human dynamics in psychology and education: Selected readings.* Boston: Allyn and Bacon, 1968.

Student ratings of instructors: A validity study. With D. Solomon. *Journal of Educational Research,* 1958, *51,* 379-83.

REPRINTED IN:

Special Reports. U.S. Office of Education, Circular No. 3, 1959.

Teaching psychology by telephone. With R. Cutler and E. McNeill. *American Psychologist,* 1958, *13,* 551-52.

Report of the university of Michigan project under the program of grants for the utilization of college teaching resources to the Ford fund for the advancement of education. 1958. Pp. 43.

Research training in the graduate curriculum. *Psi Chi Newsletter,* January 1958, 18-21.

TV for college instruction. *Improving College and University Teaching,* 1958, *6,* 84-88.

1959 *The appraisal of teaching in large universities.* (Ed.) Ann Arbor: University of Michigan Press, 1959.

Appraising teaching effectiveness. In W. J. McKeachie (Ed.), *The appraisal of teaching in large universities.* Ann Arbor: University of Michigan, 1959. Pp. 32-34.

Conceptions of human nature. In L. F. Miller (Ed.), *Digest of Proceedings,* Institute for Employee Development Officers, U. S. Civil Service Commission, 1959.

Group decision makes democracy work. *Religious Education,* 1959, *46,* 90-91.

The interactions between student anxiety and teaching approach in learning mathematics. In R. Feirabend and P. DuBois (Eds.), *Psychological problems and research methods in mathematics training.* St. Louis: Washington University, 1959.

The interaction of personality variables with teaching methods affecting college learning. In R. Feirabend and P. DuBois (Eds.), *Psychological problems and research methods in mathematics training.* St. Louis: 1959.

A program for training teachers of psychology, Mark II. With R. L. Isaacson. *American Psychologist,* 1959, *14,* 658-59.

1960 Changes in scores on the northwestern misconceptions test in six elementary psychology courses. *Journal of Educational Psychology,* 1960, *51,* 240-44.

The role of the faculty in improving the instructional program. In W. Blaketor (Ed.), *Proceedings, 1960 Judson College Faculty Workshop.* Marion, Alabama: Judson College, 1960.

Studies of teaching effectiveness. In J. K. Folger (Ed.), *Proceedings Institute on Institutional Research.* Atlanta, Georgia: Southern Regional Education Board, 1960.

Teaching methods. In W. Blaketor (Ed.), *Proceedings, 1960 Judson College Faculty Workshop.* Marion, Alabama: Judson College, 1960.

College teachers and the learning process. In J. W. Gustad, *Faculty preparation and orientation.* Winchester, Massachusetts: New England Board of Higher Education, 1960.

The instructor. In G. Finch (Ed.), *Education and training media.* USAF-NAS-NRC Symposium, 1960, *789,* 22-33.

Recitation and discussion. In O. Lancaster (Ed.), *Achieve learning objectives.* University Park, Pa.: Penn State University, 1960. Pp. 1-37.

Behavioral sciences can improve college teaching. *NEA Journal,* 1960, *49,* 79-81.

Certification of psychologists. *American Psychologist,* 1960, *15,* 51-52.

An honors program in psychology. *Journal of General Psychology,* 1960, *63,* 179-83.

The instructor faces automation. *Improving College and University Teaching,* 1960, *8,* 91-95.

REPRINTED IN:

H. A. Estrin and D. M. Goode (Eds.), *College and university teaching,* Dubuque, Iowa: Brown, 1964.

Problems of the minister's home. *Church Management,* 1960, *37,* 38-41.

Textbooks to come. *Contemporary Psychology,* 1960, *5,* 11.

To be good, teaching should be fun. With E. Bordin. *Senate Affairs,* 1960, *7,* 3-4.

"Prayer," a short choral composition with words by John Bowring. Performed by the choir of the First Baptist Church since April 1960.

The improvement of instruction. *Review of Educational Research,* 1960, *30,* 351-60.

Individualized teaching in elementary psychology. With B. Forrin and Y. Lin. *Journal of Educational Psychology,* 1960, *51,* 285-91.

Teaching tips: A guidebook for the beginning college teacher. (4th ed.) Ann Arbor: George Wahr, 1960.

The value of effective teaching in liberal arts college. In W. Blaketor (Ed.), Proceedings, 1960, *Judson College Faculty Workshop.* Marion, Alabama: Judson College, 1960.

What do the research findings from behavioral sciences suggest concerning the improvement of teaching and learning? In G. Smith (Ed.), *Current Issues in Higher Education.* Washington, D. C. NEA, 1960.

1961 Motivation, teaching methods and college learning. In M. R. Jones (Ed.), *Nebraska Symposium on Motivation,* 1961. Lincoln, Nebraska: University of Nebraska Press, 1961.

 Translated as motivation, Lehrmethoden und Lernen in Hochschulen. In Franz Weinert (Ed.), *Padagogishe Psychologie.* Koln & Berlin: Kiepenhuer & Witsch, 1967.

REPRINTED IN:

R. G. Kuhlen (Ed.), *Studies in educational psychology.* Waltham, Massachusetts: Blaisdell, 1968.

Size of class and institution as a factor in enjoyment of teaching. With E. Bordin. *Journal of Higher Education,* 1961, *32,* 339-42.

Teaching effectiveness. *Senate Affairs,* 1961, *8,* 1-3.

Understanding the learning process. *Journal Engineering Education,* 1961, *51,* 405-8.

The psychology of learning as applicable to effective college teaching. In *A regional faculty orientation program.* Harrisburg, Pennsylvania: Pennsylvania Association of Colleges and Universities, 1961.

What do research findings reveal that might increase the effectiveness of teaching? In A. Henderson, *The Annual Conference on Higher Education in Michigan.* Ann Arbor: University of Michigan, 1961.

Recitation and discussion. In O. Lancaster (Ed.), *Achieve learn-*

ing objectives. University Park, Pennsylvania: Penn State University, 1961, 1963.

Undergraduate curricula in psychology. With J. E. Milholland. Chicago: Scott, Foresman, 1961.

1962 Current research on teaching effectiveness. *Improving College and University Teaching,* 1962, *10,* 15-19.

REPRINTED IN:

H. A. Estrin and D. J. Goode (Eds.), *College and university teaching.* DuBuque, Iowa: William Brown, 1964.

Internships in college teaching. In D. L. Delakas and R. R. Taylor (Eds.), *On the threshold to academic careers.* Madison: University of Wisconsin, 1962.

Psychological content in high school social studies. In B. Berelson (Ed.), *The social sciences and the social studies.* New York: Harcourt, Brace & World, 1962.

A Review outline of psychology. With S. Komorita, Ann Neel, and M. Wagman. Paterson, N. J.: Littlefield, Adams, 1962.

Teaching scientific psychology in the denominational college: Comments. In A. A. Schneiders and P. J. Cente, *Selected Papers from the ACPA Meetings of 1960, 1961.* New York, American Catholic Psychological Association, Fordham University, 1962.

Procedures and techniques of teaching. A survey of experimental studies. In N. Sanford, *The American college.* New York: Wiley, 1962.

REPRINTED IN:

Western Interstate Commission for Higher Education and Center for Research and Development in Higher Education. *The individual and the system.* Berkeley: Center for Research and Development in Higher Education, 1967.

1963 College teaching and student motivation. In H. A. Estrin and R. W. Van Houten (Eds.), *Higher education in engineering and science.* New York: McGraw-Hill, 1963.

Problems and perils in controlled research in teaching. In E. R. Sternberg (Ed.), *Needed research in the teaching of English.* Washington, D. C.: U. S. Office of Education. Coop. Res. Monog. No. 11, 1963.

Psychological characteristics of adults and instructional methods in adult education. In R. G. Kuhlen (Ed.), *Psychological backgrounds of adult education.* Chicago: Center for the Study of Liberal Education for Adults, 1963.

Correlation of teacher personality variables and student ratings. With R. L. Isaacson and J. E. Milholland. *Journal of Educational Psychology,* 1963, *54,* 110-17.

Religion, sex, social class, Probability of success and student personality. With R. W. Carney. *Journal for Scientific Study of Religion,* 1963, *3,* 32-42.

"Lullaby," a Christmas cradle song. Composed with Linda McKeachie). 1963.

Research on college teaching. In N. Gage (Ed.), *Handbook of research on teaching.* Chicago: Rand McNally, 1963.

REPRINTED BY Council of Social Work Education for distribution to Schools of Social Work.

Translated as *Que revelan les invistigaciones sobre los metodos de ensenanza universitaria* by J. Diaz Bordenave and Carmen Coto. Lima, Peru: Instituto Interamericano do Ciencias Agricoles de la OEA, 1966.

Needed research on psychological factors in learning as related to the social studies. In R. A. Price (Ed.), *Conference on needed research in the teaching of the social studies.* Syracuse, New York: Sagamore Conference Center, Syracuse University, 1963.

W. W. Charters, Jr., and N. L. Gage (Eds.), *Readings in the social psychology of education.* Boston: Allyn & Bacon, 1963.

1964   Approaches to teaching. In N. Sanford (Ed.), College and character. New York: Wiley, 1964.

"I bind my heart," a hymn with words by Lachlean MacLean Watt (composed with Virginia McKeachie). First sung by congregation and choir of First Baptist Church, Ann Arbor, February 1964.

Dimensions of student evaluations of teaching. With R. L. Isaacson, J. E. Milholland, Y. G. Lin, Margaret Hofeller, J. W. Baerwaldt, and K. L. Zinn. *Journal of Educational Psychology,* 1964, *55,* 344-51.

The college teacher and creativity. In D. Schwartz (Ed.), *Creativity in its classroom context.* Lexington, Kentucky: Bulletin of Bureau of School Service, University of Kentucky, 1964.

Psychology and college teaching: A survey of recent experimental studies with implications for the future. In M. Whiffen (Ed.), *The teaching of architecture.* Washington, D. C.: The American Institute of Architects, 1964.

Motives and learning. *Sound seminars,* Cincinnati, Ohio, 1964 (a recording).

Ambivalance in graduate education. *American Psychologist,* 1964, *19,* 682-83.

A look at the teaching machine. *Toledo Blade Sunday Magazine,* March 15, 1964, 4-5.

E. Page (Ed.), *Readings for educational psychology.* Harcourt, Brace & World, 1964.

Research on the characteristics of effective college teaching. With R. L. Isaacson and J. E. Milholland. Final Report: Cooperative Research Project No. OE 850, Ann Arbor, Michigan, 1964.

1965 The faculty's role in policy making. *Michigan Daily,* January 26, 1965.

Automation: New media in education—Concerns and challenges. *College and University Bulletin,* 1965, *18*(3), 1-5.

The discussion group. *Memo to the faculty,* No. 14. University of Michigan, Center for Research on Learning and Teaching, 1965.

REPRINTED IN:

P. Bordinat, *On the art and craft of college teaching.* Wright State College, Ohio, 1966.

The Delta Pi Epsilon Journal, 1966, *9,* 1-5.

The learning process as applied to short term learning situations. New Brunswick, New Jersey: National University Extension Association, 1965.

Psychology. In H. N. Rivlin (Ed.), *The first years in college.* Boston: Little, Brown. 1965.

Teaching tips: A guidebook for the beginning college teacher. (5th ed.) Ann Arbor: George Wahr, 1965.

Spanish edition. (transla.) Carmen Coto Compés and Enrique Sanchez Narvaez. Mexico Hirrero Hermanos Sucesors Mexico S.A.

1966 Review of B. E. Collins and H. Guetzkow, A social psychology of group processes for decision making. *Administrative Science Quarterly,* 1966, *10,* 545-47.

Effective Teaching: The Relevance of the Curriculum. In L. E. Dennis and J. F. Kauffman, *The College and the Student.* Washington: American Council on Education, 1966. Pp. 189-91.

Research in teaching: The gap between theory and practice. In *Improving College Teaching: Aids and Impediments.* Washington: American Council on Education, 1966. Pp. 28-56.

Higher Education. In P. H. Rossi and B. J. Biddle, *The new media and education.* Chicago: Aldine, 1966.

The teacher in higher education. *Changing dimensions and demands of the profession.* California Teachers Association, Los Angeles, 1966.

Functions of APA. *American Psychologist,* April 1966, *21* (4), 372-74.

"No trespassing," a Civil Rights song, words by John Sherwood, 1966.

Instructors' manual (to accompany *Psychology*). With L. A. Siebert and J. S. Caldwell. Reading, Massachusetts: Addison-Wesley, 1966.

Personality, sex, subject matter, and student ratings. With R. E. Carney. *Psychological Record*, 1966, *16*, 137-44.

Student affiliation motives, teacher warmth, and academic achievement. With Y. Lin, J. Milholland, and R. L. Isaacson. *Journal of Personality and Social Psychology*, 1966, *4*, 457-61.

Psychology. With Charlotte Doyle. Reading, Massachusetts: Addison-Wesley, 1966.

1967 The cast of multiple models. *The Clinical Psychologist*, 1967, *20*, 108-10.

Cooperative versus competitive discussion methods in teaching introductory psychology. With D. B. Haines. *Journal of Educational Psychology*, 58, 1967, 386-90.

New developments in teaching. *New dimensions in higher education*, No. 16. United States Office of Education. April 1967.

Some thoughts about teaching the beginning course in psychology. With E. L. Walker. Belmont, California: Brooks/Cole, 1967.

Translated into Spanish and Portuguese, Brooks/Cole, 1968.

Significant student and faculty characteristics relevant to personalizing higher education. In J. W. Minter (Ed.), *The individual and the system*. Boulder, Colorado: Western Interstate Commission for Higher Education, 1967. Pp. 21-35.

The means of achieving educational objectives in the classroom. In E. Foreman (Ed.), *The improvement of instruction: The instructional process*. Macomb, Illinois: Western Illinois University, 1967.

1968 Review of A. Rez Arasteh, Teaching through research: A guide for college teaching in developing countries. *Contemporary Psychology*, 1968, *13*(2), p. 109.

Review of Joel R. Davitz, and Lois Jean Davitz, A guide for evaluating research plans in psychology and education. *Contemporary Psychology*, 1968, *13*(8), pp. 410-11.

Encyclopedia psychology. In David L. Sills (Ed.), *International Encyclopedia of the Social Sciences*. New York: Macmillan and Free Press, 1968. 17 vols. Pp. 9, 520.

Reviewed by W. J. McKeachie, R. Heine, R. Dixon, M. Hoffman, E. Douvan, and A. W. Melton in *Contemporary Psychology*, 1971, *16*(1).

Memo to new department chairmen. *Educational Record*, 1968, *49*, 221-27.

REPRINTED IN:

Academic professional development associates. *The department chairman—His many roles and functions.* Chicago: APDA. In Press.

Report of the Recording Secretary. *American Psychologist*, 1968, *23*, 854-56.

The importance of teaching. A memorandum to the new college teacher. With Committee on Undergraduate Teaching. New Haven, Connecticut: The Hazen Foundation, 1968.

Psychology at age 75: The psychology teacher comes into his own. *American Psychologist*, 1968, *23*, 8, 551-57.

Research characteristics of effective teaching. U. S. Department of Health, Education, and Welfare, Office of Education, Bureau of Research, Project #05950, Grant #OE-4-10-001, Ann Arbor, 1968. Pp. 850. With R. Isaacson, J. Milholland, and R. Mann.

Student achievement motives, achievement cues, and academic achievement. With J. Milholland, R. Isaacson, and Y. Lin. *Journal of Consulting and Clinical Psychology*, 1968, *32*, 26-29.

REPRINTED IN:

Selected academic readings. New York: Simon & Schuster, 1968.

1969   The faculty: Who they are, what they do. In Southern Regional Education Board, *The College Campus in 1969*, Atlanta, Georgia: SREB, 1969.

Field experience in the psychology curriculum. In W. C. Sheppard (Ed.), *Proceedings: Conference on Instructional Innovations in Undergraduate Education.* Eugene, Oregon: University of Oregon, 1969. Pp. 113-23.

The interaction of achievement cues and facilitating anxiety in the achievement of women. *Journal of Applied Psychology*, 1969, *53*(2), 147-48.

Achievement standards, debilitating anxiety, intelligence and college women's achievement. With Y. Lin. *The Psychological Record*, 1969, *19*, 457-59.

Student ratings of faculty. *American Association of University Professors Bulletin*, 1969, *55*(4), 439-42.

Toward an educational psychology of higher education. *Educational Psychologist*, 1969, *2*, 6, 13-14.

The organization of a large department of psychology. *American Psychologist*, 1969, *24*(7), 659-61.

State associations: A view from the board (of directors of the

APA). *Michigan Psychologist*, April 1969, *28*, 8-12.
REPRINTED IN:
Psychotherapy Bulletin, August 1969, 2, 11-12.
A public policy conference for psychologists. *American Psychologist*, 1969, *24*, 6.
Teaching tips: A guidebook for the beginning college teacher (6th ed.). Boston: D. C. Heath, 1969.

1970 Aptitude, anxiety, study habits, and academic achievement. With Y. Lin. *Journal of Counseling Psychology*, 1970, *17*(4), 306-9.
Goals and activities of male and female college students. With Y. Lin. *Education and college student survey*, 1970.
The relationship between student-teacher compatibility of cognitive structure and student performance. With Y. Lin, M. Wernander, J. Hedegard. *Psychological Record,* 1970.
Attitude change: Resistances and conflicts. In W. L. Heimstra (Ed.), *Dynamic christian growth.* Proceedings of the 17th Annual Convention, Christian Association for Psychological Studies. Grand Rapids, Michigan, 1970.
Instructors' manual (to accompany *Psychology*). With J. S. Caldwell and M. Freedman. Reading, Massachusetts: Addison-Wesley, 1970.
Psychology. 2nd ed. With Charlotte Doyle. Reading, Massachusetts: Addison-Wesley, 1970.
Report of the Recording Secretary, *American Psychologist*, 1970, *1*, 9-12.
Research on college teaching: A review. Washington, D.C. ERIC Clearinghouse on Higher Education, 1970.

1971 APA's organizational state may be critical but not *In Extremis. Professional Psychologist*, 1971, *2*, 33-34.
Student ratings of teacher effectiveness: Validity studies. With Y. Lin and W. Mann. *American Educational Research Journal*, 1971, *8*, 435-45.
Conflict and style in the college classroom—An Intimate Study. With Barbara Ringwald, Richard Mann, and Robert Rosenwein. *Psychology Today*, February 1971, *4*, 45-49, 76-79.
Land, M. L., Weebes, H., and Denham, A. (Ed.), *Selected Academic Readings.* New York: Simon and Schuster, 1971.
Sex differences in student response to college teachers: Teacher warmth and teacher sex. *American Educational Research Journal*, 1971, *8*, 221-26.

Research on college teaching. *Memo to the Faculty*. University of Michigan Center for Research on Learning and Teaching, May 1971.

Building a new program. *College and University Bulletin*, November 1, 1971, *24*(3), 3-4.

Goals and activities of male and female college students, *College Student Journal*, 1971, *5*, 12-16.

8

Toward Humanizing Social Psychology

M. BREWSTER SMITH

I am a social psychologist and have so regarded myself since long before I had any clear idea of what the field was really about. (My first secure sense of the shape of the field came only after I had been teaching it for a couple of years: the conventional course of lectures may be a deplorable mode of instructing the student, but it is an excellent way of educating the instructor!) But as a sample of one, I have been deviant, not at all typical of the field of social psychology as it has developed over the past two decades.

In an era when laboratory experimentation was the main order of the day, I did none except as a student. My research has mainly involved interviewing and survey analysis, and even so, I cannot regard myself as primarily a research psychologist. I have taught undergraduate and graduate students for almost a quarter-century at Harvard, Vassar, N.Y.U., Berkeley, Chicago, and now the University of California at Santa Cruz, for some students a good teacher but I have never regarded myself as a particularly skillful one. I have been an editor of psychological journals. I have been an academic administrator as a department chairman at Vassar and Chicago, a research institute director at Berkeley, and now at Santa Cruz as what would elsewhere be called a dean of social sciences—but throughout I seem to have retained much of the ambivalence toward administrative roles that is instilled by the research-oriented values of graduate education. I have invested a good deal of time in the affairs of the American Psychological Association and in participation in government advisory committees. I have maintained close intellectual relations with colleagues in clinical and developmental psychology and in the mental health professions without ever being a mental health professional, while, outside of psychology, I have also at one time or another been in good communication with political science, sociology, and, to a lesser extent, anthropology. All of these activities, most of which are unrepresented in what follows, are part of my identity as a psychologist.

And, with increasing clarity, I have struggled to make sense of an emerging three-way commitment: to a psychology that seeks to come to grips with human experience (and is in that sense "humanistic"), to a psychology that broadly abides by the rules of the game of science as a public, self-critical, and therefore cumulative social enterprise aimed at the comprehensive understanding of the phenomena in its territory, and to one that bears helpfully on the urgent social problems that hinge on an ingredient of human cussedness. That has made me a generalist—at a time when ever more intensive specialization has been the predominant trend. The things I have done that have pleased me most, in writing and teaching and consultation, have been efforts at conceptual mapping and clarification, of establishing relevance and cutting across established boundaries, more than the direct products of my research. To an extent greater than I sometimes like to admit, I have been an "armchair psychologist." If there is an "Establishment" in psychology and the social sciences, I am nevertheless surely a member of it, but—I hope—I am something of a maverick. Since this disorderly and atypical career seems to have made more sense, after all, than I should have had any reason to expect, it may serve the purposes of this enterprise for me to probe lightly into some of the circumstances behind the pattern of commitments that in middle life now seems reasonably clear to me. The path to where I now am was certainly not guided by much foresight and rational decision.

ONE PATH TO PSYCHOLOGY

I came from an academic family with virtually no contacts in the business world, and when I began college at Reed in 1935, I took it for granted that I would go on to some professional or graduate school. Through my father, an English professor and dean at a then inconspicuous western state university, I knew more about Ph.D. training than about the launching of any other career. Following childhood interests in natural history—especially insects and fossils, I first tentatively saw myself as a biologist; brilliant teaching that I encountered in my freshman year lured me to history. But it was the professor, not the field that had attracted me, as I learned when as a sophomore I had to put up with mediocre teaching in the subject. By then, I had begun to get seriously interested in psychology, for a tangle of reasons that I imagine is not uncommon.

There was a great teacher: William "Monty" Griffith, a huge, brilliant Rabelesian figure of a man who as I learned later regarded himself as a failure because he could never bring himself to complete his doctoral dissertation, but was then very much a success in making psychology real and interesting to bright students. There was delayed adolescent confusion (I was two years young for my class), in which late bull sessions with friends, deepening involvement in student radicalism (Depression-style), and the fascination of Portland's small Bohemia for a very proper and socially timid small-town boy came to compete all too effectively with the automatic role of good student that I had previously played so successfully, without having really made it part of my chosen self. (There was guilt and anxiety, too, about classes missed, work undone, and the resulting scholastic tailspin.) And there was a girl, a senior psychology major, my devotion to whom carried over to her field.

I could claim with some validity that psychology represented an ideal "synthesis" between the "thesis" of biology as my initial undergraduate interest and the "antithesis" of humanistic history and my family background. But it is obvious that I was mainly drawn to psychology because of preoccupation with my own inner problems. By then I was enrolled in premedical courses with the predictable goal of psychiatry in mind—but the academic collapse that cost me credit for half my junior year ruled out that possibility. In a mixture of shame at my failures, wry satisfaction at having salvaged *that* much from what threatened utter disaster, and misgivings about the future, I transferred provisionally to Stanford the following summer.

Yet I have always been grateful to Reed for letting me discover myself, however painfully. At that time we could not yet read Erik Erikson about the "identity crisis" that he has added to our vocabulary. Reed with its intensely intellectual nonconformity and its potent self-sustaining culture shared by students and faculty provided a high-risk, high-gain educational setting in which identity crises were provoked and new identities forged. For me, it was a kind of salvation, but of course I think so because the "I" that looks back was essentially formed there.

Stanford was a success, capturing me irrevocably for psychology, and I stayed on a second year for a master's degree, working with E. R. Hilgard on Kurt Lewin's new topic of "level of aspiration." (I also did a study of human learning with him: Hilgard and Smith, 1942.) From Hilgard, then young and newly from Yale, I learned valuable lessons about digging for the *psychology* in a problem, as he liked to put it: getting behind the trappings of method and stylish topic to underlying questions that are psychologically interesting. (An acute nose for psychological problems, as Hilgard has always had, is what differentiates good psychology from ritual busywork, of which there is too much.) My interests in psychology, as I remember them, were not yet clearly focused, but they turned mainly in a personality-social-clinical direction, and both my gradually relaxing Marxism and my perennially hypersensitive social conscience inclined me to social psychology. For further doctoral training the excellent choice between Harvard and Yale was opened to me. One of my

Stanford mentors, C. P. Stone, with whom I had published a minor rat study (Stone and Smith, 1941), urged Harvard; another, Lewis Terman of the Stanford-Binet—the grand old man of the department—urged Yale, and my reading with Hilgard in Clark Hull's early system-building in behavior theory might well have tipped the balance that way. But I still possessed no real basis for intelligent choice, and as I remember it I made the decision for Harvard on the flimsiest and most nonrational of grounds: a girl who was going from Stanford to Radcliffe. My father's Harvard Ph.D. probably had more to do with my choice than I then liked to admit.

Only later did I realize how decisive the choice had been. The pre-war Harvard department was a collection of dissensual prima donnas: Gordon Allport, Henry Murray, and E. G. Boring, among those who became particularly important to me. Yale in contrast was the base for a vigorous consensual research group dominated by Clark Hull and his neobehavioristic learning theory. Had I gone to Yale, I would surely have been assimilated to the "Yale school" and launched upon a clear trajectory of research agenda. At Harvard, graduate students were exposed rather to a remarkably stimulating cafeteria of choice. Like Reed, high-risk, high-gain, as I look back on it. For many, the experience was disorienting. For me, the result was that I came out more my own man.

Two major things happened on my route to psychology during my year and a quarter at Harvard before I was drafted into the Army right after Pearl Harbor. The main focus of the first year was a horrendously demanding intensive-extensive "proseminar" chaired by Boring, the great historian of psychology, and involving several other faculty in their specialties. When this had been capped off by the fearsome "preliminary examinations" for doctoral candidacy, I surely knew more book-and-journal psychology than I ever have since. It was crammed in every whichway, and I had to rely upon a cooperative unconscious to organize and digest the jumbled facts and theories—something that has always worked for me, though I gather it is not well-advised practice generally. I think that students today whose graduate training makes less heroic demands on them are missing something.

The other major happening was my first encounter with two memorably contrasting representatives of personalistic psychology, in the charismatic figures of Gordon Allport and Harry Murray. Saul Rosenzweig (1970), whose Harvard years were somewhat earlier, has felicitously matched Murray, Allport, and Boring with the id, the ego, and the superego in Freudian psychoanalysis: the fit is uncanny. At the old yellow clapboard building of the Psychological Clinic, where I had a cubbyhole and an intellectual-social home, Murray made the study of human fantasy seem a royal road to the understanding of hardly formulated human depths, and made us, students and junior colleagues, feel like bold explorers. Up in the chaster environment of Emerson Hall, Allport expounded the unique individual and fended off as best he could the hostile forces of psychoanalysis (at the clinic) and of behaviorism and positivism (elsewhere in America). He taught us how to formulate and write life histories, and (in this, joining with Murray) involved us in trying to apply the slim resources of our psychology to the real-life problems of civilian morale, in the tense period while a neutral America watched the ominous war in Europe. (Our seminar papers were supposedly circulated in Washington, and this impressed us.) He emanated an atmosphere of "high seriousness," of social and ethical concern.

In the fall of 1941 I sought to delay being drafted by joining the psychoanalyst Walter Langer in work on the psychological analysis of various countries for his brother William Langer, then head of the Office of the Coordinator of Information, the predecessor of OSS. I shudder to think of the callow hypotheses I promulgated about the character structure of the Finns and the Portuguese in this primitive attempt at "culture and personality" study from secondary sources in English. The gains were a U.S. Civil Service appointment form as junior psychoanalyst (which I still treasure as a souvenir) and staying around Harvard at a time of high intensity, when recent refugees from Hitler's Europe—especially Frederick and Gertrud Wyatt who became my life-long friends—were bringing a complex and fascinating cosmopolitanism to an already heady atmosphere. Six of us graduate students had rented a slum house near Harvard for $15 a month apiece, where by our parties we probably hastened the break-up of the Psychology Department whose tensions we sought to dispell. (The others included Silvan Tomkins, Robert Holt, and John Harding, with whom I have remained in touch over the years.) But Pearl Harbor came, and I was drafted immediately after, the first in the department to leave for the war. Characteristically, I was afraid after my warm and enthusiastic send-off that I might be rejected and have to slink back.

As a reluctant draftee in a war in which virtually all of us believed, my first experience was unacademic but psychologically invaluable: immersal in the tough and colorful culture of young working-class Americans, mainly Texans. A good contrast from Harvard, and from my whole previous life! Later on as an enlisted man and as an officer, I took a turn at several aspects of personnel psychology (which I never felt tempted to make my professional specialization); finally I joined the Chicago sociologist Samuel Stouffer's research branch of the Information and Education Division, working first with the psychologist Carl Hovland on experimental studies of the impact of orientation films on soldier attitudes, and then on sample surveys of various aspects of soldier morale, attitudes, and motivation—in the United States, in the Mediterranean theater, and at the very end of the war, in the Pacific. The assignments entailed a lot of responsibility, the work was exciting and important. We were doing "relevant" research on things like the AWOL and desertion problem among the veteran troops on the Italian front, psychoneurotic breakdown in combat, officer-enlisted and Negro-white relations in the Army, and the venereal-disease problem among troops in Italy and in the Philippines. When after four years I got out of the Army as expeditiously as I could, I was really a psychologist, not just a student of psychology.

My fate in the Army had fortunately involved me with three major strands in the making of social psychology as it emerged vigorously in the post-war years. Survey research and analysis as heavily influenced by Stouffer's group has been a primary source of data for public opinion research and descriptive social psychology, especially as practiced by sociologists. And the experimental study of persuasive communication and attitude change —another major strand carried forward in the 1950's in a highly productive program at Yale led by Carl Hovland—was a direct outgrowth of the experimental Army studies in which I had served a brief apprenticeship. I add Hovland to my list of great teachers for his uncommon gifts in Socratic questioning to bring clarity out of obscurity in the design and interpretation of research, but he did not succeed in making an experimentalist out of me. I returned to go to Harvard, not to Yale.

The third strand was "symbolic interactionist" sociology as represented by Arnold Rose, later an eminent sociologist but then incongruously an enlisted man teamed up with me, an officer, in North Africa and Italy. From our running dyadic seminar over more than a year of the kind of close association that a joint overseas assignment can develop, I "internalized" much of the Chicago tradition of social psychology as a specialty of sociology, not psychology. I also was re-educated in the social psychology of prejudice and race relations, vicariously benefitting from Arnold's just completed experience as junior collaborator in Myrdal's classic study of the Negro in America (1944). His prickly sensitivity to unjust status differences, which I felt uncomfortably on many occasions, very likely saved me from over-identifying with my officer role.

When I was finally released from the Army at the end of 1945, I was filled with a sense of urgency to disclose the "real" story that our inquiries and my privileged vantage points made me want to tell: my old romantic radicalism was still there. I had the idea of writing a popular muckraking book that would draw upon our Army data, and, after getting my Ph.D. degree, of going into applied social psychological research, maybe under the auspices of a labor union. The point of decision, when I had to wonder whether or not I was "selling out," occurred very shortly when Stouffer invited me to join with several other former members of the research branch, civilian and military, in the reanalysis and write-up of the vast data from our studies for the Army, an undertaking that eventually led to the publication of *The American Soldier* (Stouffer et al., 1949). This was a realistic opportunity and challenge that, in the balance, made more sense to me than embarking on crusading journalism, for which I had no preparation or models.

My chapters in *The American Soldier* were my first major piece of published work. I analyzed the pertinent survey data and wrote about the motivations that sustained troops in ground combat, about the special situation and the attitudes of soldiers assigned to the "rear echelon," and about the predicament of green replacement troops assigned to veteran combat units. This was good practice in the older style of survey analysis, using the IBM counter-sorter with decks of the already efficient punch cards of coded data. I still like the direct contact with emerging findings and the flexibility of analytic tactics with the counter-sorter better than the distance imposed by the efficiently programed analyses that are required by modern electronic computers. (I pay tribute to Stouffer's mastery of this research style in my biography of him in the *International Encyclopedia of the Social Sciences* (1968c).

Later on, I experienced a mixture of pride and chagrin when Merton and Kitt (1950) reinterpreted my analysis of the replacement data in their classic paper setting forth a generalized theory of "reference groups," groups to which one refers comparatively in appraising one's own situation. I had presented and discussed some provocative comparisons, drawn from surveys of divisions that were waiting in England for the invasion of Normandy: combat veteran infantrymen in veteran divisions that had seen various amounts of previous action in the Mediterranean theater versus green replacements in the same veteran divisions versus infantrymen in completely inexperienced divisions. In their willingness for combat, for example, the replacements stood squarely between the veterans and the inexperienced troops (the veterans being by far the most unwilling); in their attitudes toward their noncommissioned officers they were by far the most favorable; while in their confidence in their own ability as combat leaders they were much the lowest. I had offered a commonsense interpretation of this mixed pattern of morale indicators. In some respects, the replacements partially took over the attitudes of the veterans around them (thus their intermediate willingness for combat). But they also reacted to the fact that their new outfit and its members had the prestige of combat experience (thus, their more favorable attitudes toward their noncoms, and also their higher pride in their companies). Yet in comparison with the veterans who were available to them *for* comparison, they naturally felt ill equipped to take the lead in combat. Well and good, but I later envied the imagination of Merton and Kitt who were able to cast these ad hoc interpretations into the coherent, generalized framework of reference group theory, as following from the fact that veterans were a positive reference group for the replacement soldiers in the veteran divisions. The more general account is more elegant and simpler.

Back, then, to Harvard, where I had only the dissertation to finish to attain the Ph.D. that I still coveted. I opted to take my degree in the new Department of Social Relations, a pioneering interdisciplinary venture joining social and clinical psychology with sociology and cultural anthropology, rather than in psychology from the now residual department. During the summer of 1946 when I was winding up my writing for *The American Soldier,* I was also working with Jerome Bruner and Robert White whom I had known as junior faculty in the pre-war department. We were planning a research project on the personal dynamics of public opinion that was being generated in the new Laboratory of Social Relations at Harvard that Stouffer was shortly to join as director. I returned to Harvard in the fall, technically still a graduate student but also project director of our joint study at the clinic. Being the director helped a lot: at that point the petty indignities of the unadulterated graduate student role would have been hard to take.

The study on which I embarked with Bruner and White was the investigation of personal determinants of attitudes toward Russia that some years later, resulted in our *Opinions and Personality* (1956) which is still around in paperback. (Conflicted delay in getting things written up has always been one of my problems.) Bruner at that time was still primarily identified with social psychology and public opinion research; he was just at the point of initiating his studies of personal factors in perception that formed the bridge to his later brilliant career in cognitive research and developmental psychology. White was a careful and original psychologist of personality in the broadly psychoanalytic tradition, who combined many of Murray's interests with something of Allport's disciplined and well-controlled style. This naturally inclined him to the reformulation of Freudian "ego psychology," as in his subsequent work on competence (1959), which later influenced my thinking profoundly.

Our study had two major components. At the clinic, a large group of investigators studied the personalities and the opinions about Russia of ten adult men, in repeated sessions over several months that included intensive interviews, projective tests, and tests of cognitive abilities. The senior members of the investigating group met as a "Diagnostic Council" to arrive judgmentally at a formulation of each "case." They followed research traditions established at the clinic by Murray in his classic *Explorations in Personality* (1938), which I had read at Stanford, and had been part of the appeal of Harvard for me. Each member of the council was responsible for administering at least one procedure and for formulating at least one case. My special responsibilities among the subjects of our study were the communist "Hilary Sullivan" (Smith, Bruner, and White, 1956, pp. 154-88) and the accountant "Clarence Clark" (pp. 203-10). Significantly in terms of my persisting later interests, I selected for my part of the data collection a two-hour semi-structured recorded interview on "personal values and religious sentiments." According to our plan, the intensive clinic study was to provide us with the kind of rich qualitative data about people's opinions in the full context of their personalities that should enable us to refine and elaborate our understanding of the kinds of relationships that obtain between opinions and personality. (We well understood that the qualitative study of ten cases could not provide solid evidence to test particular hypotheses.)

The second facet of the study, an interview survey of a representative sample of adults conducted in Springfield, Massachusetts, was intended to provide quantitative evidence for some of the relationships that we thought we discerned in the earlier phases of the clinical investigation. I analyzed these data for my doctoral dissertation (1947a, 1947b).

It was the intensive, qualitative study that most fascinated me. I discovered that an interviewer who listens intently can learn a great deal about matters that are important in people's lives by asking them—and also reading between the lines; and that what one learns in such a direct, essentially *collaborative* relationship may be even more important, or at least more cleverly relevant to understanding what the other person thinks and does, than the beguiling results of inferences from projective techniques and fantasy characteristic of "depth psychology." I also learned that the psychopathologically slanted Freudian account of defense mechanisms gives an impoverished and distorted picture of the versatile adaptive strategies that "normal" people use in coping with their life situations.

Before *Opinions and Personality* took final form, the three of us had many discussions in which we progressively reformulated the "natural history of opinioning" as we eventually presented it. We discerned among the ten men whom we had come to know so well three basic modes in which their opinions bore on their processes of adaptation: *object appraisal,* according to which the opinion or attitude reflects a sizing up of the relevance of its object for the person's values, interests, and concerns; *social adjustment* (I would now (1968b) prefer to speak of *mediation of self-other relations*), according to which holding or expressing an opinion promotes a desired relationship with other people or a desired identity; and *externalization and ego defense,* according to which the person's opinions serve as a kind of projection screen for the expression or working out of one or another of his unacknowledged inner problems. The same pie could have been cut along somewhat different lines, as it has been by other theorists (e.g. Katz and Stotland, 1959). But I think our clinical, qualitative study established quite definitively that theories are simplistic and inadequate if they try to reduce the psychological basis of opinions to some single process, like projection or displacement. It also provides an explicit place (in object appraisal) for the kind of rational processes that seems essential for human dignity but had been too much ignored by clinical and social psychologists—a theme to which I returned much later (Smith, 1968a).

SOME TURNING POINTS

If I had become a psychologist by the time I left the Army, I was duly anointed when I gained the doctorate in the fall of 1947, after writing my thesis in six harried weeks (also the first six weeks of my marriage: my wife suffered cooperatively!) in preparation for my initial academic job on the Harvard faculty. I have written in some detail about my *becoming* a psychologist because these steps should have particular meaning for undergraduates. The career vicissitudes that followed are of less interest here, and I will therefore touch on only a few turning points that seem salient as I review the development of my thinking and activities as a psychologist.

One came early. As a new assistant professor in the Harvard Department of Social Relations, I thrived on the interdisciplinary atmosphere and on my new responsibilities in teaching, when I was also in charge of the tutorial system and honors program. But I found myself increasingly paralyzed by the sensed pressures to get on with significant independent research. I was reacting most unconstructively to the competitive atmosphere of the department. Hoping that I would find therapeutic help as well as useful training, I embarked with Dr. Helen Tartakoff in a personal psychoanalysis as a research candidate at the Boston Psychoanalytic Institute. (I was able to use the G.I. Bill to pay for it.) But a year of analysis left me even closer to sheer panic. When the opportunity arose, I fled to an excellent teaching and administrative position at Vassar.

In retrospect, I have never regretted having done so. I do not believe that, had I stayed with my analysis, I could have worked through the special reasons for my "hang-up" at Harvard in time to deal with the very real problems it created. Flight on relatively good terms was the best thing I could do at that juncture. I often think back on this experience as I see young untenured faculty reacting in equally unconstructive ways to the pressures of appraisal and "publish or perish." I also gained substantially from my very incomplete exposure to psychoanalysis, although I did not stay with it long enough for it to help me solve my problems. I learned experientially something of what psychoanalysis is about—which has given me a firmer sense of perspective in my occasional reading in the psychoanalytic literature. And I also learned a good deal about myself, posing issues for an informal self-analytic agenda that I have practiced from time to time ever since as they have taken new forms in my changing life situation.

I became well acquainted with the ghosts of my childhood relations with my parents, who now appeared to me loving but in essential respects very inadequate and conflicted people who held inordinately high and narrow aspirations for me. In knowing and living with myself I prefer to recognize these ghosts even if I cannot really exorcise them. I saw more clearly how some of my still recurring problems in my psychologist work-role—sometimes paralyzing self-doubt and guilt that blocked me from research and writing in ways reminiscent of my debacle at Reed—also had roots in my vulnerable past as a fat, unathletic boy two years younger than my classmates, an inadequate player of the male role all the way through adolescence. Perhaps most important, I painfully discovered the great gulf between intellectualized "insight" and real personality change, the absence of any magic, black or white, in psychotherapy. (But I continue to value insight for its own sake—being who I am, I could not do otherwise.)

Another formative experience, after three years at Vassar, was four years on the staff of the Social Science Research Council in New York, ending in 1956. In staffing several research planning committees of the council that dealt with matters as diverse as cross-cultural research on socialization and the problems of foreign students, I performed an honorable but largely unsung role of midwife to *other* people's research ideas—and learned how to write creative minutes, a knack that has since served me in good stead. I was also cultivating the interdisciplinary perspectives that had been sown in my association in the Army and in the Social Relations Department. Of course, I ran the risk of losing my standing and identity as a psychologist, as I very likely would have had I not at the same time been serving as editor of a major journal in personality and social psychology—another midwife role, but one that is more honored.

Because I was still young, and felt younger and short of self-confidence, I was more tolerant then than I could be now of the careful and meticulous busywork that predominated in my journal as in most others. While I tried to favor more substantial reports, I was necessarily chary about imposing my own private standards on the journal over which I held temporary steward-ship. As an editor for the American Psychological Association, I was perforce partly a bureaucratic functionary. The kind of personal editorial leadership exercised by Gordon Allport in an earlier era of the same journal was no longer possible, or so it seemed to me, and that was a loss.

Meanwhile, my family was growing, and the children (three boys and a girl engendered before my wife and I became aware of the population crisis) became for me, an only child, a crucial part of my education as a psychologist—though a part that I felt strongly should be kept "human" rather than "scientific." While I was still teaching at Harvard, I remember encountering All-port on the steps of Emerson Hall with the exultant news of the

birth of our first son, and my dismayed exasperation at his bene-
diction, "Marvellous, Brewster. Every psychologist should have
a child and a dog." In fact, my wife and I bought a Siamese cat
to "raise by the book," as an only half-facetious strategy for
working out what we feared might be our propensity for raising
our child by a book. (We developed a very neurotic cat, and
found it the highest praise when friends said that the young
Smiths did not act like psychologists' children.) Spock was useful,
all the same, mainly for his reassurances and medical advice.
Mostly we felt that our "child-rearing techniques" were heavily
determined by who we were, what was possible for us. If we
didn't apply much psychology in raising our children, I could
still learn much that books and journals can never provide from
them, and from self-discovery in the new role of "grown-up" that
children impose upon their parents. A whole set of assumptions
about language learning was ruled out for me by our first child's
"first word"—when at maybe eighteen months he pointed up,
sharing delight, to say "Moon!"

In 1955 circumstances cast me as an officer of the Joint Commission on Mental Illness and Health, a venture established by
act of Congress that in spite of being enmired in the baroque
interprofessional politics of medicine, psychiatry, and psychology
eventually produced an important report (Joint Commission,
1961), one that helped to shift the emphasis from the grim state
hospital to community-based approaches to the treatment of severe psychological disturbance. In working with task forces and
committees of the Joint Commission, I discovered that my perspectives and sense of strategy as a social psychologist were useful
and sometimes influential. I also began to get the hang of the
difficult and complex interrelations between scientific information, professional expertise, and the political maneuver and
accommodation that are involved in any attempt by psychologists
or allied scientists and professionals to influence public policy.
This is a matter with which I have since become increasingly concerned as I have seen more clearly that translating knowledge into
social policy is inherently a matter of politics, with the most

frustrating difficulties lying more often on the political side than in lack of knowledge.

Involvement with the Joint Commission confirmed my interest in the theoretical, pragmatic, and value-related issues caught up in the slogan-term "mental health," which had already been stimulated by Marie Jahoda (1950), my friend and associate at N.Y.U., where I held an academic position in psychology from 1956 to 1959. She was a psychoanalytically-oriented social psychologist somewhat senior to me and her interests and social values appealed to me as much like my own. At the bad extreme, insanity or psychosis is readily identified (though whether it is helpfully regarded as a *disease* in the conventional medical sense is quite another matter). But what do we mean by *positive* mental health? I participated in Jahoda's still useful attempt to deal with this problem for the Joint Commission by chairing a seminar of thoughtful humanists, psychoanalysts, and psychologists who discussed early drafts of her report (Jahoda, 1958).

My own thinking went through various changes under this stimulation, coming to a temporary equilibrium with the view, expressed in a paper (1961) that has often been reprinted, that mental health is not a scientific concept at all, but rather a "chapter heading" for whatever *evaluative* perspective on human personality we may want to develop. Just what value standards we decide to employ—whether "adjustment" or autonomy or realism or capacity for love or work or untroubled sleep—is a matter of ethics or politics, not of science, although psychology can contribute to the consideration of value choices by developing evidence about the causal antecedents of particular valued qualities and about the consequences for other values of giving priority to any particular value. A major line of social psychological research, for example, has brought to light a number of generally unwelcome features that seem to be linked empirically to the value priorities that characterize the "law and order" mentality. Because of their knowledge people who know about the "authoritarian personality"—with its ethnocentrism, punitive moralism, and black-and-white categorical thinking—are likely to make value choices that are different. They may raise their children differently and favor different social policies than they would otherwise.

This was "armchair psychology," but it represents, I think, a potentially useful kind of psychological contribution. For one thing, it punctures the claims of those who would use the language of mental health to give a scientific aura to the promotion of their *own* values, be they conformist or nonconformist. It helps to immunize us against the pretensions of the mental health professions as a new priesthood. The next turning point for me was no armchair matter, as it plunged me into field research in West Africa and brought me, once again, into a close collaborative relationship with the subjects of my research, who were the first contingent of Peace Corps volunteers to go overseas. The results of the research, and of the research experience, changed my thinking about a number of matters, including mental health.

By this time I was at the University of California at Berkeley, where I remained for nine years. In 1961, Berkeley had a summer training program for Peace Corps volunteers who were to go to Ghana as secondary school teachers, although only a minority of the group of fifty who entered training had had previous teaching experience. The clinical-counseling psychologist Nicholas Hobbs, a good friend and fellow veteran of Joint Commission battles, had taken on the important task of directing selection for the Peace Corps. He persuaded me to help out by coordinating selection during training at Berkeley, holding out the carrot that I could include experimental test procedures and would be encouraged to negotiate with the Peace Corps for a follow-up study in Ghana to see which measures actually helped to predict effective performance overseas. I leaped at the opportunity, not only because I too had caught the excitement of the Kennedy Peace Corps in its early days, but because I saw it as a chance to flesh out my thinking about positive mental health by the close study of able young people as they coped with a novel and challenging situation. I was also fascinated by the opportunity to see the new Africa firsthand.

In this first round of Peace Corps selection-in-training, primary reliance was placed on psychiatric appraisal interviews, from which it was possible to extract reasonably satisfactory ratings of mental health as evaluated by competent psychiatrists. For research purposes, I included pencil-and-paper measures of "authoritarianism," on the expectation that the supposed ethnocentrism and psychological rigidity of the volunteers who were high in this trait might be expected to interfere with their performance in Ghana. The third research measure, which was almost more than the traffic would bear given the volunteers' growing impatience with "shrinks," was developed by a brilliant graduate student, Raphael Ezekiel, who was working with me at the time on the topic of "time perspective," people's views of their personal future as a potential determinant of what they do with their present lives. He had the volunteers write brief mock autobiographies, first imagining what their lives would be like five years hence, and then sketching their lives at age forty. With the help of other graduate students as independent "judges," he had each essay rated for the degree of differentiation with which the future was presented, the extent to which the future state of affairs was produced by the person himself or just happened to him, and the presumed amount of persistent effort that would be required to bring it about. These ratings also yielded a summary score. We salted these data away as the volunteers left for Africa and their new roles.

I had been developing preliminary plans for a quasi-experimental comparison of schools with and without Peace Corps teachers, but the Peace Corps administration and I had the good sense to get me to Ghana at Christmastime, 1961-62, to scout things out before firming up my research plans. (Again the family suffered, but we had a special Christmas when I got back.) Fairly typically for field research, I found that I had a serious job before me in gaining the confidence of the local Peace Corps representative, of suspicious government officials, and, most important, of the volunteers themselves, a number of whom I accompanied on a holiday jaunt to northern Ghana. It immediately became clear that I could expect nothing from questionnaires but would probably get full cooperation in the authentic give-and-take of informal interviews. It also became clear that any kind of controlled comparison would be politically and practically unfeasible. Should I go ahead or call the study off? I decided that a full description of the volunteers' experience would still be worth getting, and, properly analyzed, it could be related usefully to our data collected during the training period. But by then I had been captivated by developing Ghana, much attracted by the volunteers whom I had begun to know as friends, and it would have taken a real disaster to make me drop the study.

The next two summers, Ezekiel and I returned to Ghana armed with an interview guide based on what I had learned on my first visit, and on tape-recorded interviews at length with the volunteers at their schools all over the country. We stayed with the volunteers, and we often did the interviewing late at night by flashlight or lantern to the accompaniment of rain-forest noises. The better part of another year was required to develop and apply an appropriate systematic and quantitative way of analyzing the information in the rich interview protocols as they were typed up—in this I had the help of an able group of graduate students. There had been thrills aplenty in our arduous field work, but the pay-off was delayed until the results of our analyses began to pour forth in computer print-out. They were internally coherent, they made sense! And, by then, we had the uncommon advantage of knowing each "unit" in our statistics as persons. (A decade later, I am still in touch with most of them—a sign that I had managed to achieve a kind of collaborative relationship in psychological research that I wish could be more prevalent.)

Ezekiel (1968) and I (1966) have written at length elsewhere about what we found, which shattered some stereotypes about the "good" Peace Corps volunteer and was useful, or ought to have been, to the Peace Corps administration. Here I want to discuss only how our findings affected my thinking about positive mental health. As it turned out, the psychiatric ratings showed no over-all relationship to any of the indices of Peace Corps performance that we developed. Neither did authoritarianism (Smith, 1965), perhaps because none of the volunteers was extremely authoritarian, perhaps also because of the markedly authoritarian atmosphere that turned out to be characteristic of Ghanaian education. Ezekiel's measure based on the mock autobiographies was the only procedure in our battery that helped to predict performance.

The results made sense in terms of what we thought we had seen in our direct contact with the volunteers in their job setting. Freedom from anxiety or minor neurotic symptoms had seemed quite irrelevant: a good many of the most effective volunteers had their quirks; some of the least effective were shockingly "healthy." What made the critical difference among these generally able and well-intentioned young people was whether or not the volunteer engaged himself fully with the task, invested himself to the hilt with unreserved commitment. The volunteers that really invested themselves took the difficulties they encountered in stride as challenges; they might be frustrated but could not conceive of being *bored*. Other, less effective volunteers were more reactive than active; they tended to devote their energies more to "adjusting" to their situations than to making the most of their opportunities. We found it impossible to classify the "real" difficulty of the situations that the different volunteers faced, since the same objective situation that was frustrating to one sort of volunteer was attractive and challenging to the other. Ezekiel's autobiography ratings seemed to have tapped, though crudely enough, the volunteer's predisposition to cope actively with the situations that he faced, with a full commitment of the self. The aspect of psychological effectiveness that we had come to focus on appeared to me closely akin to Robert White's (1959) concept of competence as based upon intrinsic motivation to have effects on one's environment.

Back to the armchair, or rather to the conference and seminar. In the mid-1960's I was the member of a Social Science Research Council Committee on Socialization and Social Structure, which had the mission of setting new directions for research on how society fits people to play its roles. Mainly, perhaps, we were educating each other, in a stimulating group that contained three psychologists and three sociologists, all good friends who had met together over a period of years. For the committee, I took on the task of examining leads in the research literature that would help us to understand the conditions that promote the development of competence, in White's sense of motivationally based psychological effectiveness, which also seemed to me to be the sense indicated by my Peace Corps study—a rather far cry from my earlier relativism about values and positive mental health (Smith, 1961). I had the help of a specially convened research conference that brought together specialists from a variety of fields who had something to contribute. In the resulting essay (1968d) that I eventually produced after much travail, I proposed that the motivational core of competence is a cluster of attitudes toward the self as potent, efficacious, and worthy of being taken seriously by self and others.

Such a cluster of attitudes sets a kind of "self-fulfilling prophecy" in operation. In the favorable case, the person has the confidence to seize upon opportunities as they present themselves. He tries. He therefore acquires the knowledge and skills that make successes more probable—which in turn lend warrant to his sense of efficacy. In the unfavorable case, he daren't hope, he doesn't try—and he is caught in a vicious circle that is likely to mire him in incompetence, fatalism, and failure. It seemed to me that many of our practical dilemmas of race, poverty, and education, among others, amount essentially to questions of how to foster the benign sort of circular process, and how to break into and disrupt or redirect the vicious sort. We have clues, very promising ones, but not answers.

A PERSPECTIVE ON RELEVANCE

With many gaps and omissions, I have brought the story to my present concerns. I am still preoccupied with trying to formulate more clearly the psychological problems underlying the general human problem of how man may become more fully the master of his fate, an "origin" of social causation in Richard DeCharms' (1968) sense rather than a "pawn." If psychology can be made to talk coherently and dependably to this issue, it should become unmistakably relevant—to the problems of our time as well as to student interests.

From the standpoint of this problem, traditional behavioristic psychology misses the mark by leaving no place for human freedom. It tends to reduce man to a reactor, not an actor, and leaves the free will that makes choice and planning and responsibility intelligible a matter of illusion or paradox. Classical psychoanalysis does little better in its unbalanced emphasis on unconscious determination. Both aspire, however, to a scientific causal analysis. In deploring the human irrelevance of behaviorism and psychoanalysis, the so-called "humanistic" psychologies of the "third force" (Rogers and Maslow and May) have tended at times to throw out the scientific baby with the bathwater. They accept human agency and choice as a philosophical postulate, but their respect for the integrity of human experience often leads them into disrespect for the canons of science as a self-critical cumulative enterprise.

I find grounds for hope for a more humanly cogent personality and social psychology in indications from several quarters that we are at the threshold of becoming able to treat self-determination—free will if you like—not as an illusion or paradox, not as a metaphysical assumption outside the grasp of science, but as an empirical variable that some people rank higher on than others, a variable that is linked to causes and consequences that can be understood and turned to the enhancement of human freedom. In my teaching, I refer to Claude Brown's *Manchild in the Promised Land* (1965) to illustrate the variable I am talking about. The "case of Claude" can be read as a dramatic story of the process by which the Harlem street boy gradually gains the conviction, utterly foreign to him at the beginning, that he can be the architect of his own life, not the pawn of a cruel fate. In the special case of this variable, the conviction is father of the fact.

A psychology that can deal with it empirically and systematically is *both* humanistic and scientific. It is to nudging psychology along in this direction that I should now particularly like to contribute.

This is the sort of ambition, of course, that in actuality one can realize only very partially and imperfectly, though it can infuse a good many of one's activities and make them personally meaningful. On a more down-to-earth, realistic scale, there are a number of ways in which a problem-focused social psychologist, a generalist with interdisciplinary inclinations, can contribute toward headway on the very serious problems that now present an unprecedented challenge to mankind as we are just coming to understand, an ominous package of threats that is also the basis for high hopes if we can only gird ourselves to facing up to them.

Psychologists can draw upon their knowledge of research and theory to help to reformulate the practical problems involving war, population, pollution, and the rest—to put them in new terms that may make them more amenable to solution. (We know from psychological research on thinking and problem-solving that putting the question correctly is more than half the battle.) They can undertake applied research that is directly focused on pieces of the urgent problems. They can use their technical research skills in carefully evaluating social programs, so that we can learn from our mistakes as well as from our successes. For my own part, I have recently been trying to bring my social psychological training to bear on pieces of the social problems that involve student protest and campus conflict, racist prejudice, and the population explosion.

As a social psychologist, I see a good deal of potential gain and little loss from taking much of our sense of direction from such human problems, so long as we approach them with a persistent effort to understand and to generalize. There are fields of inquiry —especially the physical sciences—where a heavy focus on applied work is stultifying. In psychology, such areas in which a strong intrinsic line of development dictates the required next steps are not so common. I think of aspects of physiological psychology, psycholinguistics, and the study of cognitive development and then begin to falter. In much of psychology, especially social psychology, the lines of development are far less clear. There have been obvious gains in the sophistication of our questions, in our awareness of relevant variables, and in the level of our information, but fad and fashion in concepts and methods have too often substituted for (and mimicked) the missing lines of development inherent in the emerging structure of the science at its frontier. Wherever this state of affairs prevails, it seems to me, advance in generalizable understanding is just as likely to come as a by-product of work at urgent human and social problems as it is from a head-on assault in "basic" research. (I do not at all criticize psychologists whose strong sense of scientific direction turns them away from social problems: we need more of them. For every psychologist who feels such an imperative sense of direction, however, there must unfortunately be dozens of others looking for a suitable topic for a publishable study: hence our cluttered and so often unrewarding journals.)

Since all important social problems entail conflicts of important human interests, in principle none of them could be *solved* by psychological—or social scientific—knowledge even if we were vastly more knowledgeable than we are. Any and all solutions will necessarily be forged in the political arena, with scientific knowledge only one ingredient in the process. But it can become a much more important ingredient than it characteristically has been. I therefore think it a fitting close to this account of one social psychologist's activities to invoke a favorite maxim of Kurt Lewin—a major influence on me as on all social psychologists of my generation, although I had little direct contact with him: "There is nothing as practical as a good theory."

I close with Lewin's maxim and example because it seems to me that the most difficult challenge of teaching today is to awaken students to the *relevance* of hard intellectual and scientific work and of persistent commitment to the difficult process of democratic politics. The unprecedented problems of the present world, the unsettling rapidity of change, have made many of us lose our bearings. The credentials of science, like those of the "Establishment," are suspect. A new romanticism has arisen in reaction to the previous suppression of feeling and human value, the aridity of technological society, the intractability of human problems. Yet the problems before us require head as well as heart if they are to be solved. Since so many of them hinge on human cussedness, the challenge to a humane yet scientific social psychology is immense.

REFERENCES

Brown, C. *Manchild in the promised land.* New York: Macmillan, 1965.

DeCharms, R. *Personal causation. The internal affective determinants of behavior.* New York and London: Academic Press, 1968.

Ezekiel, R. S. The personal future and Peace Corps competence. *Journal of Personality and Social Psychology,* 1968, *8*(2), *Monograph Supplement,* Part 2.

Hilgard, E. R., and Smith, M. B. Distributed practice in motor learning. Score changes within and between daily sessions. *Journal of Experimental Psychology,* 1942, *30,* 136-46.

Jahoda, M. Toward a social psychology of mental health. In M. J. E. Senn (Ed.), *Symposium on the healthy personality.* New York: Josiah Macy, Jr., Foundation, 1950. Pp. 211-30.

———— *Current concepts of positive mental health.* New York: Basic Books, 1958.

Joint Commission on Mental Illness and Health. *Action for mental health.* New York: Basic Books, 1961.

Katz, D., and Stotland, E. A preliminary statement to a theory of attitude structure and change. In S. Koch (Ed.), *Psychology: A study of a science,* Vol. 3: *Formulations of the person and the social context.* New York: McGraw-Hill, 1959. Pp. 423-75.

Merton, R. K., and Kitt, Alice S. Contributions to the theory of reference group behavior. In R. K. Merton, and P. F. Lazarsfeld (Eds.), *Continuities in social research. Studies in the scope and method of "the American soldier."* New York: Free Press, 1950. Pp. 40-105.

Murray, H. A. *Explorations in personality.* New York: Oxford, 1938.

Myrdal, G. (with the assistance of R. Sterner and A. Rose). *An American dilemma. The Negro problem and modern democracy.* Vols. 1 and 2. New York: Harper, 1944.

Rosenzweig, S. E. G. Boring and the *Zeitgeist: Eruditione Gesta Beavit*. *Journal of Psychology*, 1970, *75*, 59-71.

Smith, M. B. Functional and descriptive analysis of public opinion. Unpublished Ph.D. thesis, Harvard University, 1947a.

———— The personal setting of public opinions: A study of attitudes toward Russia. *Public Opinion Quarterly*, 1947b, *11*, 507-23.

———— "Mental health" reconsidered. A special case of the problem of values in psychology. *American Psychologist*, 1961, *16*, 299-306. Also reprinted in Smith (1969), pp. 179-90.

———— An analysis of two measures of "authoritarianism" among Peace Corps teachers, *Journal of Personality*, 1965, *33*, 513-35. Also reprinted in Smith (1969), pp. 117-35.

———— Explorations in competence: A study of Peace Corps teachers in Ghana. *American Psychologist*, 1966, *21*, 555-66. Also reprinted in Smith (1969), pp. 191-209.

———— Personality in politics: A conceptual map, with application to the problem of political rationality. In O. Garceau (Ed.), *Political research and political theory: Essays in honor of V. O. Key, Jr.* Cambridge, Massachusetts: Harvard University Press, 1968a. Pp. 77-101. Also reprinted in Smith (1969), pp. 14-32.

———— Attitude change. In *International Encyclopedia of the Social Sciences*, Vol. 1. New York: Macmillan and Free Press, 1968b. Pp. 458-67. Also reprinted in Smith (1969), pp. 82-96.

———— Samuel A. Stouffer. In *International Encyclopedia of the Social Sciences*, Vol. 15. New York: Macmillan and Free Press, 1968c. Pp. 277-80. Also reprinted in Smith (1969), pp. 61-65.

———— Competence and socialization. In J. A. Clausen (Ed.), *Socialization and Society*. Boston: Little, Brown, 1968d. Also reprinted in Smith (1969), pp. 210-50.

———— *Social psychology and human values*. Chicago: Aldine, 1969.

———— Bruner, J. S., and White, R. W. *Opinions and Personality*. New York: Wiley, 1956.

Stone, C. P., and Smith, M. B. Serial discrimination by rats at the choice-points of elevated mazes, *Journal of Comparative Psychology*, 1941, *31*, 79-95.

Stouffer, S. A., Lumsdaine, A. A., Lumsdaine, Marion H., Williams, R. M., Jr., Smith, M. B., Janis, I. L., Star, Shirley A., and Cottrell, L. S., Jr. *The American soldier*. Vol. 1: *Adjustment during Army life*. Vol. 2: *Combat and its aftermath*. Princeton, New Jersey: Princeton University Press, 1949.

White, R. W. Motivation reconsidered: The concept of competence. *Psychological Review*, 1959, *66*, 297-333.

9

Toward Better Self-Understanding

FREDERICK C. THORNE

My troubles literally started at birth in a difficult forceps delivery
with head lacerations. For the first six months, I suffered from
severe malnutrition due to inability to find a compatible formula,
and I was so undernourished that my joints had to be padded to
keep the bones from wearing through the skin. This condition
of malnutrition was alleviated when, by mistake, my grand-
mother inadvertently mixed the formula with solid cream which
was the first thing I was able to keep down. Severe eating problems continued for the next six years, as I developed intense
aversion reactions to eggs, fish, chicken, turkey, and all sour
foods. Mealtime was a continuing source of contention as my parents used everything up to physical force to get me to eat what
the rest of the family was eating.

Secondary to these nutritional problems were physical under-
development, frailty and poor health. Until age eleven, when I
grew twelve inches in twelve months, I was always the smallest,
lightest, and frailest of my age group, suffering from almost continuous upper respiratory disorders, middle ear infections, and
what would now be regarded as a psychosomatic gastric condition.

Small physical size and weakness were a great handicap
throughout elementary school. Entering first grade at age 6-6, I
stayed only two weeks before being removed because of illness

and was tutored at home for the rest of the year, so successfully that the school authorities judged me ready for grade three at 7-6. This was a psychological error, since I was to remain at height 4'6" and weight 96 pounds for the next three years, making me always the smallest and least able to protect myself physically in my class. Between ages seven and eleven, I found myself bullied and tormented by lower-class children who passed my home every day to get to school.

In any case, the years between six and about nine or ten years were a very difficult period of growth because I was constantly picked on and bullied by larger boys against whom I could not hold my own physically. I can remember winning only one fight in my life, and then only against an inferior opponent. During this period, I felt very anxious and insecure until I grew old enough to develop psychological defenses against aggression— such as learning to demand that an aggressor pick on somebody his own size.

My early psychosocial development was further handicapped by an undiscovered severe myopia involving bilateral 20/100 vision and functional blindness. I could not see the blackboard at school, recognize people further than six feet away, or see a ball until it hit me in the face. This sensory deficiency went undiscovered until the third grade where I did well with close paper work but could not participate in class work at the board.

Probably in reaction to physical inadequacy and social insecurity, I developed severe stammering and stuttering at age five which progressed in intensity until age fifteen and seriously interfered with later school work. I would know the answers but couldn't say them without embarrassing speech defects, so I would give the wrong answer. Throughout elementary school and in high school grades nine and ten, my marks were barely passing although I was recognized as a bright student.

PSYCHOSOCIAL DEVELOPMENT

My whole life has been greatly influenced by a continuing double-bind relationship with my mother which continued until her death, even though she was senile in a nursing home. A pretty, vivacious, at times charming person, my mother also was egoistical, opinionated, grandiose, bossy, domineering, selfish, and ignorant, even though she had good formal education for her times. She wanted her own way at all times in everything. She could tolerate only those whom she could dominate, and she successfully dominated all her family except myself. At about age ten, I completed a successful rebellion to throw off her domination which had started at about age four, when I discovered that Mother did not always tell the truth even though requiring truth from all others. At age nine, I ended the era of Buster Brown suits by tearing one off on the way home from school and throwing it down the sewer. At about age twelve, I accidentally discovered how to dominate my Mother by refusing to kiss her and withholding little courtesies whenever she became too difficult.

Throughout her life, Mother was beset by psychosomatic complaints and she had more symptoms than almost any woman who ever lived to be more than ninety-five years of age. She was always complaining of "sick" headaches, "aching" back, and of feeling "terrible" when anything displeased her. If someone displeased her greatly, she would accuse them of undermining her health and of trying to "kill" her.

Although I successfully threw off maternal domination about age ten, my mother never ceased to try to control me and my only sister, so that for the last fifty years all contacts with Mother have consisted of her unsuccessful efforts to reestablish her influence by giving me unending instructions as to how to behave, how to stand, what to say, what to wear, what to do, and whom to be seen with. On more subtle levels, Mother continued her needling by criticizing her children's spouses and their children, and thus ensuring constant hard feelings on the part of all those who felt dominated or criticized by her. The emotionally conflictual double bind continued into her senility when she was still giving orders and making snide remarks against those she could not control until her death at age ninety-five in May 1971.

This double-bind situation with my mother did have one beneficial effect, however, in that I early began to question "authority" and began to think things out for myself. Although strangers unhesitatingly would take my mother's side, because they could not see how such a beautiful and charming lady be in the wrong, I gradually came to perceive her actions with cold realism and was no longer taken in by her little games. I learned the hard way that all that glitters is not gold, or as it appears on the surface.

Although very emotionally disturbing to live with, the very serious interpersonal problems in my family provided very valuable psychological insights later when I finally came to understand some psychopathological constellations not hitherto well described in the literature. I later came to realize that my own family contained a veritable museum of the psychopathology of everyday life. In truth, many of my later contributions represented analyses of phenomena first encountered among my own relatives.

TOWARD CLINICAL UNDERSTANDING

Early attempts on the part of my family to secure help through the family physician, pediatric consultant, and school authorities were totally unsatisfactory under the existing lack of professional resources between 1910 and 1925. I literally received no help until age fifteen, as a high school senior, when I discovered a shelf of psychology and psychiatry books in the local public library. The first text I happened to pick up was Rosanoff's *Manual of Psychiatry,* which was fascinating to leaf through even though largely incomprehensible. From that time on, I avidly read anything psychological I could get my hands on.

These interests led me to major in psychology at Columbia College starting as a sophomore. I took every available psychology course, motivated basically by the need of self-understanding. Unfortunately, immediate personal insights were not forthcoming since Columbia then and now espoused logical positivism and objective psychology. My eight years on the Columbia campus involved another double-bind situation in that the staff and curriculum required me to give lip service to a behavioristic psychology which I didn't believe in and could not respect, so that I literally went "underground" and engaged in "bootleg" studies of psychodynamics and psychopathology. By day I fulfilled the role of an experimentalist and did my Ph.D. in psychophysics to conform to the prevailing ethic of the Columbia department. By night, I read Freud, Adler, Jung, and other clinicians, and built up a clinical library much more extensive than my experimental library.

My formal education in the graduate Psychology Department at Columbia contributed little or nothing to self-understanding except for rewarding personal contacts with Prescott Lecky who taught a pioneer class in Personality after returning from a sabbatical spent in Europe studying with Alfred Adler, to whom I was to be introduced later by Lecky. By chance, my first semester in Introductory Psychology was taught by the late William M. Marston, the only Columbia psychologist intensively concerned with the phenomena of consciousness, and who did not last long at Columbia for that and similar reasons. I found Woodworth polite but distant (and with an unresolved stammering himself), Poffenburger cordial but awed by Woodworth, Garrett hard to know but cooperative, Hollingworth intense but difficult to relate to personally, Murphy brilliant but with an unresolved negative transference to some of his more creative students, Warden personally very friendly and supportive, Lecky with the most sensitive clinical insights, Klineberg preoccupied with civil rights, and Carney Landis constricted and preoccupied with his political tenure. All this added up to a good formal education, a Ph.D without ever having made an intensive study of a single person, and the intention to go beyond the Ph.D if necessary to gain access to clinical experiences.

I am very grateful for having been at the Columbia graduate department during the era of its Golden Age when all of its "great" psychologists were there including Thorndike, Woodworth, the Hollingworths, Poffenberger, Garrett, Murphy, Warden, Klineberg, Mortimer Adler, Lecky, W. M. Marston,

Landis, Zubin, Piotrowski, Goodwin Watson, Percival Symonds, and summer session faculty such as Dallenbach and W. N. Kellogg. Collectively, these men represented a breadth and depth of resources unavailable elsewhere, and probably it was from the very heterogeneity of their viewpoints that I first became aware of the necessity for a broad spectrum eclectic approach. I sat and listened to them all, accepting what was consistent with my own developing theories, and rejecting what seemed irrelevant or invalid.

Although I resented it at the time, one aspect of the Columbia departmental attitude was responsible for my broadening my education by studying medicine. It so happened that the Columbia department collectively seemed to take very little interest in the later professional development of its students and rarely went out of its way to help them get jobs. At a time when the Yale department in the persons of Clark Hull and Yerkes had collected a group of outstanding students and was actively promoting their professional development by recommending them for the few good academic openings, the Columbia department rarely attended APA meetings, did not seem too interested in the practical development of the field, and rarely went out of their way to look up job openings and recommend students for academic positions that did open up.

After having been a laboratory assistant at Columbia College for three years in both undergraduate and graduate experimental courses, the best job I could get in 1933 was a $1500 instructorship at Long Island University offered by Dr. Richard M. Paynter, who discovered that I was a fraternity brother of his in Phi Sigma Kappa at Columbia by chance at a picnic given by Dr. Poffenberger.

While a student at Columbia, I had experienced the recurrence of study problems encountered first in grammar school, then high school, and later in medical school. Perhaps as a result of congenital severe myopia, and never early being able to see well even though corrected to 20/20 with glasses, I have never had a photographic visual verbal memory. I can learn best by doing things organically, next by hearing about them auditorily, and least by reading. I simply cannot remember names and facts which I have read. My mind is like a quart jar. To get something new in, I have to forget something old. This has always constituted a problem in passing examinations. My academic record has been checkered, with high marks only in subjects like psychology that I was interested in and failing marks in languages and dull subjects. Several Columbia professors considered me a misfit, not doing well in their subjects and advising that I should dig ditches. Such for academic counseling! I thumbed my nose mentally and went on to somewhat worthwhile successes by utilizing cleverness to cover up for real memory deficits.

Twice in my academic career I have been saved from crucial failures which would have terminated my studies—sympathetic instructors went beyond the call of duty to get me by in my weaker subjects. For example, I early mastered stuttering and stammering in English by age sixteen as self-help techniques and confidence grew, but I would stutter as badly as ever today while attempting to speak any foreign language. My own academic experiences and brushes with near failure have taught me that marks in subjects of secondary interest are not critical for ultimate intellectual development. Every academician holds his own subject dear and is intolerant of those who cannot learn it, not realizing that life pays off on optimum performances rather than on academic averages. Although my own secondary subject was mathematical, I have learned to be very tolerant of clinicians who cannot master chi square and advanced calculus. But in all this, I got no real help from the educational process at Columbia.

Several times between 1930 and 1945, I made abortive attempts to enter into personal psychotherapy or psychoanalysis in a further quest for personal understanding, and also because it was then the professional thing to do. None of these attempts turned out well, largely because none of the consultants seemed able to tune into my type of problem (which was more existential in nature) and I felt that my time and money were being wasted by invalid techniques. By this time, I knew the nature of my problems better than my consultant. More than that, I had now gained considerable clinical experience concerning the indications and contra-indications of what the known spectrum of clinical methods could accomplish.

Having come to know personally many of the "authorities" in clinical psychology and psychiatry, I became increasingly critical and disenchanted with limited systems and practices which accumulating clinical experience and research came to discredit. Many contemporary schools and systems are too limited, parochial, and even invalid, as evidenced both by the human predicament of their inventors and advocates and by general lack of therapeutic success. I have come to understand that psychotherapy is extremely difficult if not impossible in many cases with current resources. Clinical psychology and psychiatry both are oversold fields, called upon to produce cures for conditions for which there is yet no effective treatment.

LEARNING TO SOLVE MY OWN PROBLEMS

I have profound respect and sympathy for the conflicts and quandaries of all younger generations who bring sensitive minds and personalities to question the solutions of the Establishment to age-old problems of the human condition which have no perfect solutions. Forty years ago I was in the same position as the rebellious youth of today. My own experiences had taught me that a lot in life was wrong. I wanted answers which neither family nor colleagues could give me. I found out that I had to find out the truth for myself because the "authorities" simply did not have it. My adult and professional life has been dedicated to finding out this truth.

In any case, I found myself at age twenty-five with a Columbia Ph.D. and still no clinical training or experience. I had made an abortive attempt to get some clinical experience as a psychology intern under Carney Landis at the New York State Psychiatric Institute in 1933 but we parted by mutual consent after six months during which time I found that Landis wanted my services only to work on apparatus while I wanted to roam the wards and attend clinical conferences for which no arrangements were made at that time for psychology interns. At least, I did get to study some cases at the NYSPI.

This frustrating educational experience plus the inability to secure a good academic appointment in the depths of the depression in 1934 resolved me to enter medical school primarily to gain clinical training and experience. I intended at no time to specialize in medicine and planned to return to clinical psychology. Medical school was a fascinating and inspirational experience as I was thrown into the intimate study of human life in all conditions from conception to autopsy. I can truthfully say that I never was taught to study until medical school, and I believe that no one can judge medical education who has not passed through it. It provided me with organic clinical training in depth.

It was in medical school that I became personally aware of the "master clinician." My original purpose in applying to enter medical school had been the desire to gain access to case materials under all conditions from conception to death. Only in the practice of medicine can case materials be studied *in depth,* utilizing every known method under every possible condition. In medical school, my insights were carried a step further when I realized that it is not enough to just obtain access to case materials—beyond that it is necessary to become a master clinician in order to make the most of the clinical cues upon which more sophisticated diagnosis must rest. In medical school, I was exposed to clinicians of all levels of competence including a few clinicians who did consistently better in their diagnosis and case handling.

I came to understand that the critical problem of all clinical training is to discover who the master clinicians are and then to study their clinical processes in order to discover the cues upon which more valid and relevant decision processes are based. My goal was to become a master clinician myself and I was lucky enough to be exposed very early to two master clinicians in Alfred Adler and Prescott Lecky whose clinical decision processes

I attempted to analyze in depth with the limited resources which my then limited experience permitted.

My early training in experimental-statistical methods facilitated my development of more valid clinical decision processes in myself, because I came to regard each case as a separate experimental situation which had to be checked and rechecked to discover the validity of my problem solutions. I attempted to keep records to check upon how my clinical predictions actually turned out. One of the things which I discovered about myself was that I never really came to understand schizophrenics and too often my case handling with them did not work out well. I still believe that schizophrenia is an organic disorder even though such etiology has never been verified. I did best with neurotics and character disorders by actual count of case results.

It should be stressed that even after having completed my medical education at Cornell in 1938, my primary interests were still in the field of clinical psychology which I regarded as basic to psychiatry. My interests still were primarily in teaching and research in clinical psychology and I spent the winter of 1938-39 trying unsuccessfully to secure a major academic position in clinical psychology where I could develop my theoretical and research interests. I did write a *Handbook of Clinical Psychology,* which was accepted for publication in the Mosby handbook series; but the only copy of the manuscript got lost in the mails!

Frustrated in my attempts to return to clinical psychology, I secured a position in Vermont in 1939 as director of the Brandon State School and organizer of the Vermont Mental Hygiene Clinics. Already very busy in these two positions, in the World War II years between 1941 and 1945 I examined almost 50,000 men for the Selective Service System and did any other psychiatric work required to be done on the side. The situation of holding so many assignments and being the only psychiatrist available in my area of the state gave me a breadth of psychiatric experience rarely acquired.

I would probably have remained in these capacities in Vermont indefinitely had there not arisen in 1947 a political upheaval which resulted in a turn-over in the heads of many institutions. I had developed one of the most active sterilization programs for the mentally defective in the country. It was opposed by a resurgent Catholic welfare program and resulted in my removal as director of the Brandon State School. Between 1947 and 1961, when I developed an incapacitating ruptured spinal disc which required operative removal, I developed a lucrative private practice in psychiatry in the southern part of Vermont.

One of the most interesting aspects of private practice was serving as psychiatric consultant at Spring Lake Ranch, Cuttingsville, Vermont, between 1948 and 1961. Spring Lake Ranch is a psychiatric half-way house catering to patients, particularly young people, referred from many of the best private psychiatric institutions in the country. These patients often were cases in which everything else had failed, and they provided a "hard core" challenge to discover some methods which would improve their conditions. We utilized this population to test out many of the methods later described in *Principles of Personality Counseling* (1950) and *Psychological Case Handling* (1968).

I taught the first-year course in psychiatry at the University of Vermont College of Medicine between 1939 and 1953 and ran a clinical service for senior medical students at the Brandon State School between 1941 and 1947. Nevertheless, in spite of stimulating practice and teaching in the field of psychiatry, my primary interests and loyalties remained with clinical psychology. Essentially, this was because I had discovered that psychiatry did not really have all the answers in its field and that a return to the investigation and study of fundamentals was greatly needed.

THE JOURNAL OF CLINICAL PSYCHOLOGY

As early as the summer of 1933, while still a graduate student at Columbia, I had become fascinated by the possibilities in the scientific publishing business. In August 1933, Poffenberger held a picnic at his summer camp at Montrose, New York, attended by many of the greats of the department and particularly by Dr.

James McKeen Cattell. I listened as a rapt student while Dr. Cattell reminisced about the circumstances and history of his development of *Science*. He made many astute observations concerning scientific publishing and planted the seed in my mind of maybe starting a journal in clinical psychology.

In the early 1930s, it was practically impossible to get a paper accepted on clinical topics by the APA or published in an APA journal. I made several unsuccessful attempts to talk and write on clinical topics and finally decided there would have to be another kind of journal. When the *American Association of Applied Psychology* (AAAP) finally decided to publish an applied journal, I held my breath until they chose the title *Journal of Consulting Psychology* because I had determined to use the title *Journal of Clinical Psychology* (a much better title). With the start of World War II in 1941, all my plans had to be placed in abeyance until early in 1944, when I discovered that Dr. Gordon A. Allport, editor of the *Journal of Abnormal and Social Psychology* had plans for splitting it and having a separate clinical section. Quickly I decided to jump the gun and sent out a letter announcing that the *Journal of Clinical Psychology (JCP)* would start publication in January 1945.

I quickly ran into major difficulties in getting the new *JCP* started. The war was still on and printing facilities and paper were in great scarcity. Worse still was the problem of securing sufficient manuscripts to publish the first few issues. My first step was to write major figures in the field and invite them to become editorial board members and to submit manuscripts. Although I was relatively unknown in applied psychology, having been practicing psychiatry since 1939, enough prominent figures accepted the invitation for me to feel safe to proceed.

My announcement of a new clinical journal was received with a great deal of enthusiasm, and some people even began sending in subscription money, but I was soon confronted by the fact that no manuscripts were coming in. In spite of promises, I had only two manuscripts by September 1944, three by October, five by November, and six by December 1 with a January 1 publication date. In desperation, I sat down and wrote a long paper describing the status of clinical psychology in 1945. Several people read the paper and none saw anything wrong with it.

The first issue of *JCP* appeared in January 1945 and was greeted initially by enthusiasm, but by February we found ourselves in trouble. Albert Deutsch announced in bold headlines in the *New York Post* that a new instance of discrimination had been uncovered in the form of advocacy of a quota system for selecting students for training in clinical psychology! This alarm was directed at a paragraph in my lead article on the status of clinical psychology in 1945 in which I had recommended that students should be selected on a more representative basis, giving proper representation to all minorities. The paragraph, which, if read today, would be in line with the civil rights movement, was instead interpreted as an attack on the then overrepresentation of Jewish students entering the clinical field. At this point, the stuff really hit the fan. I began to receive communications from all sides, ranging from commendation to severe denunciation as a traitor to liberty. My editorial board divided into supporters and detractors who promptly resigned. I began to regret the whole thing until I discovered that in the excitement of charges and countercharges, sufficient curiosity was stimulated so that subscriptions and manuscripts began to come in in increasing numbers to the point that the new journal was never in the red at any time and became widely read right from the beginning.

Within five years, the publication business grew to such size as to become my principal source of support and to require my full-time attention as publisher, writer, editor, and researcher. I began to expand by adding monographs, books, and tests to our line. I became vitally interested in all details of journal and book production in all stages from writing the manuscript to manufacturing the completed book. Between 1945 and 1960, I literally attended to all details myself, never having even a secretary to help with subscription lists, wrapping single issues, or handling the large mail-order business. Doing this work had a strangely soothing effect and in addition saved a lot of money.

THE DIRECTIVE-NONDIRECTIVE CONTROVERSY

The availability of a publication medium made it possible for us to embark upon a personal campaign to influence the development of the whole field of clinical psychology. Following the example of Sir William Osler who had modernized medical practice by introducing the team approach in standardized medical centers throughout the world, we hoped to indicate similar directions for standardized training and practice in clinical psychology following the eclectic model.

The opening move in our program was to direct attention to Carl R. Rogers and his nondirective methods of counseling and psychotherapy which had attained great popularity in World War II and threatened to becloud larger issues. In particular, Rogers argued that diagnosis was now obsolete and unnecessary for the nondirective approach, which was advanced more or less as a universal panacea which could be learned in training as brief as three-week courses. The nondirective approach was one of the first distinctively psychological contributions, and in some places was the only method being taught.

Following an initial critical paper (1944) outlining some of the general shortcomings of the nondirective approach, we started publishing in 1945 a series of fifteen papers describing the operational characteristics of the more traditional directive techniques which we considered to constitute a fundamental body of knowledge in relation to which newer techniques must be developed, analyzed, and compared concerning their advantages and limitations. It was our intention to confront the profession with such classical clinical information retaining therapeutic values which should not be overlooked nor lost.

The result of publication of this series of articles was a confrontation and controversy between Rogerian nondirectivism and my directivism which continued from 1945 to about 1955. At no time did I intend to classify myself as directive but the designation was popularized by writers looking for terms to characterize the opposing systems. In actuality, between 1950, when our first major text entitled *Principles of Personality Counseling* appeared, and 1955, I had completely abandoned my concern with directivism as such in favor of a broad spectrum eclecticism which sought to introduce a completely comprehensive approach utilizing every new development of value in terms of its indications and contraindications.

ECLECTICISM AND PSYCHODIAGNOSIS

My interest in eclecticism stemmed from two important sources. At Columbia, I was influenced profoundly by Robert S. Woodworth (probably the first great American eclectic) who introduced me to the term and whose interests had the broadest spectrum. Also at Columbia, I first met and during 1929 and 1930 took a course under Alfred Adler, who also impressed me deeply. Adler's individual psychology dealt with a very wide range of phenomena ranging from biological inferiority to style of life and existential concerns—in fact, no other teacher ever impressed me as being so comprehensive as Alfred Adler.

Adler's teachings struck direct personal overtones in my own experience in that his formulations seemed to come closer than any other to the nature of my own personal problems. I knew at first hand about organic and physical inferiorities, the style of life concept seemed particularly relevant in my own personal affairs, and I was impressed by his concepts of social interest and movement.

But even more important in support of eclecticism was my realization from both studies and personal psychotherapy that more limited schools and systems were not comprehensive enough to solve the kinds of problems I had experienced in my own life. Only a genuinely eclectic therapist could have had any chance of dealing with the types and breadth of problems in my own life—consequently, I had direct face validation of the eclectic approach in my own life.

My first book in 1950 had been on counseling and psychotherapy because in all of the history of clinical science, treatment has evolved often far in advance of any diagnostic rationale. Therefore, the next general topic to claim my interest was a systematic approach to psychodiagnosis resulting in publication of *Principles of Psychological Examining* (1955). The eclectic approach is based logically upon thoroughgoing diagnosis, since without a valid knowledge of diagnostic indications and contraindications there can be no logical basis for clinical decision-making. The whole concept of causation (*etiology*) implies that causes can be recognized and differentiated diagnostically. The book on the principles of psychological examining reviews in great detail the theory and rationale of extending the concept of diagnosis to all phases of clinical processes.

Unfortunately, publication of this book in 1955 came at a time when the whole Zeitgeist was running against the whole concept of diagnosis. Starting with Rogers who declared that psychodiagnosis was unnecessary and even contraindicated with his nondirective methods, there developed a wave of studies critical of classical psychiatric diagnostic classifications and nomenclatures, which were at that time recognized to be invalid, irrelevant, and obsolete. Because the traditional methods of diagnosis came to be discredited, a wave of nihilism developed in relation to psychodiagnosis as a whole. Other recent developments such as behavior therapy which make no diagnostic assumptions have tended to further discredit the area of psychodiagnosis to the point where it is not even taught in some training programs nor utilized in many treatment centers.

Nevertheless, our contention continues to be that some diagnostic presumptions must underlie all clinical decisions whether such presumptions are objectified and formalized as such or not. Objectivity requires that all assumptions or presumptions must be investigated as to validity and relevance, and this inevitably must consider diagnostic relationships. We remain committed to the priority of diagnosis in all clinical processes.

CLINICAL PSYCHOLOGY AND CLINICAL JUDGMENT

Starting with the Michigan clinical assessment studies in 1950, perhaps the most significant development of the 1950s and '60s has been progressive realization that clinical psychology can be no more valid than the underlying clinical judgments. An increasing weight of research on clinical judgment and assessment procedures made it evident that classical diagnostic and treatment methods were either invalid or irrelevant. One of the first casualties was Freudian theory and particularly its projective applications which were demonstrated to be basically invalid. In 1954, Meehl presented devastating evidence indicating the superiority of actuarial methods over clinical judgment and intuition.

The first reaction of the profession to the implications of clinical judgment research was one of disbelief as many clinicians continued to trust their intuitions, claiming that increased years of experience made possible refinements of judgment not possible with actuarial methods. When cumulative research continued to undermine the validity of even refined clinical methods, the next reaction was one of nihilism as many psychologists reported that they would not enter the field of clinical psychology again if given another chance. Other clinicians abandoned psychodiagnosis completely, preferring to use methods not requiring extensive case study and diagnosis. Many gave up clinical work completely, escaping into teaching and administration.

My own reaction to these developments was to insist upon a return to fundamentals, starting over again to investigate the validity of all clinical methods right from the beginning and calling for basic research to differentiate the bases for valid clinical decisions. In 1960, I submitted a questionnaire to one thousand clinical psychologists asking them to submit protocols reporting the nature of the worst clinical errors made during their careers. The resulting data became the basis for the book *Clinical Judgment* (1961), which summarized the literature and cited some common clinical errors. In 1971, we again brought the clinical judgment literature up.to date in a chapter for a new book on clinical assessment. Our latest position is that clinical psychology is synonymous with clinical judgment and that all training in clinical psychology should be training clinical judgment.

FORMULATING A COMPREHENSIVE SYSTEM
OF CLINICAL PSYCHOLOGY

One of the major criticisms directed against my eclectic approach
was that it involved no systematic theoretical rationale and was
simply a shot-gun approach using whatever happened to be available on a haphazard basis. Such a criticism does not do justice to
the broad spectrum of the eclectic orientation since this approach
is based on logical applications of the methods concerned with the
pros and cons of various theories. To combat such criticisms, I
determined to write up my conceptions of the theoretical rationale of all clinical science with particular application to clinical psychology.

The first step was to tabulate the operational foundations of
all the major schools of psychology in order to differentiate their
assumptions, subject matter, and operational methods, and this
information, along with the conclusion that no single method
was capable of dealing with all the phenomena of clinical psychology, was published in our book *Personality* (1961).

Personality also included the first presentation of our theory
that raw behavior occurs phenomenally only in the form of psychological *states,* defined as cross-sections of the stream of psychic
life (being, existence, experience). Our review of the literature
indicated that personality structures or traits can explain only
about 25 per cent of behavior variance at best, with the balance
being determined by state and/or situational factors. In fact, the
whole concept of "personality" is regarded only as a semantic
abstraction with the same level of validity as "mind." This book
outlined for the first time our conception of the relationships between consciousness, functions of self, and psychological states.

In 1955, we published *Tutorial Counseling,* subtitled *How
To Be Psychologically Healthy,* which summarized the mental
hygiene literature and indicated the value systems which I believe to underlie mental health.

The capstone of my system of clinical psychology consisted of
three books, all written in a burst of creative energy in 1966-67.

The basic theoretical ingredients of my new integrative psychology had been written piecemeal, starting in with my revision of Prescott Lecky's *Self-Consistency* (1951) in which I introduced some of my own interpretations of unification theory. In later papers and chapters in the 1960's, I had written progressively more in depth about integration theory, pointing out that psychiatric concepts of integration had never been developed in their ultimate implications and suggesting that integration (unification) was the central process underlying all behavior. In 1967, all these separate writings about integration were brought together in *Integrative Psychology* which also developed a comprehensive "state" psychology in detail. Integration was now defined as the central drive or need, since higher behaviors are impossible except in integrated states. State theory requires an integrative psychology to explain how states become organized in such infinite variety and complexity.

Our elaboration of a comprehensive integrative psychology required extensive revisions of our early *Principles of Personality Counseling* (1950), now out of print, which was accomplished in the two-volume *Psychological Case Handling* (1968). The concept of case-handling was adopted to emphasize that healing or therapy do not exist in fact unless healing or therapeutic effects can indeed be demonstrated—i.e. everything is basically case-handling until healing effects can be demonstrated. In this book, we reinterpreted all the standard methods of case-handling in terms of the new integrative psychology, showing that all behavior modification depends upon either stimulating new integrations or preventing or reversing disintegrative factors. All disorders are now interpreted as breakdowns of integration and/or control, and the central problem becomes one of reintegrating along more healthy patterns. *Psychological Case Handling* consistently reflects my eclectic method of selecting methods according to their indications and contraindications.

Between 1961, when our theory of the role of integration or unification as the central process of psychic life was first formulated, and 1967, when we made a more systematic presentation of its implications in *Integrative Psychology,* we started the systematic collection of observations of state phenomena which led to the formulation of new diagnostic classifications and nomenclatures for psychological states in general (1967) and existential states in particular (1970). This work led us to a collaboration with Peter E. Nathan in developing systems analytic methods for clinical process diagnosis which we consider as one of our most important contributions.

THE OBJECTIVE MEASUREMENT OF PSYCHOLOGICAL STATES

Although our original concept of the psychological state stemmed directly from the psychiatric concept of mental status (implying that any observations are valid only for the moment of study), we were also influenced by the failure of traditional personality structure and trait theory to come up with valid measurements of psychological states. It became evident that most clinically significant behaviors involve not traits but rather situationally stimulated state phenomena. It also became quickly evident that psychological space was very incompletely measured by classical personality structure and trait factors.

Accordingly, in 1965 we embarked on an entirely new measurement concept based on the objective study of all the various levels of factors potentially organizing integrated states. The basic idea was to develop a set of state measures sampling a much wider spectrum of behaviors than formerly attempted and thereby greatly broadening the range of possible etiological factors brought under study. This series of tests was called *The Integration Level Test Series,* and it was constructed by deliberately selecting eight different levels of factors potentially organizing clinically significant behaviors.

As a first approach to state measurement, we selected the area of sexuality since sexuality exists only as a state phenomena. The development of *The Sex Inventory* is described elsewhere (1965), but briefly we first attempted to derive a subtle-indirect scale based on selected MMPI items. We were unsuccessful and were forced to develop a new set of two hundred items using direct-obvious questions to sample sexual states openly. Although still available currently only as a research instrument, *The Sex Inventory* appears to measure sexuality as a state better than any other available instrument.

The second step in state measurement was an attempt to sample cognitive-ideological factors using *The Ideological Survey,* a two hundred-item inventory based on the conflicting ideologies involved in Ayn Rand's objectivist philosophy and its opposing welfare state ideology. This effort represented a first attempt to map out ideological space as a determiner of cognitively integrated psychological states which had hitherto been largely ignored in psychological experimental methodology.

Other inventories for which factorial standardization was completed in 1972 included studies of psychophysiological supporting systems (*The Personal Health Study*), femininity patterns (*The Sex Inventory, Female Form,* and *The Femininity Study*), social status and role-playing factors (*The Social Status Study*), Freudian and other developmental factors (*The Personal Development Inventory*), Murryan need systems and Adlerian life styles (*The Life Style Analysis*), and existential factors (*The Existential Study*).

The grand research design here is to factor analyze the eight individual inventories by sampling various factors separately, in order to identify the principle factors in each instrument, and then to construct a master inventory in which all important primary factors are represented, which will be factor analyzed again to discover possible second-order factors cutting across more peripheral group and specific factors.

MY FEUDS WITH THE PROFESSION

My early contacts with the American Psychological Association were quite frustrating to me as a young student. Enthusiastically interested in clinical psychology, I found no opportunities in the APA to express my concerns and few people who even seemed to want to talk things over. My early attitude was one of eager willingness to go along with the APA and become an active part in shaping the new profession of clinical psychology. Between 1932 and 1945 I tried to vent my concerns but no one seemed to be listening.

By 1945, when I started the *Journal of Clinical Psychology,* I had already determined to function in the role of a loyal opposition to the APA, utilizing an independent podium to state things which I could not find expression for within its official deliberations. A review of the Editorial Opinions which I wrote over the years in *JCP* will reveal the multitude of issues with which I have confronted both the APA and also individual professionals who seemed to me to be getting off base. Although many of the points at stake will now seem to be dead issues because they have since been unsatisfactorily resolved, many of them were associated with delicate and sensitive differences of opinion concerning how the field should develop.

My most loyal supporters, over the years, have been post-graduate clinicians out working in the field. *JCP* has been the post-graduate professionals' journal over the years. That it has had some influence is indicated by the fact that in 1945, 0 per cent of clinicians were labeling themselves as eclectics but by 1970 over 50 per cent of the APA division's twelve members were identifying themselves with eclecticism. The professionals out in the field, who are best acquainted with actual working conditions, had never had the official professional representation which they deserve.

Perhaps the most important professional development between 1960 and 1970 involved the cumulative impact of research in the clinical judgment area which provided increasingly cogent evidence that much was wrong in the field of clinical training. When the majority of the best trained clinicians are unable to make valid and relevant judgments and predictions, something must have been grossly wrong with their training. Realization of this situation caused us to give special emphasis and encouragement to clinical judgment studies in *JCP,* and also to focus on the failure of basic science psychology and clinical teachers to come up with valid foundations for clinical practice. We have repeatedly issued the call to return to fundamentals—back to psychodiagnosis to discover what is the matter with the bases for clinical decision-making.

The pattern of the 1970s is already becoming clear. Confronted with their clinical-training shortcomings, many academicians and APA professionals have turned to nihilism, hair-pullings, and hand-wringings, proclaiming that clinical psychology is dead and that all psychologists should return to the safer areas (safer from criticism and actuarial evaluations) of academia and laboratory research on minutiae. Indeed, the 1970 APA presidential address was given over to chanting eulogies over the demise of clinical psychology, to calls that clinical training programs should be abandoned in university departments, and that we should return to the laboratories. Our message is that we ought to retire to pasture those academicians and professionals who have proven so invalid and irrelevant in the past to clear the way for a new generation to return to fundamentals and work out the salvation of the field with techniques which are more valid, relevant, and workable. We need to dispense with the cold dead hand of the ultra-conservative establishment, to get out from under the restrictive control of the methodologists, to come into our birthright of actual clinical practice where the action is.

MY FAMILY AND SOCIAL LIFE

On August 1, 1936, I married Eleanor Murdoch Chalfant of Pittsburgh, Pennsylvania, a graduate of Bryn Mawr College with graduate training in psychology and occupational therapy. Eleanor turned out to be just what I needed as a working teammate, capable and willing of turning her hand to anything that needed to be done. Many times we have moved boats and refrigerators together, and painted walls. Eleanor is an excellent cook and homemaker, able to put on a full-course banquet at a moment's notice.

We have two children, Peter born in 1938, and Patricia Anne born in 1940. Peter turned out to be an outdoor type, most interested in dogs, hunting, and fishing. He worked for me in the publishing business for about ten years before retiring to the logging business which is more to his interests. Peter has four children.

Patsy early showed an intuitive interest in psychology but did not major in the subject because she did not like the objectivism taught at Bryn Mawr. Nevertheless, she maintained her interests in the field by starting to read proof for the journal and eventually becoming managing editor for *JCP* and *Psychology in the Schools.* Patsy had her first child in 1970, so Eleanor and I have five grandchildren as of this writing.

Some of our happiest hours were at Lake Champlain, where for many years we held Grand Isle workshops in psychology every Monday afternoon during the University of Vermont summer session. They were attended largely by the summer session staff. Every Monday afternoon we would get together and discuss psychology for several hours while drinking and engaging in gay repartee, followed by a picnic supper and more discussion. These sessions were truly worthwhile for all concerned.

Personally, I have not been much of a socialite or "joiner." I work and think best alone, and large masses of people irritate and annoy me. In the private practice of psychiatry, I ran across so much human inefficiency and suffering that I craved solitude in leisure hours. Many of my books and papers have been written drifting alone in the middle of Lake Champlain in my old cruiser where I could look up and be refreshed by the scenery when I sensed mental fatigue.

My editorial work has been facilitated by the fact that I have speed (if not power in depth) intelligence, being able to think and decide very fast. For example, I read very rapidly and can glance over a journal manuscript to tell whether it is publishable within five minutes and I can edit a whole manuscript in not too much longer. In the years when I ran the whole publishing business alone, I was doing work in one to two days which it took one or two people a whole week to accomplish.

Even more important has been steadiness of purpose, in that I learned what I wanted to be at about age sixteen in high school and have stuck to psychology steadfastly ever since. I am convinced that a person does not have to be highly intelligent to succeed if he merely sticks to a job and works hard over long periods. Once I had visualized the idea of a scientific publishing venture with the possibility of influencing more people editorially than I could even by teaching, I determined to let nothing tempt me off into other pathways even though several times I became very much interested in academic or business ventures. I have stuck to one career throughout my life and its saving grace was in involving sufficient variety to keep me interested. Perhaps my most intense motivation has been that I had to make a go of it if it was humanly possible within the limits of my abilities.

ON MY OWN SHORTCOMINGS

On reading other autobiographical efforts, I have been continually impressed with the fact that most writers spend most of their time delineating their successes and very little time on their failures. So I have made up my mind to be very frank about my own "hang-ups" because I believe that my readers deserve to know something about my failures as well as my presumed successes. My lifetime colleague and friend, Dr. William A. Hunt, has always insisted that you cannot understand a man's work without knowing a great deal about the person who lies behind what happens.

First, let me state that I have never been in a psychotic state or even had a severe psychoneurotic reaction. I have never had any spells, fits, or convulsions. Physiologically, I have had a very labile autonomic nervous system, resulting in a wide gamut of psychosomatic symptoms when fatigued or under even moderate stress. Fortunately, upon studying medicine, I learned that all these symptoms were functional in nature and could be ignored, which I swiftly proceeded to do.

I early developed certain sociopathic reactions incident to being myopic. I was allowed to escape written homework and study for the first few years of schooling because an ophthalmologist said that close work might ruin my eyes further and also because I was relatively small and frail and had to learn to use my wits to get by. In other words, I used to try to use my wits to get something for nothing, experimenting with dishonesty, deceit, and cheating to try to make up for what I hadn't honestly learned. Only when I learned that the costs were too high did I abandon such tactics. However, this sociopathetic strain proved to be of great help in later years in understanding and working with severe sociopaths.

The biggest hang-up of my life, as the reader may guess from what has gone before, was in trying to understand and get along with my mother, who was a very difficult person to get along with, and who "bugged" me all the time and continues to influence me after her demise because of the habitual reactions which I built up in relation to her. In short, the extreme ambivalence which I developed in relation to my mother involving elements of dislike, disrespect, anger, and even hate, undoubtedly has conditioned and warped my reactions to all mankind. Mother was a person who never allowed herself to be ignored, and from whom you could never get away no matter how much you disliked what she did because she always demanded interactions. She was a person who could be extremely charming and yet I doubt whether anyone ever really liked her. Certainly everyone who was ever intimately exposed to her selfish, domineering machinations came to dislike her intensely and so did my father even on his death bed. It took me some years, and a great deal of progressive frustration, before I discovered that the world didn't seem to give a damn about me and that anything I got I would have to earn myself. Also, I have had to beware of perfectionistic tendencies in myself, particularly in relation to my expectations of others. It took me many years to learn that while perfectionism may pay off in relation to the physical world where exact causal relations exist, in the social world there are many ways to Rome and preference for any one may reflect only personal preferences rather that a black-white dichotomy of right versus wrong.

Since early adulthood I have recognized that I am somewhat of a difficult person to live with, both because of certain temperamental qualities and because of my high expectations of myself and other people. I have often cited the analogy that people are like abrasive wheels of different degrees of hardness, e.g. the harder wheel tends to wear down softer wheels. Being an extremely complex person myself, it requires someone of approximately equal complexity to understand me empathically and this not everybody is able to do. In any case, I can be very critical, competitive, and demanding at times, and I am completely capable of making the person who does not and/or cannot deliver very uneasy. I have to watch myself to give the other fellow living space and not to crowd him too much psychologically and competitively.

Many people have thought I am too serious and sober because of my constant philosophical and existential preoccupations. I have always been vitally interested in the important issues of life and have wanted to talk about them with all who would listen. For example, as a young student I naïvely imagined that one of the purposes for attending the annual conventions of the American Psychological Association was to get to know and gain inspiration from any revered elder statesmen of the field. To my consternation, I discovered that most people simply wanted to drink and carouse around. I have never been a country-club personality, and small talk can be most difficult for me, particularly with persons of limited intellectual repertoire. I have gone for years at a time without finding anybody who seemed to understand what I was interested in or wanted to talk about it. As a result, I was forced to learn some "lines of talk" to get along with the average people in my community and, at times, this has been quite forced and unnatural for all concerned.

At times, I have wondered whether I was actually temperamentally suited to the practice of psychiatry where all kinds of misfits and incompetence are the daily diet. Being somewhat existentially insecure myself, I found myself at the same time being fascinated and also repelled by the depths of human failure and degradation which I daily encountered. I found myself torn by the conflict of wanting terribly to help unfortunate people while at the same time coming to despise them for what they did. There came a time when my revulsion against human stupidity and degeneracy began to overweigh my compassionate feelings, and then I decided it was time to stop practicing psychiatry (1961).

A related hang-up has recurred many times over the years in the form of a conflict between principles and expediency. As a young person I was very idealistic and a strong believer in "principles." I had been taught that one should never sacrifice ideals or principles. In real life, to the contrary, I painfully discovered that the Establishment usually operates according to expediency and political considerations. Several times in my life I have had bruising jousts with the Establishment over issues of principle. I differed with the psychological and psychiatric establishments over the validity of their theories and practices. I jousted with state government over how institutions should be planned and operated. I jousted with the Roman Catholic Church over the sterilization of the mentally defective and disordered. I have jousted with political parties over short-sighted policies. I have jousted with discrimination and unfairness wherever encountered. My head is bloody but unbowed, but I am getting a little tired from the continuing necessity for controversy in the interests of progress. I have learned that there are times to be expedient and times to stand firm.

In this connection, some people who have known me best may have wondered about an abrupt change in my existential philosophy and interests which occurred about 1950. As a young student and physician, I was again quite idealistic and even socialistic, having resolved to devote myself to the care of the unfortunate. Between 1930 and 1950, I devoted myself principally to the care of mental defectives, epileptics, delinquents—mental cases of all sorts—giving more if anything to the lower classes than to the upper. In 1950 I experienced a sort of conversion experience in which the insight suddenly came to me, "Why have I been spending my life on the unfit and the infirm where what I can accomplish is limited at best when what I am more interested in are the superior and the more creative?" I suddenly realized that the unfit and the infirm were not really what makes civilization advance—that it is the essential man who can do the necessary things, who is most important and should be studied and cultivated. I suddenly decided that I would spend the rest of my life working with the fit and the competent. In this connection, about 1960 I became aware of Ayn Rand and her objectivist philosophy and found that she had verbalized many of the things which I had belatedly come to see as most important. I was confronted with the issue of "Whither is mankind going?" and came to believe that the ultimate value of a man is in terms of what he can actually do. I came to understand that such abstractions as "love," "hate," "aggression," and "fear" are all referential terms which have no actual meaning except with reference to specific actions and situations. Some of my critics have felt that this change of direction was for the worst, but I have felt that it involved an essential reorientation.

Since 1960, my concerns with "Whither mankind?" have led me to become increasingly concerned and dismayed over the social convulsions which seem to be engulfing the world. Mankind appears to be entering another of its cyclic periods of confusion and turmoil where it is running mindlessly off in all directions like a chicken with its head cut off. I must confess extreme impatience with nondirectivism, permissiveness, Christian passivity and forgiveness, compulsory togetherness, anti-intellectualism, nonjudgmentalism, carrying principles to the point of absurdity, and other excesses in the name of democracy and freedom. I perceive the futility of arguments and persuasion, and can conclude only that the only resolution of truth will be in the actuarial costs of acting out any way of life. Those who are in error will have to pay the costs of their stupidities and it will all serve them right. I am too old to be bothered as long as I run my own life sanely. So I believe in rational self-interest. So what? It is my life; let others run their lives to suit themselves.

Although truly enjoying stimulating human contacts, in my adult life I have become more and more of a loner because it is the only way in which I preserve the time and energy necessary to accomplish what I really want to do. Early in my work career, I found myself tending to become overcommitted, to accept too many assignments, and to invest myself in things which really were not that important. Many people were clamoring for my time and attentions, and I soon found that I had to ration my resources in terms of the highest priorities.

For one thing, I have done my best thinking in solitude and I have had to reserve large blocks of time for my editorial duties and creative writings. I can work efficiently only in quiet aesthetic surroundings where I can hear myself think. It has been best for me to be alone for long periods of time and I have come to resent invasions of privacy.

More importantly, I tend to become overstimulated by people to the point where my thinking is unbalanced by impulsivity. When alone, my thinking is much more logical because I am not overacting emotionally to other people. Many of my most excessive statements, of which I have later become very regretful and embarrassed, have come in reaction to public appearances or disturbing human contacts where I have overacted emotionally in ways which I would not repeat after due rational consideration. I have come to distrust my emotional enthusiasms and resentments which, although occasionally creative and constructive, have too often been too impulsive and unbalanced.

One of the most difficult tasks for me has been to restrain myself and be polite or tactful in situations where it is easier to speak my mind. One of the reasons why I have rejected academic or institutional assignments and remained a lone wolf is that I have always tried to tell it as I saw it—I would rather express myself frankly no matter how the cards may fall. In 1967, I accepted the co-directorship of an NIMH Hospital Improvement Project at the Dannemora State Hospital, which we found in a state of disorganization and mismanagement. Rather than condoning the existing situation at the hospital expediently, we plowed in and worked out a plan to reorganize the entire institution, replacing the old authoritarian custodial management with a modern therapeutic approach. Repeatedly, it was necessary to speak out against individuals and situations which appeared to be blocking progress.

AN OVERVIEW OF MY LIFE

I am satisfied with my existence and could not have done any different than what I did if I had to live over again. My greatest successes and my greatest failures have been due to the same traits and motivations. I like to think of myself as an iconoclast with all the profits that original thinking can bring and all the losses of popularity which stepping on other people's cherished beliefs can bring.

My most creative moments have come in moments of frustration and conflict. Over and over again, when things have not been going well, I have found myself lying awake at night, mulling over my problems and then suddenly developing a new insight making possible a breakthrough with some problem. I have learned to trust my brain as an efficient computer. I have developed the technique of programing my mind before going to sleep, by reviewing in depth all aspects of the problem at hand. Time and again, I find that after reviewing the various aspects of a problem over and over again, the answer pops unbidden into my head when I am least expecting it. I have learned that when I am troubled by very practical life problems and cannot go to sleep because I am so worried about them, that is the time when I am likely to come up with some productive solution. I have found that anxiety and conflict seem to be a necessary precondition for problem-solving and that I should not become too involved with the stress incident to reaching new solutions.

I must attribute most of my creative success to the validity of my subconscious inner processes. I have learned to free associate almost automatically, starting out on a topic with no idea of what I am going to say next and often being surprised when I produce a new construct purely out of inner processes which I really cannot understand or control. The right answer just comes out, and I would really be powerless if the wrong answer came out in the same way.

One thing which really intrigues me (in relation to behavioristic or psychological theories) is the fact that I persisted in following my own destiny and developing my own life style in opposition to very strong forces advocating conformance and/or adjustment. My own parents were very perfectionistic to standards and my mother in particular demanded utter conformance to her dictates. In college I persisted in my studies after several professors told me I didn't belong there. In graduate school I developed my own viewpoints in opposition to the prevailing positions. My whole professional career has been one of loyal opposition to the Establishment. It has cost me a great deal in terms of professional prestige and recognition to advocate unpopular positions just because I happened to think they were most valid. Many of my contemporaries have ignored me and my work, but I have always thought "So what?" I am inclined to think that whatever success I may have achieved was due to the fact that I persisted in being an individual thinker, working out my own solutions at all costs.

And so it is that now I find myself at odds with many of the trends of contemporary life. To a degree never before reached in my experience, during the last ten years I find myself surrounded by nuts, kooks, misfits, extremists, bleeding hearts, militants, queers, deviates, and whole armies of peculiar characters all intent on doing their own things under the stimulus of modern progressive and humanistic philosophies. Where they are going or what they are achieving, I often fail to see. I find myself falling back to an increasing degree upon dependence on the great natural psychobiologic forces underlying life in all its manifestations.

I feel that only that which is truly compatible with Nature can survive and that all the other nonsense must inevitably perish. My job for the rest of my life as I see it is to try to discover what the great natural truths really are and to try to see that they are put into practice. So, my bequest to the young: Continue to struggle after TRUTH.

REFERENCES

Lecky, P. *Self-Consistency*. (rev. ed.) New York: Island Press, 1951.

Meehl, P. E. *Clinical vs. Statistical Prediction*. Minneapolis: University of Minnesota Press, 1954.

Thorne, F. C. *Principles of Personality Counseling*. Brandon, Vt.: Journal of Clinical Psychology, 1950.

Thorne, F. C. *Principles of Psychological Examining*. Brandon, Vt.: Journal of Clinical Psychology, 1955.

Thorne, F. C. *Personality*. Brandon, Vt.: Journal of Clinical Psychology, 1961.

Thorne, F. C. *Clinical Judgment*. Brandon, Vt.: Journal of Clinical Psychology, 1961.

Thorne, F. C. *Tutorial Counseling*. Brandon, Vt.: Clinical Psychology Publishing Company, 1965.

Thorne, F. C. *Integrative Psychology*. Brandon, Vt.: Clinical Psychology Publishing Company, 1967.

Thorne, F. C. *Psychological Case Handling*. Vols. I and II. Brandon, Vt.: Clinical Psychology Publishing Company, 1968.

10

Working Paper

ROBERT I. WATSON

Methodological Note. After I had given in to my vanity and agreed to write an autobiography, several months elapsed before I saw clearly how to proceed. During this period of groping I found myself again remembering a variety of past experiences—recurrent memories that were already part of my subjective life. I decided that I might take advantage of this "spontaneous" recall.

This was all the more congenial because of my particular, and what to many would be atrocious, work habits. All of my books and most of my articles were written by a "scrap method." That is to say, I have long followed the habit of jotting down whatever occurred to me in connection with whatever I was working on whether this resulted in a sentence, a paragraph, or a page, then classifying it, by major category, and filing it away in one of many folders, the classification for which emerged as the work proceeded. More often than not, to my still recurring surprise, the "stuff" seemed to fit together at least for a first draft.

Why not, I reasoned, use precisely this technique for an autobiography? I resolved to record these recurrent memories that must in one way or another be significant even though my interpretation of them might be riddled with rationalization and self-deception. Further, after getting them down on paper, I resolved to try as best I could to see that I did not later polish to deceive.

When I was fifteen I decided to become a bridge-tender. I was already a high school dropout, so any occupation at a higher level seemed to be out of the question. As I saw it, the work consisted of a few minutes' furious activity followed by much longer periods of inactivity. The "guided reading" of high school and college was not for me except for a half-day a week in continuation school required of each individual under sixteen having so-called "working papers" so he would not slip back into illiteracy.

Fifteen is the age when reading is obsessive and all literature new. As I saw it, I could use these blessed periods of freedom for reading—reading anything and everything. To this very day, I cannot but feel that the one sure sign of the progress of civilization is that we have libraries from which books may be borrowed free. One habit was established at this age—keeping lists and evaluative notes on what I read. My isolation from sources of guidance other than my own may have instigated this habit, but, as Allport has said, habits become autonomous, and my current predilection for drawing up various lists of references was launched.

I never did get to be a bridge-tender. My first job was as mail boy with a large manufacturer of cotton thread located in one of the industrial towns of northeastern New Jersey. When reaching sixteen, however, I escaped to the beginning of a white-collar career, although at first still functioning as a mail boy. This was with one of the nation's largest insurance corporations in Newark, New Jersey, where after six months I became a very junior clerk, a position I held for about four more years. Although the pay was meager, the hours were relatively short and I managed to indulge my interest in reading and in music via the radio and a few precious records.

A high school diploma was out of the question but there was

an alternative. By a semester or two of cram courses at night I managed to pass enough of the New Jersey regents course examinations to secure the "equivalent" of a high school diploma. Naturally, I selected the examinations each easiest to master by reading a book. English, history, and something called economic geography were prominent. Three weaknesses thereby began. I was deficient then and now in mathematics and in the natural sciences and I have only partially overcome a weakness in foreign languages.

A minor miracle then occurred. In its wisdom, the state of New Jersey decided that at least two years of college would be necessary before one could attend a law school within its boundaries. It so happened that New Jersey Law School, located in Newark, was the very profitable private property of an individual. So as not to interfere with the flow of new students, the owner decided to inaugurate a program of two years of college study under the severely pedestrian name of New Jersey Law School Pre-legal Department. Since by now we were in the first years of the Depression, the night courses were quite popular. I entered the second class accepted at this fledgling institution and took courses for two years. Despite its somewhat grimy location in a converted brewery, the student body and faculty created a very intellectually stimulating environment.

The faculty was young and enthusiastic. Although they maintained a cynical façade it was not too hard to see that many of them saw it as a bold venture with glorious possibilities. True, there were more than the expected share of "flawed" individuals, those fired from other jobs, restless academic wanderers, and A B D's aplenty, but for a while at least they worked together.

The academic program was severely limited at first. Of the sciences only geology was taught. There were no courses in languages or mathematics, so the social sciences and English dominated the curriculum. Fortunately for me, psychology was offered in the first year. Up to this time the only book that I had read on the subject was a very very dull volume by Henry J. Watt in some English self-improvement series. My first teacher was

Frederick J. Gaudet, who some years later transferred to Stevens Institute of Technology in Hoboken, from which he has recently retired. Brilliant, suave, and the epitome of a sophisticated academician, he made a deep impression on me and I decided, then and there, that I would make psychology my career. I had not come to the Pre-legal Department with a firm conviction that I wanted to be a lawyer—I had merely seen it as the only way to a professional career of any sort. Perhaps prophetic of what later happened, the subject which I found next most interesting was history. The second member of the Psychology Department, Charles Webster St. John, had taken his degree at Clark University. Through his help, I secured a scholarship to go to Worcester for my junior year. This was the Clark that still had in its department Walter Hunter and Carl Murchison. However, most undergraduate courses were taught by Vernon Jones and John Paul Nafe, one of Titchener's last Ph.D.'s. During that year I took French, German, experimental psychology, and modern history which, by then, was my official minor. The course in experimental involved our moving through Titchener's qualitative manual. Years later, this experience would become important, because when I came to Washington University to help found their clinical psychology training program, Professor Nafe, then chairman at Washington, was more receptive to my appearance than he would have been to another because, as he put it, "any clinical psychologist who went through Titchener's manual could not be entirely lost to psychology."

The summer after my Clark year I joined a group of graduate students from Clark who were working in what is now Marlboro State Hospital in Marlboro, New Jersey. With no guidance and little rationale, except a vague feeling that personal attention was essential, each of us worked 'round the clock with small groups of deteriorated schizophrenics. Since this was in the mid-thirties, this must have been one of the pioneer attempts at intensive reaching out to these patients. But nothing came of it.

Since I had not saved enough money, I could not return to Clark that fall even with a Jonas G. Clark scholarship and instead stayed on for a year at the hospital as an attendant. By then New Jersey Law School Pre-legal Department had metamorphosed into Dana College and offered a four-year college degree. I returned home therefore and went to school for my senior year at Dana and graduated in its first class. Our Commencement speaker was Norman Thomas, and I, as salutatorian, also spoke. As I remember it, my talk was the more pessimistic of the two.

During my senior year Professor St. John had become ill and I began to teach his classes. Since he did not return, what was meant to be a week or two stretched on over five years. Only a year or two older than my students I did the only thing I could think of to increase my age and dignity—I grew a mustache.

Fortunately for me, Columbia University's laissez-faire policy concerning its graduate students extended to the point that practically anyone with minimum qualifications would be allowed to enter. My problem, of course, was that I did not even meet those qualifications since I came from the first graduating class of an unaccredited institution. As it was, I was first accepted only as a special student.

The focal point of the first-year graduate program was the course by Robert Woodworth in systematic psychology. For convenience's sake it was taught in the evening and consequently all first year graduate students took this course at this time. About fifty graduate students were in this course. Five of us finished with a Ph.D., although in varying years. I went through the usual offerings—Poffenberger for physiological, Garrett for statistics, Landis for abnormal, Murphy for social, Warden for comparative. I also did some work in anthropology, studying with Franz Boas and Ruth Benedict. I did venture across that "widest street in the world" to Teachers College to take Rudolf Pintner's course in intelligence testing, only to have academic credit refused on the grounds that it was inappropriate to my degree.

The staff-student research seminars were a tremendous source of stimulation to graduate students. Here it was Professor Woodworth who made the deepest impression. It was the catholicity of his knowledge which then seemed to us to cover all of psychology, his reasoned judgments, expressed firmly and yet gently, that awed us.

Many of the professors were relatively unapproachable. This was not the case with Carl J. Warden who, during the years with which I am familiar at Columbia, attracted a large and profoundly heterogeneous group of students—ostensibly to work in comparative psychology—which actually included such individuals (in the years just ahead of me) as Meredith Crawford, Bob Thorndike, and Ted Riess. In general, the atmosphere of the department bred heterogeneity that might be further illustrated by the fact that my best friends as students were Saul Sells and Joe Stone. All of us have gone on to quite different careers.

My dissertation was based on material obtained from my teaching at what by then was the University of Newark. It involved retesting undergraduates for their knowledge of elementary psychology with groups extending over a five-year period. Since I was teaching full time, it took me five years to complete the Ph.D., which was achieved in June 1938. Before then I had begun looking for a job.

A more unpleasant facet of Columbia's laissez-faire policy now came into prominence. Almost to a man, when old grads of Columbia of those years gather they revert to what surely is their major complaint about their graduate school days—the casual disinterest on the part of the faculty in our placement. Our favorite illustration of how it should have been done was the Yale Department of Psychology whose members were seen as working hard at strategic placement of their graduates.

As any provincial New Yorker would, I concentrated on finding an appointment within the city limits or, at the worst, within commuting distance. I was interviewed at such diverse places as Bard College and Brooklyn College, but the worst happened and I was a failure the day I received my degree because the only job I could find was at the University of Idaho, Southern Branch, in Pocatello.

In many ways my two and a half years in Idaho were interesting and rewarding, although the outdoor aspects of life there—the hiking, hunting, and fishing—were completely ignored. The nearest city of any importance was Salt Lake City some 185 miles away. Boise, the capital, was over two hundred miles away and the main campus of the university in Moscow (whose name produced the usual jokes about from whom one was taking orders) was over five hundred miles and relatively inaccessible to boot. The social geography created a situation that led me into a variety of clinical activities for which I was not prepared. For example, Mooseheart, the home for orphaned children of members of the Order of the Moose, requires intelligence testing before a child is accepted—and I was to carry out the testing. Although I had taken Pintner's course in intelligence testing, I had had no practical experience. It came down to this. At least I was no worse prepared than anyone else in a neighborhood of two hundred square miles. So, quite unexpectedly I had to teach myself something about clinical procedures and to begin a small therapeutic practice. Although it probably resulted in considerable misinformation, I remember slaving over the Rorschach manual then available only in German! Of course, most of my time was taken with the more customary activities of teaching introductory, abnormal, and experimental psychology. One of my earlier publications was a laboratory manual for use in this last course; it was called quite deliberately *Manual of Standard Experiments in Psychology* and was designed so as to use the least expensive equipment obtainable.

My experiences in Idaho were important for other reasons. I met and collaborated with Vivian E. Fisher, a pioneer psychologist-psychotherapist. It was through him that I arranged to spend a summer as research associate at Idaho State Hospital in Blackfoot. Out of this relationship came a series of articles concerned with the meaning and measurement of so-called "affective tolerance." We collaborated on two papers and in publishing the inventory, and I continued this work for a series of three or four more papers that appeared during the years thereafter.

When the opportunity came in February 1941 to accept appointment in the Student Counseling Bureau of the College of the City of New York, I seized it quickly. Not only did I increase my salary almost 50 per cent (from $2,200 to $3,000) but I was still enough of a city person to think that I was returning to civilization.

In December 1941 I applied for a commission in the United States Naval Reserve. I went on active duty in May 1942 and started immediately to evaluate would-be naval aviation cadets. Except for the longer hours and wearing a uniform, there was no other immediate change in my style of life. I simply took the same train from the New Jersey suburbs and then the Hoboken ferry, but downtown instead of uptown. I had not a single moment of indoctrination, then or later. For this small favor I am grateful, although, possibly, it did leave me more readily thinking as a civilian in uniform. Although on active duty for three years, eleven months, and twenty days, I marched in formation only once and I never took the obligatory weekly physical exercises. A certain amount of small shrewdness and petty adroit maneuvering must be acknowledged.

During the first two years on active duty I was concerned with aviation cadet selection. By then, psychologists were being more and more used in connection with many other aspects of Navy life. I heard unofficially I was being sent to "Siberia," an outlying field of Corpus Christi Naval Air Station located on the vastness of the King Ranch. (Why I was to land there is irrelevant to the story.) I carried out some unofficial negotiations and arranged to transfer to the neuropsychiatric service which resulted in a billet at Bainbridge Naval Training Center, Bainbridge, Maryland. Here my primary task was on the receiving line, where I gave a one-minute psychiatric-psychological examination consisting of three or four key questions and an immediate decision to investigate further or to let events take their course. The remainder of my time was taken with some in-depth examinations of an hour or two, and sitting on boards which decided whether a recruit would go on to service or return to civilian life.

For the first time since going on active duty I had some leisure that could be devoted to more general psychological activity. The only reading resource, however, was a substantial run of issues of the *Psychological Abstracts*. Since I had to make do with what I had, I decided that I would begin to prepare a bibliography preparatory to what proved to be my first two books in clinical psychology. Another officer attached at that time to Bainbridge was Chauncey M. Louttit who generously encouraged me in this endeavor. I say "generously" because at the time his was the only available book in the field and therefore I was a potential competitor.

As the end of the war approached, my thoughts naturally turned to finding a civilian occupation again. After two or three leaves in order to investigate possibilities I accepted appointment as director of the Bureau of Measurement and Guidance and an assistant professorship in the Department of Psychology of Carnegie Institute of Technology, Pittsburgh. This opening came about because Laurance Shaffer had decided to go to Teachers College, Columbia. As anyone who knows Shaffer will understand, I found the bureau a thoroughly organized and efficient activity. I continued working in counseling activities and teaching the usual array of undergraduate courses appropriate to my interest and experience.

One day early in 1947 I received an unexpected visitor in the person of Edwin F. Gildae, head of the Department of Neuropsychiatry of Washington University School of Medicine, St. Louis. He dropped in to inquire if I would be interested in appointment in his department as a psychologist responsible for the Division of Medical Psychology and to work in the dean's office, replacing Carylye Jacobson. I spent the next five years as assistant dean of the medical school and associate professor of medical psychology.

My duties as assistant dean can be put very succinctly—I selected medical students and then, once they were enrolled, served as their adviser and, of course, in the process, defending my judgment of them. For the freshmen students I was charged with the responsibility of offering a course in medical psychology. I cannot say that I was very happy with the results, although perhaps part of my sense of frustration came about because in the scheme of things this course was allotted twelve out of approximately twelve hundred class hours leaving a rather overwhelming majority of the hours devoted to somatic considerations. Most of my teaching was on the main campus, where, with Philip Du Bois, I helped to direct the newly founded clinical psychology program of the university. We were later joined on the committee by Saul Rosenzweig who accepted a dual appointment at the medical school and in the Department of Psychology.

For the first time I had graduate students and interns in psychology. The Division of Medical Psychology, of which I was a part, became a rather closely knit, harmonious group of staff, graduate students, and interns. This was a new and stimulating experience for me since I had been something of a loner before that time. The first doctoral dissertation I directed was in the field of gerontological psychology, carried out by Bettye M. Caldwell. Besides Bettye, who at the time was also on the staff of the medical school, Ivan Mensh joined the staff in medical psychology the year after I arrived, and Samuel Granick and James Palmer a year or so later. Joe Matarazzo was our first intern. He remained on for another year as the first and, so far as I know, the only man to take a year's Ph.D. "minor" in medicine. He then joined the staff. Interns, of course, came and went but I must mention two for whom I developed a special fondness, Evelyn Mason and Benjamin Pope. Associated with the division in a more peripheral manner as consultants were two young statisticians, Goldine Gleser and Jane Loevinger. In view of the brilliance of their later work is it any wonder that relationship with them increased my conviction that I was a statistical dolt!

I continued to work on the two books whose bibliographies had been prepared in part during the war years, and in 1949 *Readings in the Clinical Methods in Psychology* and in 1952 *The Clinical Method in Psychology* made their appearance. *Psychology as a Profession* (1954) was also largely written while I was still at the medical school. I also began to work on *Psychology of the Child* but its publication was delayed until 1959, some years after I had arrived at Northwestern. In the meantime I continued the usual variety of research articles, chapters in books, and a series of methodological studies on psychotherapy in collaboration with Ivan Mensh and Edwin F. Gildae.

Interest in the topic and awareness of the need for a particular volume, of course, motivates the would-be author. But I suspect many authors have deeper, less obvious reasons for writing a book. Certainly I had in almost every instance a "private" reason for proceeding with a particular book that had nothing to do with its feasibility, its sales value, my professional advancement, or any other mundane consideration. What I wanted from each book was an answer to a question or questions that writing the book might help to answer. Moreover, as might have been inferred already, the amassing of knowledge is a salient, defensive maneuver on my part and all writing helps to meet this need.

In working on books in clinical psychology this appeared most baldly since I was also trying to see that if knowing what I thus learned verbally about clinical methodology would translate into more sensitive and adroit clinical interaction on my part. It didn't.

In my writing *Psychology of the Child* (1959) I had from the very beginning the goal of satisfying myself whether the literature on "academic" child psychology could be reconciled with psychoanalytic contentions. My limited answer to myself would be that the two streams of evidence at least are not incompatible and that many research findings from academic psychology can be integrated under psychoanalytic rubrics. To a somewhat lesser degree, the second edition some years later helped me to answer how integration with the Piagetian literature could be related to the main stream of child psychology.

When I was first appointed assistant dean there was a possibility that I was the youngest assistant dean of a medical school in the United States. It took me five years to realize, the situation being what it was, that if I lived long enough, I would die the oldest associate dean of a medical school in the country! In a medical school a hierarchy is a very real and living thing. In certain respects my status among 750 full-time, clinical psychologists was that of number three man—below the dean and another assistant dean. And yet, in another sense, for many day-to-day decisions I was not even on the hierarchy since I lacked the M.D. degree. I must confess sometimes mentally comparing the situation to that of a poker game in which the other players were allowed to use the joker and I was not.

This problem was by no means the decisive factor that brought about my move to Northwestern University in 1953. Although I had found time to write the books and articles I have already mentioned, I had to do most of the work after ten o'clock at night and on weekends. Illustrating of the sheer intensity of the tempo was that events had conspired to give me time for a total of but three weeks' vacation in the five years. I wanted that form of leisure which is freedom to work on what one wishes. The final incident which hardened my resolve to make the move came when a young ophthalmologist with whom I was to collaborate in studies of squint died of a heart attack certainly exacerbated by overwork.

At Northwestern I found a relatively small department. The person I had known best before arriving was William A. Hunt, since we had been in the Navy together. Among other senior members of the department were Benton J. Underwood and Carl Duncan and, a year or two later, Donald Campbell. Essentially there were three graduate programs, with Carl and Ben in general charge of the experimental program, Don in charge of the social program, and I with the responsibility for the clinical program, although, naturally, Bill Hunt maintained his interest in this last field. A stalwart in the clinical program was Janet Taylor, who supervised perhaps more Ph.D. dissertations than any other member of the department during these years.

The publication most decisive for my future work was "A Brief History of Clinical Psychology" which had appeared in 1953. Research articles of mine, although presumably respectable enough, caused no great response on the part of others. There had been the usual request for reprints, incidental mention in related literature, and so on, but there was really no particular impact. This particular article seemed to strike a responsive chord. It has since been reprinted a half-dozen times and I had more requests for reprints than I had had for all my other articles combined. While still very much actively engaged in clinical teaching, research, and practice, I began to wonder in the early years at Northwestern if my strengths did not lie in the area associated with this particular publication. Increasingly thereafter my publications were to take a historical turn. My teaching responsibilities in the general field of personality made it quite possible to stress historical aspects and I proceeded to do so.

It was in about 1959 that I decided explicitly to become a historian of psychology in the sense that I resolved thereafter this would be my major area of research and publication. But there were many obstacles. For one thing, there seemed to be little in the way of company and hardly any precedent. Heretofore psychologists had turned to history for a text, article, or monograph and then went back to other, more absorbing interests. The only ones who had been consistent in their interest were aging psychologists who confused an interest in their extended present with an interest in the past. And yet I knew that scattered around the country there had to be a handful of individuals with similar interests.

In 1960 I attempted to stimulate interest in the field by publishing a paper that was meant to serve as a challenge, "The History of Psychology: A Neglected Area." To show how much could be done I emphasized how little had been done. For example, among other findings I reported that approximately 60 psychologists out of 16,000 consider the history of psychology among their several interests. No one could argue that this was an impressive number.

Another step also taken in 1960 was the result of a meeting in Evanston involving David Bakan, John C. Burnham, the historian, and I. We decided to take advantage of a provision in

APA convention programing that allows individuals to publish an announcement that at the annual meeting a "special interest group" was to meet. In September 1960, fifteen or so individuals showed up! In subsequent years, however, the number increased to about fifty. In my more pessimistic moments I said our purpose was to huddle together for warmth. Actually, the meetings were quite stimulating and gradually those interested in history came to know one another.

A newsletter containing news and notes about meetings, publications, and courses taught was first published by the group in October 1960. This also tended to bring individuals working in history a bit closer together. Quite deliberately the group was without officers, dues, or even an official name. Many of us found this state of affairs congenial. When the possibility of a formal division within the APA was first broached, I demurred. The argument that convinced me that such a step was necessary was the comment of one young psychologist to the effect that a division of the history of psychology would give a stamp of authenticity to work in this area—that it would help bring recognition that the history of psychology is a form of specialization. We decided at our meeting in 1964 to proceed with a petition for divisional status. In September 1965 the governing body of the APA approved the formation of the Division of the History of Psychology with a charter membership of 211. This has grown, so that today there are approximately 400 members.

The next development in which I participated came about in part because of an affiliation I have with a publishing enterprise in clinical psychology. I had been on the Editorial Board of the *Journal of Clinical Psychology* since 1951. At our meeting in 1962, Frederick C. Thorne, editor and chief stockholder of the journal, proposed to us that we consider founding some additional journals. As a first venture in this area, he suggested organization of what eventuated as *Psychology in the Schools*.

The next year or so I spent thinking through and organizing a prospectus for a historical journal. In 1963 a plan was presented to the group and their financial backing was secured. The next year was spent soliciting articles and arranging for a multi-disciplinary board of editors drawn from psychology, anthropology, sociology, neurophysiology, neurology, psychiatry and psychoanalysis, and history itself. In January 1965 the first issue of the *Journal of the History of the Behavioral Sciences* appeared.

Certain expectations turned out to be all too true—the first few years were touch and go financially, numerous suspiciously yellowed-page manuscripts came in along with a horde of papers of the genre that could be epitomized by the title "My Three Hours with Freud." However, with the steadfast cooperation of the Editorial Board, a gradual stability and a certain standing in the field emerged.

During the sixties Edwin G. Boring had an important influence upon me. My relationship is epitomized in the dedication of *The Great Psychologists* (1963a)—"To E.G.B. my teacher, under whom I never studied." His erudition, his helpfulness, even his narrowness expressed in the grand manner, were important to me. The latter can be illustrated by our first interaction in 1956. The occasion allows me to deliver a story that has never appeared in print and, since it appeared on a postcard, would not be in his carefully preserved letter correspondence. It was on the occasion of his requesting that I prepare for the *American Journal of Psychology* an obituary for Lightner Witmer. After making the request he seemed to feel that he must justify his not doing it himself. So he went on to explain, "After all, I knew his work until 1896 but then he went into clinical psychology and naturally I lost track of him." I might add that in 1896 Professor Boring was ten years old.

Some years later, Boring agreed to read critically the next to last draft of my *The Great Psychologists* (1963a). Anyone who knew him would have guessed correctly that his comments were often longer than the material on which he was commenting. In many ways he did much for the burgeoning specialty of the history of psychology. He lent his support to the history of psychology group, the Division of the History of Psychology, and to the *Journal of Clinical Psychology*, the last both by joining the Editorial Board and by submitting an article for the first issue. Just for fun Donald Campbell and I embarked on editing his papers. In this endeavor we were ably abetted by the late Gordon Ierardi of John Wiley & Sons, our mentor on publishing matters. In this connection, let me tell a part of a story that is new. When the idea was broached to Boring in Cambridge by Ierardi that we edit a collection of his papers, he supported the venture with the statement that "only modesty would have prevented me from suggesting it myself," as we have already reported in the Preface to the volume (1963b), but we did not go on to report that under his breath he was heard to mutter "and Tolman had to collect them himself."

At Northwestern I had continued to work in the general clinical area, directed my share of dissertations, and carried out the numerous administrative duties that fall to a director of clinical training. Increasing administrative responsibility is part of that almost inevitable development of a clinician who remains in an institutional setting. Attracted to clinical activities he discovers that his reward for service and for skill consists of inexorably moving in the direction of less and less clinical contact. For the clinical facilities with which I was affiliated I ended up as the consultant to the director of training who saw the staff psychologist, who saw the psychological trainee, who saw the patient!

Acceptance of an appointment as professor of psychology at the University of New Hampshire beginning in 1967 was influenced by several considerations. I was already familiar to some extent with their plans for the Ph.D. program that they were in the process of installing because, along with Fillmore Sanford, I had made a consultant visit two or three years before to meet with the graduate council, the department, and the administration concerning their plans. Although many individuals contributed to these plans it was Eugene Mills, now academic vice president and then chairman of the department, and Raymond Erickson, just now retired as chairman, who offered the leadership. They impressed me tremendously and events have served only to increase my admiration and friendship.

What they were seeking was a classic department involving general experimental psychology, with degrees in physiological, cognitive and perception psychology, social psychology and personality, and the one that was particularly intriguing to me, history and theory of psychology. If I were to move to Durham it would give me the opportunity to establish the pioneer Ph.D. program in this field. Evanston was changing as Chicago kept creeping northward and I found a multi-university somewhat less to my liking than it had been in the past. But it was the opportunity to work full time in the history of psychology that was so much of an inducement that I could not but accept the appointment.

Another step toward professionalization of the emerging specialization of the historian of psychology was taken when funds were secured by Josepf Brozek and I from the National Science Foundation for the Summer Institute on the History of Psychology (1969, 1970). This institute was held in June 1968 at the University of New Hampshire the summer after I arrived. The thirty participants, twenty-five post-doctoral and five pre-doctoral, seemed to find it stimulating. So too did the five or six instructors whose services we had arranged. We were careful to include among their number both a historian of science and a psychiatrist so as to signalize the fact that our specialization had relation to other areas as well.

One direct outgrowth, instigated by Julian Jaynes, one of the instructors, was an inter-disciplinary society, *Cheiron: The International Society for the History of the Behavioral and Social Sciences.* It held its fourth annual meeting in June 1971. Although the international aspect is still more of a hope than it is an accomplishment, *Cheiron* has proved to be inter-disciplinary in scope.

We in the Department of Psychology spent the next years getting organized in a preliminary fashion. One major development was the selection of the department by the administration to apply for a departmental development grant from the National Science Foundation. After some years of assiduous planning this grant was received. It began in 1970.

To go back to history as a field, a point of view that I developed in clinical psychology was to have its counterpart in work in history years later. I had coined (or unconsciously plagiarized) an aphorism, "Clinical enrichment is research contamination." It expressed my awareness of the necessity of attempting on the one hand to do justice to the sheer idiographic subtleties of the psychological functioning in a person that is a patient and on the other hand to conduct research with due attention to the demands for rigorous quantification and careful delimitation of the research variables. The line that I tried to walk was that of a balance of the two in which I saw the clinical psychologist as being as rigorous as the qualitative data permitted—but no more. A similar point of view is being expressed in my work in history through my determination to use quantification as a tool in the study of history but not to the extent that it excludes the qualitative material that is essential to the historian. The goal again is rigor, but not rigor that distorts.

In their doctoral dissertations several current graduate students have found or will find use for quantifying devices—for example, content analysis and statistical manipulation. On the other hand, I support enthusiastically other dissertation topics unequivocally not quantitative in nature.

It is my position that psychologists have something positive to contribute not only to the study of history of psychology but also to the study of history in general. He is perhaps better equipped with certain skills than the typical historian. His expertise in quantitative methods, his knowledge of social and dynamic psychology, and his familiarity with personality research and theory may well serve in the future to give new breadth and depth to other aspects of history.

The first of the history of psychology Ph.D. dissertations at the University of New Hampshire was completed in 1970 by Barbara Ross. It was entitled "Psychological Thought Within the Context of the Scientific Revolution: 1665-1700." Dr. Ross applied content analysis categories, cast in prescriptive variables terms, to the relevant articles in the *Philosophical Transactions* for this temporal period. When her quantitative findings were combined with the usual narrative approach, she demonstrated, prescriptively speaking, that the basic attitudes and modes of conception of the seventeenth-century scientist included a behavioral view of man, thus tending to cast doubt on the more conventional view that psychology as a science was a product of the nineteenth century.

The Great Psychologists (1963a) followed a predominantly biographical approach. Returning to my theme of having a private reason for writing, I wanted to see how far I could go using the individual as the vehicle of history. Although the book seems pedagogically successful in that it meets an educational need, i.e. it sells rather well, I was not fully satisfied. I had become convinced during the writing that the Great Man approach cannot be *the* framework for historical writing and research, important though it may be as a subsidiary tool. I was also convinced that the Zeitgeist or climate of opinion approach was so empty of meaning as to be no more than a subsidiary approach in the same sense as the biographical. This made me restless. I wanted another framework.

Thomas Kuhn's work on the paradigmatic sciences gave me an important clue. He argued that mature sciences are guided by paradigms. In one of his meanings, a paradigm is a universally accepted model that serves for an appreciable time as a framework of that science. He considered all sciences once and some sciences now to be pre-paradigmatic, i.e. to lack this guidance. In view of psychologists' quarrels about what is basic in psychology and our national provincialisms I readily agreed with his position that psychology was pre-paradigmatic. If not paradigmatic, what served in its place as guiding themes? At the outset I assumed a plurality because if the guidance function was monolithic then it would be paradigmatic in the sense just defined. What seemed necessary were trends numerous enough to deal with at least some of the complexity of psychology and yet not so numerous as to make them so specific as to be relatively meaningless. After some years of cutting and filling, I came up with a list of themes that I call "prescriptions." Since it is impossible to go into detail let me say crudely that thirty-six prescriptions emerged, sometimes arranged in terms of eighteen contrasting pairs. To quote a more formal statement about their nature:

A prescription is an attitude taken by a psychologist toward one or another aspect of his psychological concerns. By conceiving prescriptions in attitudinal terms, in effect, I am opening up the possibility of placing them in the setting of social psychology. The major function of prescriptions is conceived to be orientative or attitudinal in that it tells the psychologist how he should behave. A quantitative prescription is manifested by a psychologist when, faced by a psychological problem, he forthwith starts to ask how he might quantify it without necessarily first inquiring whether the problem is suitable for quantification. Moreover, in order to be of historical value, the prescriptions isolated for study must have existed over some appreciable period of time. The rational and empirical prescriptions have served a guidance function for centuries while more specific manifestations such as logical empiricism have been of historical moment for much shorter temporal periods. Empiricism and rationalism then are the prescriptions; logical empiricism a manifestation of them (1971b).

Prescriptive attitudes may show a variety of interrelationships in a particular formulation and differ according to the particular temporal and national setting. Locke espoused an empirical view of human nature in an England that was overwhelmingly rationalistic in outlook. Rationalism was then dominant, empiricism barely counter-dominant. "Contrast," "dominance," "polarity," "gradation," "integration," "implicitness," "contentual," and "methodological" express in capsule form some of the ways in which temporal changes in prescriptions may be expressed.

A program of research on prescriptive theory has begun to emerge. First there was a paper that was an account of the then current status of psychology in the United States (1965) in a symposium in which others offered papers on the French, English, and German psychology. This symposium took place at the International Congress of Psychology in Washington in 1963. In my paper, some, but not all, prescriptive trends were utilized but merely as aspects of an implicit framework. My own thinking was not at all clear on many issues. For example, I treated "manifestations" and "prescriptions," as I later called them, as equivalent. So far as prescriptive theory is concerned, the paper gave me confidence that, using the beginnings of prescriptive theory as a basis, I, at least, could make sense out of the current scene in psychology in the United States.

Then the opportunity arose for me to give a rather lengthy paper as a formal address. This paper, "Psychology: A Prescriptive Science" (1967), meant to establish my theoretical position along with an account of whatever scraps of evidence I had at that time. It was a prolegomenon of further work, not a summarization of past accomplishments. In the meantime I was working on a book in the history of modern psychology which naturally opens with the seventeenth century. Since prescriptive theory was the means of organization, it helped me to answer the question whether it would work for the seventeenth century as it seemed to do for the twentieth. In order to get something in print about it a few years later I "lifted" from this manuscript a paper on Descartes (1971a).

In the meantime students and others were writing dissertations and carrying out factor analytic studies using prescriptive theory which produced further evidence interpreted as positive in nature. Then the time arrived not only to state a further "refined" view but also to compare the approach with other ways of interpreting the history of psychology. The paper being published as I write this is the result (1971b).

All of this is a far cry from a textbook account of a formal programatic design. It more resembles prospecting by drilling test holes here and there in a terrain that we have some reason to believe will have positive results.

Another project on which I am now engaged originated in a sort of gossipy game that Garry Boring and I had played. The context was of our common editorial interest in necrologies (my territory, I gathered, was to be the sociotropes while he reserved the biotropes for himself). In 1966 I wrote a letter mentioning by name some of the psychologists whom I thought would be remembered a century from now. He responded with an almost entirely different list. After a certain amount of argument back and forth we decided we just couldn't agree on living psychologists. So at some point we switched to psychologists of the past and found that there was much more agreement. If we could agree why not submit a list in more formal fashion to a larger panel? So we pooled our files for individuals who contributed to psychology from the seventeenth century coming onward with over a thousand names resulting, submitted the names to individuals we considered knowledgeable, and asked for their evaluation. The study of eminence was published in 1968.

After the study was finished, Garry wrote me that the five hundred or so psychologists who topped the panel ratings would make a rather neat basis for a book of short biographies which he proposed to write. This stirred me to think about what further I might do with our findings. *Eminent Psychologists: Primary and Secondary References* with approximately 12,000 primary and 36,000 secondary references to appear in a year or so is to be the result. The references to be reported are, of course, selective, but include indications about the more complete locations of individual bibliographies. The other secondary references include autobiographies, biographies, past and current critical studies both in books and journals, citations in encyclopedias, handbooks, and so on.

This volume, of course somewhat pedestrian in nature, is my present low-key work. I have found that I function best when I work simultaneously on two (or more) problems each at a different level of complexity and involvement. The demanding problem gets me worked up to a certain level of excitement that cannot be maintained indefinitely—the less-demanding is the laborious but lazy-going activity of my other hours.

What else? Well, historians of psychology still lack a monographic outlet and several of us are working on this problem. A book in the history of personality theory is under way, and I shall return to work on my book on early modern psychology. Two other books have a few scraps in my folders. And then . . .

REFERENCES

Readings in the clinical method in psychology. (Ed.) New York: Harper, 1949.

The clinical method in psychology. New York: Harper, 1952. (Paperback reprint, Wiley, 1963)

A brief history of clinical psychology. *Psychological Bulletin,* 1953, *50,* 321-46.

Psychology as a profession. New York: Doubleday, 1954.

Psychology of the child. New York: Wiley, 1959. (Second, Oriental, and Spanish editions in later years)

The history of psychology: A neglected area. *American Psychologist,* 1960, *15,* 251-55.

The great psychologists: From Aristotle to Freud. Philadelphia: Lippincott, 1963a. (2nd ed., 1968; 3rd ed., 1971)

With Donald T. Campbell (Eds.). *History, psychology and science: The collected papers of Edwin G. Boring.* New York: Wiley, 1963b.

The historical background for national trends in psychology: United States. *Journal of the History of the Behavioral Sciences,* 1965, *1,* 130-37.

Psychology: A prescriptive science. *American Psychologist,* 1967, *22,* 435-43.

With Edith L. Annin and Edwin G. Boring (Eds.). Important psychologists, 1600-1967. *Journal of the History of the Behavioral Sciences,* 1968, *4,* 303-15.

With Josef Brozek and Barbara Ross. A Summer institute on the history of psychology: I, II. *Journal of the History of the Behavioral Sciences,* 1969, *5,* 307-19; 1970, *6,* 25-35.

A prescriptive analysis of Descartes' psychological views. *Journal of the History of the Behavioral Sciences,* 1971a, 7, 223-48.

Prescriptions as operative in the history of psychology. *Journal of the History of the Behavioral Sciences,* 1971b, 7, 311-22.

11

Some of My Doing

WILSE B. WEBB

It is a personally engrossing task to put these pieces together into some coherent pattern: Yazoo City, Mississippi; Cambridge, England; Iowa City; Okinawa; University of Florida. Or Hull-Spence learning theory; aircraft accidents; clinical tests; sleep. Or teaching; department chairing; association presidencies and politics. Or the hundreds of pages in some one hundred papers and three books that include: "The Use of the Wechsler-Bellevue Intelligence Test in the Study of Mental Deterioration" (1942); "The Motivational Aspect of an Irrelevant Drive in the White Rat" (1949); A Checklist Technique for Evaluation of a Training Program" (1949); "A Qualification of the Use of Analysis of Variance" (1950); "The Problem of Teaching Internships" (1952); "Some Relations Between Two Statistical Approaches to Accident Proneness" (1953); "Leadership, Followership, and Friendship: An Analysis of Peer Nominations" (1955); "Elements in Individual to Individual Communication" (1957); "Antecedents of Sleep" (1957); "The Choice of the Problem" (1961); *The Profession of Psychology* (1963); "Sleep Patterns of Young Adults: An EEG Study" (1964); "Micro-sleep Responses in the Rat" (1965); *Sleep: An Experimental Analysis* (1968); "A 'Couple' of Experiments" (1969); "The University-wide Department of Psychology" (1970).

However interesting and challenging this may be to me, there is a prior question that should be raised before this becomes a public matter. Is this ego trip necessary? If not necessary, since it could hardly meet that classification, of what possible purpose could it be? The question is first a general one about biographies. I know why I read them. I read about famous or infamous or wise people (who are sometimes neither famous nor infamous) to learn from them—not so much to learn facts or skills or solutions, but to learn about courage and grace and daring and hope and style. Sometimes even less—to simply vicariously experience life on a broader and more extravagant plane than will ever be possible for me. For example, the life of Madame Pompadour.

But even in matters of psychology, without false modesty, I cannot really consider myself famous or infamous or wise. Marginally so, yes, but not first rank. Not a name that will echo in the corridors of history nor be heard beyond the lives of a few students and friends. On the other hand, I have been productive, I have been voted into transient positions of leadership, and I have lived a good life as a psychologist. More importantly, I am a partisan of psychology. I find it important, exciting, and endlessly challenging. I would defend it, reform it, scold it, praise it. In short, I am in love with it. Perhaps that is enough. I can at least try to express some of this joie de vivre so that a student may have some vicarious vision of it.

This story will be divided into three parts: personal growth and times; beliefs about the profession of psychology; and working at being an experimental psychologist. The first of these segments is purely autobiographical, and I don't believe it is particularly useful in the sense of how to become a better or worse psychologist. The other two sections are amazingly independent. My beliefs about psychology as a profession have grown independent of my laboratory and teaching and vice versa. The former have been accretions and expressions of being an administrator and a political person within the organizations of psychology and the university. The latter has been an intellectual trip generally unrelated to broader concerns of psychology. The analogy of the physicist running for political office would not be inappropriate. Because he is a physicist, he is undoubtedly different from a lawyer, but neither being a politician nor a physicist has a major influence on the two aspects of his life.

PERSONAL AFFAIRS

Nobody starts out to be a psychologist. Today, maybe, one must begin in his sophomore year to make grades and to take courses to get into the graduate school of one's choice. Or even today one may become "hooked" on psychology through a course in high school or becoming acquainted with a not now unrare psychologist. But not in Yazoo City, Mississippi, in the 1930's. I am sure those days affected me but did not direct me toward psychology.

I can see some of the effects. There, and in other small southern towns, one acquires a thing about lost causes. A statue in Yazoo City to the Confederate dead says, "As at Thermopylae the greater glory was to the vanquished." You read a lot to make the world bigger in such a small town. You know everybody. When your high school class has about fifteen people in it, you know everybody. When your town has six thousand people (half black and half white) you know everybody. You grow up believing that you can and should talk to anyone. There is also something about an agrarian world that has to do with time. It is very complex, but part of it has to do with working very hard in cooperation with the natural process of growing in time. You can't plant and you can't pick whenever you want to, and you can't make it grow any faster than it will.

I went to Louisiana State University (because everyone else was going to Ole Miss and my mother was from Louisiana). I don't even remember how I happened to take a course in psychology. Mostly, I was celebrating life, which was comprised of fraternities, beer, girls, football games, running an off-campus humor magazine. However, I did take some psychology courses. But there is no doubt, however, that the accident of psychology for me was midwifed by Harry Capps—a lonely, lost, neurotic Ph.D. of Carney Landis from Columbia. He had done his Ph.D. on epilepsy and was now teaching vaguely interested swamp children of LSU. He paid attention to me, talked to me, put psychology in front of me. (He killed himself in November of 1941 as a protest against our involvement in World War II.)

I graduated in 1941. I didn't have the foggiest notion of what to do. I went to work in the Mississippi State Mental Hospital for the summer. During the summer, I received a telegram from the University of Tennessee offering me an assistantship ($30 per month) in psychology. That was arranged by Capps. However, a friend from Jackson, Mississippi, who was an art major at Iowa suggested that I go to Iowa as a fraternity house adviser (room and board). I knew him and the idea seemed more interesting than going to Tennessee, so I went to graduate school in Iowa. In those days when you went to graduate school, you were not "admitted."

Iowa simply was more college to me at the time. I registered for courses since that presumably was what one did. Names in books began to become people. A course with Kurt Lewin (pronounced "Leveen" at the time) and one with John McGeouch on verbal learning. Carl Seashore slipped in and out like an aging ghost.

Pearl Harbor was bombed while I was playing bridge in the fraternity house. A few weeks later, fate (and the machinations of John Flanagan) kindly posted a notice on the bulletin board announcing a place for psychology students in the Army Air Force Selection Program. The Iowa male graduate students marched out en masse. My days of glory were somewhat blunted by not being able to pass the eye examination for "volunteers." I had to get myself hurriedly drafted, thus following my compatriots to San Antonio Aviation Classification Center six weeks after they had arrived.

Memories of the peoples, places, and times of the four years of the war are overwhelming even in recall. I moved from private to master sergeant to officer candidate school to ultimately studying pilot combat efficiency on Okinawa. This last involved going in the lead navigation planes (Air Force fighter pilots were miserable navigators over water) on strike missions against Japan and China from Okinawa. I was scared green.

I would certainly not wish my experiences to be an endorsement of war, but I recognize the value of those years for me. I met and became friends with people who were among the best psychologists of the time as they entered the wartime program as officers. They and my future colleagues and friends who were beginning in psychology were to become the psychology of my time. Through them I saw that psychology was not an abstract set of statements in a textbook but that it existed in people and in places. I could see that a scientist and a science could exist outside a classroom or a laboratory and was of people's doing. Personally I was made less provincial, less self-centered, and more confident of my place in the world. Finally, I was given the rare chance in our society of finding out if I am brave. I am not, particularly.

I returned to Iowa in early 1946, married (in 1942), with a child, and a very different person than when I had left. I was going to become an experimental clinical psychologist. I ended up a believer in Clark Hull and a disciple of Kenneth Spence. I wish I could say that this was an intellectual and evaluative choice. I know that it was not. My wartime friends were in learning, and those that I liked best at Iowa were in learning. I joined them in courses with Spence, Judson Brown, and Gustav Bergman.

And that's all it took. I know I cannot capture in the net of words the source of influence of Kenneth Spence on me, although the influence is clear. It was not, for me at least, at an interpersonal level. I found him somewhat mirthless and reserved. He seemed to want, indeed need affirmation, admiration, and loyalty but was not easily able to accept it. I always felt he wanted to be warmer and more human than his social skills permitted.

Nor were the facts that he taught me influential, although I believe his schema for ordering the behavioral world is still sound and worth learning. No, the influence which has been with me ever since was his mind and his commitment. He had a conceptual brilliance guided by a deep-rooted empiricism. His concepts were elaborate and complex but never misty and always grounded in data. They were always testable and never mere verbal descriptions. Most critically, there was an impelling urge to understand more, to correct misconceptions, or, more often, to replace mere words with proven facts, trying to lay a track across the miasma of thought with data. No man standing in the presence of this urge to know could ever again be satisfied with his own efforts.

I graduated in about eighteen months and in September of 1947, I finally went to the University of Tennessee where that year psychology was emerging from the Department of Philosophy and Psychology into its own individual department. In late spring, John Paul Nafe, a magnificent carrier of Titchner, offered me a position at Washington University in St. Louis. Not only was it challenging, but the salary was a magnificent boost (from $2800 to $4200 as I remember).

Washington University was five good years of teaching made better by two summer schools at the University of Southern California. I ran rats as I had been properly taught, consulted on aircraft accidents, and got an Office of Naval Research contract in technical training. Unfortunately (or perhaps fortunately) I was not to be promoted in my fifth year to associate professor and, more out of bewilderment than anger since I was publishing, a popular teacher, and, I thought, all I needed to be, I took a position as the head of the Aviation Psychology Laboratory at the School of Aviation Medicine in Pensacola, Florida. That time was made good by the presence of new Ph.D.'s being assigned in the Medical Service Corps for their tour of military duty. Working on the selection and training of naval aviators, I survived as an administrator by learning to ask two questions: for those emerging from their Ph.D. and wishing to continue their basic research, I would ask, "But what does this have to do with naval aviation?" And for those who wished to plunge into problems of the "real world" on particular problems of naval aviation, I would ask, "How will this generalize?"

After five years good fortune struck again and I became the department head of the University of Florida in 1958. I've been there since, but the time has been embellished by two fellowships to Cambridge, England. I resigned as chairman in 1969 and was appointed a graduate research professor.

Are there any lessons here? It has been a time of good fortune and good friends. Perhaps I've had some part in bringing those about. If so, it has been based upon confidence—not a confidence in myself, but in the essential belief that people really want things to work out as well as possible and given half a chance, they will try to make them do so. Given such a base of being with and working with people (and they are always involved), it gives a person a hell of a lot of confidence. This, by the way, is a simple extension of reinforcement theory.

I suspect there is one other aspect. I never have learned to say no—to a person, to a problem, or to a party. I must add that over the last few years, although I still find myself cognitively saying "yes," the behavior turns out "no."

THE PROFESSION OF PSYCHOLOGY

First, I would use the term "profession" to set the stage for my beliefs and concern about the profession of psychology. Webster's *Seventh New Collegiate Dictionary* lists these definitions of the word in historical order: *"profession* n. 1: the act of taking the vows of a religious community 2: an act of openly declaring or publicly claiming a belief, faith, or opinion: Protestation 3: an avowed religious faith 4a: a calling requiring specialized knowledge and often long and intensive academic preparation b: a principle calling, vocation, or employment c: the whole body of persons engaged in a calling."

My personal position prefers the definition 4a; the current scene of psychology seems to me to drift toward 4c, or more dismally, into the definition of "professionalism": "the following of a profession for gain or livelihood."

First, let me openly declare my belief about psychology: (1) Our primary task is to determine behavioral principles. (2) We must in turn teach these to the users of these principles. It is as simple as that.

Of course, I shall elaborate. I have this undoubtedly oversimplified idea about societal roles. It goes like this: in the nuclear family group, in circumstances of dispersed cultures such as frontier movements or nomadic tribes, all jobs are done by that limited group: food production, housing, teaching, enforcement of rules. As groups become more complex, by convenience and necessity, critical activities become parcelled; some workers exclusively tend to the food needs, others manufacture required tools and goods, others begin to administer justice, and others take on the processes of education of the young. I believe you can see the emergent groupings of agriculture, manufacturing, law, religion, and education. Complexities and numbers further produce transportation, bartering, and personal amusement services. Eventually, the complexities and the tasks produce experts to aid in the refinement of these processes and we find the emergence of the arts and sciences. Ultimately, the arts and sciences themselves become so complex that they may develop an autonomy which often makes difficult their interaction with their original purpose.

I do not consider this process as a description of the emergence of psychology. I feel that psychology developed so late in the process that it was a combined result of sheer curiosity (which had always been present). It was largely a child of philosophy and a step-child of religion and further extended from unanswered questions of several extant disciplines, physics and physiology in particular. Rather I present my view of history of the development of societal roles to make the point that society has already "assigned" the major behavioral services prior to the emergence of psychology: e.g. education, law, medicine, manufacturing. However, the *behavioral sciences* were lacking. Now I believe that the previous methods of behavioral control are failing (education, slavery, religion, legal control, for example) and the tasks are becoming so complex as to require a science of behavior for these control systems. We happen to be available for that purpose.

To restate this. The "assigned" roles and programs of our society which involve behavior have primarily developed to cope with social requirements. They have reached the point of needing improved ways. However, the various programs are so deeply involved in the process of production that they need a science to aid them in coping with their procedures. Unless we respond, these programs will develop their own sciences and we will be without a purpose. We will aid these programs best by improving their ways of proceeding, rather than attempting to provide their already organized services.

I have written elsewhere more specifically about the practice of psychology (Webb, 1970a), and about how departments of psychology in universities must meet their problems of training (Webb, 1970b). Let me quote from one of these about my specific feelings regarding the future of practice in psychology.

The issue here is not whether there will be practitioners using psychological information and techniques. Where knowledge and need combine there is inevitable utilization. Rather there are two questions: Who will practice psychology? and What manpower and resource priorities will be given by psychologists to practice itself?

The deciding of who shall practice psychology depends on what we mean by practice. If we mean any application of psychological principles or procedures which can lead to more effective human behavior, then to argue that such practice and principles shall be the sole prerogative of psychologists is not only ridiculous but immoral. Teachers, parents, pastors, politicians, physicians, managers, engineers, indeed almost all those engaged in human interaction, are continuously faced with needs and opportunities to "apply psychology." To argue that they must call in psychologists to be effective would be both absurd and evil.

We would probably agree that only psychologists should practice dangerous psychology techniques (whatever they may be). I would further think that we would tend to restrict this to PhDs. The assumption here is that danger exists, that the benefits exceed the danger, and that training and screening of PhD psychologists makes them more responsible in accepting and minimizing the danger.

For those other practices based on training requirements for effectiveness or time necessary for application, we are faced with two alternatives—training more psychologists or training others more fully and buying their time. One position proposes to follow the first procedure, training people to become psychologists at various levels of performance. An alternative is to train individuals within the various professions to perform specific psychological tasks associated with those professions. This is not a new idea; in fact, it exists in many forms. There are, for example, guidance counselors, psychiatric nurses and social workers, special education teachers, rehabilitation counselors, personnel selection technicians, pastoral counselors, psychiatrists, industrial engineers, consumer researchers, etc.

We have not settled, however, which is the more viable model. The arguments for "setting our own practice standards and training requirements," "autonomous professional integrity," and "protection of the public" are offset by manpower pools, professional entrenchments, public images and, most important, the need for contextual training and know-how for effective performance in highly varied settings.

What priorities are to be given within the profession to practice? We may affect practice in three ways: efforts at restriction of practice, training and research, practice itself. Choosing among these I would give, in the light of my previous argument, the lowest priority to restrictive activities. At best these activities are engaged in for the "protection of the public" and at worst the protection of the psychologist.

". . . I would give the highest priority to the matter of teaching and research, since I believe that this is the most effective means to enhance practice itself. I believe it is our best manpower response to improving the methods of practice. Simply, there will always be more of "them" than of "us," and I, at least believe procedures are best improved by research. Practice in and of itself is a process that ends in its execution. Teaching others and devising improved methods of practice has an endless effect and is a multiplicative affair.

"As for practice itself, I will not argue against it, but only against priorities which would interfere with our jobs of teaching and research. With proper priorities and perspective, practice is vital to the well-being of psychology. Certainly there have been and are likely to continue to be socially necessary technological applications which are (a) not yet teachable, (b) not yet recognized in their importance, and (c) which require training and application time which cannot be afforded by other professions. It would be wrong if not impossible to fail to provide these activities. Moreover, the day-to-day interaction with contextual settings such as mental health and industrial and educational arenas offers continuous challenges and enrichments for teaching and research. Only when technological application or practice becomes an end

in itself and absorbs our limited training and manpower resources
or warps our programs of training and research into limited objectives would I feel that our priorities are misaligned (Webb,
1970a).

I recognize that what I have said so far is mostly referent to the
problem of rendering clinical services. I feel, however, one may
generalize these comments to all aspects of professional psychology: the extent to which the psychologist is the doer, not the
creator and the trainer, is the extent to which he aborts his role
as an effective psychologist. If, for example, an industrial psychologist solves a particular problem and this problem solution has
no generality, he has been a tinker, not a psychologist. If he then
continues to act as the problem-solver rather than replace himself with a technique or if he teaches someone else to do the task,
he is not even a tinkering psychologist, he is a personnel manager,
a shopman, an engineer, or what have you.

I have been fortunate to be in the kitchen in these matters—
nine years with the Air Force and the Navy as an applied psychologist, a department chairman concerned with a complex of
training programs, and a part of the apparatus of the APA as it
has struggled with these problems. This may not guarantee the
credibility of my beliefs but at least they have been tempered by
perspective and reality.

I have been heavily involved in the organization of psychology.
I have been president of the Southern Society for Philosophy and
Psychology and the Southeastern Psychological Association. In
the apparatus of the APA, I have been chairman of the Policy
and Planning Board, the Convention Committee (now Board), a
member of the Board of Directors, and I am currently on the
Education and Training Board. I have been a member of the
Council of Representatives and the president of the Division of
Teaching.

I am lucky to be able to finish this section about administrative things by reverting to a personal point of view. I recently
survived a "retreat," which is one of the euphemisms for an "encounter" group, centered on departmental administration. I
learned a lot and was told a lot about the way I act. The three

things I remember most clearly (and of course I remember the good things or have reworded them into good things), were as follows: I come off as confident, making things happen, and involving people. Since I've already written about the confidence bit, I will comment briefly on the latter two aspects.

I find more often than not in approaching problems, be they short-term approaches such as committee meetings or more long-term prospects such as running departments, that there's a strong tendency to end up solving or dissolving the problem with words, but doing very little about it. Resolutions, discussions, appointments of committees to further discuss the problem may be satisfying, but unless they result in active changes they are seldom satisfactory.

Most of the time, it seems to me, problems really amount to points of immobilization or impasse resulting from complexity or confrontation. I have found that frequently if you can abandon the search for some grand or complete distal solution and seek a proximal action that can be initiated, the problem can at least be changed. Once movement can be accomplished, new solutions or at least new perspectives emerge and the old problem may be put aside.

As for the involvement of people, I would suggest this: people seldom can or will be persuaded to do something that they don't want to do or can't do well. On the other hand, things that people can or want to do are oftentimes useful in solving a problem or pushing a project along. I think projects or problems are seldom solved by grand schemes that ignore the talents and desires of the individuals involved in those schemes. Rather the scheme has to be organized around the people rather than the people around the scheme. If you then go ahead and pick up the few remaining pieces and do the things that the most people involved don't care about doing, most of the time the program can be pulled off.

SCIENCE AND ME

Then there is the other side of the coin; following the analogy, the head side. This is a description and evaluation of me as a data-gathering person, or my attempts to be a scientist. I shall do this in three parts: my present thoughts about science, comments on my two attempts to verbalize about this process, and then a capsule and evaluation of my behavior.

The simplest and for me the most useful bedrock definition of science would be simply: science is the minimization of error. I recognize the paucity of this definition and will try to qualify it further. However, like any good, very loose clothing, it fits well in the sense of being comfortable.

At the other end of a definitional continuum I must thank a theoretical physicist: Serge DiBernadetti. One day at Washington University, probably after an armwaving initial lecture on science (I tend to begin all courses in praise of science), I decided I really didn't know what *real* science was. As a consequence, I went over to the nearest real scientist that I knew—a theoretical physicist—and asked him what science was. He paused about one second and said, "Of course, science is fun!"

Over the years, I've perhaps elaborated on only these two important statements about science. I can perhaps best summarize these elaborations by going over my response to a conversation which I had with a younger colleague a few weeks ago. Because I teach a course called Contemporary Theories (I have noted that most chairmen end up teaching either introductory psychology or history since these seem to be the only two that they can keep up with), he came to me for commiseration. He had asked second-year graduate students to identify such terms as "Fechner," "Zeitgeist," "positivism," "Brunswik," and the like. He said, "They are packed with facts and can do triple interaction analyses of variance, but they seem to have no perspective." He then said, "Why don't we start a course in philosophy of science?" Strangely enough, for me, I heard the word "we" and said, "Let's think about it." I've been thinking about it since.

What would I really want to say about science, and a course about the science of psychology? I find that this is not one thing but many things.

First, *it*, science, is certainly a body of facts (or as close as we have been able to come to facts) and is a particular set of methods for collecting and analyzing facts in one's particular domain of interests. But that seems to me to be the tip of the iceberg.

These facts and procedures are creations of individuals struggling to capture beautiful butterflies of their time, driven by beliefs about their pursuit. As such, to me, to know about science and its real meaning is to know about these individual efforts of describing their selected world in the great flow of time. In short, history.

Certainly, also it is to know and be concerned about the "classical" philosophy of science. It is foolishness to wander through the terrain of knowing and believing and the seeking of facts while ignoring the attempts of full-time minds to cut epistemological and ontological paths. To ignore such people as Russell, Whitehead, Carnap, Feigel, and Bridgman, to name a few, is like trying to find a treasure without a map.

But still more important to me is to observe the stubborn and brilliant assaults on common ideas by long successions of brilliant people and to observe the emergence of new ideas and approaches in the brilliance of human creativity. This is to follow the assault on the problem of sensation by Locke, Fechner, Berkeley, Brentano, Wertheimer, and the psycho-physicists such as the contemporary Stevens, or the struggles with individual differences by Binet and Cattell into the contemporary work of behavior genetics or to observe the individual genius of such men as William James, Ebbinghaus, or Pavlov. This is some combination of history and philosophy of science—perhaps it is what people mean by a history of ideas.

I must admit I'm not sure what can be learned from the pursuit of a history of ideas and the men in that history. Two things, however, are quite obvious: a belief in the mind of man and a personal humility.

I have written on two occasions about a part of the process of science: about the choice of the problem to research (Webb, 1961) and on getting started on a problem (Webb, 1968a). Each of these was in response to the challenge of a presidential address, for the Southern Society for Philosophy and Psychology and the Southeastern Psychological Association, respectively.

Both are cramped into the confines of the now of "doing an experiment" in contrast to the historical and broader perspective and interpretation championed above. However, they were cries of anguish about two very real problems of experimenting. They were concerned with the triviality of so many experiments, and oddly, and perhaps somewhat in contrast, the matter of going ahead and doing an experiment. I waive a claim to profundity, but I did try to speak to two very real problems that I had observed in my years of teaching about and doing experiments.

In the *Choice of the Problem*, I stated that some six criteria, either independently or in combination, were the typical bases for justification, the initiation, approval, or funding of experiments. These were curiosity, confirmability, compassion, cost, cupidity (personal gain), and conformity. I evaluated and rejected these as adequate criteria for the development of a valuable experiment. I concluded that "Unfortunately . . . there is a . . . probability that a studied meeting of these guidelines will pay off (but) in small change." I then suggested that more appropriate bases for experiments or problems were "knowledge, dissatisfaction and generalizability." I said that "You must know thoroughly the body of research and techniques of experimentation . . . related to a given area." In addition, "You should disbelieve, be dissatisfied . . . with what you now know." I noted that these two statements were not incompatible since the latter should be an active process of knowing and then knowing differently. Finally, I stated that one should evaluate the generalizability or extensity of one's experiment. I quoted Poincaré in his *Methods of Science*: "What then is a good experiment? It is that which informs us of something besides an isolated fact. It is that which enables us to foresee, i.e., that which enables us to generalize. . . . It is needful that each of our thoughts be as useful as possible, and this is why a law will be the more precious the more general it is. This shows us how we should choose. The most interesting facts are those which may serve many times."

My second foray into "how to do" science was concerned with how experiments get started and my basic premise was a simple one: "that most research is initiated by research that precedes it, one's own research or someone else's." I noted that most experimental findings were not definitive in character. I quoted from the discussion section of experiments verbatim: "It appears, then"; "were assumed to reflect"; "indicated that"; "we can tentatively conclude that"; "one may argue that"; "the results are open to two and possibly three interpretations." I then examined the "why" of this tentativeness which I felt in turn permitted, indeed provoked, further experimentation. I noted that both dependent and independent variables almost inevitably permitted extensions or improvements; that the relationships between variables typically permitted further interpretations; that experiments were always done in particular context and variations in these contexts were fruitful sources for further experiments; that by-products in the form of chance observations or new techniques were nearly always inherent in each experiment; that accidents did occur which provoked further experimentation; that your skills may interact with other areas or other skills may interact with your knowledge base to permit more refined experimental work.

I was quick to note that following these experimental procedures did not necessarily lead to good experimental work. I merely felt that they were sufficient conditions to provoke experimental work.

My own chasing of the beautiful butterflies has been flawed by at least one major fault. This fault can be labeled a lack of persistence. On the polite side, I could blame this on a need for new challenges; an overresponsiveness to the problems at hand; limitations of time resulting from trying to be an administrator, teacher, father, politician, and bon vivant. On the darker side, there is perhaps a superficiality, a reaching for the quick and dirty, a need to shift when the going gets rough. I don't know. I suspect it may be a combination of all of these things and more.

Certainly a part of my early flitting around across topics was of the times and a matter of possibility. In the early 1940s, one could pick up almost any article, certainly understand it, and possibly see how to improve or extend it. In each person there was the potential of a renaissance man—a man interested in *all* new facts. Today, of course, this is impossible. To be able to read with comprehension any journal in its entirety is a feat beyond my imagination—even a specialized journal in one's own area.

I have often thought about Clark Hull who bravely took on and conquered tests and measurements, and then hypnosis (or vice versa) and rode bravely into the area of learning—just as it was burgeoning. I suspect he was trapped not so much by interest or challenge but by the massive increase in technology and technical facts and their resultant complexities.

But let me stop avoiding the promise of encapsulating and evaluating my performance. The record on various tracks is approximately as follows in terms of journal articles: Learning and Motivation (18); Applied Psychology and Accident Research (12 plus 25 technical reports); Tests and Measurements and Statistics (13); Peer Ratings (7); Psychology and Science (6 plus 1 book); Miscellaneous (5); Sleep (45 plus 2 books and 7 chapters).

About half of the pre-sleep papers (circa 1960) were joint authorships; two-thirds plus of the sleep papers had joint authorships; approximately 90 per cent of these articles have been reports of experiments; and about 10 per cent have been critical reviews or position papers.

So much for the capsule. What about their value? In each instance, I considered each paper worthwhile at the time. I had found out or thought of something that I didn't think other people knew, and I wanted to let them know. In retrospect, I must admit that very often the purpose behind this was not educational but a matter of demonstrating my own cleverness. Furthermore, each article was the culmination typically of varying amounts of effort in terms of data collection and writing. That put an effective value tag on the effort from my point of view.

But more critically, have they been valuable to others?

I may best talk about these in two parts—the non-sleep and the sleep papers. There is a sufficient time perspective for the non-sleep papers to look back with some assurance. Doing so, I would certainly have to say that there is little enduring value in them. As estimates, since I certainly have not kept score, I would say that about one-half of the research reports got into an annual review; about one-fourth were referenced in an ensuing text or so. I am reasonably sure that few if any have been referenced in the last year or so; I receive perhaps one or two reprint requests a year from this group of papers. (There are three exceptions: a paper on emotions (1948) seems to deal with an unsolved and long-term problem; the choice of the problem (1961) has been reprinted at least three times, and the peer-nomination paper on leadership and followership (1955) has been reprinted at least twice.)

But then I think that most of us should not expect much endurance from our research papers. We are, after all, as researchers in a cumulative process in which each finding should be an improvement upon and hence a beginning of the eclipse of previous findings.

I would guess that three-fourths plus of these papers had *some* direct effect. This is a feeling cumulated from seeing the article referenced in other articles, conversations at conventions, and occasional letters. Certainly my doctoral dissertation (The Role of an Irrelevant Drive in the Rat, 1948) spawned a half-dozen articles which showed a faulty interaction between hunger and thirst as a probable cause of the obtained effect.

All in all, it has been a little disappointing, particularly in regard to the work on drive as cues (or rather non-cues), accidents, and peer-nomination methodology. But then perhaps this says something about the sociology of science. I've noticed that unless one carries one's own spear into battle, few people will pick it up.

It is far too soon to evaluate the papers on sleep. Most have been written in the last five years, all in the last ten. In spite of this, I am a little more certain about the immediate effect of this work. I am one of the few first-class psychologists involved in the area, and I am bringing twenty-five years of research experience to the area. Perhaps more importantly, the work has been well financed and I have persisted in my efforts to almost the exclusion of any other research in the past ten years. Objectively, a number of the papers are referenced in almost any new text in the area of sleep and in almost any paper that is in the area that I have been working. One paper has run through more than five hundred reprint requests.

It is again likely, however, that few of the papers on sleep will have a half-life of more than three to five years. Technology is advancing rapidly in the area, and bright minds are thinking ahead daily. If I make an enduring impact, it will be at a theoretical level, and I am only now learning enough to begin to think of the forest beyond the trees.

ENVOI

I turned the preceding over to a tried and true friend and withheld my asking for comments until we had eased our minds with the fruit of the vine. I shall end with my recall of what he said: "It all may be true, but it sure ain't you. You sound like a mild-mannered contemplative senior citizen calmly sitting in the fading sunset of yesterday's flashes of glory. In fact, last Tuesday I saw you firing heavy verbal artillery on stage against a women's liberation speaker. You told me you were on your way to record a poetry reading for your weekly poetry program on radio. I know your sleep laboratory has grants of about $100,000 a year. At a party, you are the one likely to be booming away about almost anything. In many a dull meeting, I've seen you toss a verbal bomb just to stir things up. Frankly, I see you as an attractive, energetic, and ambitious guy, although I admit I don't know what your ambitions are. Psychology just happened to have been the ball park that you played your game in."

SCIENTIFIC PUBLICATIONS

1942   The use of the Wechsler-Bellevue intelligence test in the study of mental deterioration. *Proceedings of the Iowa Academy of Science 49*, 450-51 (Abstract).

1946   Some comments on Marion Bartlett's "Suggestibility in Dementia Praecox Paranoid Patients." *Journal of Consulting Psychology 34*, 97-100.

1947   The role of irrelevant drive in response evocation in the white rat. *American Psychologist 2*, 303 (Abstract).

A note on the Rabin ratio. *Journal of Consulting Psychology 11*, 107-8.

1948 A study of random bar pressing activity in the white rat. *American Psychologist 8*, 33 (Abstract).

A motivational theory of emotions. *Psychological Review 55*, 320-25.

1949 The motivational aspect of an irrelevant drive in the behavior of the white rat. *Journal of Experimental Psychology 39*, 1-14.

With Bloomberg. Variations within a single drive continuum as cues in spatial discrimination in white rats. *Journal of Experimental Psychology 40*, 628-36.

Some considerations of the use of statistics in abnormal psychology. *Journal of General Psychology 40*, 95-102.

With Haner. Quantification of the Wechsler-Bellevue vocabulary sub-test. *Educational and Psychological Measurement 4*, 693-707.

A check list technique for evaluation of a training program. *Personnel Psychology 1*, 465-70.

Occupational indecision in college students. *Occupations 27*, 331-33.

1950 A test of "relational" vs. "specific stimulus" learning in discrimination behavior. *Journal of Comparative Psychology 43*, 70-72.

With Lemon. A qualification in the use of analysis of variance. *Psychological Bulletin 47*, 130-36.

With Rappaport. An attempt to study intellectual deterioration by premorbid and postpsychotic testing. *Journal of Consulting Psychology*, 95-98.

1951 With Dehaan. Wechsler-Bellevue splithalf reliabilities in normals and schizophrenics. *Journal of Consulting Psychology 15*, 68-71.

A study of "place" and "response" learning in a discrimination behavior. *Journal of Comparative and Physiological Psychology 44*, 263-68.

With Teel. Response evocation on satiated trials in the T-maze. *Journal of Experimental Psychology 41*, 148-52.

1952 The problems of teaching internships. *American Psychologist 1*, 20-21.

Self-evaluations and group evaluations. *Journal of Consulting Psychology 16*, 305-7.

Response in absence of the drive of acquisition. *Psychological Review 59*, 54-61.

Corrections for variability: A reply. *Journal of Consulting Psychology 16*, 156.

With Lemon. A sequel to the notes of Patterson and Diamond. *Psychological Bulletin 49*, 131.

1953   With Jones. Some relations between two statistical approaches to accident proneness. *Psychological Bulletin 50*, 133-36.

With Nolan. Cues for discrimination as secondary reinforcing agents. *Journal of Comparative and Physiological Psychology 46*, 180-89.

1954   With Malt. Pseudo conditioning of the response to electroconvulsant shock in humans. *American Psychologist 9*, 489 (Abstract).

Medical needs and absenteeism in a healthy population. *Industrial Medicine and Surgery 23*(9), 416-17.

1955   With Nolan. Students, supervisor, and self-ratings of instructional proficiency. *Journal of Educational Psychology 46*, 42-46.

With Hollander. Leadership, followership, and friendship: An analysis of peer nominations. *Journal of Abnormal and Social Psychology 50*, 163-67.

The problem of obtaining negative nominations in peer ratings. *Personnel Psychology 8*, 61-63.

Humpty Dumpty and the symbols of statistics. *Psychological Reports 1*, 43-47.

A method for evaluating training programs. *Research Reviews*, 18-21.

Self-evaluations, group evaluations, and objective measures. *Journal of Consulting Psychology 19*, 210-12.

The illusive phenomena in accident proneness. *Public Health Reports 70*, 951-56.

Drive stimuli as cues. *Psychological Reports 1*, 287-98.

1956   The prediction of aircraft accidents from pilot-centered measures. *Journal of Aviation Medicine 27*, 141-47.

With Hollander. Comparison of three morale measures: A survey, polled group judgments, and self-evaluations. *Journal of Applied Psychology 40*, 17-20.

A procedure for obtaining self-ratings and group ratings. *Journal of Consulting Psychology 20*, 233-36.

With Wallon. Comprehension by reading versus hearing. *Journal of Applied Psychology 40*, 237-40.

With Izard. Reliability of responses to pictures of peers. *Journal of Projective Techniques 20*, 344-46.

With Kaspar. The ability to reproduce task cues and the ability to perform the task. *Perceptual and Motor Skills 6*, 291-94.

1957   Elements in individual-to-individual communication. *Journal of Communication 7*, 119-24.

With Bowers. The utilization of student learning as a criterion of instructor effectiveness. *Journal of Educational Research 51*, 17-23.

With Wallon. The effect of varying degrees of projection on test scores. *Journal of Consulting Psychology 21*, 465-72.

Applied research: Variations on a theme. (Comment) *American Psychologist 12(4)*, 225-26.

Antecedents of sleep. *Journal of Experimental Psychology 53*, 162-66.

1958   With I. J. Goodman. Activating role of an irrelevant drive in absence of the relevant drive. *Psychological Reports 4*, 235-38.

With Miller and Seale. Further attempts at coding aircraft accidents. *Journal of Aviation Medicine 29(3)*, 220-25.

1959   With M. Schwartz. Measurement characteristics of recall in relation to the presentation of increasingly large amounts of material. *Journal of Educational Psychology 50*, 63-65.

With Rogers and Gallagher. Effect on extinction of restricting information in verbal condition. *Journal of Experimental Psychology 57*, 219-23.

1960   With R. Wherry, Jr. Vigilance in prolonged and repeated sessions. *Perceptual and Motor Skills 10*, 111-14.

With F. Brown. A study of set effects in the verbal conditioning experiment. *Psychological Reports 6*, 50.

1961   The choice of the problem. *American Psychologist 16*, 223-27.

An overview of sleep as an experimental variable. *Science 134*, 1421-23.

The profession of psychology (Ed.). New York: Holt, Rinehart and Winston.

1962   The effects of prolonged learning on learning. *Journal of Verbal Learning and Verbal Behavior 1*, 173-82.

With Wipf. Proactive inhibition as a function of the method of reproduction. *Journal of Experimental Psychology 64*, 421.

The profession of psychology. Editor and chapter contributor. New York: Holt, Rinehart and Winston.

Some effects of prolonged sleep deprivation on the hooded rat. *Journal of Comparative and Physiological Psychology 66*, 791-93.

With H. W. Agnew, Jr. Sleep deprivation, age and exhaustion time in the rat. *Science 136*, 1122.

1963   With W. Stone. A note on the sleep responses of young college adults. *Perceptual and Motor Skills 16*, 162.

With Jeanneret. Strength of grip on arousal from full night's sleep. *Perceptual and Motor Skills 17*, 759-61.

With S. C. Gresham and R. L. Williams. Alcohol and caffeine: Effect on inferred visual dreaming. *Science 140,* 1226-77.

1964   With B. Flanagan. Disinhibition and external inhibition in fixed interval operant conditioning. *Psychonomic Science 1,* 123-24.

With H. Aades. Sleep tendencies: Effects of barometric pressure. *Science 143,* 263-64.

With H. W. Agnew, Jr. Reaction time and serial response efficiency on arousal from sleep. *Perceptual and Motor Skills 18,* 183-84.

With H. W. Agnew, Jr., and R. L. Williams. The effects of stage four deprivation. *Electroencephalography and Clinical Neurophysiology 17,* 68-70.

With R. L. Williams and H. W. Agnew, Jr. Sleep patterns in young adults: An EEG study. *Electroencephalography and Clinical Neurophysiology 17,* 376-81.

With R. A. Levitt. Effect of aspartic acid salts on exhaustion produced by sleep deprivation. *Journal of Pharmaceutical Sciences 53,* 1125-26.

With R. A. Levitt. Effect of pentobarbital sodium on sleep latency and length of sleep in the rat. *Nature 204,* 605-6.

1965   With R. F. Dillon. Threshold of arousal from "activated" sleep in the rat. *Journal of Comparative and Physiological Psychology 59,* 446-47.

Our dreams. *New Society,* February, 6-8.

The nature of natural sleep. *Bulletin of the British Psychological Society 18,* 1-10.

With F. Johnson. Microsleep responses in the rat. *Psychonomic Science 3,* 499-500.

With R. A. Levitt. The effects of early deprivation on later sleep stress resistance and weight gain. *Nature 208,* 1128-29.

With H. W. Agnew, Jr. The effects of a restricted sleep regime. *Science 150,* 1745-47.

With R. L. Williams and H. W. Agnew, Jr. Sleep patterns in young females. *Electroencephalography and Clinical Neurophysiology 20,* 264-66.

1966   With H. W. Agnew, Jr., and R. L. Williams. The first night effect: An EEG study of sleep. *Psychophysiology 2,* 263-66.

With H. W. Agnew, Jr., & H. Sternthal. Sleep during early morning. *Psychonomic Science 6,* 277-78.

With D. Svorad and Smieskova, A. Sleep differences in the EEG picture of sleep in man and mouse. *Ceskoslovenska fysiologie 15,* 133-34.

With R. L. Williams and H. W. Agnew, Jr. Effects of drugs and disease on the EEG patterns in human sleep. Proceedings of the IV World Congress of Psychiatry, Madrid, September. *Excerpta Medica International Congress Series,* 150.

With R. L. Williams. *Sleep therapy.* Charles A. Thomas.

1967   With H. W. Agnew, Jr., J. C. Parker and R. L. Williams. Amplitude measurement of the sleep electroencephalogram. *Electroencephalography and Clinical Neurophysiology 22,* 84-86.

With J. Kersey. Recall of dreams and the probability of stage 1-REM sleep. *Perceptual and Motor Skills 24,* 627-30.

With H. W. Agnew, Jr., and R. L. Williams. Sleep patterns in late middle age males: An EEG study. *Electroencephalography and Clinical Neurophysiology 23,* 168-71.

With H. W. Agnew, Jr., and R. L. Williams. Comparison of stage four and 1-REM sleep deprivation. *Perceptual and Motor Skills 24,* 851-58.

With H. W. Agnew, Jr. Sleep cycling within twenty-four hour periods. *Journal of Experimental Psychology 74(2),* 158-60.

With R. L. Williams and H. W. Agnew, Jr. Effects of prolonged stage four and 1-REM deprivation: EEG, task performance, and psychological responses. *SAM Reports,* July, SAM-TR-67-59.

1968   A "couple" of experiments. *American Psychologist 23,* 428-33.

With H. W. Agnew, Jr., and R. L. Williams. The effects of sleep therapy on the EEG sleep pattern. *Psychosomatics 9,* 135-39.

With J. R. Ross, H. W. Agnew, Jr., and R. L. Williams. Sleep patterns in pre-adolescent children: An EEG-EOG study. *Pediatrics 42,* 324-35.

With H. W. Agnew, Jr. The displacement of stages 4 and REM sleep within a full night of sleep. *Psychophysiology 5,* 142-48.

With I. Karacan, W. Heine, H. W. Agnew, Jr., R. L. Williams, and J. J. Ross. Characteristics of sleep periods during late pregnancy and the postpartum periods. *American Journal of Obstetrics and Gynecology 101,* 579-86.

With I. Karacan, S. M. Wolff, and R. L. Williams. The effects of fever on sleep patterns. *Psychophysiology 5,* 225.

Sleep: An experimental approach. New York: Macmillan Company.

With H. W. Agnew, Jr. Measurement and characteristics of nocturnal sleep. In L. E. Abt and B. R. Riess (Eds.), *Progress in clinical psychology,* Vol. VIII, *Dreams and dreaming.* New York: Grune and Stratton.

1969   The nature of all night sleep patterns. *Activitas Nervosa Superior 11,* 90-97.

With J. Friedmann. Length of sleep and length of waking inter-relations in the rat. *Psychonomic Science 17*, 14-15.

Twenty-four hour sleep cycling. In A. Kales (Ed.), *Sleep. Physiology and pathology. A symposium*. Philadelphia: J. B. Lippincott.

Partial and differential sleep deprivation. In A. Kales (Ed.), *Sleep. Physiology and pathology. A symposium*. Philadelphia: J. B. Lippincott.

1970 The practice of psychology and the university training program. In *Journal of Professional Psychology 1*, 253-58.

A university-wide model of the department of psychology. *American Psychologist 25*, 424-27.

With J. Friel. Characteristics of "natural" long and short sleepers: A preliminary report. *Psychological Reports 27*, 63-66.

With H. W. Agnew, Jr. Sleep stage characteristics of long and short sleepers. *Science 168*, 146-47.

Length and distribution of sleep and the intrasleep process. *International Psychiatry Clinics 7*, 29-31.

Individual differences in sleep length. *International Psychiatry Clinics 7*, 44-47.

1971 With H. W. Agnew, Jr., and R. L. Williams. Effect on sleep of a sleep period time displacement. *Aerospace Medicine 42*, 152-55.

With J. Friel. Sleep characteristics of "natural" long and short sleepers: Personality and EEG characteristics. *Science 171*, 587-88.

With J. Friedmann. Some temporal characteristics of paradoxical (LVF) sleep occurrence in the rat. *Electroencephalography and Clinical Neurophysiology 30*, 453.

With J. Friedmann. Attempts to modify the sleep patterns of the rat. *Physiology and Behavior 6*, 459-60.

With H. Swinburne. An observational study of the sleep of the aged. *Perceptual and Motor Skills 32*, 895-98.

Sleep behavior as a biorhythm. In W. P. Colquhoun, NATO symposium on the effects of diurnal rhythm and loss of sleep on human performance. In press.

Sleep behavior as a biorhythm. In W. P. Colquhoun (Ed.), *Biological rhythms and human performance*. New York: Academic Press. In press.

With Agnew. Sleep latencies in human subjects: age prior wakefulness, and reliability. *Psychonomic Science 24*, 253-54.

With Agnew. Variables associated with split period sleep regimes. *Aerospace Medicine 42*, 847-50.

12

An Eclectic in Psychology

PAUL THOMAS YOUNG

An autobiography can be a history of significant events in the life
of an individual or a history of intellectual and professional development and achievements. This chapter gives an intellectual
history with just enough personal data to set the stage for action.
The story describes changing interests, research problems, laboratory techniques, and decisions during a career in experimental
psychology.

FAMILY BACKGROUND

My intellectual history began in Los Angeles in 1892. Like other
children I naïvely accepted the manners, attitudes, beliefs, and
values of my parents. Father was a Presbyterian minister active
in religious, educational, and philanthropic work. Since his life
style and achievements have been recorded in a book by his
daughter-in-law, it will not be necessary to repeat the record
(N. M. Young, 1967). There were four sons and a daughter in the
family. I was the second son.

It is not easy to evaluate the influence of early family life upon
my personality and career but several things stand out promi-

325]

nently: there was a major emphasis in the home on religion and
the Protestant ethic. Father preached a fundamentalist Christianity which we were taught to accept. Father and Mother instilled
a New England type of puritanical ethics: we were not to smoke
or drink or know anything about sex. We were to attend Sunday
school and church regularly, to be prudent in all things. Father
was frugal in financial matters. I recall that while a student at
Occidental Academy and College I had an allowance of $2.00 per
week and turned in a weekly account of expenditures and balance
(if any). There was, I think, a fair compromise in our home between freedom and discipline.

A second impression of early influences was a strong and consistent emphasis on education. Father was a graduate of Lafayette
College and Union Theological Seminary. Mother was an alumna
of Mount Holyoke College. In 1887 Father called together a group
of ministers and laymen who founded Occidental College. He was
always interested in the welfare of the College and in 1906-7 acted
as president. The five Youngs hold degrees from Occidental College and all went on to postgraduate study, three obtaining a
Ph.D. and two a M.A. degree. Four were elected to Phi Beta
Kappa and three now hold honorary degrees. The Youngs were
thus an intellectual and academic family group.

A third impression of early influences was an active interest in
music. We acquired a variety of instruments and formed various
ensembles: a brass quartet, a mandolin and guitar group, and
several combinations of orchestral instruments. Each of us played
a few instruments including the piano and organ. An appreciation of music continued throughout college years and developed
in later life.

A major impression from early childhood is bound up with the
unfortunate fact that Father and three of his children were
afflicted with a rare yet benign form of progressive muscular dystrophy. For my entire life I have had to cope with physical weakness and limitations; this has influenced my career in ways too
numerous to mention (1971).

EDUCATION

At the turn of the century during horse-and-buggy days in Los Angeles I attended the old Thirtieth Street School located across the street from our church. Somehow I learned to read, write, and do arithmetic despite wretched penmanship and spelling. At one time I wanted to quit school and was adamant about it, but my parents insisted that I continue. The difficulty, I now believe, was the repeated frustrations from an inability to cope with physically normal children on the playground.

After getting a certificate from the grammar school I attended Occidental Academy (1906-10) and Occidental College (1910-14) in Highland Park. In the academy I found geometry a subject of great interest. I worked out a proof of the Pythagorean theorem and attempted to trisect an angle and to solve other problems. This was fun.

Geometry fitted in well with a mechanical bent. As a boy I attempted to make a perpetual motion machine! I repaired clocks, made a toy automobile that ran by clockwork, made fire balloons, giant kites, musical instruments. Some of my later xylophones and marimbas were of good quality, being made of rosewood which I imported from Guatamala.

At Occidental College I began to question the religious doctrines taught at Sunday school. Professor Calvin O. Esterly, fresh from studies at Berkely and Harvard, offered a course in biology that aroused great interest. He outlined in detail the evidence supporting the Darwinian theory of evolution and later described Mendel's pioneer studies of heredity. In the laboratory we dissected a crayfish and then a cat. The theory of evolution contradicted what I had been taught at home. So I began to read and study on my own in an attempt to reconcile the facts of organic evolution with the doctrine of special creation.

At Occidental College the subjects that interested me most were biology, physics, astronomy, mathematics, and philosophy. Although I had elected a major in economics and history, I was more interested in the natural sciences. Languages were off bounds; I struggled with Latin, Greek, German, and French but never enjoyed or mastered any of them. I liked to write, however, as a form of self-expression, but I hated the memorizing required in courses on history and literature.

In philosophy I was interested in three courses: psychology, ethics, and comparative religions. The psychology course was taught by Professor Thomas G. Burt. We used as a text George Trumbull Ladd's book on descriptive psychology. I doubt whether this course influenced me in moving toward a career in psychology but I recall that after graduation, in the summer of 1914, I wrote an essay on "superception" which I later realized was a very naïve groping toward Wundt's doctrine of apperception.

After graduation at Occidental I spent two years in graduate study at Princeton University (1914-16), two at Cornell University (1916-18), and a post-doctoral year as a student in the University of Berlin (1926-27).

DECISIONS AT PRINCETON

In the summer of 1914 Germany invaded Belgium and started World War I. I was deeply impressed by the course of events and continued to speculate about the kind of international organization that would make wars impossible. Despite the war I held to my plan of entering the graduate school at Princeton University. My brother, Arthur, who had been studying economics at Princeton, helped me in getting oriented.

When I arrived at the beautiful and impressive graduate school (which Dean Andrew Fleming West had succeeded in locating on a hill away from the undergraduate campus) I was uncertain as to what courses to follow. I had several conflicting interests. During my first year at Princeton I enrolled in courses in philosophy and psychology, and in a course in theology offered at the Princeton Theological Seminary.

The philosophy courses were excellent. I soon abandoned

theology; in the philosophy courses there was an atmosphere of intellectual freedom which contrasted with the dogmatism of theology. I appreciated this freedom, but was not won over to a career in philosophy.

During both years at Princeton I attended the psychology seminar of Professor Howard Crosby Warren. Professor Warren was proud of the fact that he had succeeded in establishing psychology as a separate department apart from philosophy. There was a psychological laboratory on the third floor of old Nassau Hall in which I did some experiments on tone.

Members of the psychology seminar read papers on topics that interested them. Professor Warren argued for his double-aspect view of the mind-body relation. He claimed that there are not two orders of existence—mental and physical—but a single order which is revealed in two aspects.

Attending the seminar was a Mr. Henry L. Eno, who was interested in the electrical theory of consciousness. He had purchased a number of storage batteries to produce a powerful electromagnetic field around the head of his subjects to discover whether consciousness would be changed by an electromagnetic force. I recall putting my head in the electromagnetic field during a few simple tests of sensitivity but no disturbance was noticed. Mr. Eno appeared to have plenty of money and later he contributed to the construction of Eno Hall, the first psychology building on the Princeton campus.

When my turn to read a paper came around I examined the nature of belief, confidence, and faith. I related these factors to desire and behavior. This interest in human motivation doubtless arose from my personal experience. There had been a conflict over religion and science. There were emotional problems related to my physical disability and life plans. There was an interest in social problems and human welfare. In my experience emotions, feelings, desires, plans were in some way interrelated. I wanted to study them. Alexander Bain had argued that there is a "primitive credulity." The child assents uncritically to what he is told until something happens that causes him to doubt. Belief and doubt are thus psychologically opposed while belief and disbelief are logically opposed. Psychology is different from logic. Two propositions may be logically incompatible yet either may be accepted as in wishful thinking. These views, of course, were thoroughly discussed and criticized by members of the seminar.

I recall a course in physiological psychology offered by J. T. Metcalf who had recently completed a doctorate at Yale University. We worked through the text of Ladd and Woodworth: *Elements of Physiological Psychology* (1911). Here was solid information about the senses, the nervous system, and a bit about the affective processes. The course was followed by one in abnormal psychology and a clinic in psychopathology at the Trenton State Hospital. The clinic was conducted by a Kraepelinian psychiatrist, the late Dr. Clarence B. Farrar. After describing a mental disorder Dr. Farrar brought in patients to illustrate the symptoms. The clinic was impressive.

Life in the Princeton Graduate School was delightful. Meals were served in the great hall where Dean West presided with dignity at the head table. We wore academic gowns at dinner. I recall a Sunday evening discussion group called the Hour Glass, to which selected faculty members were invited to lead discussions of religious, social, and ethical problems. The group included physicists Arthur H. Compton and Alan T. Waterman, economists Wilson Compton, William W. Cumberland, and Arthur N. Young, and others.

I think it is fair to say that at no time while at Princeton did I decide to prepare for a career in psychology. I simply worked on courses of study that interested me. This laissez-faire philosophy led to decisions to drop theology and to specialize increasingly in psychology rather than philosophy. One result of the laissez-faire philosophy is that there has been little difference between work and play. What I did was enjoyable. So I decided to study psychology further.

A MOVE TO CORNELL

In discussing plans for further study Professor Warren advised me to move to Cornell and study under Edward Bradford Titchener whom he regarded as the leading psychologist of the country.

In the spring of 1916 I met Titchener when he came to the Princeton campus to preside over a group of experimental psychologists. This group had been meeting from year to year on different campuses. After Titchener's death in 1927 the group was organized as The Society of Experimental Psychologists, which has become an honor society for experimental psychologists.

At the time the society was organized I was asked to continue as a charter member but voluntarily withdrew from the group. I have never been a joiner. Throughout my career I have avoided situations that would be embarrassing on account of my physical limitations. I am sure that this reticence along with feelings of inferiority have delayed my professional advancement.

Titchener was a large man, typically with a huge cigar projecting from his massive beard. I timidly told him I wanted to move to Cornell to study some problem related to feeling and emotion. After chewing his cigar for a moment he said that I might study the problem of "mixed feelings." I did not know what a mixed feeling was nor how it differed from green cheese but thought it prudent to acquiesce. Subsequently I found out that a mixed feeling was an alleged experience in which pleasantness (P) and unpleasantness (U) coexist.

In the summer of 1916 I studied psychology at the Marine Biological Laboratory at Wood's Hole, Massachusetts. At Princeton I had taken a course in general physiology with Professor E. N. Harvey, known for his brilliant work on luminescence. Professor Warren had advised further study of physiology and kindly arranged a tuition scholarship for me at Wood's Hole. There was no fixed program. I observed developing eggs of the sea urchin, studied the reactions of drosophila to light, and incidentally became acquainted with several biologists including Jacques Loeb, a mechanistic physiologist who was attempting to explain behavior in biochemical and neural terms.

At Cornell in Titchener's heyday psychology was exciting and challenging. There was a group of serious-minded students and a staff which in addition to Titchener included Edwin G. Boring, Karl M. Dallenbach, and Harry P. Weld. The main program for advanced students was a two-year course called Systematic Psychology. This course covered almost everything that was known at the time about experimental psychology. There were numerous references, many in German and French, which we attempted to read; to cover all was impossible. I studied in detail the classical volumes of William James, read Oswald Külpe's text, which had been translated by Titchener, and many other books.

As minor studies I elected a course in physiology planned for first-year medical students which was offered by Sutherland Simpson and a course in mental tests offered in the Education Department by William S. Foster.

Titchener's evening seminars were exciting. Members of the staff and graduate students read papers which were then critically discussed. Titchener explained at the start of the series that all papers must be worthy of publication which standard, he said, was low enough! Professor Weld usually read and approved the papers of graduate students before they could be presented at the seminar.

When it came my turn to read a paper I attempted to evaluate Titchener's claim that psychology must be defined by a point of view (Titchener's of course!) rather than by a specified field of subject matter such as mental phenomena. I collected numerous definitions of psychology and by contrast many definitions of physics. I gave full scope to Titchener's view that psychology deals with the sum total of human experience regarded as dependent on an experiencing organism and contrasted this view with Ernest Mach's definition of physics.

At the time Titchener and Watson were engaged in a controversy over the nature of psychology as the behaviorist views it. I had become personally acquainted with John Broadus Watson at Princeton when he was attending Dr. Farrar's clinic on psychopathology at the Trenton State Hospital. Watson had sent me one of his manuscripts for criticism at the time I was preparing my paper and I think my interest in the definition of psychology dates back to this time. Ultimately I settled for an eclectic approach and in this have been influenced by Warren, Titchener, Boring, Külpe, James, Watson, Lashley, Skinner, the physicist Mach, and others.

AFFECTIVITY AND CONSCIOUS MEANING

My doctoral experiment was an attempt to elicit pleasantness and unpleasantness simultaneously while getting introspective reports from the observers during a relatively brief period (1918a). Mixed feelings had been reported in published protocols but if P and U are dynamically opposed, they should not be *felt* at the same moment. As it turned out the introspections revealed a distinction between affectivity (definitely *felt* P or U) on the one hand and cognitive meaning on the other. In the so-called "mixed feelings" one or both of the "feelings" was a judgment referred to an object and the "feeling" was localized at the place of the object or referred to a situation. In everyday life we hear about mixed emotions but this does not mean that two or more emotions are actually experienced simultaneously.

One of Titchener's seminars was devoted to the nature of meaning. We discussed Titchener's context theory. At the time Titchener was engaged in a controversy with the Würzburg school over imageless thought. Titchener argued that meaning is not observed as an existential process or content of experience. Meanings are "carried by" sensory and imaginal content; they depend upon an experienced context or upon brain processes. Titchener argued that the study of meaning belongs to biology or to common sense or to semantics but not to psychology. I did not accept this view because I wanted a dynamic psychology that dealt with meanings, feelings, values, attitudes, motives, loyalties, and the like, and that had practical and social significance.

While I was studying at Cornell the United States entered World War I. Robert M. Yerkes called together a group of psychologists at Harvard to consider what psychologists might do to help win the war. I attended the meeting. The outcome of the meeting was the development of the Army Alpha and Beta tests of intelligence, which were used extensively for selection and classification of Army personnel. The military psychologists contributed to the war effort in other ways.

At this time I was engaged in doctoral research and not physically qualified for military duty. Faculty members, including Edwin G. Boring, were leaving the campus for military service. Boring's departure made an opening in the teaching staff. I then became Titchener's teaching assistant. I had previously been appointed Sage Scholar in Psychology and the additional income eased my financial situation.

Titchener lectured in an academic gown in the Oxford style. His lectures were clear, illustrated with demonstrations, well organized, and delivered without notes. The lectures were attended by staff and graduate students who sat in the front row. After a lecture there were informal discussions in a smoke-filled anteroom which was called a demonstration laboratory.

As a student at Cornell I never fully accepted Titchenerian psychology. But I retain a great respect for the rigorous, scientific training of the Cornell laboratory. I admired the erudition, the command of languages, the intellectual integrity of the big chief. Titchener used to say, "Learn one system of psychology well. Then you will have something to tie to." We learned Titchener's system but many of his students departed from it not to return.

While working on my dissertation I had weekly conferences with Titchener in his home. These were always helpful and right to the point. On Sunday evenings Titchener conducted a little orchestra. I played trombone, often attempting cello parts since there was no cello. This was fun, but musically not much! After the music we discussed topics that ranged through the universe but never involved technical psychology. In these meetings I became acquainted with Mrs. Titchener, a charming lady, and with the rest of the family.

VIBRATING BARS

From childhood onward I had been interested in things that produce musical tones. At Princeton I considered making a career in acoustics or the industrial side of music. And in the psychological laboratory I made some observations on tonal thresholds using a variable organ pipe and studied the vibrations of piano strings. At Occidental, in a laboratory course in physics, I had studied the vibration of xylophone bars that produced two tones.

At Cornell I made some observations on tunable bars using a stethoscope. I utilized tunable bars in some observations on difference tones (1918b, 1922). Interest in difference tones arose from the discovery that intense difference tones were produced when two bars in the top octave of a glockenspiel were struck simultaneously.

TEACHING AT MINNESOTA

I gained a Master of Arts degree from Princeton in 1915 and a doctorate in psychology from Cornell in the spring of 1918. The war was then in full swing but approaching an end. I was uncertain what to do next and, being concerned about my health, I decided to take a year off to work in a wholly different field.

At that time the American Museum of Natural History was making an excavation of the prehistoric Indian pueblo in Aztec, New Mexico. Through Earl Morris, who was in charge, I arranged to assist in the digging as a laborer and thus to earn a small amount of money. I obtained bulletins and reports from the American Bureau of Ethnology in Washington which I studied with interest. At Aztec I lived in an old adobe house on a rise above the beautiful Animas River and boarded at a nearby farm house. This change of location made it possible to visit other prehistoric sites in the Great Southwest. I enjoyed the simple outdoor life.

Then came the influenza epidemic of 1918. For weeks I was bedfast with the flu. After the war ended on November 11, 1918, I moved home to Los Angeles for recuperation.

In 1919 Robert M. Yerkes had agreed to reorganize the Psychology Department at the University of Minnesota but he withdrew to continue work for the military services. He recommended

Richard M. Elliott to take his place. The general plan was to bring together a group of psychologists with different orientations. The new appointees included Karl S. Lashley, William S. Foster (my teacher at Cornell), Mabel Fernald, Charles Bird, and, of course, Elliott himself. Herbert Woodrow remained from the previous department.

Nothing else being in sight I had agreed to accept a $600 assistantship in the reorganized department but shortly after arriving in Minneapolis I received an offer of an instructorship at $1800 from Ohio State University. Minnesota promptly matched this offer and I became a full-time member of the Psychology Department there. I was financially on my own.

Charlie Bird, a social psychologist, and I shared an office in the public health building which housed the entire department. My job was to conduct discussion sections in elementary psychology and to assist Foster in the beginning laboratory. Laboratory work was required in the first course but the requirement was soon dropped. The flood of students was so great that the laboratory work had to be made optional.

While at Minnesota I did some experiments on pleasantness and unpleasantness examining these affective processes in relation to the perception of odors and in relation to the dynamic conflict of habituated reactions. Also in connection with the laboratory course I developed a differential color mixer with stationary disks (1923). The work in colorimetry was continued for several years but my interest in it proved not to be permanent.

The liberal intellectual atmosphere of Minnesota was agreeable. I spent evenings matching Lashley run rats and talking with him about behavioral psychology. Lashley gave the impression that understanding animal behavior, including human, was a matter of prime importance. Calvin P. Stone, whom I have always respected, was a graduate student working with Lashley at that time.

In 1921, during my second year at Minnesota, I received an offer from Madison Bentley to go to the University of Illinois at a salary of $2500 with the rank of associate in psychology. Subsequently I learned that this was a mongrel rank, now abolished, a kind of cross between an instructorship and assistant professorship, but since I did not like the bitter cold of Minneapolis winters I was glad to move southward.

THE UNIVERSITY OF ILLINOIS

At Illinois I found a small closely knit department. Madison Bentley was head and the only full professor. The departmental office was one large room, number 209 of old University Hall. Bentley had a big desk in this office and there were seven or eight smaller desks scattered about the room for instructors. In the room were desks for Coleman R. Griffith (who later became provost of the University), Glenn D. Higginson, Carl Rahn, Alice Sullivan and Elizabeth Möller (both from Cornell), Harriet Anderson, and Walter Zuschke, in addition to mine. Students came to the office for conferences usually about examinations and grades but occasionally to clarify a point in text or lecture.

My job at Illinois was to conduct discussion sections in Psychology I and a section of the laboratory course. Later I gave lectures in the beginning course and was in charge of the laboratory. Lecturing was a challenge, for there were usually crowds of students. I recall one group of nearly five hundred students crowded into a room that had originally been a chapel and was then taken over for band practices in the late afternoons! In the lectures I made a point of having demonstrations, motion pictures, slides, and group participation whenever possible. It was not easy to hold the interest of these undergraduate groups.

The laboratory on the fifth floor of old University Hall was prim and orderly. It was reminiscent of the Cornell laboratory only smaller. In glass-covered cases were the traditional kinds of apparatus: Hipp chronoscopes, König tuning forks, Helmholtz resonators, Zwaardemaker olfactometers, a Galton whistle, etc. There was a room for haptics, a Mach tilting board, several dark rooms, a room for vision, a cabinet filled with colored papers and disks. Most of the equipment had been imported from Germany and was used for study of the special senses. There was a small wood-working and machine shop which I appreciated.

In the laboratory I made a point of introducing experiments that were unique to psychology: one on human maze-learning (which I brought down from Foster's laboratory at Minnesota), an experiment on Emmert's law of projection of visual after-images, an experiment on mental set, and others.

Madison Bentley had taken his doctorate at Cornell during Titchener's early years there and had stocked the Illinois department with Titchener's students. After Titchener's death Bentley became head of the Cornell Psychology Department.

Bentley was a gentleman and a scholar. He was meticulous about facts, talented in editorial work, and a stickler for the correct use of words. I found him friendly and easy to get along with even when I did not agree with his brand of psychology.

DEFINING THE FIELD OF PSYCHOLOGY

The textbook in Psychology I was Bentley's *The Field of Psychology*. In this text Bentley developed his doctrine of "psychosomatic functions." The trouble with this theoretical system, it seemed to me, was that the "psyche" of the "psychosomatic functions" was precisely Titchener's "dependent experience" and the "soma" was a highly sophisticated series of mental faculties, certainly not the "nervous system" of Pavlov, Watson, Lashley, and many neurologists. The factual evidence for Bentley's "psychosomatic functions," however, appeared to be sound and well documented but the system itself was neither a functional mentalism nor a consistent behaviorism.

During these early decades of the century psychology was divided into schools. In addition to Titchener's structuralism there was a Chicago school of functionalism with doctrines propounded by James Roland Angell, and others. Then there was Watson's radical behaviorism. In Germany there was *Gestalt psychologie* initiated by Wertheimer, Köhler, Koffka, and others, as a protest against traditional associationism and sensationism.

In England and America there was William McDougall's hormic purposivism. And, of course, there was Freudian psychology.

In 1923 I read a paper at the annual meeting of the American Psychological Association in which I formulated a definition of psychology based on phenomenology (1924). Re-reading this paper after half a century I still believe that a phenomenological approach to the definition of psychology is sound.

I have never abandoned the concept of consciousness. I continue to believe that the science of psychology has a unique responsibility to analyze and interpret subjective phenomena such as perceptions, mental images, the experiences of memory and thought, the awareness of feelings, and emotions. I believe it is appropriate to postulate dispositions that determine mental life: memory traces, habit systems, mental sets, goal orientations, beliefs, values, and other dispositions. I recognize that man is an animal, a biological organism, living within a sociocultural environment with abilities to perceive real events and to remember, imagine, think, reason, and act as well as to feel and react emotionally. Human behavior is rational to a limited extent. There is today a crumbling faith in man's rationalism and a tendency to view human nature as it actually is.

EXPERIMENTS ON ORGANIC SET

A common inference about human behavior is that activities are controlled and regulated by motives. What is a motive? In everyday life a motive is regarded as a persisting intent to act in a particular manner, for example, an intent to mail a letter or to take a trip. Human motives may be communicated by words or symbols and a motive can obviously exist without communication.

In the laboratory a motive can be established by verbal instruction. For example, in year V of the Stanford-Binet intelligence test a child is given three commissions: "Here's a key. I want you to put it on that chair over there; then I want you to shut (or open) that door, and then bring me the box which you see over there. . . ." If the child understands the instructions and carries out the three commissions, he passes this unit of the test at mental age five. The instruction produces a temporary *set* of the organism which regulates immediate action.

In the 1920s we made several studies of organic set, testing 822 children in the Urbana and Champaign schools. These exploratory studies were followed later by two doctoral theses (Gundlach, Rothschild, and Young, 1927; Compton and Young, 1933, and Thomas and Young, 1942).

The apparatus was a vertical board with ten miniature electric lamps arranged in a circle. The lights were flashed one at a time in sequence. The subject was instructed: "Note carefully the *order* and *position* of the lights as they appear. After the lights have been flashed point in *order* to the places where the lights appeared. . . ."

A subject's performance in carrying out this task depends on a good many factors: the age of the subject, the number of lights flashed, the interval between successive flashes, the amount of practice in the task, the configuration made by the lights, the delay between presentation and execution of a task, and others.

In a doctoral study R. K. Compton presented spatiotemporal patterns by point stimulations to the eyes, ears, and skin, after instructing his subjects to reproduce the patterns immediately by pressing keys that were appropriately placed. In another doctoral study W. F. Thomas presented spatiotemporal patterns visually by flashing lights. Subjects were instructed to reproduce the patterns immediately by pressing keys or pedals or by using special head keys.

In both studies it was found that the main source of difficulty was the configuration, or gestalt, made by the point stimulations. Compton found that if a pattern was difficult when presented in one sense modality, it was also difficult when presented in other modalities. Thomas found that if a pattern was difficult when reproduced by one motor system, it was also difficult when reproduced by other motor systems. Of course, the sensory mode of presentation and the motor mode of reproduction markedly influenced difficulty but the main source of difficulty was the organizing and holding of a central set.

This kind of research on organic set is important and should be extended. After closing my laboratory in 1963, I learned that Albert Michotte at the University of Louvain had made similar studies of the organization of point stimulations, their transposition, and relation to Gestalt psychology (Michotte, 1952). But he was not aware of my work nor I of his.

BERLIN, 1926-1927

In 1926 I was awarded a National Research Council fellowship in biological science for post-doctoral study abroad. My project was to study the *physiology* of pleasantness and unpleasantness. This was before the pioneer studies of Olds and Milner, Neal Miller, and others; and I knew nothing of Berger's brain waves and electroencephalography.

In the spring of 1926 I wrote Wolfgang Köhler, director of the Psychologisches Institut der Kaiser Wilhelm Universität, concerning my project and desire to spend a year at the University of Berlin. Köhler replied: "We have no special instruments for work in that direction, since nobody here has done such work, and I must confess, that I have no personal experience in this field. . . . I don't think it would be worth while only to work out a scheme which you have conceived in America. That would be possible without the trip. Perhaps after looking around here for a short while, you will see some new aspect of your own problem." That is exactly what happened.

On the way to Berlin I attended the Eighth International Congress of Psychology in Groningen, Holland. There I met a number of psychologists whose names were familiar. I read a paper on the nature of observation in the field of affective psychology. I argued for a functional type of report in the form "I like it" or "I dislike it" rather than an attempt to observe the "what" of hedonic experience. I had found that introspective reports were biased by laboratory atmosphere and that statistically uniform and reliable results were obtained from naïve subjects when asked to report their likes and dislikes for chemically controlled odors (1927, 1931).

After arriving in Berlin I spent a month studying German in the Institut für Ausländer. This training was necessary before enrolling as a student in the university. I had little talent for languages and wanted to improve my German as a tool for psychological research. The instruction at the Institut was excellent.

I attended courses of lectures by Köhler and Wertheimer. I became acquainted with Lewin and his students. This was the heyday of Gestalt psychology. I found that *Gestalt theorie* fitted well with my previous research and theoretical views. I attended other lectures, including a series by Einstein, heard some symphony concerts, lived with a military family in Halensee, and altogether had a very profitable year.

When I finally got around to the physiology of pleasantness and unpleasantness I did not know how and where to begin. I was familiar with the physiological "methods of expression" including work on the psychogalvanic reflex but these traditional approaches offered little hope of arriving at the central neurology of affective processes. So I decided to make an out-and-out behavioral approach to the problem.

I decided to study the preferences of rats for different kinds of grain. N. R. F. Maier gave me three white rats he had used as subjects in his experiments on reasoning. I bought several kinds of grain at a local market. I had the rats, the grain, a table, and that was about all. I began by presenting a pair of grains in an open field and arranging conditions such that neither grain had an advantage in space and time. Then I devised several preliminary forms of preference-testing apparatus (1928a).

These first observations showed clearly that each animal developed stable and consistent choices. Moreover, the three rats were strikingly uniform in their preferences despite minor differences. For each animal the grains arranged themselves into a hierarchy, or transitive series, from the least to the most acceptable. I realized then that we were in business! The relative likes and dislikes of rats for foodstuffs can be studied objectively and quantitatively! After returning to Illinois I improved the apparatus and refined the technique for testing food preferences of animals.

This postdoctoral year at Berlin marked a turning point in my career. It was the termination of my formal education and the beginning of a serious career in experimental psychology. Without hardly realizing it I had embarked upon a career of teaching, research, and writing in the field of experimental psychology. Experiments in psychology were fun! I worked for the satisfaction derived from trying to understand animal, including human, behavior and I hoped that my efforts would have some ultimate social significance.

SOUND LOCALIZATION

While at Berlin I carried out an experiment on sound localization. I had long been interested in space perception but this particular study was suggested by Stratton's classical work on vision without inversion of the retinal image (Stratton, 1896; Stratton, 1897).

With the help of Kurt Lewin we made a pseudophone that acoustically transposed the positions of the outer ears (1928b). The pseudophone produced a discrepancy between visual and auditory perceptions of position and direction. As in the well-known mirror-drawing experiment the pseudophone produced a need for adjusting to incompatible sensory information (Figure 12-1).

With the subject's eyes closed, and the pseudophone adjusted, an acoustic stimulus on the right was regularly heard as a phantom on the left and vice versa. With eyes open, however, there were two striking phenomena. First, there was sometimes an experienced discrepancy between visual and auditory localizations. For example, while I was facing the street a motor vehicle would be seen moving silently from left to right and a bodiless phantom would be heard moving from right to left. There was complete dissociation between visual and auditory localizations. Second, when a visible source was attentively fixated the sound was referred to the place of the source and no discrepancy was experienced. Both phenomena were observed at the very start of the experiment by all observers.

FIGURE 12-1   Author with pseudophone.

Habituation to pseudophonic hearing in the laboratory and on the streets of Berlin resulted in consistent visual-auditory localization. It was possible to go for hours along the Kurfürstendamm without experiencing any discrepancy between visual and auditory positions. Sometimes, however, an unexpected sound would be heard and search revealed the fact that the auditory localization had been right-left reversed. After more than fifty-eight hours of habituation to the pseudophone, tests in the laboratory showed a consistent right-left reversal when eyes were closed and knowledge of the position of a source eliminated.

The experiment shows that the brain can integrate discrepant information from eye and ear. When a sounding object is attentively fixated, vision dominates hearing. The visual-auditory type of sound localization is obvious enough in the ventriloquist's illusion and in localizing voices of speakers seen on screen or television. There is commonly a *cognitive* identification of the voice with speaker typically without a precise auditory placement of the voice.

After returning to Illinois I continued studies of sound localization using trumpets like those on the pseudophone as artificial pinnae. The trumpets were anchored to a frame above the subject's head or in another room (1928b, 1931, 1937a). This technique of detaching the pinnae artificially from the head eliminated influences of head movements on sound localization. I found, in agreement with previous investigators, that when head movements could not change the binaural stimulus-pattern the phantom was localized on an arc behind the head outside the field of vision. Within this restricted auditory space the subjects could consistently and reliably distinguish between right and left positions and intermediate right-left directions. A distinction between front and back was impossible.

These experiments suggest that purely auditory localization is important when the source of sound is not visible and especially when it is behind or above the observer. Vision ordinarily dominates hearing in localizing the sources of sound. This finding confirms Stratton's result in his study of vision without inversion of the retinal image.

THE MOTIVATION OF BEHAVIOR

After returning from Berlin the years were filled with activities too numerous to mention. From a personal point of view my marriage to Josephine Kennedy in the summer of 1929 was an event of outstanding importance. Josephine's educational and religious background had been similar to mine. She had obtained an M.D. degree from the University of Illinois College of Medicine in 1918, the same year that I acquired a Ph.D. from Cornell. I was proud of the fact that she was valedictorian of a medical class made up largely of men. Josephine was socially popular and in constant demand as a speaker. Her outgoing nature tended to compensate for my tendency to avoid social contacts and work long hours in the laboratory. She helped me in many ways, reading and criticizing manuscripts, attending meetings on various campuses, even running rats in a dark room, all the while providing a comfortable home environment for our many friends and growing family.

In 1932 while spending a sabbatical year at Stanford University we adopted a daughter, Rosemary Adele (Mrs. Lawrence Lee Mitchell), and in 1934 a son, Stewart Adams.

At the time of my marriage I was offering an advanced course on human and animal motivation and the time seemed ripe for bringing together the materials from different sources. So I obtained sabbatical leave for the academic year 1931-32 and moved to Stanford University to develop a text for my course.

Woodworth in 1918 had introduced the term "drive" to American psychology. F. A. Moss adopted the term and in 1924 published an experimental paper on animal drives. The concept of drive was promptly taken up by other investigators of animal motivation and "drive" became a substitute for "instinct"—a concept which at the time was in disrepute. There was a growing literature on animal drives and this needed to be brought together.

Scattered through the literature were studies of social motivation—competition and cooperation, incentives of praise and reproof, and the like. A review of the experimental psychology of motivation by C. M. Diserens and J. Vaughn (1931) proved to be helpful.

My research had dealt in good measure with human motivation. Studies of organic set were concerned with the programing of sensory information and the establishing of motives. Studies on pleasantness and unpleasantness had led to a dynamic formulation of hedonic experience and a functional view of affective process. Work with food preferences of rats, palatability, and appetite emphasized the importance of hedonic porcesses in motivation and development.

At the time, I was teaching a text by L. T. Troland (1928) on human motivation. He had formulated an hedonic theory of motivation.

My book, *Motivation of Behavior, the Fundamental Determinants of Human and Animal Activity,* was published in 1936 by John Wiley and Sons. The book brought together empirical results from a rapidly expanding field of experimental psychology. The book went through twelve printings before going out of print. Today, of course, there are many excellent works in the field of motivation but for a while *Motivation of Behavior* had little competition.

FOOD PREFERENCE, PALATABILITY, APPETITE, AND DIETARY HABIT

After returning from Berlin in 1927 I continued experiments on the food preferences of rats. I developed a technique known as the brief-exposure serial method of testing preferences. With this technique two test foods are exposed side by side and positions are interchanged from trial to trial. Exposures are brief but long enough to determine an animal's choice. During repeated trials an animal usually develops a consistent habit of choice.

In the 1920s and following years there was a controversy concerning the self-selection method of feeding animals and human beings. In this method the subject is allowed to choose freely from the components of a complete diet presented in separate containers. Curt P. Richter and others had utilized the self-selection method of feeding. Richter argued that the "appetites" of the rat are indicators of metabolic needs and that the self-selection method of feeding combined with surgical techniques can reveal the functions of endocrine glands in regulating metabolism and behavior. Nutritionists, however, were adamant that the appetites of animals, including man, were fallible and undependable guides to correct nutrition. Nutritional and hedonic values are clearly different and may be opposed.

I adopted the self-selection, or cafeteria, method of maintaining groups of rats while continuing to test food preferences with the brief-exposure serial method. The simultaneous use of these two methods of observing food selections raised a lot of problems and yielded some interesting results.

One study, in collaboration with James P. Chaplin, was especially illuminating (Young and Chaplin, 1945). We housed groups of rats in large cafeteria cages offering the animals a free choice among the separate components of a complete Richter diet. Two dietary components were sucrose (cane sugar) and casein. We ran brief-exposure preference tests between these foods and found that the rats developed and maintained a uniform and consistent preference for the sweet-tasting sucrose. Then we produced a metabolic need for protein by removing casein from the cafeteria cages. A severe and increasing protein starvation developed but the animals maintained the preference for sucrose day after day. Metabolic need for protein did not change the original preference!

At that point in the experiment we introduced another method of testing preferences. Sucrose and casein were presented in widely separated containers. At the choice point the rats could not see, smell, touch, or taste the test foods. They had to *learn* to run to one food or the other during successive trials. Under these conditions the rats promptly and consistently developed a preference for casein which clearly agreed with their increasing need for protein. For a while it was possible to demonstrate simultaneous incompatible preferences! On one apparatus the animals preferred sucrose; on the other, casein! This exciting experiment raised a question concerning the nature of preference and appetite.

In everyday life an appetite is regarded as a desire or craving for food or for a particular kind of food or for sex or something else. Now the criterion of appetite used by Richter and many others was the quantity of food ingested per day by an animal. This criterion agrees with the common sense notion that the better one likes a food the more of it one eats. But the over-all quantity ingested *per diem* does not take account of the fact that the level of "appetite" varies with the duration of deprivation and the degree of approach to satiation. Appetite is a variable motivation. A food like sucrose is highly palatable but an animal is quickly satiated on it. Young and Chaplin found as a fact that the *per diem* mean intake of casein was slightly greater than that of sucrose in the cafeteria cages. (On intake as a measure of acceptability and preference, see Young and Green, 1953.)

A distinction must be drawn between appetite and palatability as determinants of food preference and choice. Actually there are several different determinants of choice. "Palatability" refers to the hedonic response to foodstuffs that are perceived through the head receptors, especially through taste and smell. "Appetite" refers to a motivation that has also an intraorganic, chemical, and neural basis. Specific appetites are acquired on the basis of internal motivation effects. Preferential *habits* are learned on the basis of experience and they may function autonomously as determinants of choice. When a man refers to his food preference he may be reporting an attitude or bias based on previous experience with foodstuffs (1967a).

In the 1960s with the help of assistants, R. G. Burright, K. R. Christensen, C. H. Madsen, R. H. Schulte, and C. L. Trafton, we published a series of studies dealing with the psychophysics of palatability, taste preferences, fluid intake, and dietary habits (1966, 1968; for references, see 1965). Recent theoretical papers have interpreted preference as an evaluative choice and the acceptance-rejection of foodstuffs as primary evaluative reactions.

An interesting finding in the experiments of the 1960s was the discovery that positive and negative hedonic intensities summate algebraically. For example, if a compound solution contains a positive solute (sucrose) plus a negative solute (quinine hydrochloride), the level of palatability varies directly with the concentration of the positive solute and inversely with the concentration of the negative solute. The two components summate algebraically in their hedonic effect. With high concentrations of quinine in the compound no amount of sugar will make the solution acceptable.

In these studies with the up-and-down psychophysical method the quantitative relations are surprisingly exact. These data should be examined by anyone who holds to the traditional doctrine: *De gustibus non disputandum est.*

Our finding of the precise algebraic summation of positive and negative hedonic intensities is exciting because it implies that positive and negative affective arousals are incompatible and do not coexist. Therefore, the objective studies of food preferences with rats led to a conclusion that was reached long ago by the maligned introspective method: pleasant and unpleasant *feelings* (not meanings) are incompatible and do not coexist. It is obvious that a rat cannot accept and reject a taste solution at the same instant. It is not so obvious that the level of acceptability depends upon the precise quantitative interaction of positive and negative determinants.

From the point of view of scientific method the finding demonstrates that subjective and objective approaches to a complex problem yield results that are congruent and mutually supporting. This, of course, is an argument for an eclectic approach to psychology rather than an approach that adheres to a strictly predetermined point of view. Today I think it is widely recognized that complex behavioral problems should be examined from different points of view, in different aspects and contexts.

The studies of James Olds and others on the neurophysiology of pleasantness and unpleasantness also confirm the findings of behavioral and introspective studies. What is observed from one point of view thus helps us to understand what is observed from another standpoint.

TEACHING AND WRITING

A good way to learn about a subject is to teach it. My education has been furthered by teaching various courses at the University of Illinois and elsewhere. I have taught courses in social psychology, physiological psychology, genetic psychology, and the history of psychology in addition to the introductory course and the laboratory in experimental psychology.

My main effort in teaching, however, has been concerned with motivation and emotion. In the 1920s I took over Ruckmick's course entitled Feeling and Emotion. In 1929 I began alternating this course with another entitled Motivation. In 1946 these courses were merged into one entitled Emotion and Motivation. This course brought together my experimental and theoretical interests in dynamic psychology and I continued to develop the course throughout my teaching career.

Along with teaching I prepared suitable textbooks and wrote about a dozen encyclopedia articles on the topics of motivation and emotion. I also wrote numerous reviews of books and articles.

I mentioned above my *Motivation of Behavior* which was published in 1936. In 1939-40 I arranged a sabbatical leave and spent the year as visiting fellow at Yale University in the Institute of Human Relations. This year made it possible to organize the content for a book entitled *Emotion in Man and Animal, its Nature and Relation to Attitude and Motive.* This book, published by John Wiley and Sons in 1943, went through seven printings before going out of print.

In 1947-48 I arranged another sabbatical leave to study as research fellow at Harvard University. I had hoped at that time to prepare a dynamic social psychology but the project was never finished. The book was intended to be a text for my full-year introductory course entitled Human Nature. The course presented a view of man as a biological organism living within a sociocultural environment. Although I worked long hours on the text, it turned out to be too biological and not sufficiently social. The book was never completed.

My research in social psychology has been meager (there are only three studies: 1937b, Young and Thomas, 1938, and Young and Yavitz, 1946). I reluctantly abandoned the project of a text on dynamic social psychology and turned to the preparation of a text for my course on motivation and emotion.

In 1961 John Wiley and Sons published *Motivation and Emotion, A Survey of the Determinants of Human and Animal Activity.* The book appeared a year after my retirement but I am pleased to note that it has been well received and is being used widely as a text.

These books recognize that man is an emotional and feeling creature as well as a rational one. This is important in considering social problems. In the current social unrest and turmoil over problems of war and peace, exploding populations, poverty, pollution of the environment, crime and violence, revolution, and others, I am sure that one must view human nature as it actually is—partly rational, partly emotional, partly dominated by habit, partly spiritual. To be a good citizen a student needs to have a sound understanding of the psychological nature of man.

IN RETROSPECT

In 1963 I closed my laboratory and moved to Claremont, California. My wife had died in 1962. In California I married Marvie N. Davis.

As I look back on my career I think it fair to say that the kind of psychology I have tried to develop is naturalistic, biologically and socially oriented, empirical, realistic, and definitely experimental. I have been aware of Freudian psychology but have more or less ignored it. My approach to behavioral problems has been eclectic and multidisciplinary.

During my career I have been fortunate in obtaining financial support from the American Medical Association, The Rockefeller Foundation, the Research Board of the University of Illinois, the Quartermaster of the United States Army, and the National Science Foundation. Without these grants it would have been difficult or impossible to carry on the experiments.

After retirement I have continued writing and there have been several recognitions. In 1961 my alma mater, Occidental College, conferred the degree of Doctor of Science with this citation: "Paul Thomas Young, Bachelor of Arts, Master of Arts, Doctor of Philosophy, son of a founder of this college, Occidental alumnus, devoted scholar and teacher, psychologist, author, American man of Science, you have profoundly deepened and extended man's understanding of himself." This was sweet music!

In 1965 I received the Distinguished Scientific Contribution

Award of the American Psychological Association. The citation mentioned a life-long study of hedonic processes in behavior, clarification of acceptance and appetitive behavior, and examining composite stimuli and preference, and said, "Current renewed interest in hedonic theory rests in good measure on his experimental demonstrations and theoretical arguments." There was a $1000 prize with the award and an invitation to present a paper at the 1966 meeting of the American Psychological Association (1967b).

On September 3, 1967, at the seventy-fifth anniversary celebration of the founding of the American Psychological Association, I was pleased to be included in a group of senior psychologists who were honored for "a distinguished lifetime's contribution to psychology as a science and as a profession."

Although these recognitions have been gratifying I am humble enough to realize that my total contributions add up to only a few bits of information in a complex and rapidly expanding field of knowledge known as experimental dynamic psychology.

REFERENCES

1896 G. M. Stratton. Vision without inversion of the retinal image. *Psychological Review 3*, 611-17.

1897 G. M. Stratton. Vision without inversion of the retinal image. *Psychological Review 4*, 341-60 and 463-81.

1918 (a) An experimental study of mixed feelings. The localization of feeling. *American Journal of Psychology 29*, 237-71; 420-30.
(b) Tunable bars, and some demonstrations with a simple bar and a stethoscope. *Psychological Bulletin 15*, 293-300.

1922 Series of difference tones obtained from tunable bars. *American Journal of Psychology 33*, 385-93.

1923 A differential color mixer with stationary disks. *Journal of Experimental Psychology 6*, 323-43.

1924 The phenomenological point of view. *Psychological Review 31*, 288-96.

1927 With R. Gundlach and D. A. Rothschild. A test and analysis of "set." *Journal of Experimental Psychology 10*, 247-80.
Studies in affective psychology: III, The "trained" observer in affective psychology. *American Journal of Psychology 38*, 175-85.

1928 (a) Studies in affective psychology: VI, Preferential discrimination of the white rat for different kinds of grain. *American Journal of Psychology 40*, 372-94.

(b) Auditory localization with acoustical transposition of the ears. *Journal of Experimental Psychology 11*, 399-429.

1931 With W. L. Morgan and E. H. Kniep. Studies in affective psychology: XI, Individual differences in affective reaction to odors. XII, The relation between age and affective reaction to odors. *American Journal of Psychology 43*, 406-21.

The role of head movements in auditory localization. *Journal of Experimental Psychology 14*, 95-124.

1933 With R. K. Compton. A study of organic set: Immediate reproduction of spatial patterns presented by successive points to different senses. *Journal of Experimental Psychology 16*, 775-97.

1937 (a) Reversal of auditory localization. *Psychological Review 44*, 505-20.

(b) Laughing and weeping, cheerfulness and depression: A study of moods among college students. *Journal of Social Psychology 8*, 311-34.

1938 With W. F. Thomas. Liking and disliking persons. *Journal of Social Psychology 9*, 169-88.

1942 With W. F. Thomas. A study of organic set: Immediate reproduction by different muscular groups, of patterns presented by successive visual flashes. *Journal of Experimental Psychology 30*, 347-67.

1945 With J. P. Chaplin. Studies of food preference, appetite and dietary habit: III, Palatability and appetite in relation to bodily need. *Comparative Psychology Monographs 18* (3), 1-45.

1946 With J. A. Yavitz. Activities in which college students experience success and failure and those in which they wish to be more successful. *Journal of Social Psychology 24*, 131-48.

1952 Albert Michotte (autobiography). In E. G. Boring, H. S. Langfeld, H. Werner, and R. M. Yerkes (Eds.). *A History of Psychology in Autobiography, IV*. Worcester, Mass.: Clark University Press.

1953 With J. T. Greene. Quantity of food ingested as a measure of relative acceptability. *Journal of Comparative and Physiological Psychology 46*, 288-94.

1965 *American Psychologist 20*(12), p. 1088.

1966 Hedonic organization and regulation of behavior. *Psychological Review 73*, 59-96.

1967   Nellie May Young, *William Stewart Young: Builder of California Institutions.* The Arthur H. Clark Company, Box 230, Glendale, California 91209. Library of Congress catalogue card number 67-18217.

(a) Palatability: The hedonic response to foodstuffs. In C. F. Code *et al.* (Eds.), *Handbook of Physiology,* Section 6, Alimentary Canal, Vol. 1. Baltimore: Williams & Wilkins.

(b) Affective arousal: Some implications. *American Psychologist* 22, 32-40.

1968   Evaluation and preference in behavioral development. *Psychological Review 75,* 222-41.

1971   Heredity of progressive muscular dystrophy: Reflections on a case study. *Social Biology 18,* 260-67.

Biographical Index

Adams, Henry E. (1931-   ), is professor of psychology at the University of Georgia and has published extensively on clinical psychological topics. 66

Adams, Henry F. (1882-   ), is professor of psychology emeritus at the University of Michigan. He was one of the pioneers in advertising psychology. 42, 51

Adler, Alfred (1870-1937), was an early pupil of Freud who later founded his own school of individual psychology and originated such concepts as inferiority complex, style of life, and organ inferiority. 245, 249, 255, 261

Adler, Mortimer (1902-   ), professor of experimental psychology at Columbia College, was best known for his work at the University of Chicago in collecting the great ideas of man. 245

Allport, Gordon W. (1897-1967), was the most eloquent spokesman for the idiographic rather than the nomothetic orientation to an adequate understanding of personality. He was professor of psychology at Harvard from 1942 until his death. 115, 217, 218, 223, 227, 252, 276

Angell, James (1869-1949), was the president of the American Psychological Association in 1906. Along with James he was a leader in the school of psychology called Functionalism. 338

Atkinson, John (1923-   ), in a series of books (most recently with David Birch), has illumined new ways of thinking about human motivation. He is professor of psychology at the University of Michigan. 179, 180, 182

Attneave, Fred (1919-   ), is professor of psychology at the University of Oregon. He was the first to use information-theoretic concepts applied to pattern perception. 80

Bain, Alexander (1818-1903), occupied the "Chair of Logic" and English at the University of Aberdeen. His two major works, *The Senses and the Intellect* and *Emotions and the Will*, were among the first textbooks in psychology. 329

Bakan, David (1921-   ), is now professor of psychology at York University in Canada. Formerly he had taught at the University of Chicago, Harvard University, and elsewhere. His areas of publishing are research methodology and the history of psychology. His book, *Sigmund Freud and the Jewish Mystical Tradition*, is a highly original work. 287

356]

Bass, Bernard M. (1925-   ), is director of the Management Research Center at the University of Rochester. He has also held professorships at Louisiana State University and the University of Pittsburgh. 60

Beach, Frank A. (1911-   ), is professor of psychology at the University of California, Berkeley. He works in the area of animal behavior with special emphasis on the sexual, maternal, and hormonal factors. 141, 142, 143, 144, 152

Beebe-Center, J. G. (1897-1958), was a life-time lecturer in psychology at Harvard University. He was best known for his experimental approach to affectivity. 115, 120

Benedict, Ruth (1887-1948), was a professor of anthropology at Columbia University and a poet. She wrote *Patterns of Culture* and *The Chrysanthemum and the Sword*. Her work had cross-disciplinary impact upon sociology and psychology. 279

Bentham, Jeremy (1748-1832), was the father of English utilitarianism with its doctrine of the greatest good to the greatest number. 116

Bentley, Isaac Madison (1870-1955), took his degree with Titchener. He was author of *Field of Psychology*. 336, 337, 338

Bergman, Gustav (1906-   ), was a German born and trained philosopher who was identified with the Vienna Logical positivists. He moved to the United States in the 1930s and originally worked with Kurt Lewin at the University of Iowa, but in the early 1940s he began a long collaboration with Kenneth Spence in examining the philosophical foundations of neobehavorism. 303

Bird, Charles (1893-1957), was pro-

fessor of psychology at the University of Minnesota. His research interests centered on attitude measurement, personality structure, and the techniques of human learning. 336

Boas, Franz (1858-1942), trained in Germany, was a pioneer anthropologist who continued to teach at Columbia University long after reaching emeritus status. He is the author of *The Mind of Primitive Man* and *Anthropology and Modern Life*. Although interested in all aspects of anthropology his impact in cultural anthropology was immense, overshadowing the work of all contemporaries in the United States. 8, 279

Borenblatt, Lloyd (1923-   ), is associate professor of psychology at New York Univesity. 174

Boring, Edwin G. (1886-1968), student of Titchener, was professor of psychology and director of the Psychological Laboratory at Harvard University. His research ranged widely and seminally. By consensus, his most important work was his *History of Experimental Psychology* first published in 1929 and revised in 1950. He was president of the American Psychological Association in 1928 and honorary president of the Seventeenth International Congress of Psychology in Washington, D.C., in 1963. 94, 95, 96, 106, 115, 217, 218, 289, 290, 295, 332, 333, 334

Bronfenbrenner, Urie (1917-   ), is one of the leading students of Russian and American education and child-rearing practices. He has been professor of psychology, child development, and family relations at Cornell University since 1948. 175

Brown, Judson S. (1910-   ), received his Ph.D. at Yale in the later part of the Clark Hull regime (1940). He

Clark, E. L. (1895   ), served for many years as director of admissions and associate professor of psychology at Northwestern University. He is now retired in Vermont. 58, 59, 64

Cofer, Charles (1916-   ), one of the first students of psycholinguistics, is professor of psychology at Pennsylvania State University. 181

Cole, Lawrence (1897-   ), was for many years head of the Department of Psychology at Oberlin College. He is author of an introductory textbook, *Human Behavior*. 182

Coombs, Clyde (1912-   ), one of the founders of the field of mathematical psychology, is head of the Mathematical Psychology program at the University of Michigan. He has stimulated the development of mathematical psychology through his books and through post-doctoral training institutes for psychologists all over the world. 175, 190

Crawford, Meredith P. (1910-   ), was director and is now president of HumRRO (Human Resources Research Office), a research organization in Washington, D.C. He had been professor of psychology and dean at Vanderbilt University. Research administration and military psychology are his specialities. 280

Crissey, Orlo (1904-   ), is former director, Personnel Evaluation Services, General Motors Institute. 197

Cronbach, Lee (1916-   ), one of the leading educational psychologists of our time, is now Vidadachs Professor of Education at Stanford University. 178

Dallenbach, Karl M. (1887-   ), was professor of psychology at Cornell University, specializing in the study of the sense organs. He was editor of the *American Journal of Psychology* for many years. 103, 246, 332

Danielson, Lee (1920-   ), is professor of industrial relations at the University of Michigan. 174

Davage, Robert (1923-   ), has carried out elegant studies of teaching both at Pennsylvania State University and, currently, at Hunter College. 189

Davenport, Charles B. (1866-1944), was known for his research in eugenics and heredity. 7

DeCharms, Richard (1927-   ), is professor of psychology at Washington University. 235

Deutsch, Albert (1905-61), was a sensationalistic feature writer for the *New York Post* and other newspapers, and was noted for his civil rights exposés. He wrote books and articles for the layman on mental illness, psychiatric services, and related problems. 253

Diserens, Charles M. (1889-   ), was professor of psychology at the University of Cincinnati, concentrating his interests in the psychology of music. 346

Donahue, Wilma T. (1900-   ), is chairman of the division of gerontology at the University of Michigan. 51

Douvan, Elizabeth (1926-   ), is Catherine Neafie Kellogg Professor of Psychology at the University of Michigan. 174

Doyle, Charlotte (1937-   ), is chairman of the Department of Psychology, Sarah Lawrence College, and co-author (with McKeachie) of the introductory psychology textbook *Psychology*. 184

Du Bois, Philip H. (1903-   ), professor of psychology at Washington University, is best known for his work in statistics and psychological tests. He is author of *An Introduction to Psychological Statistics* and of *A History of Psychological Testing.* 284

Duncan, Carl P. (1921-   ), is professor of psychology at Northwestern University. His research field is thinking and problem solving and learning. He is the editor of *Thinking: Current Experimental Studies.* 58, 286

Ebbinghaus, Hermann (1850-1909), was a German psychologist who pioneered in the scientific study of memory. 46, 312

Erickson, Raymond L.. (1925-   ), is professor of psychology at the University of New Hampshire. Research in verbal learning is a major interest. 290

Eriksen, Charles W. (1923-   ), is professor of psychology at the University of Illinois and has done extensive work both in visual perception and in personality. 77

Escolona, Sybille K. (1918-   ), is serving as a professor of psychology at the Albert Einstein College of Medicine, Yeshiva University. 144

Ezekiel, Raphael S. (1931-   ), is an assistant professor of psychology at the University of Michigan researching on the study of time perspectives and competence. 231, 232, 233

Fehrer, E. (1909-   ), is professor of psychology at Brooklyn College working in the field of visual perception. 96

Felfoldy, Gary L. (1946-   ), is a graduate student at Yale University. He will receive his Ph.D. in psychology in 1972. 78

Fernald, Mabel (1883-   ), specialized in mental imagery, correction of special disabilities, and psychometric techniques with the division of psychiatric services in the Cincinnati public schools. 336

Fernberger, S. W. (1887-   ), was professor of psychology at the University of Pennsylvania. He edited the *Psychological Bulletin* and *Journal of Experimental Psychology.* 99, 106

Festinger, Leon (1919-   ), is professor of psychology at the New School for Social Research. He is best known for his theory of cognitive dissonance but presently works on visual perception. 83, 175, 178

Fisher, Vivian E. (1897-1951), was associated with New York University and the Blackfoot State Mental Hospital in Idaho. He wrote several books on psychotherapy and abnormal psychology. His brother was Vardis Fisher, the novelist. 281

Flanagan, John C. (1906-   ), during World War II directed and developed the Air Force Classification program in which many psychologists served. After the war, he founded and directed one of the largest and most successful psychological consulting groups, the American Institute for Research. 302

Foley, John P., Jr. (1910-   ), is a management consultant. Trained principally in experimental and comparative psychology at Indiana University and Columbia, he moved from university teaching to industrial psychology during World War II. His research and publications range over many areas, including cross-cultural studies. 8

Fowler, Raymond D. (1930-   ), is professor of psychology and chairman of the department at the University of Alabama. He is a past-

Fowler, Raymond D. *(Cont.)*
president of the Southeastern Psychological Association. 63

Frazier, Charles H. (1870-1936), introduced (with William Gibson Spiller) the operation for the relief of a trigeminal nerve. He was a professor of clinical surgery at the University of Pennsylvania from 1900 to 1922. 98

Freud, Sigmund (1856-1939), was the founder of psychoanalysis and the most creative thinker in the history of psychological science. 44, 113, 245, 261, 339, 352

Garrett, Henry E. (1894-   ), after taking his degree at Columbia, remained there for thirty years, and, on retirement, became a visiting professor at the University of Virginia. Statistics applied to the problem of mental organization is his major approach to psychological problems. 245, 279

Gaudet, Frederick J. (1902-   ), until his recent retirement, was professor of psychology and the director of the Laboratory of Psychological Studies at Stephens Institute of Technology. Before 1941 he had taught at Dun College, which became the University of Newark. 278

Gesell, Arnold (1880-   ), was concerned primarily with developmental morphology of behavior, clinical methods of developmental diagnosis, and cinema analysis of infant behavior. He was chairman of the University Department of Child Development at Yale School of Medicine, was an attending pediatrician at Grace-New Haven Community Hospital, and the director of the Clinic for Child Development. 7

Gibson, Ralph (1923-   ), is professor of psychology and pediatrics at the University of Michigan. 174, 189

Gilbert, William M. (1911-   ), is professor of psychology and director of the Counseling Center at the University of Illinois. 51, 53

Gildae, Edwin F. (1898-   ), is professor of psychiatry emeritus and former head of the Department of Psychiatry and Neurology at Washington University School of Medicine. 283, 285

Gilliland, A. R. (1887-1952), was professor and for a while chairman of psychology at Northwestern University. He was a founder and the first president of the Midwestern Psychological Association. 58

Gleser, Goldine C. (1915-   ), is professor and director of the Psychology Division at the University of Cincinnati College of Medicine. Her major research efforts are in the areas of research design and statistical analysis. With Lee Cronbach she wrote *Psychological Tests and Personnel Decisions.* 284

Goldstein, Kurt (1878-1965), was a famous German neurologist who emigrated to the United States. His work on the effects of brain injury on perception and behavior was as important to psychology as it was to neurology. 124, 150

Granick, Samuel (1916-   ), is a clinical psychologist in private practice in Elkins Park, Pennsylvania, and a research associate at the Philadelphia Psychiatric Center. He has published on problems in gerontology and clinical psychology. 284

Griffith, Coleman R. (1893-   ), is the author of *Principles of Systematic Psychology.* He was a professor of psychology and provost at the University of Illinois. 337

Guetzkow, Harold (1915-   ), has dedicated his professional career to peace. He is professor of political science and psychology at Northwestern University. 174, 175

Guilford, Joy P. (1897-   ), is an American psychologist renowned for his contributions to the measurement of personality traits, especially intellectual abilities. He also developed psychophysical scaling and testing methods. 95

Gurin, Gerald (1922-   ), is program director of the Institute of Social Research and professor of higher education at the University of Michigan. 174

Gustad, John W. (1922-   ), is president of Kansas State College at Fort Hayes. He has written numerous articles on counseling psychology. 63, 181

Hake, Harold W. (1919-   ), is professor of psychology at the University of Illinois and is a specialist in visual perception. 77, 87

Harding, John S. (1919-   ), is a clinical psychologist teaching at Cornell University. His research emphasis is in racial and religious prejudice, child guidance, and mental health. 219

Hariton, Theodore (1921-   ), is vice-president of Psychological Services, Organization Resources, Counselors, Inc. 174

Harper, Robert S. (1922-   ), is professor of psychology at Knox College. He has written an elementary psychology text and articles on teaching. 46

Harrell, Thomas W. (1911-   ), is a professor in the School of Business Administration at Stanford University, where his specialty is industrial psychology. 57

Hartshorne, Hugh (1885-1967), completed with Mark A. May a classical study of dishonesty under the general title *Studies in Deceit.* 42

Hebb, Donald O. (1904-   ), is professor of psychology at McGill University. He is a major theorist in the field of learning and perception. 83, 141, 142

Heidbreder, Edna (1890-   ), is professor of psychology emeritus at Wellesley College. Her book *Seven Psychologies* has been a standard reference for decades. 46

Heiser, Ruth B. (1909-   ), is in private practice in Cincinnati as a psychologist. 48

Helmholtz, Hermann von (1821-94), was the German physicist and physiologist who invented the opthalmometer and opthalmoscope. He revised Young's three color theory, described mechanisms of focusing and binocular vision in the eye, and investigated color vision and color blindness. 94, 337

Hesterly, S. Otho (1931-   ), is associate professor of psychology at the University of Arkansas School of Medicine. 66

Heyns, Roger (1918-   ), is professor of psychology and education at the University of Michigan. He was chancellor of the University of California, Berkeley, for six years. On January 1, 1972, he became president of the American Council on Education. 54, 174, 179, 180, 181, 182, 186, 189, 194

Hilgard, Ernest R. (1904-   ), has interests in experimental psychology, learning theory, and conditioning. He is a professor emeritus in the Department of Psychology at Stanford University. 216, 217

Hobbs, Nicholas (1915-   ), is provost of Vanderbilt University. He is a former American Psychological Association president. 59, 60, 230

Hoffman, Martin L. (1924-   ), is professor of psychology at the University of Michigan and editor of the *Merrill-Palmer Quarterly*. 174

Hollingworth, Harry L. (1880-1957), was chairman of the Department of Psychology at Barnard College for over thirty-five years. While his major systematic contribution was the theory of redintegration, his research covered such diverse problems as the effects of drugs and alcohol on performance and the nature of the judgment process. His textbooks ranged from advertising and vocational psychology to abnormal and developmental psychology and the psychology of thought. He was president of the American Psychological Association in 1927. 6, 8, 245

Holt, Robert R. (1917-   ), concentrated his studies in computer analysis of verbal texts while teaching at the New York University. He is a clinical psychologist specializing in experimental study of ego-psychology. 219

Hovland, Carl Iver (1912-61), held the position of professor and chairman of the Psychology Department at Yale University. His research projects dealt with learning, communication, and personnel selection and training. 219, 220

Hull, Clark L. (1884-1952), was a professor of psychology at Yale, where he greatly advanced conditioned reflex concepts and directed the research of many behavioristically oriented psychologists. 7, 52, 217, 246, 299, 303, 315

Hunt, Howard F. (1918-   ), is professor of medical psychology at the College of Physicians and Surgeons of Columbia University. He is a clinical psychologist. 82, 83

Isaacson, Robert (1928-   ), a physiological psychologist with broad interests in psychology and undergraduate instruction, is professor of psychology at the University of Florida. 182

Jacobson, Carlyle F. (1902-   ), first worked in problems of comparative psychology at various institutions including Yale. Particularly noteworthy were his studies of the effect of frontal lobotomies in primates which led to its use as a therapeutic surgical technique in humans. Jacobson then served as assistant dean at Washington University School of Medicine and later executive dean of the New York State medical schools. 283

Jahoda, Marie (1907-   ), has concentrated her research in the area of ideologies and prejudice. She was a member of the Department of Scientific Research in New York. 229

James, William (1842-1910), was the dean of American psychology. His *Principles of Psychology*, published in 1890, is still quoted today. He was the brother of Henry James, the novelist. It is said of the brothers that Henry wrote like a psychologist while William wrote like a novelist. 117, 118, 312, 332, 333

Janis, Irving L. (1918-   ), is a professor of psychology at Yale University specializing in attitude change and decision making. 144

Jaynes, Julian (1928-   ), was educated at Yale and worked closely with Frank Beach, particularly in studies of ethology. He spent considerable time at Harvard University and is now at Princeton University. 291

Jenkins, Adelbert (1934-   ), is assistant professor of clinical psychology at the New York University Medical Center. 189

Johnson, Donald M. (1909-), is professor of psychology at Michigan State University. He has written books on thought processes. 55

Jung, Carl G. (1875-1961), was an early pupil of Freud who later founded his own School of Analytic Psychology studying primordial archetypes and the racial unconscious. 245

Kantor, J. Robert (1888-), professor of psychology at Indiana University from 1923 until his retirement in 1959, is best known for his systematic development of interbehavioral psychology. Among his many books are *Principles of Psychology, An Outline of Social Psychology, An Objective Psychology of Grammar, Problems of Physiological Psychology, The Logic of Modern Science, Interbehavioral Psychology; A Sample of Scientific System Construction,* and *The Scientific Evolution of Psychology.* 8

Katz, Daniel (1903-), a leading organizational and social psychologist, is professor of psychology at the University of Michigan. 182, 189, 225

Kellogg, Winthrop N. (1888-1948), was a comparative psychologist at Indiana University who attained renown when he took a young chimpanzee into his family shortly after the birth of his own child and compared their development. 246

Kelly, E. Lowell (1905-), a former president of the American Psychological Association, is professor of psychology at the University of Michigan. 186, 187, 188, 190

Kelman, Herbert (1927-), a social psychologist, is Cabot Professor of Social Ethics, Harvard University. 189

Kessen, William (1925-), is a professor of psychology and a research associate of pediatrics at Yale University. 143

Kleemeier, Robert W. (1915-64), was professor of psychology at Washington University in St. Louis. He published many studies in the field of aging. 51

Klineberg, Otto (1889-), was a professor of psychology at Columbia and other universities whose early studies refuted racial differences and who became a civil rights activist. 245

Koffka, Kurt (1886-1941), along with Wertheimer and Köhler, founded the Psychologische Forschung which became the organ of the Gestalt school. His book *Growth of the Mind* emphasized that the learning process is a part of Gestalt psychology. He was the leader of Gestalt psychology. 338

Köhler, Wolfgang (1887-1967), believed that physics would open the door to biology and eventually aid the understanding of psychology. He was interested in the laws that underlie the formation of perceptions and other aspects of Gestalt psychology. Along with Wertheimer and Kaffka, Köhler was a founder of Gestalt psychology. 95, 338, 341, 342

Kohn, Martin (1922-), was a research psychologist and principal investigator at William A. White Institute. He is presently a consultant for the New York State Division of Youth. 143

Kuhn, Thomas S. (1922-), is a Harvard Ph.D. in physics who, under the influence of James C. Conant among others, became inter-

Kuhn, Thomas S. *(Cont.)*
ested in the history of science. He
is the author of *The Structure of
Scientific Revolutions*, perhaps the
most important and controversial
book in the history of science in the
last ten years. He is now professor
of the history of science at Princeton University. 293
Külpe, Oswald (1862-1915), became a
"Dozent" at Leipzig after receiving
his degree there. He was an assistant
to Wundt and contributed to experimental studies on the higher
thought processes. 332, 333

Lacey, John I. (1915-   ), was the
chairman of the Department of
Psycho-physiology and Neurophysiology at Fels Research Institute. He
is presently a professor of psychophysiology at Antioch College. 152,
153
Ladd, George Trumbull (1842-1921),
studied and presented lectures on
physiological psychology at Yale.
His book *Elements of Physiological
Psychology* stemmed from these lectures. 328, 330
Laird, Donald A. (1897-   ), was long
a leader in applied and industrial
psychology. 42
Land, Edwin H. (1909-   ), is the
discoverer of the polaroid process
and president of Polaroid Corporation. A brilliant scientist and inno-
vator, he was much impressed by
Boring's introductory psychology
lectures at Harvard. 119, 124
Landis, Carney (1897-1962), was simultaneously principal research psychologist at the New York State
Psychiatric Institute and professor
of psychology at Columbia University from the early 1930's until his
death. He was most noted for research on emotional reactions, but

he also published on abnormal psychology and sex. 119, 120, 121, 122,
123, 124, 245, 246, 248, 279, 302
Lange, Carl (1834-1900), was a Danish
physiologist who stressed vasomotor
changes as the basis of emotion.
William James expanded Lange's
research to include peripheral behavior and to develop what is now
called the James-Lange Theory of
Emotion. 117, 118
Langfeld, Herbert S. (1879-1958), was
an American psychologist who published extensively on personality
theory and who wrote introductory
and experimental texts. He was a
professor and director of the psychological laboratory at Princeton
from 1927 to 1947. 95
Lashley, Karl S. (1890-1958), was professor of psychology at Harvard and
director of the Yerkes Laboratory of
Primate Biology. 47, 333, 336, 338
Lauer, Donald W. (1919-   ), is associate professor in the Department of
Psychology at Indiana University
and is an accomplished musician.
174
Lawrence, Douglas H. (1918-   ), is
professor of psychology at Stanford
University and is a specialist in
learning and perception. 83
Lecky, Prescott (1892-1941), an American psychologist teaching at Columbia University, was stimulated
by studies under Alfred Adler to
develop the self-consistency theory
of personality development. 245,
249, 259
Leeper, Robert (1904-   ), has been
in the Department of Psychology at
the University of Oregon since 1937.
182
Lesser, Gerald S. (1926-   ), was the
director of the Laboratory of Human Development at Harvard University. 143

Lewin, Kurt (1890-1947), was trained in Berlin and after an established career there immigrated to the United States in 1933. After two years at Cornell he went to the Child Welfare Station at Iowa and in 1945 he moved to MIT as director of the Center for Group Dynamics. Lewin developed his own "field" theory concerned with the dynamics of a person in his "life-space." In essence, the "vectors" and "valences" which directed a person were derived from a "psychological" or "perceived" environment. His thinking has been strongly influential in both child and social psychology. 216, 237, 302, 342, 343

Lewis, Donald D. (1922-   ), is professor of psychology and chairman of the department at the University of Southern California. 58, 60

Lewis, Michael (1937-   ), is a research psychologist for educational testing service at the Center for Psychological Studies, Princeton, New Jersey. 152

Lindsley, Donald B. (1907-   ), is professor of psychology at UCLA. He has done extensive research on neural mechanisms of behavior. 58

Loeb, Jacques (1859-1924), was a physiologist and one of Watson's teachers. In 1890 he formulated the theory of tropism—that the behavior of simple organisms or plants is a forced movement of a physical-chemical nature. 331

Loevinger, Jane (1918-   ), a statistician, is research associate professor at the Graduate Institute of Education and research associate at the Social Science Institute at Washington University. Test theory is her major field of research and writing. 284

Louttit, Chauncey M. (1901-56), was

for many years at the University of Indiana. He was the author of *Clinical Psychology of Children's Behavior Problems,* a pioneer volume in clinical psychology which first appeared in 1936. 283

McCall, Robert B. (1940-   ), was the chairman of the Department of Psychology at Fels Research Institute. He is presently associate professor at Antioch College, researching cognitive development and early experience. 156

Maccoby, Eleanor (1917-   ), is professor of psychology at Stanford University and is a leading developmental psychologist. 181

McConnell, James (1925-   ), is professor of psychology at the University of Michigan. He is a science fiction writer turned experimental psychologist. 182

McDougall, William (1871-1938), was a British psychologist who taught at Harvard and Duke universities. He was an early and major contributor to social psychology. 7, 55, 95, 96, 339

McGeoch, John (1890-1942), followed the functionalist tradition of Chicago. He taught at Wesleyan, was chairman of the Department of Psychology at the University of Missouri as well as at Iowa, where he died. His book *The Psychology of Learning* which was primarily devoted to verbal learning, did much to maintain and stimulate work in the area of verbal learning. 54, 302

McQuitty, Louis L. (1910-   ), is professor of psychology and dean of the College of Arts and Sciences at the University of Miami. 55

Mach, Ernst (1838-1916), published research on visual space perception and experimented on time sense. He

Müller, Georg E. (*Cont.*)
gen in Germany. His contributions
were in learning and psychophysics.
46

Murphy, Gardner (1895-   ), successively occupied academic and research posts at Columbia University,
at the College of the City of New
York, and at the Menninger Foundation. On retirement he became a
visiting professor at George Washington University. Although his research has ranged widely he is perhaps best known for his work in
personality theory and social psychology. Among his numerous books
are *Experimental Social Psychology*
and *Historical Introduction to
Modern Psychology*. He was president of the American Psychological
Association in 1944. 96, 106, 245, 279

Murray, Edward J. (1928-   ), is professor of psychology at the University of Miami. His interests lie in
the area of motivation and adjustment. 143

Murray, Henry (1893-   ), headed
the psychological clinic at Harvard.
He is best known for his development of the Thematic Apperception Test and for his need-press
theory of motivation. 115, 217, 218,
223, 261

Nafe, John Paul (1888-1970), was professor of psychology at Clark University and Washington University,
St. Louis. From the time of his retirement in 1953 until his death, he
was a consultant in research at
Florida State University. Tactual
sensitivity and its neural correlates
was his lifelong research interest.
278, 304

Nathan, Peter E. (1935-   ), is professor of clinical psychology and director of clinical training at Rutgers
University. He is best known for developing systems analysis method
and flow charts for objectifying psychodiagnosis. He developed the
Boston City Hospital check list for
studying symptoms objectively,
which demonstrated the invalidity
of classical diagnostic classifications.
260

Newcomb, Theodore (1903-   ), is a
leading social psychologist. He is
Walgreen Professor of Psychology
and Sociology at the University of
Michigan, where his research on attitudinal and personality development of college students has led to
creation of small residential colleges
within larger universities. 182

Newell, Allen (1927-   ), is professor
of systems and communication science at Carnegie-Mellon University.
188

Olds, James (1922-   ), is now a professor at the California Technological Institute. His work on self-
reinforcement centers in the brain
has offered a physiological basis for
modern hedonism. 117, 341, 350

Osgood, Charles E. (1916-   ), is professor of psychology at the University of Illinois and director of its
Institute for Communications Research. His special field is psycholinguistics. 83

Palmer, James O. (1918-   ), is associate professor of psychology at
UCLA. Group therapy and projective techniques are two of his major
interests. With Michael J. Goldstein
he published *The Experience of
Anxiety*. 284

Pavlov, Ivan P. (1849-1936), was the
great Russian physiological psychol-

ogist who pioneered the study of the conditioned response. 7, 47, 115, 312, 338

Paynter, Richard H. (1890-   ), was professor of psychology at Long Island University and later was chief clinical psychologist for the Veterans Administration New York Regional Office. 246

Peak, Helen (1900-   ), has recently retired from the Catherine Neafie Kellogg Chair at the University of Michigan. 182

Pennington, Leon A. (1908-   ), is now in private practice in Danville, Illinois. He was a professor of psychology at the University of Illinois, where he wrote books on general, military, and clinical psychology. 55, 56, 57, 62

Pepinsky, Harold B. (1917-   ), is professor of psychology at Ohio State University. He has written several books and numerous articles on psychological aspects of productivity. 61

Pillsbury, Walter B. (1872-1960), taught psychology at the University of Michigan for forty-five years and was chairman of the department. 5, 41, 51, 52

Pintner, Rudolf (1884-1942), was professor of psychology at Teachers College, Columbia University. He did extensive research in testing the intelligence of deaf children and, with Donald G. Paterson, developed the Pintner-Paterson Scale of Performance Tests. 279, 281

Piotrowski, Zygmunt A. (1904-   ), received his Ph.D. from the University of Poznan in Poland and shortly thereafter emigrated to the United States. He is recognized as one of the leading authorities on the Rorschach Test and currently is a professor of psychology at Jefferson

Medical College in Philadelphia. 124, 246

Poffenberger, Albert T. (1885-   ), was professor of applied psychology at Columbia University and was a president of the American Psychological Association. He is well known for his research efforts on work and fatigue. 245, 246, 251, 279

Pope, Benjamin (1914-   ), is now director of the psychology service at the Sheppard & Enoch Pratt Hospital in Baltimore. He had been professor of medical psychology at the University of Maryland School of Medicine. With Winfield H. Scott he wrote *Psychological Diagnosis in Clinical Practice*. 284

Pratt, Carroll (1894-   ), is professor of psychology emeritus at Princeton, where he went after many years at Harvard. A distinguished psychophysicist, he was a leader in the field of experimental aesthetics. 115

Pressey, Sidney L. (1888-   ), was professor of psychology at Ohio State Universty from 1921 until his retirement in 1959. He was a pioneer in education psychology. 64

Ray, Wilbert (1901-   ), has recently retired as professor of psychology from Bethany College. 182

Reitman, Walter (1932-   ), one of the leading students of computer simulation of psychological processes, is professor of psychology at the University of Michigan. 188

Richards, Thomas W. (1907-   ), is chief psychologist of the Kennedy Child Study Center in Santa Monica. His *Modern Clinical Psychology* was one of the earliest books in the field. 58, 59

Richter, Curt P. (1894-   ), presently serves as the director of the psycho-

strong laboratory-centered program which was one of the largest producers of Ph.D.s in the first half of the century. 42, 46, 58, 302

Seashore, Robert H. (1902-1951), was professor of psychology and chairman of the department at Northwestern University until his death. He was the son of C. E. Seashore. 58, 59

Sells, Saul B. (1913-   ), is research professor at the Texas Christian University and director of the Institute of Behavioral Research. He was with the School of Aviation Medicine at Randolph Air Force Base as a research psychologist and continues to specialize in aviation psychology and in studies using multivariate design. Along with Charles Berry he edited *Human Factors in Jets and Space Travel.* 100, 280

Shaffer, Laurance F. (1903-   ), is professor emeritus of psychology at Teachers College, Columbia University and is chairman of the board of Psychological Corporation in New York City. He is author of *Psychology of Adjustment*, the book that made it possible to create the course in the subject, and was president of the American Psychological Association in 1953. 283

Shepard, John F. (1881-1965), taught psychology at the Universty of Michigan for forty-five years. 51, 52, 173, 184

Shepard, Roger N. (1929-   ), is professor of psychology at Stanford University. 143

Sherif, Muzafer (1906-   ), received an M.A. from Istanbul in 1929 and then took his M.A. at Harvard in 1932 and his Ph.D. at Columbia in 1935. After teaching in Turkey he returned to this country and currently is professor of psychology at Penn State. He is well known for his work in group processes. 119

Sigel, Irving E. (1921-   ), is professor of psychology and director of the development of psychology program at the State University of New York, Buffalo. 150

Simon, Herbert (1916-   ), one of the nation's leading behavioral scientists, serves on the President's Scientific Advisory Committee and is professor of computer science and psychology at Carnegie-Mellon University. 188

Skinner, B. Frederic (1904-   ), is a neo-behaviorist and the developer of operant conditioning. Under Skinner's brilliant leadership, behaviorism has become an American ideology. Probably the most influential and best known of living American psychologists, he is professor at Harvard. 83, 115, 333

Skodak, Marie (1910-   ), was a pioneer school psychologist and is a leader in professional affairs both nationally and in Michigan. 197

Spearman, Charles E. (1868-1945), applied his knowledge of mathematics and thereby laid down the foundation of factor analysis to the study of intelligence. He is well known for his Theory of Two Factors. 6, 7, 12

Spence, Janet Taylor (1923-   ), is professor and chairman of the Department of Psychology at the University of Texas. Her work on anxiety opened up a research area that received a tremendous amount of attention from fellow psychologists. She considers her major field of research to be experimental psychopathology. 58, 286

Spence, Kenneth (1907-67), received his Ph.D. from Clark Hull at Yale and became his heir apparent and leader of the neo-behaviorists. He

Spence, Kenneth *(Cont.)*
was chairman of the Department of Psychology at the University of Iowa from the early 1940's through the late 1960's. He personally produced seventy-two Ph.D.s who were highly productive of the tradition of Hullian learning theory throughout the 1940's and 1950's. He was one of the dominant theorists of the time. 299, 303

Sperling, Philip (1916-   ), since 1967 has been evalution officer of AID, in the Department of State. 174

St. John, Charles Webster (1889-1933), was educated at Clark and Harvard universities. He taught and served as dean at the University of Puerto Rico before going to Dana College, Newark, in 1928, where he was department head until his death. 278, 279

Stern, (Louis) William (1871-1938), studied at Berlin with Ebbinghaus. He is noted for his differential psychology, educational psychology, and his psychophysical work. He also invented the tone-variator that bears his name. 14

Stevens, Stanley Smith (1906-   ), is professor of psychophysics at Harvard University and is an authority on sensory scaling and psychoacoustics. 76, 77, 312

Stone, Calvin Perry (1892-1954), was a professor of psychology at Stanford University. His chief research projects have been in the field of comparative psychology, emphasizing sex behavior, learning, and abnormal behavior. He has been editor of the *Journal of Comparative and Physiological Psychology* and of the *Annual Review of Psychology*. 217, 336

Stone, L. Joseph (1912-   ), is a professor of psychology and chairman of the department at Vassar College. His primary field of research has been in child personality development and the production of documentary films. With Joseph Church he published *Childhood and Adolescence*, a textbook that has also proven of value to the general reading public. 280

Stouffer, Samuel Andrew (1900-1960), emphasized statistical techniques as they apply to sociology and related fields. He was a professor of sociology and director of laboratory of social relations at Harvard. 219, 220, 221, 222

Stratton, George M. (1865-1957), served as a professor at the University of California, Berkeley. He was interested mainly in visual space, emotion, international relations, and racial comparison. 343, 345

Strong, Edward K. (1884-1963), was director of vocational interest research at Stanford University for over thirty years. The Strong Vocational Interest Blank was a landmark in interest measurement. 57

Symonds, Percival (1893-1960), was professor of psychology at Teachers College, Columbia University. 246

Taylor, Donald W. (1919-   ), is dean of the graduate school at Yale University. He formerly had worked extensively on problem solving. 82, 83

Taylor, Harold C. (1905-   ), was the director of the W. E. Upjohn Institute for Employment Research and is now retired. 48

Terman, Lewis M. (1877-1956), was a pioneer in intelligence measurement. His Stanford-Binet Test is a standard intelligence test. 42, 217

Thomas, William F. (1912-   ), is associate director and professor of the Student Counseling Center at the University of Wisconsin. 340

Thompson, Robert (1927-   ), is professor of psychology at Louisiana State University. He has published many articles on neurological factors in memory. 60

Thorndike, Edward L. (1874-1949), was professor of educational psychology at Teachers College, Columbia University, and was best known for his work in the psychology of learning and particularly for his Law of Effect. 42, 47, 245

Thorndike, Robert L. (1910-   ), has spent most of his professional life at Teachers College, Columbia University, and is now professor of psychology and education there. With Elizabeth Hagen he published *Measurement and Evaluation in Psychology and Education*. 280

Titchener, E. G. (1867-1927), founded the school of structuralism. Using introspection as a method, he based his theory on the view that sensations, images, and feelings provide the building blocks out of which conscious experience is fashioned. Brilliant, authoritative, dogmatic, he was as much feared as revered by his colleagues. 116, 117, 118, 278, 304, 331, 332, 333, 334, 338

Tolman, Edward C. (1886-1959), was an American psychologist associated with the purposive school of psychology. As an experimentalist, he investigated the concepts of motivation and helped to reestablish psychological theorizing through his concept of intervening variables. 95, 145, 290

Tomas, Vincent A. (1915-   ), is professor of philosophy at Brown University. 50

Tomkins, Silvan (1911-   ), is a research professor at Rutgers University. In 1947 he was a research associate with the College Entrance Examination Board, Princeton. 219

Troland, Leonard (1889-1932), was a professor at Harvard and a recognized authority on experimental psychophysiology. An authority on vision, he played a major part in the development of technicolor. An accident while mountain climbing ended his career before it came to full fruition. 94, 115, 346

Tulving, Endel (1927-   ), is professor of psychology at Yale University. He has been particularly concerned with the role of organization in memory. 79

Underwood, Benton J. (1915-   ), is professor of psychology at Northwestern University, where he has been since obtaining his degree at the State University of Iowa in 1942. Learning-retention has been and continues to be his research interest, which he carries out in a thoroughly programmatic style. He is the author of *Experimental Psychology*. 54, 58, 286

Vaughn, James (1898-1957), was associate director of psychology at the University of Cincinnati. His main concern was with motivation of human behavior, especially the effects of competition on behavior. 346

Volkmann, John (1906-   ), is currently professor of psychology emeritus at Mount Holyoke. A recognized authority in the field, he has made numerous contributions to psychophysics. 118, 119

Walker, Edward (1914-   ), is professor of psychology at the Univer-

Walker, Edward (*Cont.*)
sity of Michigan. A past-president of the Midwestern Psychological Association and holder of a National Institute of Mental Health Career Research Fellowship, Walker's research and theory have challenged traditional theories of behavior and stimulated generations of graduate students. 180, 181, 182, 184

Wapner, Seymour (1917-   ), is G. Stanley Hall Professor of Psychology and chairman of the department at Clark University. 51

Warden, Carl J. (1890-1961), taught most of his academic life at Columbia University until retirement in 1955. He worked consistently in the field of comparative psychology and in collaboration with two of his students wrote the three-volume *Comparative Psychology*. 245, 279, 280

Warren, Howard C. (1867-1934), was an American psychologist who asserted that methods of introspection were indispensable in scientific psychology. He supported the double-aspect theory of the body-mind relationship. Although he felt that observations of overt behavior alone offered inadequate materials for research, he was sympathetic to the behaviorism of John B. Watson. 329, 330, 331, 333

Watson, Goodwin (1899-   ), is professor of psychology at Teachers College, Columbia University. 246

Watson, John B. (1878-1958), was the father of behaviorism. Leaving his laboratory at Johns Hopkins University, he joined the J. Walter Thompson Co., where he had a distinguished career in advertising. 47, 115, 116, 332, 333, 338

Wertheimer, Max (1880-1943), along with Köhler and Koffka, was a founder of Gestalt psychology. 312, 338, 342

Wertheimer, Michael M. (1927-   ), is professor of psychology at the University of Colorado and has done research on various cognitive processes. 83

Whipple, Guy M. (1876-1941), was an American psychologist who wrote extensively on educational psychology and mental testing. 93

White, Robert (1904-   ), is a professor of psychology at Harvard. His interests are in abnormal psychology, development of personality, and social relations. 222, 223, 233, 234

Wickert, Frederic R. (1912-   ), is a professor of psychology at Michigan State University. 48

Wiggam, Albert E. (1875-1957), is a psychologist-biologist who wrote many popular books on biology and psychology. His newspaper column "Exploring Your Mind" was internationally syndicated. 42

Wimberly, Stanley E. (1915-71), was professor of psychology at and vice president of Florida Atlantic University. 51

Wolf, Katherine (1907-   ), was professor at the Child Study Center and the Department of Psychology at Yale University concentrating her studies in child development and personality research. 144

Wolfle, Dael (1906-   ), has for many years been executive officer of the American Psychological Association. 180, 181

Woodrow, Herbert (1883-   ), is professor of psychology emeritus at the University of Illinois. 336

Woodworth, Robert Sessions (1869-1962), was the dean of American psychology as professor at Columbia, where he taught for over fifty years, including about fifteen years after official retirement. He wrote many influential books, but perhaps the most important were *Dynamic Psychology*; his textbook, *Psychology*, which went through five editions; and, above all, *Contemporary Schools of Psychology*, first published in 1931, and his *Experimental Psychology* of 1938. 7, 184, 245, 255, 279, 330, 346

Wundt, Wilhelm Maximilian (1832-1920), was the first experimental psychologist who did not have another principal interest. This he stated in the Preface to his *Principals of Physiological Psychology* with his declaration to "mark out a new domain of science." 328

Wyatt, Fred (1911-), is director of the Psychological Clinic and professor of psychology at the University of Michigan. 175, 219

Xoomsai, Tooi (1910-), is professor of psychology and dean emeritus of the University of Chiang Mai, Thailand. 51

Yerkes, Robert Mearns (1876-1956), is regarded as the leader in the American movement of comparative psychology. He was director of the Yale Laboratories of Primate Biology for twenty-one years. 7, 246, 333, 335

Young, Paul C. (1892-), is professor of psychology emeritus at Louisiana State University. He was an early researcher on hypnosis. 60

Zubin, Joseph (1900-), pioneer clinical psychologist at Columbia University and the New York State Psychiatric Institute, is best known for hard-nose criticism of the theories and practice of clinical psychology and relentless advocacy of objectivism in studying abnormal behavior. 246